OUTSIDE AGITATOR

OUTSIDE AGITATOR

JON DANIELS AND TH

CHARLES W. EAGLES

The University of North Carolina Press • Chapel Hill & London

IVIL RIGHTS MOVEMENT IN ALABAMA

Library of Congress Cataloging-in-Publication Data

Eagles, Charles W.
    Outside agitator : Jon Daniels and the civil rights
movement in Alabama / Charles W. Eagles.
      p. cm.
    Includes bibliographical references and index.
    ISBN 0-8078-2091-1 (cloth : alk. paper).—
ISBN 0-8078-4420-9 (pbk. : alk. paper)
    1. Daniels, Jonathan Myrick, 1939–1965. 2. Civil
rights workers — Alabama. 3. Afro-Americans —
Civil rights — Alabama. 4. Murder — Alabama —
Selma Region — History — 20th century. 5. Civil
rights movements — Alabama — History — 20th century. 6. Alabama — Race relations. I. Title.
E185.98.D3E24   1993
323'.092 — dc20   92-50817
                                 CIP

Charles W. Eagles, professor of history at the University of Mississippi, is author of several books, including *Democracy Delayed: Congressional Reapportionment and Urban-Rural Conflict in the 1920s,* and editor of *The Civil Rights Movement in America.*

97 96 95 94 93   5 4 3 2 1

TO MY MOTHER

AND

IN MEMORY OF MY FATHER

You are here to cause trouble, that's what
you're doing. You don't live here. You are an
[outside] agitator, and that's the lowest form
of humanity.

— Sheriff Jim Clark

A martyrdom is always the design of God,
for his love of men, to warn them and to lead
them, to bring them back to his ways.

— T. S. Eliot

CONTENTS

A section of illustrations appears
following page 144

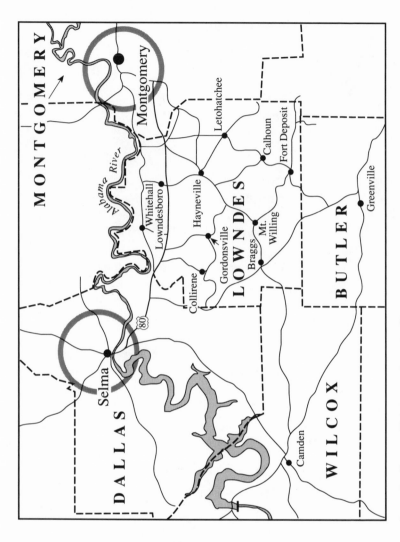

Lowndes County, Alabama, and surrounding area.

Jon Daniels was one of many white northern college students who went south in the 1960s to work for the civil rights movement. Daniels's involvement, however, had an unusual and tragic ending: on August 20, 1965, Tom L. Coleman, a fifty-two-year-old white man, shot and killed the activist in Hayneville, Alabama.[1] Beginning earlier in the week, rioting in the Watts section of Los Angeles overshadowed Daniels's death and caused it to receive limited national attention. The country was also preoccupied with the American military buildup in Southeast Asia. Similarly, five weeks after the tragedy, the trial of Tom Coleman gained comparatively little national publicity because of a major newspaper strike in New York City.

The killing of Jon Daniels late in the summer of 1965 was in many ways the last atrocity of the first, southern, nonviolent phase of the civil rights movement.[2] Though shocking, the shooting was not unique. It followed the deaths of a score of other civil rights workers — including Medgar Evers, James Chaney, Michael Schwerner, Andrew Goodman, Lemuel Penn, Jimmy Lee Jackson, and Viola Liuzzo. Daniels's death occurred, however, as the focus of the civil rights movement was shifting away from the South, where nonviolent demonstrations sought basic political rights, and toward urban areas in the North and the West, where increasingly violent protests for economic rights became central. The previous spring, the Reverend Martin Luther King, Jr., had led his last major southern protest, the Selma-to-Montgomery march for voting rights. By August 1965 most of the major civil rights legislation had already been enacted, including the Voting Rights Act signed by President Lyndon B. Johnson just days before the shooting in Hayneville.

The now largely forgotten events of 1965 warrant attention for at least three reasons. First, the story combines several approaches to studying the civil rights movement and then extends them to new topics. Initially, valuable historical accounts of the movement stressed biographies of important leaders (such as Martin Luther King, Jr.), the major national civil rights organizations (such as the National Association for the Advancement of Colored People, the Student Nonviolent Coordinating Committee, and the Congress of Racial Equality), and major events (such as the sit-ins and the Selma march). Later works, providing a different perspective, have emphasized the significance of grass-roots change in individual communities such as Greensboro, North Carolina, Tuskegee, Alabama, and St. Augustine, Florida. Some important studies have focused on the opposition — groups like the White Citizens' Council and other forces of white massive resistance.[3] This book will for the first time examine the life and work of a civil rights activist who was not a leader, consider the background and motivations of one opponent of the movement, and place both accounts within the context of a local community. As the title suggests, the book combines the record of Jon Daniels with an analysis of the reaction of southern whites who regarded him and the civil rights movement as outside agitators.

Second, the story of Coleman's slaying of Daniels contains a number of ingredients common to the movement for racial justice in the South.[4] Following his Christian conscience like many others, Jon Daniels volunteered in the movement out of a commitment to significant and immediate change in southern race relations. An Episcopal seminarian from New Hampshire, he went to Alabama seeking freedom for blacks and for himself. He sought to help blacks liberate themselves from white dominance, to assist them in their struggle for equality before the law, and to promote black political participation. For himself, Daniels sought — away from the influence of family and school — the personal freedom to define himself through his Christian witness.[5]

Third, in 1991 the Episcopal church took the first major step toward adding Daniels to its Calendar of Lesser Feasts and Fasts as a martyr of the church. When that action is confirmed in 1994, the church will thereafter commemorate the life of Jon Daniels on August 14, the day of his arrest in Fort Deposit. A full appreciation of his ultimate sacrifice requires a knowledge of his background and character, as well as an understanding of the man who killed him and the larger historical context in which the shooting occurred.

Lowndes County, Alabama, where Daniels died, was a bastion of white minority dominance. For half a century, no black had voted or served on a jury in Lowndes. Known for the violence used by whites to maintain their control, "bloody" Lowndes presented Daniels and other civil rights workers with almost insurmountable obstacles. In the summer of 1965 Lowndes County was in the throes of a social revolution. Seeking to overturn the county's long-established pattern of race relations, the southern freedom movement protested discrimination, struggled to educate and organize blacks to fight for their rights, and helped them to register to vote so they could begin to protect themselves. The entrenched white social order feared any breach in the racial status quo;

all residents, black and white, seemed instinctively to understand that the movement would drastically alter life as they had known it, not just in the area of race relations but also as it concerned jobs, income, education, politics, agriculture, law enforcement, and daily interpersonal relations. The whites, who still retained economic and political power, naturally opposed the civil rights movement.

Tom Coleman, a native of Lowndes County, represented the consensus among Lowndes whites that violent resistance to racial change was justified. Like his friends and neighbors, Coleman found the prospect of any radical alteration in southern race relations so intolerable as to be inconceivable. To defend his community and to prevent change, he resorted to violence against "outside agitators." Shortly after shooting Jon Daniels, Coleman turned himself in to local authorities and was charged with the crime. Six weeks later, an all-white jury in Lowndes County found him not guilty of manslaughter in Daniels's death.

The story of Jon Daniels and Tom Coleman in many ways represents, albeit in extreme forms, the forces promoting and resisting change in southern race relations; events similar, if usually less tragic, to the events of August 20 occurred in other southern communities. However representative Daniels and Coleman may have been of larger forces, they were nevertheless real individuals with distinctive personalities who were caught in specific circumstances. The explanation of how Daniels and Coleman came to be at opposite ends of a shotgun outside a country store must go beyond general, and often stereotyped, portrayals of national civil rights organizations, student activists, southern rednecks, bullying southern sheriffs, and the rural South.

The narrative begins by exploring Daniels's odyssey from childhood and youth in New Hampshire to college at the Virginia Military Institute to seminary studies in Cambridge, Massachusetts. It then describes his civil rights activities in Selma before and after the famous march, as he tried to integrate the local Episcopal church and help blacks organize. The story moves on to the troubled history of "bloody" Lowndes, the county's repressive culture of racial segregation, and the less-sophisticated life and personality of one of its respected white citizens, Tom Coleman. Finally, it demonstrates how the white community in Lowndes disposed of criminal charges against Coleman in Daniels's death.

Limited largely to one rural southern community, this account does not attempt to explain the entire civil rights movement. An examination of the individuals involved in one death in Lowndes County should provide insight into the powerful forces clashing in the broader movement for equal rights in the South and the challenges facing others involved in the struggle.

OUTSIDE AGITATOR

FROM KEENE
TO CAMBRIDGE

1

When Jon Daniels went to Alabama in 1965, he had no
experience in the Deep South and knew little about southern race relations. Except for four unusual years at the Virginia Military Institute
(VMI), he had always lived in New England; his first meaningful contacts with blacks were provided by his seminary fieldwork in Providence,
Rhode Island. He joined the civil rights movement out of a dedication to
serve others, a commitment to Christian justice, and an existential need
to clarify his own life's purpose, and he pursued his witness with a
perseverance and a courage learned at VMI. Unlike many other northern
students involved in the movement, he did not come from a radical
environment or even from a politically active family, and he had no
personal political agenda. Daniels's embrace of the cause of civil rights
did, nonetheless, grow out of his background, which instilled values that
he expressed by going to Alabama and created needs that he fulfilled by
participating in the movement. Key early influences on Jon included his

parents and several close friends, as well as his avid reading, his interest in music and drama, and his developing religious faith. His father and mother naturally helped shape his values and interests, while friends, including his younger sister, provided companionship. In school and church Jon developed a keen appreciation for books and ideas, for music and pageantry. In perhaps unconventional ways the Virginia Military Institute, seminary in Cambridge, and eventually the civil rights movement in Alabama were all parts of a life that took root in the small New Hampshire town of Keene.

Jon's parents, Phil and Connie Daniels, were both Vermonters who had met at the state university. After graduating, Constance Weaver spent six years teaching French and Latin in public schools in Vermont and New Hampshire, while Philip Brock Daniels attended medical school at the University of Vermont and completed his internship. They married and settled in Keene in 1932.[1]

The young couple elected to live in Keene because it was the right size, had a community hospital, and was a convenient distance from their families in Vermont. They managed to find a house directly across from the police station where Phil could also see patients. Moreover, the location made it convenient for the police to call Dr. Daniels when they had a medical emergency; Daniels soon became the official city physician, a position that helped him establish his professional status in the community. After three years, Connie and Phil moved to their permanent home on Summer Street. Their first child, Jonathan Myrick Daniels, was born on March 20, 1939.[2]

In 1942 Phil Daniels joined the army as a captain in the medical corps and left home for training. Jon and his mother followed when they could and lived briefly in Arkansas, Kentucky, and Washington, D.C. A daughter, Emily, was born in 1943. In October 1944 Captain Daniels left for Europe with an armored division, and just days before the war ended he suffered serious wounds in the feet and lower legs, for which he received a Bronze Star and a Purple Heart. Hospitalized until late 1945, he officially left the army in mid-1946 and returned to private practice in Keene.[3]

Located in southwestern New Hampshire less than fifteen miles from both Vermont and Massachusetts, Keene had a population of fifteen thousand. Settled by congregationalists, it became the seat of the new Cheshire County in 1771. By 1850 railroads connected it to Boston, New York, and Burlington, Vermont. During the nineteenth century woodworking was the town's largest industry. In the twentieth century the economy diversified, and by the time of Jon Daniels's birth it had over fifty industries manufacturing chairs, glue, toys, shoes, textiles, paper boxes, and other merchandise. In fact, all boxes used to package JELL-O were then made in Keene. Perhaps its best-known product, started in the 1890s, was Wright's Silver Polish. In 1941 two more advanced industries — the New England Screw Company and Miniature Precision Bearings — moved to Keene. In 1939 the Keene Normal School, which had served the area since 1909, became Keene State College.[4]

Though Keene had an unusually diverse and stable economy, it was in other ways a typical New Hampshire town. Nearby Monadnock Mountain and Lake Spofford brought tourists in the summer and fall. Visitors would have noticed the Congregational church that dominated the large town square and might have been impressed by the many tall elms along the 172-foot-wide Main Street. Everyday life in Keene was normally tranquil. Jon Daniels's peaceful surroundings included within just a few short blocks the town square, the public library, the Congregational church, and an elementary school. By the time he entered the first grade at old Tilden Elementary, the unusually friendly and courteous boy freely roamed the neighborhood, ventured to the stores on the square, and visited the library.[5]

Phil Daniels exerted a strong influence on his son. Jon's slight build came from the Daniels family, but he also obtained from his father a seriousness of purpose, a commitment to service, and an interest in books and music. Phil Daniels had grown up in Linden Hill, Vermont, where his own father was superintendent of the local schools. His mother was a Phi Beta Kappa graduate of Middlebury College. The strict Baptist family permitted no smoking, card playing, drinking, dancing, or other frivolities and dedicated themselves to their church and schools. The victim of childhood asthma, Phil spent a lot of time reading instead of engaging in sports or other activities his family might have disapproved of. In college the family restrictions loosened and he joined a fraternity. Always a good student, he graduated from medical school with honors.[6]

Although a family doctor, Phil Daniels gradually gained a reputation as an obstetrician. Dedicated to his patients, he earned the love and respect of his community. Once after delivering a baby in the hospital, Dr. Daniels volunteered to sit with the couple's other small child in their home so the father could visit his wife and new baby. On another occasion, he took time to be in the operating room when one of Jon's close friends had his appendix removed; while the boy was anesthetized with a spinal, Daniels provided reassurance and explained the surgical procedure to him. "If ever a member of the medical profession placed service above self in ministering to his fellow man, it was Dr. Philip B. Daniels," the local newspaper declared at the time of his death.[7]

Daniels's concern for his patients meant that he was constantly away from home. Seldom, for example, did all the family members dine together, and they frequently ate holidays meals in a restaurant because of both parents' busy schedules. A two-week summer vacation remained their only significant time together, although several times a year they also attended musical performances at Tanglewood in Massachusetts. The physician's hectic pace contributed to a lack of tranquility in the Daniels home.[8]

One oft-told story revealed much about Phil Daniels's personality. While he was returning to his office after lunch, his Ford station wagon stalled on a busy street. Traffic backed up behind him, but still the car would not start. Finally, the driver behind him started blowing his horn. The doctor, though upset, removed his key from the ignition, got out of his car, and walked back to the driver who was honking. "If you'll go up and start my car," he told the man, "I'll be glad to sit here and blow that damned horn." Controlling his temper, he made his point and defused the situation with a touch of wit. From his father, Jon Daniels acquired his own sense of humor, appreciation of self-discipline, and quiet decisiveness.[9]

Phil Daniels succumbed to kidney failure during Jon's junior year in college, a time of considerable uncertainty because Jon had yet to figure out what he wanted to do with his life. His father's death deprived Jon of valuable support. In addition, the son now had to assume greater family responsibilities when he needed to deal with his own problems. Even in death, however, Jon Daniels found in his father a model of hard work and selfless devotion to serving others. Phil's example inspired Jon to consider a career in medicine.

Perhaps a greater influence on Jon Daniels was his mother, a strong-willed, energetic woman. Active in Keene's civic and social life, Connie Daniels served terms as president of the county and state medical auxiliaries and of the aid societies at local hospitals; she also participated in the Daughters of the American Revolution, the country club, the League of Women Voters, and the Congregational church. Her many activities resulted largely from social ambition. She wanted to cultivate the town's better people, and she encouraged her children to associate only with youngsters from proper families and worried when they found friends among less reputable groups. Her extensive social commitments and ambition for her family may, in part, have derived from the Daniels's non-Keene roots, which meant that she and Phil always remained outsiders. They probably developed as well from a strict upbringing. Constance Weaver, whose ancestors had settled in Salem, Massachusetts, in the 1620s, grew up in small rural Vermont communities where her father, a graduate of Phillips Exeter and Yale Medical School, worked as a country doctor of modest means. Steadfast Episcopalians, the Weavers raised their children in nearly puritanical fashion. Except for music, especially singing, Connie and her brother engaged in few activities other than studying; certainly, sports and parties were not allowed. Connie found new freedom when she entered the University of Vermont. Later as the wife of a doctor, she wanted to be and do many of the things previously denied her.[10]

To avoid conflict, young Jon Daniels usually obeyed his mother. Thus, in many ways he became the son she wanted — well mannered, adept in the social graces, and well groomed. In his early teens, however, the strong-minded, independent, and bright adolescent began to rebel against a home life that he frequently found constricting and tense. Jon resented the time his mother spent away from home pursuing her social and civic interests and reacted against her efforts to discipline him. When she objected to his smoking cigarettes, to his choice of friends, to his careless school work, and to his general disobedience, he usually responded with verbal jabs. His sister joined in the revolt, and the pair sometimes teamed up to frustrate their mother's demands. Nevertheless, Jon carefully sought an acceptable balance between defiance and conformity and seldom went too far.[11]

Jon Daniels's rebellion took many forms. For example, in high school — from the ninth grade until his senior year — he dated a girl of whom his mother disapproved; she felt that the girl's family was not up to her standards (they owned a local bakery). The couple broke up only when the girl started going out with one of Jon's friends. In school, where Jon had been a superior and favored pupil, he paid less attention to his studies. In junior high he confessed to being a "thorn in the flesh of" his teachers, and during the last report period in the ninth grade he received an F in Latin, his mother's specialty. Poor grades sparked repeated clashes with Connie Daniels, who expected her son to perform to his ability, yet his academic work did not improve. In high school Jon was often tardy, occasionally skipped class, and saw his grades fall. Like a number of students, especially his friends from the "wrong" families, he smoked cigarettes on the school grounds and went to a nearby pool hall; sometimes he slipped away for coffee and a cigarette in the back of a drug store. Outside of school Daniels's impetuosity led to several speeding tickets.[12]

One escapade finally landed him in serious trouble during his junior year. When a friend acquired an old car and managed to get it running, Daniels agreed to go for a drive as soon as the friend's driver's license became valid. One evening shortly after midnight, Jon crept out of his second-floor bedroom window onto the roof and climbed down a ladder placed there by his friend. They then went for an uneventful cruise around town to christen the "new" car. On returning home, Jon made his way up the waiting ladder. While swinging onto the roof, he slipped on the frost-covered shingles and fell to the concrete walk below. Before leaving, his frightened companion helped him get back up the ladder and into his room. In agonizing pain, Jon managed to awaken his sister, in the next bedroom, who tried to make him comfortable. About three o'clock in the morning Phil Daniels heard some noise from Jon's room and went to investigate. He took his son to the hospital for X-rays and subsequent treatment for his broken leg and assorted bumps and bruises. Jon remained in the hospital for four weeks and was discharged the day before Christmas.[13]

The accident, which could have been fatal, and the lengthy recovery apparently had a salutary effect on young Daniels. The hours in bed in the hospital and later at home gave him time to think seriously about his life, what he had been doing with it and what he hoped to do. In the high school literary magazine that winter, a very brief story by Jon, entitled "The Shadow," speculated about reality and the way the human mind works. Awaking from a nightmare, the narrator wondered just "what is hiding in the eerie shadows of the night." In terror he felt "that deadly presence reaching in; an irresistible, insidious force, to claim my life," but then, "like a shaft of light shining into the gloom of a black cellar, there steals into my soul a ray of hope, an idea which can explain all." Daniels seemed to be acknowledging the "shadows" in his own life and his longing for a "light" to alleviate his doubts and worries. As he later stated, "When dawn finally arrived, belatedly, I found myself a trifle behind the eight ball." It was a sobering time for the sixteen-year-old. According to his mother, he was a changed person after the experience: he was less undisciplined, unhappy, and openly rebellious and his grades improved, though Latin and chemistry still stumped him.[14]

Despite his teenage rebellion, Jon had fun growing up in Keene. One of his close friends was his sister Emily, four years younger than he. They often played together, and especially in their disagreements with their mother they were steadfast allies. As a youngster many other children and adults liked Daniels, but, except for a brief involvement in Cub Scouts, he did not participate in the typical boyhood activities. Asthma and allergies combined with his lack of interest in team sports to limit his athletic activities. In the summer he did not like mowing lawns or attending camp. An intense and introspective personality led him instead to read widely and think seriously about questions often beyond his years. Music, drama, books, conversation, and friends occupied most of his out-of-school time.[15]

Music had a central role in Daniels's life. He took piano lessons though often would practice only when forced by his mother sitting on the piano bench beside him. Able to pick up almost any instrument and play it moderately well, he occasionally performed on the glockenspiel and the sousaphone. For three years he played the clarinet and the tuba in the high school band, sometimes as a soloist, and for two summers he attended the New England Music Camp in Maine. He also sang tenor in his high school's a cappella choir as well in church choirs. When not practicing or performing, he played music on the family stereo. He favored classical music and symphonies but liked some kinds of popular music too. As a high school senior he admitted that he "detest[ed] much modern music, especially 'rock 'n roll' and the trash that Elvis Presley sings."[16]

Daniels's other major extracurricular activity was dramatics. The Keene Children's Theatre provided uncommon opportunities for young people between the ages of nine and fourteen, including Jon and Emily Daniels. In addition to acting, Jon worked on costumes, scenery, and sound systems. At school he joined the Dramatics Club and took part in many productions. Later he became involved with a summer stock theater group in Keene. Both drama and music allowed him to excel in performance, and the pageantry of the theater and the precision and beauty of music appealed to his aesthetic sensibilities.[17]

Reading before the first grade, Jon Daniels always read avidly on his own. Typical of unathletic, introspective boys, he spent much of his time absorbed in books (television had not come to Keene by the early 1950s, and when it did his parents did not buy a TV set). Often with records playing, he spent afternoons and evenings with his own thoughts and dreams about the books he was reading. In his twenties Daniels wrote that in the fourth grade books began to unlock "a great door to magnificent adventure" and that he "early loved to especially read exciting tales of valiant knights and fair ladies and dreamed beautiful, fantastic dreams of myself as a great hero." His eclectic tastes included science fiction, good literature, philosophy, religion, and biography, many far beyond his age level. Unlike some bookish teenagers, though, Daniels did not hide his reading interests or his fascination with ideas. Among his classmates he gained a reputation as a serious boy.[18]

His earnest book column in the high school literary magazine, the *Enterprise*, confirmed his image as an intellectual. "Inside the Covers" assessed books he had recently read and recommended works to his fellow students. The tenth grader began his column, "First of all, let's be serious." High school students were "old enough to think for themselves," to realize the problems in the world, and to consider what they could do about them. To act, however, required a philosophy, and reading could help to find new ideas, "to break down and combat false or poor ones you may have, and to strengthen any good ones."[19]

Daniels's intellectual bent undoubtedly struck many of his peers as peculiar. What one friend called his genuinely elegant style — handsome, well mannered, and well groomed — struck other students as affected and goody-goody. His invariably friendly and sometimes even gregarious personality helped counter their disapproval and teasing. Daniels also defended himself with his biting wit. With a phrase he could cut right through pretense and pomposity, thereby alienating some while entertaining others. Though his sensitivity usually prevented his humor from being wounding or cruel, his quick reactions to people and situations and his self-assurance made it penetrating. Daniels's tastes and style as a teenager did not make him a social outcast but limited his real comrades to a group of similarly inclined young people.[20]

By his middle teens, Daniels had developed a small circle of close friends — Gene Felch, Carlton Russell, Tony Reddington, Gary Howard, and Max Young. All of them were a year ahead of him in school but shared his intellectual predilections, his appreciation for music, and many of his other interests. Felch also suffered from asthma and was not particularly athletic, read a great deal, had a seemingly natural curiosity, and played musical instruments. Russell and Daniels became close after attending the New England Music Camp together. Russell was a fellow sousaphone player in the high school band and edited the high school literary magazine the year Daniels started writing for it. Reddington went to the same elementary school as Jon for a few years; he was bright and shared their intellectual interests and fondness for music. Gary Howard and Max Young were the least literary and intellectual of the group.[21]

Although they often included girlfriends in their activities (as the handsome son of a prominent physician, Jon Daniels was particularly popular with girls), the teenage boys spent much of their time playing chess, hashing over the problems of humanity, and listening to and performing music. They frequently congregated at one of their homes for long bull sessions about the latest movie or play or book, but usually the talk would turn to their ideas about how to solve world problems. Perhaps common in the 1950s, their discussions related more to philosophy and religion than to politics or economics; conscious of the atomic bomb hanging over the world, they were more concerned with figuring out who they were than with confronting social ills. Carlton Russell, for example, could not understand how someone as bright as Gene Felch could be a

Catholic. Tony Reddington, a Unitarian, especially questioned religion and faith. Later, in their college years, when gathered on holidays and in the summer, they increasingly covered more sophisticated topics — such as the works of Camus, Niebuhr, and Kierkegaard. Whatever the subject, the young men constantly challenged themselves.[22]

An eleventh-grade essay by Daniels exemplified the issues that he and his friends addressed. Seeking to "stimulate and provoke" thinking and to make his readers come "face to face with reality," he agreed with Henry David Thoreau that many luxuries and modern conveniences actually hindered "the basic fulfillment of our mortal existence." Life might be easier with gadgets and machines, he admitted, but in the process people lost "the eternal vigilance and moral stamina which we need in the great struggle for survival — merely because there is no longer that struggle." Instead, the modern world offered an abundance of leisure, which — like supposedly too much work — threatened to make people dull and easy prey for the work of the devil. Warning against materialism, Daniels feared a "down hill slide" toward a moral decay similar to that which, he thought, had destroyed the Roman Empire.[23] No doubt he had discussed the major points of the essay with his friends as he tried to work them out in his own mind.

Daniels shared with his friends an interest in religion, which was important in his life even as a teenager. From an early age, he had developed a strong interest in theology; he planned to be either a minister or a doctor. Before reaching junior high, he had read Lloyd C. Douglas's *The Robe* and Henry M. Robinson's *The Cardinal*. The latter introduced Jon to the inner workings of the Catholic church — its doctrines, rituals, and liturgy. On numerous occasions he talked with Gene Felch's mother about *The Cardinal* and quizzed her about her Catholicism and the church.[24]

Daniels's developing interest in religion became explicit in his writings for the high school literary magazine, where his very personal comments on matters of faith hinted at his own search for belief. For example, he praised Thomas B. Costain's *The Silver Chalice*, the story of early Christians in the Roman Empire. Not only did he appreciate its "thrilling action and entrancing beauty," but he also found the story about the artisan who built the chalice an "inspiration and an invitation to a greater faith and a stronger belief in Jesus Christ." Nonfiction with religious themes also received his recommendation. One book described Christians, Jews, and other religious groups in Eastern Europe. Caught up in the cold war, Daniels admired the "breathtaking exploits of modern day heroes and martyrs." Their faith, he declared, united them in "resistance to Communist atheism, to fighting, often dying for their beliefs behind the Iron Curtain."[25]

In his middle teens, Daniels became involved with a youth group at St. James Episcopal Church in Keene because the Congregational church did not sponsor a Boy Scout troop. In high school he started attending the church's Sunday evening youth group. Before long he wanted to switch his membership to the Episcopal church, but his parents objected. His mother in particular wanted to avoid a disruption in the family or the community and thought that it would be difficult to support two churches, especially since her husband had so little time for church anyway. Prevailed upon by his parents, Jon Daniels postponed the move until his senior year in high school.[26]

Many factors must have contributed to his decision to join the Episcopal church. For one thing, he had the example of his maternal grandfather, who was a dedicated Episcopalian. A more direct influence was the Reverend J. Edison Pike, the local Episcopal rector from 1953 to 1959. Phil Daniels was the Pike family's physician, and the two households occasionally socialized together. Jon, therefore, got to know Pike outside St. James at the same time that he was developing an interest in religion and the Episcopal church. Finding the rector an interesting and compatible tutor, Jon often stopped by his office or the rectory for informal talks. Pike discouraged Jon from severing his ties with the Congregational church until he was ready to leave for college so the move would not create any rivalry among the Keene churches or provide grist for the local gossips. (Pike sponsored Daniels's confirmation in the Episcopal church in 1958).[27]

Jon Daniels's teenage rebellion also probably disposed him to change his denomination. By rejecting the Congregational church, he could repudiate his parents' control over him in a way that could hardly be condemned. Of greater importance, however, was his deep attraction to the ritual and pageantry of the Episcopal church. A person who enjoyed Arthurian legends, writing and playing with words, and the theater could naturally be drawn to the formal liturgy, classic ceremony, and rich heritage of the Episcopal church. In contrast, the plainness, restraint, and dryness of the Congregational church's services would have had little appeal for him.[28]

Daniels had given many indications of his attraction to the Episcopal faith. For example, his enjoyment of *The Cardinal* and *The Silver Chalice* suggested his inclination to pull away from the Puritan tradition in New England and toward the Episcopal church, if not the Catholic church itself (he wrote sympathetically about a Catholic priest in his melodramatic and romantic short story, "In Memoriam"). And he declared that Paul I. Wellman's *The Chain*, a novel about an Episcopal priest, was "magnificent" and "inspiring." His joining the Episcopal church came, therefore, as no surprise to his family and friends, who knew that the ministry appealed to him as well.[29]

Jon Daniels's change in denomination occurred at the same time that he started thinking seriously about college. Though naturally a bit apprehensive, he looked forward to greater freedom and the opportunity to grow on his own. His parents preferred that he attend an Ivy League school and become a doctor, and Daniels, who had neither ruled out medicine nor settled on another career, did apply for admission to Harvard and Yale. His high school record did not meet the standards of the more selective schools; at graduation, he ranked fifty-fifth in a class of fewer than two hundred. In addition to elite universities, Daniels in January 1957 sought admission to the Virginia Military Institute in Lexington. When VMI accepted him, he decided to head south for his college education. A gentle, intellectual, undisciplined young man, he seemed to his baffled friends the most unlikely candidate for the physical rigors and regimented life of a military institution. Even his family remained a little puzzled by his choice.[30]

VMI did, however, hold special appeal. Although not crucial to his decision, Daniels had probably first heard of it from a Vermont friend of his father who was a VMI alumnus. Moreover, Tony Reddington had the year before attended a military college in Vermont, and his example may have encouraged Daniels. Phil Daniels's valiant service in World War II also greatly impressed on his son the importance of the military and patriotism. In addition, Rev. Pike gave his imprimatur to the military by continuing to serve as a chaplain in the U.S. Air Force Reserve. A southern institution such as VMI would not have seemed as alien to Jon Daniels as it would have to some of his contemporaries in Keene because of his fond memories of his early sojourns in the South when his father served in the army.[31]

Just as the ritual and liturgy of the Episcopal church had attracted Daniels, so VMI's uniforms, formations, ceremonies, and traditions must also have been alluring to him. The heroic qualities associated with the military tradition also fit comfortably with his appreciation of literary epics. Perhaps more important, the strict military discipline fascinated Daniels, who was lackadaisical about his studies, habitually late, and still somewhat rebellious. He realized, and certainly his mother agreed, that he could benefit from the order required of cadets at VMI. The institute's austere, regimented life also promised quite a change from the clutter and disarray of the Daniels home, which would be replaced by an impersonal set of rules to be followed by all. Whereas the Episcopal church provided spiritual order, the military training at VMI would instill greater self-discipline in his everyday behavior.[32]

Located toward the southern end of the beautiful Shenandoah Valley of western Virginia about halfway between Charlottesville and Roanoke, Lexington in the 1950s had a population of a little over five thousand. In addition to VMI, it was home to Washington and Lee University; each school had about one thousand male students and their campuses adjoined each other. For Jon Daniels, VMI and Lexington were important parts of a culture significantly different from his native New England. He really had no experience in the South, knew no southerners, and lacked any understanding of southern race relations.

The nation's first state military college, VMI opened for classes in 1839 and became known as the "West Point of the South." It was steeped in southern traditions. Cadets and faculty had served in the Civil War, some under one of the professors, Thomas Jonathan ("Stonewall") Jackson. VMI had been burned and nearly completely destroyed by Union forces in June 1864. The war was memorialized annually in a formal ceremony: the corps of cadets marched in full-dress uniform to the cemetery, where the names of cadets killed in the battle at New Market were called, taps played, and volleys fired overhead. Whenever cadets left the barracks through the Jackson Arch, they always saluted the statue of Stonewall Jackson. They also saluted the Lee Chapel containing Robert E. Lee's tomb as they walked from the campus to town. Two Confederate symbols — the flag and "Dixie" — were common at VMI.[33]

Jon Daniels entered this bastion of the Confederacy and the Lost Cause in September 1957. He could not have expected what he found. The college historian has written that "entering new cadets . . . find it a sudden shock, unimagined even by the best prepared to face it." During orientation week, when Daniels and his "Brother Rats" were indoctrinated in the institute's procedures and traditions, Jon met many southerners (more than half the cadets were from Virginia and only twenty-six came from New England) and discovered the military system. The real shock came the next week when the three upper classes returned to VMI and began to initiate Daniels and the other new cadets.[34]

In the "Rat system," upperclassmen sought to instill the qualities deemed necessary to be a successful cadet and later a soldier or civilian. The system emphasized some of the very qualities that Jon Daniels felt he lacked — self-control and self-reliance, humility, neatness and orderliness, respect for authority, punctuality, consideration for others, and a military manner. Exotic methods were employed to train the Rats, though physical hazing had been virtually eliminated. Every new cadet, for example, had to eat his meals in a rigid posture called bracing. Rats paid for their mistakes with push-ups, running, and intense verbal harassment by upperclassmen. Daniels found life as a Rat almost unbearable. "What with 'bracing' (a rigid and painful position of attention), all the abuse from upperclassmen, and too much studying to be done in too little time — in short a perpetual rat race — the life of a Rat is somewhat less than ethereal bliss," he wrote. In effect, VMI was "pure, unadulterated hell."[35]

Like most Rats, Daniels performed poorly in the first semester. In the second semester his grades improved, but the military routine continued what he described as "its deadening effects on the poor cadet." Occasionally he ventured out of the barracks for a few concerts and for trips, sponsored by the English Department, to the opera and museums in Baltimore and Washington, D.C. The chairman of the department encouraged Noland Pipes, a junior English major from Louisiana, to befriend Daniels because both cadets were considering entering the Episcopal ministry, hated much of VMI, and had other interests in common. Daniels also sang with the VMI Glee Club and participated in the local Episcopal church's Canterbury Club. For most of his first year, however, Daniels experienced the usual fears, frustrations, and angers of a Rat. He concentrated on surviving the next "resurrection" (forced early morning runs around the parade grounds carrying rifles), worried about what an upperclassman would order him to do, and had little time for studying, forming real friendships, or thinking about the outside world.[36]

Many of his classmates had not expected Daniels to survive the first year because they thought he was completely out of place at VMI and too weak and too soft for its rigors. Moreover, the slight if not frail cadet (weighing 142 pounds and just under six feet tall) was unprepared for the physical challenges confronting him. Eighteen of his Brother Rats left VMI within the first ten days; 44 out of 346 Rats quit by the end of the semester (more than half of them from outside the South). The Rat system broke one of Daniels's roommates and he had to withdraw. To the surprise of many, and perhaps to himself, Daniels stuck it out. The experience may have given him some idea of what it was like to be a second-class citizen and to be oppressed by another group; later as an upperclassmen, he never enjoyed harassing Rats. More important, however, by outlasting the rigors of VMI he surely acquired the confidence that he could handle anything that came his way.[37]

For Daniels life at the institute improved after his first year. Still governed by VMI regulations, he attended the required church services every Sunday, faced regular military inspection on Thursday afternoon, participated in military drills, engaged in intensive physical training, and endured barracks inspection on Sunday morning, but he coped more successfully with the routine. Though he disliked the military, Daniels was always well scrubbed, pressed, and shined for inspection. Taking pleasure in evading some of the rules, he studied after lights out and in later years courted disaster by keeping a bottle of J&B scotch stashed away in a hollowed-out Civil War dictionary. His interest in academics increased and his grades improved sufficiently for him to make the dean's list regularly, his participation in extracurricular affairs widened, and his friendships with some of the other cadets grew. In effect, he created his own satisfying world within but separate from VMI.[38]

Daniels particularly enjoyed singing and traveling with the Glee Club but turned down trips to study and write. A member of the Timmins Music Society, he found its lounge on the fifth floor of the library to be a cultural haven. He spent many hours in the Timmins Room listening to his favorite music and discussing it with others. For a brief time he also worked on the student newspaper.[39]

Two of Daniels's closest acquaintances, James J. Wilson and Walter R. ("Buzz") Bossart, were his roommates for three years. In their spare time, the trio always seemed to have a game of hearts going. Wilson, in particular, had much in common with Daniels. A fellow Yankee from New Brunswick, New Jersey, he was a history major and, therefore, also a member of the beleaguered liberal arts minority. He and Daniels shared an intense dislike of VMI's regimented life, enjoyed having a beer in the local hangouts, and spent a lot of time talking and drinking with friends in their room. Several times they went to Washington to visit friends and sightsee. Another Yankee, from Mount Lebanon, Pennsylvania, Bossart majored in chemical engineering. Daniels, Wilson, and Bossart were known as "Rat Daddies" because they looked out for new cadets and tried to protect them from the harassing upperclassmen.[40]

Daniels also developed close associations with a clique of about a dozen English majors in his class. The young men's appreciation of literature brought them together as kindred spirits in an environment dominated by engineers and scientists. They all belonged to the Raymond E. Dixon English Society, which Daniels described in the 1961 VMI yearbook as "a monument to humanism in a wasteland of hypertensive steam tables [athletes], desiccated frog hairs [scientists], and quidsubsolar gas laws [engineers]." The society pledged itself to the "preservation of the arts against insuperable odds." For Daniels it was truly a supportive association in the intellectually and socially inhospitable institute, and by his senior year he had become its president. More than just belonging to the Dixon society and taking classes together, the English majors constituted a self-conscious group whose members studied together in a collegial but highly competitive spirit. As their mentor, Colonel Herbert Nash Dillard, the chairman of the English Department, encouraged his students to view themselves as an elite group. An energetic evangelist for the liberal arts, Dillard intellectually inspired and personally cultivated his cadets. Daniels particularly enjoyed his course on the English romantic period.[41]

In addition to appreciating literary ability, the coterie of humanists in the class of 1961 prized verbal pyrotechnics, especially acidic comments, biting wit, and challenges to any sacred belief. They regularly jousted verbally in the classroom, library, and barracks, and throughout Jon Daniels more than held his own. After the intensified rivalry of their senior year, Daniels ranked third academically in a class of twenty-three English majors.[42]

When they first met Daniels in his Rat year, some of his friends and acquaintances thought he was immature, delicate, and even a bit effeminate, but he soon demonstrated the strength of his personality and ideas. As time went on, many cadets considered him a true intellectual. He seemed unusually perceptive about human inadequacies, including his own, yet he was compassionate, never mean, and often humorous in his criticism.[43]

Under the tutelage of Dillard and other professors, and in competition with fellow English majors, Jon Daniels blossomed intellectually as his knowledge broadened and deepened. Unusually receptive to new ideas, he often surprised some faculty members by reading and later commenting on books they had casually mentioned in conversation with him. As one professor observed, he was "not a dilettante, but someone with intellectual curiosity." In addition to excelling in literature, Daniels pursued courses on the major ideas and prominent writers in Western civilization and took a year-long survey of the fine arts (the latter included laboratory sessions in which Daniels could "dabble a bit" to discover his own, albeit limited, talents). He also immersed himself in philosophy, where he was drawn to the existentialist philosophers. In advanced French literature courses he encountered André Malraux, Albert Camus, and Jean-Paul Sartre.[44]

Daniels's intellectual growth had the not-unusual effect of challenging his faith and his inclination toward the Episcopal ministry. New and competing ideas caused him to reevaluate the religious beliefs that he had rather easily accepted in Keene. Plagued by doubt more than disbelief, he grappled with but found no satisfying answers to his religious questions. In his Rat year, though singing in the church choir and serving on the cadet vestry of the Robert E. Lee Memorial Episcopal Church in Lexington, Daniels abandoned his nightly prayers; even his church attendance became irregular. The institute's mandatory church attendance grated on him, and he often ducked out of the cadet's Sunday church formation to return to his room to sleep or study. A number of his acquaintances at VMI never knew that he had planned to enter the ministry because by his sophomore year he claimed to be a nonbeliever. His friends ragged him about the hypocrisy of his continuing limited participation in Lexington's Episcopal church while claiming to reject the church and religion. When he did attend services, Daniels sometimes went with James Wilson to the Catholic church.[45]

Daniels's senior thesis revealed his philosophical self-examination and his need for personal action to define himself. It explored "the problem of the absurd in selected writings of Albert Camus." Like Camus, Daniels apparently felt, as he described modern man, "alone, isolated from his heritage and from the solace of a comfortable conviction in his own deathlessness," and he "suspect[ed] that his actions, his existence, are ultimately without sanction if not without value." Although he found "troublesome" and "disturbing" the questions Camus raised, Daniels did not try to avoid the issues by repressing his doubts; rather, he pursued them directly in a sober, intellectual way. He argued that the "absurd" was a modern human dilemma resulting from a confrontation between the rational need to understand the world and the irrational incoherence of that world. Existentialists such as Camus knew that the struggle with the absurd could end only at death, yet they refused to opt out through suicide. Instead, the existentialists stressed the importance of the individual's freedom and responsibility to "become" through personal involvement in the world.[46]

For Camus, according to Daniels, "the individual creates his own system of values, simply by the emergent act of volition," and the absurd, therefore, became "a springboard for ethical consideration." Apparently Camus attracted Daniels precisely because "he is an intellectual, an artist, with the propensity for contemplation associated with 'the man of thought,' yet he is a man of positive and energetic action." Camus lauded the rebel and Daniels agreed. "Rebellion confronts evil," he declared, "and all it can accomplish is to receive new impetus. The rebel must do what he can, knowing that his success will be only limited." Daniels valued Camus's emphasis on intellectual liberation, human decency, and the need for personal action in the face of absurdity.[47]

By his senior year at VMI, then, Daniels had grown significantly intellectually, but he had yet to find the appropriate arena in which to exercise his freedom through positive action. The institute's rigid discipline had both prevented him from fully defining himself and trained him to cope with an arbitrary and absurd world. Though upsetting to many of his initial beliefs, the writings of the existentialists encouraged him and gave him the strength to endure the harsh conformity of VMI while permitting his intellectual independence and his search for meaning in his own life. As one professor observed, Daniels displayed an "unusual degree of adaptability . . . in that he has been able to maintain independence of spirit and openness of mind" while also succeeding as a cadet.[48]

Having decided against a career in the ministry, he groped for an alternative. For someone as introspective as Daniels, the uncertainties must have been especially troublesome, if also exciting. An academic career, perhaps in literature, initially seemed possible; however, by his junior year his thoughts had turned to medicine. Unquestionably, he was affected by his father's career, which was ending in 1958–59 as Phil Daniels died slowly of kidney failure. Jon also became aware of "the lamentable inadequacy of my scientific background" in the summer of 1959 "while attempting an intelligent reading of Joyce's *Ulysses*." As a result, the next year he took several biology and chemistry classes and spoke of going to medical school. His decision to double up premedical courses with English ones took him further out of the mainstream of cadet life and deeper into his studies.[49]

The ministry and medicine both tugged at Daniels in his senior year. At the urging of his English professors, he sought Fulbright, Woodrow Wilson, and Danforth fellowships. The English faculty considered him "extremely conscientious," "exceptionally well qualified," the "best student in his class," and very articulate, even if his prose sometimes suffered from "over-seriousness and . . . a bit of pomposity." He was accepted for graduate study in English at Harvard and received a Danforth Fellowship. In Cambridge he hoped to "continue my peripatetic explorations in the humanities" and concentrate on either the seventeenth-century or romantic poets; he still held open the possibility that he "might channel my affinity for medicine into intensive scholarship and criticism" in literature.[50]

Before leaving VMI, Jon Daniels had to deliver the valedictory address at graduation exercises. His classmates *elected* him because they respected their Yankee colleague. As one student commented, Daniels was known to be "honest, outspoken, [and] talented." Perhaps more important, the other seniors thought highly of him because he was atypical, independent, and apparently unaffected by VMI's militarism. He could be trusted to speak his mind and thereby voice many of their own complaints about the institute. Preparing the speech was difficult because Daniels could not say things he did not believe, and he had mixed feelings about VMI. Although he had grown intellectually, the institute had not provided him the room to become his own person and to find value in his life.[51]

For himself and his classmates, Daniels expressed his mixed emotions — "relief and reluctance." He was relieved to leave a place where all had had "bitter experience[s] . . . and periodic disenchantment[s]" and where the "joy of learning . . . sometimes seemed more harsh than pleasant." His reluctance derived from the roots each cadet had inevitably, and perhaps unwillingly, planted at VMI. The New Hampshire native observed, "Not even the weed can welcome the prospect of being uprooted." Daniels also acknowledged some regret at leaving behind the "only glamor that some us will ever know." Perhaps most significantly, he still suffered the anguish of the existentialists and confessed to being personally disturbed "by a question that still cannot be answered. When IS the man — a man? We have spent four years in preparation for SOMETHING. What that something is, who we are, we do not know." Nonetheless, he wished his colleagues "the joy of a purposeful life" full of "decency and nobility" and urged them to "greet the unseen with a cheer."[52]

After saying good-bye to VMI and his friends in Lexington, Daniels chose to work in Washington, D.C., rather than return home for the summer. In Keene his family had been struggling emotionally and financially since his father's death. Though Jon's presence could have helped ease some of the tension, he was reluctant to give up his independence. In Washington, Senator Norris Cotton, who had been influenced as a boy by Daniels's maternal grandfather, helped him secure a job as a Senate postal clerk. Daniels became interested in government, law, and political science but still could not make up his mind and was plagued by indecision. He even had doubts about getting a doctorate and teaching English.[53]

In the fall of 1961 Daniels nonetheless entered graduate school in Cambridge. He soon disliked Harvard because he found his fellow students and the English faculty pretentious, coldly careerist, and not very interesting intellectually. In his first semester, he enrolled in four literature courses and ended up taking incompletes in two of them. In the second semester, a comparative literature course examining continental influences on the English Renaissance "was the only one I give a damn about." His major research paper on the style and themes in three sequences of love lyrics initially excited him, but within a few months he commented, "Flower catalogs and pretty euphemisms for good old fashioned lust are not precisely my cup of tea. Another 'dainty pap' and I'll jump out the window. I'd rather talk about the weather." Disillusioned with the study of literature, he realized that he was more interested in the ideas and philosophy found in writings than in the aesthetics of literature and that he wanted to be involved in the world of action. The "obfuscations" in literary criticism reminded him of the definition of scholarship as " 'shedding false light on non-problems.' H'ray for our team," he concluded in mock battle with the literary lights of Cambridge.[54]

In spite of his doubts, Daniels was exhilarated "to feel the toughening and sharpening of my critical processes." The work of I. A. Richards especially impressed him. Deemphasizing the biographical background and the social context of literature, Richards stressed the need to analyze carefully the specific text itself to, as Daniels put it, "see more fully what 'happens' in a piece of writing." Daniels thought that he gained from Richards "a decisively more acute awareness of the logic or total design informing an artifact and of the need for close logic in critical study." Finding the British critic's ideas helpful outside the classroom as well, Daniels discovered that he "listens more carefully to conversations, too," and, more generally, he "learned to notice things I never saw before."[55]

Personal and family difficulties continued to distract Daniels and no doubt contributed to his disenchantment with graduate school. Several weeks of counseling helped him deal with what a counselor assessed as his delayed grief over his father's death and his indecision about his future. More immediate family troubles may have caused even greater turmoil for Daniels. His sister was hospitalized during Christmas vacation and early in the new year. He made numerous trips to New York and Keene to help her, to confer with her doctors, and to advise his mother. Emily's hospitalization also drained the family's limited finances, exacerbating Jon's concern.[56]

In the spring of 1962 Daniels nevertheless concluded that his year in Cambridge had been "both rewarding and difficult." Although "increasingly sure of my commitment to teaching," he was uncertain of what he wanted to teach. His rapidly receding commitment to literature competed with a renewed interest in religion. His reading of many sermons in his course on seventeenth-century English literature actually helped rekindle religious concerns. In addition, his roommate encouraged him to read. C. S. Lewis and other religious writers in the Anglo-Catholic tradition. Still uneasy in his faith, he had been irregularly attending the Church of the Advent in Boston, and there on Easter he had, as he later described it, a reconversion experience. Thereafter, Daniels began to resolve his religious doubts and gain reassurance about his professional goals. Soon he decided to study for the ministry. His decision was reinforced and made easier by Harvard, which coincidentally recommended that he not continue his graduate studies in English.[57]

Hurt by Harvard's rejection but at the same time relieved to be extricated from the English Department, Daniels early in the summer of 1962 returned to New Hampshire. To help his mother financially and to wait to start seminary, he decided to work in Keene for a year. He still chafed under his mother's dominance and his sister's demands, and he at times found the Daniels home "still a madhouse." He became frustrated that, although "nothing ever *really* happens around here, something is always happening or (worse yet) about to happen."[58]

Fortunately for Daniels, he became involved in activities outside the home. He worked as an office assistant for a company that repaired and serviced electric motors. By early fall, however, he had grown to despise the job and his employer and left to work at the hospital in Keene — first as an orderly and then, after a short training program, as a surgical technician. The latter assignment served as one last test of his decision to pass up a medical career.[59]

During his year back in Keene, Daniels also had a rather brief, passionate love affair with an older woman. He was "delighted with the unexpected joy in it" and at times found himself "smirking and simpering like a fifteenth century lover." "I sometimes think God made a damn fool here!" he confessed to a friend — "Not to pass the buck, of course." He did not, however, just delight in his newfound love. Because the woman was more than twenty-five years his senior, their relationship caused him considerable distress as well as raising the ordinary questions about the appropriateness of their liaison.[60]

Daniels had difficulty reconciling his selfish romantic and sexual involvement with his growing understanding of real Christian love. He fretted about the once abstract but now real and personal differences between "agape" and "eros" and tried to sort out his masculinity in relation to his faith. Agape, he found, was "so cussed reluctant" and insufficiently valued, while eros was so "headstrong." The former "must be constantly commanded into being, and the other whipped into discretion." Always doubting and questioning, he wondered if his feelings were really admirable. Quoting C. S. Lewis ("we must get over wanting to be needed"), Daniels worried that to need someone amounted to wanting to be needed, that eros was closely tied to jealousy. "Must we not in the love of Christ (what I must insist with myself is the only real love)," he asked, "work always and solely for the perfect freedom of the beloved?" Increasingly confident in his faith, he found some solace in the belief that "[w]ithout Grace, the cause would indeed be lost."[61]

In the summer and fall of 1962 Jon Daniels became more active in the local Episcopal church and took serious steps toward enrolling in a seminary. He quickly became friends with the new rector of St. James, the Reverend Chandler McCarty, who in late 1959 had replaced Ed Pike. Daniels joined the choir and started teaching a youth Sunday school class, which he found "equivalent to a week's supply of iron pills." In

late September he began the complicated process of applying for seminary. As the first step, he met with the bishop of New Hampshire and the
diocese's Board of Examining Chaplains to discuss his plans, as admission to an Episcopal seminary required their approval. He also successfully underwent physical and psychological tests. Daniels officially
became a postulant for Holy Orders on April 3, 1963. Under the sponsorship of St. James Episcopal Church and with the backing of McCarty and
the diocesan officials, he applied for admission to the Episcopal Theological School (ETS) in Cambridge, Massachusetts. In the late spring he was
accepted for study beginning in the fall.[62]

In his application to ETS, Daniels — always intensely self-critical —
described himself as insecure and anxious but also intelligent and sensitive. He worried that he was too concerned about what others thought of
him and that his sensitivity encouraged him to control his emotions very
tightly. Talented in abstract and theoretical work, he could be so self-
critical as to become pessimistic and depressed or, as he put it, "almost
paralyzed by doubt." On the other hand, Daniels was optimistic and
positive about himself. "Perhaps because of an intense awareness of my
own limitations," he suggested, "I am decidedly more inclined to gener-
osity than to aggression." In addition to being courteous and honest, he
counted among his strengths "critical perception, communicability, sympathy, and empathy." He hoped that he used his abilities to reassure
people and help them understand themselves instead of to judge them. In
seminary he wanted, of course, to prepare for the ministry, but he also
hoped to "work out the salvation of my own soul." He expected that his
studies would relieve some of his doubts, strengthen his faith, and increase his knowledge, and he held open the possibility of further graduate
work in theology after finishing the program at ETS.[63]

In September 1963 Daniels entered the Episcopal Theological School,
located on a small campus just a few blocks from Harvard Square. Established in 1867 by the Diocese of Massachusetts and opened on January 1,
1868, the seminary sought to "educate men who shall combine personal
faith in Christ with thorough scholarship, and who shall be equipped to
deal with the theoretical problems and the moral and social needs of our
own day." Since 1914, when ETS became formally associated with Harvard University, its students could take courses at Harvard, use its libraries and other facilities, and attend many events on its campus. As the tie
to the formerly Unitarian Harvard Divinity School might suggest, ETS
was a "low church" Episcopal seminary; its liturgy and ritual were closer
to Protestant churches than those of the "high church" seminaries, which
had a greater affinity for the Roman Catholic church.[64]

When Jon Daniels arrived at ETS, the seminary had two dozen professors, most of whom lived on or near the campus, and about 125 students. The seminarians were predominantly northerners, with nearly half of them from Massachusetts, New York, Pennsylvania, and Ohio. More than 50 percent of the students were unmarried and lived in two dormitories on campus. Most of the married students without children lived in apartments in a building next door. Fewer than a dozen students were women. The predominantly upper-middle-class, white, male student body lived and studied in a very proper, cordial atmosphere. Student life was centered almost exclusively at the seminary, rather than in Cambridge or nearby Boston, primarily because students lacked the money for theaters, restaurants, and other entertainments.[65]

At ETS, where everyone knew each other, Daniels was liked and widely respected. He remained slightly detached, concentrated more than most on academics, and gave little time to typical diversions such as watching football on television. Many students were impressed by his intensity and scholarly inclination, though to some these qualities seemed excessive and boring. If he formed few close friendships at the seminary, he did have many acquaintances because he had the unusual ability to attract people with his smile, sense of humor, and friendliness and then engage them rather quickly in serious discussion, often about his reading and studies. Those who did get to know him found him concerned about the welfare of others.[66]

Most ETS students were preparing for the parish ministry. Over and above the course work, a seminarian was expected to know Greek and to pass a written examination on the contents of the Bible and the Book of Common Prayer. Each student was also required to devote part of a summer, usually after the first year of study, to clinical pastoral training and had to become involved in some kind of supervised religious fieldwork during the three-year program. At the end of the three years, a seminarian faced general examinations testing the student's comprehension of the subjects studied and the ability to integrate the variety of disciplines involved in seminary education.[67]

Daniels threw himself into the ETS program. In addition to German, which he had studied at Harvard, he took the usual courses on the Old and the New Testament and church history. He also took an introduction to theological education and the ministry with Dean John B. Coburn. The Old Testament course, taught by the Reverend Harvey H. Guthrie, delighted Daniels, and he especially found church history "exciting." The reading requirements at the seminary struck him as "*enormous*"; however, the overall academic program "was not a bit more demanding" than Harvard had been, and he liked it much better. "Millions of books!" he told his mother. "I love it and hopefully pray for real growth."[68]

In his first year at ETS, Daniels and the rest of the juniors, as the first-year students were called, took their courses together. In the formal and polite classes, Jon's quick mind and sharp wit soon became known among his peers, who began to think twice before disagreeing with him. In addition to his verbal abilities, his intellectual strength impressed his colleagues; his inquisitiveness pushed professors to go beyond their usual lectures and students to explore their assignments more thoroughly. His intensity may have bothered the less able students. Occasionally, he offended some by assuming a rather dogmatic stance on issues and by advocating a more high-church position than was customary at ETS. Often in a minority in debate, he seldom compromised or adjusted his views.[69]

A major component of the seminary training involved regular services in the seminary's small chapel. The seminarians were expected, but not required, to attend weekday Morning and Evening Prayer and to participate in the celebration of Holy Communion on Sunday and Wednesday. On Sunday, however, the chapel was usually almost empty because the seminarians had left campus for their assigned fieldwork in local parishes. Most seminarians worked in churches in the Boston area and left ETS for only a few hours on Sunday. In their first year Daniels and his friend Harvel Sanders drew an assignment to work in an inner-city parish in Providence, Rhode Island. It was unlike anything Daniels had known in Keene or at VMI. A native of a small Missouri town and a graduate of the state university, Sanders too had no experience in an urban setting.[70]

Early every Saturday morning they boarded a train for Providence, where they worked with the Reverend Alan Mason in one of four experimental urban programs sponsored by the Episcopal church. As the white, working-class parishioners of Christ Church moved to the suburbs, the local rector tried to serve the increasingly black neighborhood (then about 40 percent black), but his congregation gave him little encouragement; in fact, few parishioners attended Sunday services. Mason, Daniels, and Sanders were sent to work with the parish and the neighborhood. On Saturdays Daniels and Sanders visited in the area and worked in an ecumenical arts program for youngsters with a dozen students from the Rhode Island School of Design and Brown University. For the first time Daniels gained experience with blacks. The next day he worked with the acolytes in Christ Church, while Sanders taught a Sunday school class; sometimes they participated in the worship services. They arrived back in Cambridge late on Sunday.[71]

For Jon Daniels the work in Providence provided an invaluable introduction to race relations, urban society and its special problems, and the church's urban role. Though he found the project tiring, time-consuming, and "often discouraging with respect to human resources," he believed that it would be "crucial to my own 'holy history.' " When he entered ETS, he had never considered a parish ministry but expected to go into the teaching ministry. The Providence fieldwork, however, "opened unexpected horizons" by demonstrating the importance of parish work and persuaded him that he "could serve my Lord with a glad heart in a slum." He enjoyed the challenging work in Providence and urged his seminary to support the new program.[72]

At the end of his first year at ETS, Daniels entered the required summer clinical pastoral training program. In part because they did not have cars and could not travel in their work, he and Michael Stichwey, another friend and classmate, were assigned as interns to the Institute of Pastoral Care at Willard State Hospital in upstate New York. Five seminary students and one minister lived and worked in the hospital for twelve weeks. Willard housed about two thousand psychotic and neurotic adults in an isolated but scenic area on the eastern shore of Seneca Lake. There Daniels and his five colleagues studied personality development and human behavior under the direction of the Reverend Edward A. Tulis, Willard's supervisor of chaplains and an ETS graduate.[73]

Each intern was assigned to work on a ward with the clinical staff and the chaplain. The patients' aberrational, unpredictable behavior could be frightening to one so inexperienced as Daniels, because, without needles, uniforms, or tests as a defense, he had to relate to them with his own mind and feelings. Accustomed to dealing with people and problems either with his wit and intellect or with his polished manners, Daniels had some trouble reconciling the volatile emotional atmosphere with the world he had known. Tulis, through reviews of Daniels's written reports from each session, sought to improve his pastoral skills. In time, Tulis found that the seminarian obtained favorable responses from a variety of patients, interpreted their cases accurately, and provided them "sufficient emotional support and sustained interest for the interpretations to become viable."[74]

In seminars the interns learned about alcoholism, theories of personality development, counseling techniques, the problems of aging, and specific neuroses and psychoses. Following the seminars they entered a more personally threatening activity: a group dynamics session, led by Tulis, in which they exposed their strengths and vulnerabilities to the others as they talked about their personal feelings and experiences. In the group, Tulis reported, Daniels often revealed more about himself than he could comfortably manage. He displayed occasional defensiveness and seemed ill equipped to handle an exploration of his feelings, though he did not seem to realize this, and the others, especially Tulis, quickly learned to rescue him. The intense training may actually have given him unwarranted confidence in dealing with new and threatening situations,

because it encouraged him to continue to rely on his intelligence, personality, and customary style, instead of increasing his awareness of his own
and others' emotions. At the end of the program, Tulis concluded that Jon
Daniels would "make a sensitive, articulate, thinking clergyman" because he had a "fine intellect," "acute sensitivity," and a "warmly gregarious personality." Sensing that Daniels had not yet developed a clear
understanding of himself, however, Tulis perceived his need for personal
growth.[75] Daniels would continue to seek experiences that would allow
him to grow existentially; he was developing his ideas and values but
needed an opportunity to put them into action.

In September 1964, Daniels returned to Cambridge for his "middler"
year at ETS. Most seminarians were a bit more secure and happy in their
second year because they had successfully completed one year and the
clinical training program, had more self-assurance, and had acquired
confidence about their future in the clergy. Resuming his academic
training, Daniels took courses in the exegesis of the New Testament,
homiletics or the art of preaching, and Greek. He found more exciting,
however, an introduction to theology course and a class on the history of
the medieval church taught at Harvard Divinity School. Instead of the
more mundane fare in pastoral theology or homiletics, he relished grap-
pling with such topics as the Atonement, the Resurrection, the meaning of
righteousness, and the Holy Spirit. Intellectually demanding, he emphasized the proper use of language in examining issues. On at least one
occasion he caused a small uproar in theology class when he criticized a
fellow student's paper as an example of inferior analysis. Several classmates argued that he had more interest in disparaging others, scoring
points, and having fun at their expense than he had in theology. After the
class ended, Daniels apparently held no grudges, but his critics became
more wary of debating with him; Daniels's intellectual and verbal talents,
his aggressiveness, and his lack of patience with others irritated some
students.[76]

Some classmates also reacted negatively to his growing conservatism,
which struck some as dogmatism. Though he came out of a New England
Congregationalist background, he was moving away from the low Episcopal church toward the high. Increasingly he appreciated the beautiful
music, rich and ordered liturgy, and elaborate ceremonies of the high
church. The incense, candles, vestments, singing, and other aspects of
worship provided a full aesthetic experience that he liked. When with
some friends from ETS he attended the Anglo-Catholic Church of the
Advent on All Saints Day in 1963, he responded positively to the proces-
sions, architecture, stained glass, paintings, and other facets of the high
church service. On occasion he even attended services at the Catholic

monastery near ETS and spoke of eventually moving to the Roman Catholic church. At the low-church seminary, Daniels's high-church inclinations proved somewhat unpopular and led him to be increasingly defensive about church affairs.[77]

If Daniels underwent a shift toward the high church, he also became more conscious of the social implications of his faith. In his second year at ETS, he and Harvel Sanders resumed their work in the transitional parish in Providence. Late in the fall of 1964, the diocese bought a tenement house for three tenants near the church and Alan Mason moved there. Staying on weekends in one of the other tenements, Daniels and Sanders became even more deeply involved with the local community. On Saturday evenings, for example, they helped arrange drop-ins at the church house for teenagers in the neighborhood; the program became so popular that the floor sagged under the weight of the crowd and a steel beam had to be inserted to support it. The unusually time-consuming fieldwork meant that Daniels had little social life at the seminary and he had to work harder on his studies during the week. His urban ministry, however, had a major impact on him: for the first time he confronted the enormous social problems involving race and poverty, and he could begin to see in concrete terms how the gospel might apply in a community suffering from poverty and powerlessness. His commitment to Christian social action grew.[78]

In the early 1960s, political and social issues had no great appeal on the ETS campus and Daniels showed no particular interest in political action or radical causes. Early in 1965, however, interest in the civil rights movement began to develop in reaction to events in the South, especially in response to the declarations of the Episcopal bishop of Alabama. Bishop Charles C. J. Carpenter had announced that he would not welcome any civil rights workers, particularly Episcopalians, into his diocese. Episcopal church protocol, recently reaffirmed by the church's national executive council, gave the bishop just such authority to bar religious activity by Episcopalians in his diocese, but Episcopalians at ETS and elsewhere began to question the practice. The ETS student government, the St. John's Society, voted to condemn the church's policy. In a student-faculty meeting, Jon Daniels vigorously defended the traditionalist position that stressed the bishop's authority, and he opposed outside Episcopalians' going into Alabama without Carpenter's approval. His theology professor, William Wolf, spoke strongly against Daniels's views, disagreed with the church's stand, and asserted that the bishop's right in this case was just an overlay for states' rights. Though Wolf prevailed, the debate caused an increased awareness at ETS of the southern civil rights movement and the church's role in it.[79]

In the early spring of 1965 concerns at ETS for the civil rights movement suddenly escalated. The immediate spark was the call by the Reverend Martin Luther King, Jr., for clergy to march in Alabama from Selma
to Montgomery. On March 7, soon after local police stopped peaceful
demonstrators in a bloody confrontation in Selma, King sent out hundreds of telegrams asking "clergy of all faiths . . . to join me in Selma for
a ministers march to Montgomery on Tuesday morning, March ninth."
By Monday afternoon ETS student Jack Lawton and his wife had decided to accept King's call and began asking other students to join them.
Interest seemed to grow spontaneously.[80]

The St. John's Society's executive committee, including Jon Daniels,
met in the afternoon of March 8 and endorsed participation by ETS
students. Quickly more than six hundred dollars was raised. After some
frantic discussion and argument, eleven ETS students agreed to heed
King's call. Although most at the seminary approved of their church's
involvement in the march, some questioned whether a one-shot witness
would be effective and others suggested that the students should stick to
their studies. Jon Daniels, who just weeks before had opposed such
action, was now convinced by events that participation in the Selma
protest — even over the objections of Bishop Carpenter — was necessary.
At first excited, he believed that the idea of going to Selma was "impractical" and satisfied himself with contributing to the funds being collected
at ETS. At Evening Prayer, however, the Magnificat had a special effect
on him. As he wrote three months later, "as usual I was singing the
Magnificat with the special love and reverence I have always felt for
Mary's glad song. 'He hath showed strength with his arm.' As the lovely
hymn of the God-bearer continued, I found myself peculiarly alert, suddenly straining toward the decisive, luminous, spirit-filled 'moment.' . . .
Then it came. 'He hath put down the mighty from their seat, and hath
exalted the humble and meek. He hath filled the hungry with good
things.' I knew then that I must go to Selma."[81]

SELMA

2

The Reverend Martin Luther King, Jr., wanted clergy of all faiths to assemble in Selma, Alabama, in early March 1965 to help with a black voter registration drive. He planned to lead a peaceful protest march from Selma to the state capitol in Montgomery. King hoped that the demonstration, by focusing national attention on the discrimination against southern blacks at the polls, would prod Congress to enact federal voting rights legislation. The voting rights campaign would be King's last major protest activity in the South.[1]

Jonathan Daniels and hundreds of clergy and seminarians from across the nation responded to his call. Daniels, and many of the others, participated for the first time in a civil rights movement that had been growing for over a decade. No one event, of course, began the modern American civil rights movement. Countless lawsuits challenging racial segregation preceded the Supreme Court's 1954 decision in *Brown v. Board of Education*, which struck a major blow at segregation not just in education but by implication throughout American society. The Court's decision also provided great constitutional and moral support for local, indigenous movements for equal rights. The first local effort to capture the nation's attention was the black boycott of segregated municipal buses in Montgomery, Alabama.[2]

In 1955–56 Martin Luther King's leadership of the Montgomery bus boycott first brought the young black minister to national prominence. The boycott's success and the subsequent development of his Southern Christian Leadership Conference (SCLC) propelled King into the leadership of the burgeoning civil rights movement. The movement, which was always larger than King, soon included sit-ins by college students, freedom rides sponsored by the Congress of Racial Equality, and other protests. After struggling for several years to establish the conference and develop his nonviolent protest strategy, King and SCLC in the early 1960s moved into a series of southern communities to lead massive, nonviolent protests to achieve greater civil rights for black Americans. In late 1961 King assumed leadership of a protest movement in Albany, Georgia. Inspired by workers with the Student Nonviolent Coordinating Committee (SNCC), young blacks in the southwestern Georgia town had begun to challenge local segregation in transportation facilities and municipal services. When the Albany movement fell into disarray, King and SCLC joined it and led more demonstrations. The local law enforcement authorities, however, responded nonviolently with a restraint that foiled the nonviolent tactics of the black demonstrators. Even with King's personal involvement, the Albany protests collapsed, and his nonviolent methods failed in their first major application since Montgomery. Moreover, some began to doubt King's leadership ability.[3]

From the Albany experience King and his advisers learned to choose their targets more carefully. They achieved greater success the next year in Birmingham, perhaps the most segregated city in the South. SCLC timed the protests to start after the local election and took advantage of the violent racial hostility of the city's public safety commissioner, Eugene T. ("Bull") Connor. According to the plans of King and his aides, Birmingham would be made a national symbol of discrimination, would reinvigorate the stalled civil rights movement, and would spur passage of federal laws dealing with public accommodations, in addition to solving some of the city's dire racial problems. When the demonstrations began in April, Bull Connor responded viciously. Hundreds were arrested, including King, who spent a couple of weeks in jail. The crisis received national attention and helped prompt President John F. Kennedy to call for what became the Civil Rights Act of 1964.[4]

King's focus next shifted to voting rights in the South. In 1964, only

40 percent of southern adult blacks were registered to vote, as opposed to 70 percent of the white population. The percentages for blacks were lowest in Alabama (19.3 percent) and Mississippi (6.7 percent). Selma's Dallas County had a black majority in population, but in the early sixties *less than 1 percent* of its registered voters were black. In April 1961 the Kennedy administration had filed its first voting rights lawsuit against the Dallas County registrar; additional suits followed. In November 1964, King and SCLC chose to start their push for voting rights in Selma, where the repressive actions of local courts and officials had stymied the federal government and had stopped the momentum of SNCC's early efforts.[5]

When King arrived in Selma, the Alabama town was nearly 150 years old. Though the site of Selma had seen explorers and temporary settlers as early as Hernando de Soto in the sixteenth century, Andrew Jackson's defeat of the Creek Indians in 1814 permitted a land rush and the first real settlements in the fertile Black Belt of Alabama. William R. King, later vice-president of the United States, helped organize the Selma Land Company in 1819 and gave the town its name. Located on the northern bluffs of the Alabama River, Selma was incorporated in 1820. By 1840 the surrounding Dallas County had twice as many slaves as whites and cotton production was booming. Selma served as an important slave market and point of loading for cotton shipped via the Alabama River to Mobile. The town grew even faster after the railroad came in 1853. During the Civil War, Selma was the Confederacy's second most impor- tant military depot — with a foundry, an ironworks, and several factories. Federal forces captured and burned parts of the town in early April 1865. Later the same year voters nonetheless decided to make Selma the seat of Dallas County.[6]

While the county grew slowly in the late 1800s and hardly at all in the next five decades, Selma progressed steadily. Much of the town's busi- ness was tied directly to the cotton production of the Black Belt. By 1920 it had more than 15,000 citizens, many of whom worked in cotton gins and warehouses or in businesses serving the rural population. The coun- ty's population, which had reached almost 20,000 by 1940, remained 75 percent black, but whites held the power. Under the 1901 state constitu- tion, blacks lost the right to vote as a result of a poll tax and a literacy test. Whites frequently resorted to violence to maintain complete control of Dallas County. Between 1882 and 1913, they lynched nineteen blacks in the county; twelve of the lynchings occurred in or near Selma. Though outwardly completely segregated, sexual liaisons occurred between the races; an observer reported estimates that one out of five blacks in Selma was the product of an interracial union.[7]

Two events in 1940 spurred the development of Selma: the modern Edmund Winston Pettus Bridge over the Alabama River opened for U.S. Route 80 to Montgomery, and the U.S. Army Air Corps started the Selma Army Air Base (later renamed Craig Air Force Base) just east of town. The bridge reinforced Selma's role as a transportation and distribution center for that section of the Alabama Black Belt, and the air base, even in the postwar period, employed scores of civilians and pumped hundreds of thousands of dollars into the local economy. In addition to the lumber mills, cotton gins, and fertilizer plants typically associated with an agricultural area, the Selma economy by the 1960s had expanded to include factories making cigars, bicycles, furniture, bricks and concrete products, mattresses, and clothing; one plant produced magnesium ingots. Early in 1965 the Hammermill Paper Company announced plans to construct a multimillion-dollar pulpwood mill a few miles outside of Selma.[8]

At the time of King's arrival, Selma seemed to some an unusually pleasant and attractive southern community, especially for the town's score of millionaires and for the more than four hundred members of the all-white country club. The *Selma Times-Journal* lauded it as "a beautiful city, with its wide streets, well-kept residences and magnificent, century-old oak trees," and some of the prosperous white sections were particularly attractive. According to the *Times-Journal*, Selma "maintain[ed] the friendliness, hospitality and culture of the Old South, which is coupled with the progressiveness of the New South." Pointing with pride to the town's three hospitals, numerous churches and schools, eight playgrounds and two golf courses, and many businesses, one observer considered it "an ideal, quiet, cultured city." Community leaders boasted about their "city of opportunity!"[9] It may have been for whites, but it was not for most blacks.

Selma's black residents were poor and powerless in a town controlled by white segregationists. The Citizens' Councils of Alabama, the leading diehard segregationist organization, had started in Selma in 1954, and in the early 1960s the largest chapter was in Dallas County. Sheriff James G. Clark's posse enforced strict segregation. Blacks knew their place and appeared helpless in the face of their subordination to whites. Although after World War II whites may have seldom resorted to violence, all knew that the color line existed. As one student of Selma has suggested, "on the surface, during daylight hours, the blacks and whites followed the rules, smiled at each other, talked and joked as if everything was just as the whites believed it was and ought to be." Many whites treated blacks paternalistically, and most managed to blind themselves to the injustice around them. A very few whites, however, had begun to have some awareness of the massive self-deception. Commenting on the racial situation in Selma, one local white later admitted that for the "charmed group known as the American upper middle class . . . Selma is a delightful place to live. . . . But our lives are spent mostly in certain sections; more than half our town we seldom see, except when we take the cook or the houseboy home. Perhaps we have been mistaking a part for the whole. Perhaps a majority of our citizens are not a part of the graceful living we take for granted."[10]

Along the unpaved streets in the black part of Selma, almost unknown to whites, the civil rights movement started to emerge in the early 1960s. The U.S. Department of Justice in 1961 charged the voting registrars in Dallas County with racial discrimination and, when two resigned, took the remaining one to court. While the case dragged on, workers with the Student Nonviolent Coordinating Committee arrived in Selma in 1963 to begin organizing in the black community. Led by SNCC, Selma blacks challenged segregation in public accommodations (outlawed by the federal civil rights law passed in 1964) and led a number of marches to the county courthouse to register to vote. Hundreds were arrested. In July 1964 a local judge effectively quashed the nascent movement by banning all demonstrations. Although only 300 out of 15,000 potential blacks voters had registered by the end of 1964, SNCC had at least begun the vital job of awakening and mobilizing the black community.[11]

After careful planning, Martin Luther King and SCLC opened the Selma campaign with a mass meeting on January 2, 1965. King announced their intention to register voters in Selma and the Black Belt and, if barred by local officials, to pressure the governor, the legislature, and even Washington for relief. SCLC and SNCC cooperated in organizing demonstrations, and King returned for another mass meeting on January 14. The next day he led the first march to the Dallas County courthouse, but no black was allowed to register. During a second march on the sixteenth, Sheriff Clark attacked and arrested one black woman while his deputies jailed scores of other demonstrators — it was the dramatic response SCLC wanted. More arrests and violence followed. Among the many arrested in the coming days were several hundred school children and King himself.[12]

When the protests spread to other Black Belt towns but prompted few changes in voter registration procedures, King and SCLC decided to apply pressure on the state and federal governments with a march to the state capital. On the afternoon of Sunday, March 7, six hundred marchers left Brown Chapel African Methodist Episcopal (AME) Church in Selma for the walk to Montgomery, even though Governor George C. Wallace had prohibited such a protest on Highway 80. The marchers advanced peacefully through downtown Selma and across the Pettus Bridge, where they encountered a large force of state troopers and Dallas County possemen. After allowing the demonstrators to kneel for prayer at the end of the bridge, the officers gave them two minutes to turn around and return to Selma. Only a minute passed, however, before the troopers without warning attacked the marchers with clubs, fists, and tear gas. The mounted possemen quickly joined the fray. More possemen met the marchers on the Selma side of the bridge and chased them with whips and nightsticks into a nearby black neighborhood. Scores of blacks were injured and more than fifty were taken to local hospitals.[13]

The events of "Bloody Sunday" in Selma horrified the nation. That night Martin Luther King, who had not been in Selma for the protest, called for a second march to Montgomery two days later. Using a new tactic, he asked for clergy of all faiths to join him in the peaceful march.[14]

In Cambridge, Massachusetts, on the following Monday evening, Jon Daniels joined the ten other students from the Episcopal Theological School who had decided to respond personally to King's call. Their bags hastily packed, they quietly congregated with their supporters in the chill outside the dormitories and prepared to leave. Just before getting into cars, someone suggested that a prayer be offered for the departing seminarians. Among the well-wishers, the Right Reverend Arthur Lichtenberger, an elderly former presiding bishop of the Episcopal church, seemed the natural person to give the prayer, even though Parkinson's disease affected his speech. His wife broke the tension by observing, "Well, he'll say a blessing but he'll stutter." After the prayer, the eleven seminarians rode to Logan Field in Boston for the flight south.[15]

Daniels and his fellow seminarians arrived in Atlanta in the middle of the night. Emotionally, they resembled soldiers preparing for battle — though anxious, even fearful, they were at the same time excited about the prospect of participating in the march to Montgomery. Some were silent, while others chatted nervously. An inveterate smoker, Jon Daniels had innumerable cigarettes while sitting rather quietly. They spent the rest of the night at SCLC headquarters in Atlanta with others who were also heading to Selma for the march. Those who could sleep bedded down on sofas, in chairs, and on the floor; some slept in King's office.[16]

The next day the Episcopalians participated in Morning Prayer before setting out for Selma. During the more than five-hour bus ride, Daniels learned something about the situation he would find in Alabama. Veterans of the movement began singing protest songs, and the newcomers quickly joined in. Though morale was high, the mood on the bus turned more sober when in Birmingham the driver refused to go any further because he feared the bus would be attacked. After some words between the driver and the local dispatcher, a new driver arrived and the bus continued on its way, but the incident alerted Daniels and the other passengers to the real physical dangers that they might encounter. Explicit warnings came from a young woman who briefed the group on what to say and do to avoid violent clashes with opponents of civil rights both in Selma and on the march.[17]

The bus did not go to the Selma bus station but instead dropped Daniels and the other northerners off at the edge of a black neighborhood several blocks from downtown. From there they walked to Brown Chapel, which served as an unofficial headquarters for the march activities, and joined Martin Luther King and hundreds of others who had been gathering since the morning. Like good foot soldiers, Daniels, James Capen, Judith Upham, Stephen Weissman, and their colleagues from ETS waited for the march to begin. Finally, with King in the lead, the march began. Two thousand people proceeded to downtown Selma, then up and over the Edmund Pettus Bridge. Under a federal court order barring any march, they were stopped abruptly on the Montgomery side of the Alabama River. They sang "We Shall Overcome," were led in four prayers, and then, to avoid violence, turned around and crossed the bridge into Selma. There was no violence but there was no real march either.[18]

Jon Daniels and the other would-be demonstrators returned to safety in Selma's black community. Immediately after the aborted effort, some of the marchers began returning to their homes, but Daniels, Judy Upham, and others stayed for several more days. One marcher who decided on the spur of the moment to remain for another day was the Reverend James Reeb, a Unitarian minister from Boston who had flown to Atlanta on the same plane as the ETS seminarians. That evening a group of local whites attacked Reeb soon after he left a black restaurant, and he died the next day.[19] Reeb's death made even clearer to Daniels the dangers facing him and the other marchers.

For Wednesday, SCLC had scheduled a march to the Dallas County courthouse by the more than four hundred visiting clergy, and after Reeb's death it was also to include a prayer vigil to honor the slain minister. Daniels joined the throng that left Brown Chapel at noon. Heading toward the courthouse, they had marched only about a block before they were stopped by the mayor of Selma and the local police. Declaring an emergency in the city, the mayor banned further marches; in doing so, he hoped to prevent any clashes between the marchers and the nearby state troopers and sheriff's posse. Behind a rope across the street, the police in effect isolated the marchers in the black neighborhood around Brown Chapel. The demonstrators responded by holding a massive rally in front of the police. Soon they decided to maintain a vigil in the street until they were allowed to march to the courthouse. That night Daniels joined the hundreds sleeping in the street at what became known as the "Berlin Rope."[20]

The vigil continued for the rest of the week, even during a chilling rain. At one point Daniels found himself in a puddle at the front of the protesters standing face-to-face with the Selma police. Roused by a fiery Episcopal priest, part of the line moved forward and left Daniels just a few inches from a policeman. In the tense, hostile atmosphere, a young black female student who had been next to Daniels asked him to move back, but instead he reached back and pulled her to the front. The policeman said to Daniels, "You're dragging her through the puddle. You ought to be ashamed for treating a girl like that." Daniels replied angrily that it was the policeman's fault that they were having to stand there. Then, feeling ashamed, he *apologized* to the officer. Soon the youngsters around him were singing to the policemen, "I love ———," substituting their badge numbers for names. Though dumbfounded at the turn of events, some of the policemen eventually relaxed enough to talk with the demonstrators and even to share cigarettes. Daniels's witness was beginning to work; the seminarian had succeeded, however temporarily and slightly, in breaking through the hatred of Selma's Berlin Rope.[21]

Prevented from marching to Montgomery or even downtown to the courthouse, Daniels and hundreds of others cordoned off by the policy near Brown Chapel continued their vigil. They slept in the streets and on the grass and ate food provided by black families in the neighborhood. When not actually manning the Berlin Rope, they spent most of their time meeting new people, discussing the civil rights movement, attending mass meetings at Brown Chapel, and waiting to march. As new recruits, they mainly stood around and waited for hours while the leaders planned and negotiated. When they could forget the very real dangers awaiting them outside their little preserve, the atmosphere around Brown Chapel sometimes resembled a picnic.[22]

Even while Daniels was preoccupied with the civil rights demonstrations, the church continued to have great importance for him. He regularly said Morning and Evening Prayer, and on one occasion he and other Episcopalians attended a celebration of the Eucharist in front of Brown Chapel. The day after the foreshortened march to Montgomery, Daniels joined nearly a score of other Episcopal seminarians and clergy to call on the local Episcopal rector. Church protocol suggested that a visit to the rector would be proper, so a delegation of Episcopalians ventured away from Brown Chapel to St. Paul's Episcopal Church, one block on the other side of Selma's main street. The group spoke with the Reverend T. Frank Mathews for more than an hour about the demonstrations in his town and the situation in the church. In an intense discussion with the visitors, Mathews admitted that he knew very few blacks except for the ones who worked around the church. When asked if there was anything wrong with the races worshipping separately, he said, "No, I see nothing wrong with this." Someone suggested that a racially mixed group might come to St. Paul's the next Sunday and asked what would happen. Mathews replied by asking rhetorically what they would do if someone with measles came to their church. Reminded that, as one participant recalled, "blackness wasn't catching," Mathews said that the church's reaction would depend on who the ushers happened to be, because some would permit them to enter but most would bar any integrated group. He could do nothing about the policy, he confessed, if he wanted to keep his job. Coming away from the meeting believing that Mathews was a moderate who thought something should be done, Daniels believed that the local rector needed the support of the visiting clergy.[23]

The next Sunday Jon Daniels and an integrated group did go to St. Paul's for the eleven o'clock service. Reporters and television crews covered the event. To the ushers it appeared to be a staged demonstration by a disorderly crowd of preachers, beatniks, and assorted other rowdy characters. In fact, all of the visitors were not Episcopalians and the group did include, according to one seminarian, "several beatniky-looking guys in blue jeans and sneakers. It was, in effect, a demonstration." At first the ushers barred the entire group from entering the church but finally relented and agreed to admit only the clergy, regardless of race. Rejecting the ushers' offer, the visitors said the general confession on the steps of the church and then crossed the street and said Morning Prayer by themselves. Within half an hour, the large, frustrated group left the area.[24]

Already absent from Cambridge for almost a week, Daniels and his remaining seminary colleagues felt pressured to return to their studies. He and Judy Upham, the last two from ETS, planned to fly back on Monday, but they missed their ride to Montgomery and thus remained in Selma one more day. That evening, Daniels participated in the long, emotional march in memory of James Reeb. Finally authorized by a U.S. district court, the solemn demonstrators quietly proceeded from Brown Chapel to the Dallas County courthouse. The march concluded in time for Daniels to see President Lyndon Johnson's televised appeal to the Congress and the nation for a new civil rights law to protect the right to vote. Responding in part to events in Selma, Johnson dramatically moved to put the moral, and eventually the legal, authority of the federal government behind the campaign to secure equal voting rights for southern blacks. His words naturally thrilled and excited Daniels.[25]

Daniels watched the president's speech in Rosa Scott's apartment in the George Washington Carver Homes next to Brown Chapel. He spent the rest of the evening talking with Mrs. Scott, Judy Upham, and the Reverend Morris Samuel, a white Episcopal activist from Los Angeles. Buoyed by the day's events, Daniels and Upham considered the prospect of remaining in Selma. While the two seminarians realized the impracticality of staying, Scott impressed on them the perils confronting blacks if all the whites departed. She was frightened. Samuel was troubled by what he called the "wham-bam-thank-you-ma'am ministry" practiced by so many clergy who came to town just for the march; he had already decided to stay longer and encouraged the two Cambridge seminarians to join him. As a result of their long discussion, Daniels and Upham resolved to continue their work in Selma. As Daniels explained it a few weeks later, "something had happened to me in Selma which meant I had to come back. I could not stand by in benevolent dispassion any longer without compromising everything I know and love and value. The imperative was too clear, the stakes were too high, my own identity was called too nakedly into question. . . . I had been blinded by what I saw here (and elsewhere), and the road to Damascus led, for me, back here."[26] Daniels had found the existential opportunity that he had been looking for — a chance to create his beliefs and to become his real self through action. Moreover, away from family, professors, and other authorities, his work in Selma would be an extraordinary liberating and defining experience. He would be on his own. First, however, he and Judy Upham had to fulfill their pressing obligations at ETS.

When they got back to Cambridge, Daniels and Upham first sought out Joseph Fletcher for advice on how to obtain permission to return to Alabama. During the spring semester Daniels was enrolled in Fletcher's Christian ethics class, also known as "Fletcher's Dirty Books" because it approached contemporary social problems through modern fiction. Fletcher, an influential senior professor who gained renown the next year as the author of *Situation Ethics*, supported their decision to go back to Selma. He believed that an individual had the moral responsibility to respond to specific circumstances, not by following formal ethical rules but by applying Christian love in each particular context; Daniels and Upham seemed to have done just that in deciding to go back to Selma. Daniels especially appeared to have found in Selma an opportunity for self-discovery and self-fulfillment.[27]

The next day the two seminarians spoke with other faculty members and students about their plans. After questioning them closely, acting dean Henry M. Shires concluded that they had made the best decision. In the evening the eleven seminarians who had gone to Selma reported to the St. John's Society, and Judy Upham explained what she and Daniels hoped to do. Most students and faculty were excited to hear about their experiences in Selma, and most supported the continued efforts of Daniels and Upham. Some, however, considered such activity inappropriate for people who were supposed to be studying and preparing for the priesthood, and a few southerners at ETS did not approve of their colleagues' intervention in their region. A minority believed that their obligation to the seminary outweighed any concern they had for the civil rights movement. Harvel Sanders wondered how Daniels could forsake their important interracial work in Providence for that in Selma; to Sanders, the two endeavors seemed similar and the one in Providence was well under way. After some debate, the faculty decided that the two seminarians should be allowed to continue their academic work in absentia. They would be expected to submit papers from Selma during the rest of the semester and then return to Cambridge for their final exams.[28]

Judy Upham was a year behind Daniels at ETS. Born in 1942 in Tulsa, she grew up in Oklahoma and Ohio where her father worked as a patent lawyer for an oil company. Though her family moved often, she had a typical upper-middle-class childhood and adolescence before majoring in economics at Radcliffe College. After her junior year she worked near St. Louis in an Episcopal summer camp for inner-city children, and the experience persuaded her to go into social work for the church. A lifelong Episcopalian, she moved a few blocks in Cambridge in the summer of 1964 and entered ETS as one of a handful of women seminarians.[29]

Upham first met Jon Daniels that fall. Though they had no classes together, they went to an occasional movie and frequently chatted over coffee; early in 1965 she helped him repaint his dormitory room. By the time they went to Selma in March, they had become good friends. She was very attracted to Daniels, but he had other girlfriends and was not romantically interested in her. In fact, Upham admitted, part of her initial reason for going to Selma was to be near Jon Daniels. Even in the emotionally charged environment of Selma, however, their association never developed beyond that of close friends and co-workers. In Upham's words, theirs was a "very verbal, non-physical relationship," one of mutual trust and respect.[30]

Before returning to Selma, Daniels and Upham secured the sponsorship of the Episcopal Society for Cultural and Racial Unity (ESCRU). One hundred Episcopalians, mostly clergy and nearly half from the South, had met in 1959 at St. Augustine's College in Raleigh, North Carolina, to form an organization capable of responding to the growing racial crisis in the nation. An unofficial, controversial organization of Episcopalians, ESCRU immediately took a militant stand against segregation. Its original statement of purpose said: "We commit our selves to establish total participation in the Church for all persons without regard to race, class, or national origin; to give mutual support to all who act in this ministry of reconciliation; and to express this concern at parish levels and in a more creative witness through the community at large."[31]

In 1960 ESCRU was the first national religious organization to endorse the lunch counter sit-ins, and later in the year it boldly criticized all barriers to interracial marriage. In 1961 the society joined the freedom rides and sponsored a direct-action prayer pilgrimage from New Orleans to Detroit. It also protested racial segregation in an Episcopal hospital in New York and the exclusion of blacks from Atlanta's Lovett School, a prestigious private institution with close ties to Episcopalians. ESCRU participated in the 1963 March on Washington, in the funeral of Medgar Evers, and in the Selma-to-Montgomery march of 1965. Daniels and Upham first met ESCRU's executive secretary, the Reverend John B. Morris, of Atlanta, at the time of the march. When they decided to continue their civil rights work in Selma, Morris agreed to have ESCRU sponsor them.[32]

After spending only three days in Cambridge to prepare for their trip, Jon Daniels and Judy Upham set out for Alabama in her red Volkswagen beetle. The St. John's Society had given them some money, one professor's wife provided food, and another faculty member told them to use his credit card to call him. Upham took a bottle of Drambouie for Daniels's birthday the next day. They spent the first night in New York with her brother, then broke the long drive again with a short visit to VMI before heading into the Deep South. It was Daniels's first experience virtually alone in the region, and he was shocked by it. Some distance from Atlanta, they stopped late at night to buy gas and a couple of Cokes. The Massachusetts plates on Upham's car seemed to "glow in the night," and whites in the store stared at the two northerners. When Daniels noticed a "White Only" sign over the door, they decided to forget the Cokes and drive on. Down the road they stopped for coffee at an all-night truck stop. A sign over the counter declared: "ALL CASH RECEIVED FROM SALES TO NIGGERS WILL BE SENT DIRECTLY TO THE UNITED KLANS OF AMERICA." The confrontation with southern racism made Daniels sick. "It was lousy coffee," he recalled in disgust. "But worse than chicory was the taste of black men's blood. It was cheap: only twenty-five cents. At least Judas went for thirty."[33]

After their experiences on the road, Daniels and Upham were relieved and happy to pull up to Canterbury House at Atlanta University, where they spent Saturday night with the black chaplain. They were refreshed by the sleep and fellowship provided, and they finally got some good coffee. After participating in a celebration of the Eucharist on Sunday morning, they drove the rest of the way to Selma. On the outskirts of town they met the long-awaited march that had just that afternoon left Selma for Montgomery. They had arrived in time to join Martin Luther King for the historic event.[34]

While Daniels and Upham were in Cambridge, the demonstrations and arrests had continued in Selma and Montgomery. To obtain the right to march the forty-four miles to the capital, SCLC entered federal court to sue the state officials who had barred the march. Frank M. Johnson, Jr., a federal district court judge in Montgomery, ruled in favor of SCLC and approved its plan to limit the number of marchers to three hundred on the two-lane sections of Highway 80 but to place no limit on the four-lane sections. After Governor Wallace blasted Johnson's decision and refused to use the National Guard to protect the marchers, President Johnson federalized nearly two thousand Alabama guardsmen to provide security along Highway 80. Two weeks after Bloody Sunday, therefore, King led more than three thousand peaceful marchers from Brown Chapel, over the Edmund Pettus Bridge, out of Selma, and along the highway through the rural Black Belt toward Montgomery. The dramatic, but nonviolent, first day of the march covered only seven miles.[35]

Daniels did not immediately join the march. He and Upham drove directly to the George Washington Carver Homes, where Rosa Scott had agreed to let them live in her apartment. Initially, she gave them one bedroom; after the seminarians awkwardly explained that they did not sleep together, each shared a room with some of Scott's children. On Sunday evening Daniels drove to the place where the march had stopped for the night and helped ferry demonstrators back to Selma; only three hundred were allowed to march after the first day, so hundreds more had to return. That day he and Upham had also visited acquaintances and learned about on events in Selma during their absence. They spent several hours unpacking the Volkswagen and arranging their belongings — books, typewriter, clothes, and groceries. Unable to take part in the march because of the court's limit on numbers, they continued on Monday and most of Tuesday to settle in and rest after their long drive.[36]

Daniels managed to gather with the marchers on Tuesday night when they camped in Lowndes County thirty-four miles from Selma. The entire route was protected on the ground by National Guardsmen and overhead by helicopters and observation planes, but Daniels nevertheless "stood guard duty at the encampment" as part of a force organized by Morris Samuel. Except for the campsite's incredible mud caused by the day's heavy rains, he faced little danger. When the march resumed,

Daniels returned to Selma. By Wednesday night the demonstrators had reached Montgomery County, where once again Highway 80 became four lanes. For the rest of the trek the number of marchers mushroomed and by Wednesday night included Daniels.[37]

After a speaking trip outside of Alabama, King rejoined the demonstrators on the outskirts of Montgomery for the last night of the march. By then several thousand strong, the throng was entertained by an array of celebrities, including Mike Nichols, Floyd Patterson, Shelley Winters, and Tony Perkins. Joan Baez, Dick Gregory, Harry Belafonte, Peter, Paul, and Mary, Tony Bennett, Alan King, Nipsey Russell, and Sammy Davis, Jr., sang and joked for the crowd until after midnight. In the audience, Jon Daniels was disappointed by the festivities. The stars were "good, some of them kind of thrilling," he admitted. Yet during the entertainment he "began to feel a little as if I were at a circus." He would have preferred a more sober time of reflection on both the significance of the march and the future of the movement.[38]

On Thursday, March 25, King led more than twenty thousand — Jon Daniels among them — to the steps of the state capitol and then provided the inspiration Daniels had wanted. In an emotional address, King proclaimed: "We are on the move now. . . . We are moving to the land of freedom." Rhetorically, he repeatedly asked, "How long will it take?" Presciently, King acknowledged that the movement still faced "a season of suffering" in combating intransigent racial discrimination in parts of the South, yet he answered, "it will not be long, because truth pressed to earth will rise again. . . . Not long, because no lie can live forever. . . . Not long, because you still reap what you sow." Daniels found the speech "moving" and decided that King was "certainly one of the greatest men of our times."[39]

After the rally, Daniels chatted with several people who had come down from ETS for the final day of the march. One was Professor Harvey Guthrie, who had taught Daniels Old Testament. As they prepared to say good-bye, Daniels asked for Guthrie's blessing. In front of the capitol, surrounded by hundreds of people, Daniels knelt while Guthrie placed his hands on Daniels's head and blessed him. Soon the professor was on his way north, and Daniels and Upham were heading toward Selma to start their work. Later that night Viola Liuzzo, a white woman from Detroit, was murdered on Highway 80 as she drove through Lowndes County from Selma to Montgomery to transport marchers back to Selma. Her death made Daniels wary of driving in Alabama and reinforced his sense of the real dangers around him.[40]

Soon after the successful completion of the march to Montgomery, Daniels and Upham realized that only a few nonsouthern whites had remained with the civil rights movement in Selma. The thousands of other marchers had returned to their jobs and families; the clergy had gone back to their home congregations and the entertainers had flown to Hollywood and New York. The remaining hard work in the movement was left to local blacks, some workers with SCLC and SNCC, and the few whites like Jon Daniels and Judy Upham who had discovered a new commitment to civil rights in Selma. The two seminarians would stay in Selma until the middle of May, when the semester ended at ETS; they had to go back to Cambridge then to turn in papers and take final exams. Later, after a brief vacation, Daniels would return in July by himself. In March the newcomers, though dedicated and enthusiastic, surely lacked expertise in their new environment.[41]

Daniels had little experience in the South. He had, after all, been in Selma for only a week, and most of that time had been spent with non-southerners who were similarly caught up in the civil rights movement. He may have thought that Selma resembled his New England hometown, but the similarities were only superficial; Keene was not in Alabama's Black Belt. Yet his childhood experiences in the South, however slight, had been important to him. As a high school senior he had written, "Although I was only five at the time I retain, with distinct clarity, more memories of that period than of any other time or place. . . . I remember countless now cherished incidents that occurred during those years." The New Hampshire youth went on to say, "I think of the South as my adopted home and because of this, I cannot help but sympathize with her — in fact I must confess that I have a great affection . . . for the gallant and valorous but misguided Johnny Rebs."[42] Four years at VMI must have added to his belief that he understood the South and was a part of it. Though Daniels may not have realized it, the VMI experience was not the best introduction to the South because the military aspects were at least as strong as any southern qualities and the cadets did not represent a cross section of southern white society. What VMI did provide him was confidence that no task could be as difficult and challenging as the life of a cadet that he had survived.

If generally ignorant about the South, Daniels was also unacquainted with southern blacks and racial discrimination. Apparently, Keene, New Hampshire, had only one black family when Daniels was growing up. George Miller was a black man who took tickets at the local theater. Though Daniels and his friends always called him "George," he referred to the little boys as "Mr. Daniels" and "Mr. Felch," and they never thought about the distinction. Only as an adult did Daniels begin to understand that prejudice had been involved in his relationship with George Miller.[43]

The all-white VMI student body and faculty did not appreciably expand Daniels's personal contact with blacks or his understanding of race relations, though he did regularly observe blacks in menial jobs, especially the "stoop niggers" who cleaned the dormitories.[44] Harvard and ETS offered little more than VMI. During seminary, his fieldwork in a Providence ghetto afforded him his first opportunity to get to know blacks and to learn firsthand about black-white relations. Though valuable in sensitizing him to the corrosive effects of racism on an inner-city community, the Providence experience could not have provided adequate preparation for dealing with the tense and troubled racial situation in Selma in the spring of 1965. Daniels, therefore, returned to Alabama with few tools other than his wits and his personality. But he also had other vital sources of strength. The personal courage that he had gained at VMI and his growing faith constituted a powerful force undergirding his Christian witness in Alabama.

Though Daniels knew little about the South, he felt comfortable with the Episcopal church, so working on race relations with St. Paul's in Selma seemed a natural project for him when he returned to Alabama. At the time of the great march, he had been frustrated by the church's refusal to admit the integrated group including visiting Episcopalians to its services, but he did not give up. He must have assumed that the faith he shared with Selma's Episcopalians would provide a common ground on which they could reconcile their differences on civil rights. Rational persuasion and the gospel would be his tools in dealing with the local rector and his parishioners. He hoped that his own Christian witness and discussions with the minister and members of the congregation might help to bridge the gap between the races in Selma and to change the attitudes of the parish. Symbolically, the church was important because the hypocrisy of white Christians refusing to allow black Christians to enter their church was a blatant and embarrassing form of racial prejudice; it highlighted the conflict between the professed brotherhood of man and racial segregation. St. Paul's Episcopal Church was a particularly significant focal point because many of its members were leaders in the white community. To admit blacks to worship at St. Paul's would concede their fundamental humanity and their equality before God, undercut arguments for their inferiority, and set an example for the rest of white Selma. To Daniels, the integration of the Selma Episcopal church was a logical step, but to many parishioners it posed a powerful threat to the way they viewed the world. The task was, therefore, greater than the seminarian expected, and it had a more troubled history than he could have imagined.

St. Paul's had been organized in 1838. Its present Gothic Revival style building was constructed in the 1870s after the original one had been destroyed in the Civil War. Located in downtown Selma one block from the main street and within a few blocks of the town's main Presbyterian, Baptist, Methodist, and First Christian churches, St. Paul's was far from the largest church in Selma, but in the early 1960s it had almost five hundred communicants. The congregation was probably the wealthiest in Selma, with many businessmen and professionals, few hourly wage earners, and virtually no low-income members. It was also, according to the bishop coadjutor, "about as conservative — even reactionary — a congregation of any size [as] we have in the Diocese."[45]

St. Paul's members responded to the developing civil rights movement in ways similar to other white southerners. After the *Brown* decision in 1954, the church operated for a few years a private school for grades one through four. Though it contended that the new school had nothing to do with the race question, no blacks ever attended. In 1960 the church vestry passed, with only one dissenting vote, a resolution criticizing the integration of the Diocesan Youth Convention. Declaring "social integration of the races to be primarily political" and hence not an appropriate concern of the church, it protested that "certain elements are exerting undue efforts within our Church to foster the concept of integration of our young people" and that "the continued social integration of our young people . . . will hamper the effectiveness of our Youth Activities and weaken its structure." Some of St. Paul's parishioners particularly objected to the role of the National Council of Churches (NCC) in the civil rights movement and suspected that it had ties to international communism.[46]

By 1963 many members of the church began to worry that Negroes might try to attend their worship services. Over the years some blacks had without controversy occasionally attended weddings and funerals at St. Paul's and had worshipped there before 1954, but in the 1960s their attendance at regular services was an entirely different matter. In May the vestry adopted a resolution setting policy for dealing with black visitors. They were to "be ushered to the South Transept door, be requested to fill out a visitor's card and be seated in the South Transept, first, the North Transept second, and the front pews last, in that order." In other words, black worshippers would not be permitted to enter the church through the main entrance or to sit anywhere they wished. The policy further provided that the minister should later meet with the visitors to determine why they had come and apparently to persuade them not to return. No blacks appeared at St. Paul's in the spring and summer of 1963, but the vestry continued to discuss the matter.[47]

On Sunday, October 6, 1963, the vestry, fearing that blacks might try to attend a service at St. Paul's that morning, met at ten o'clock in a special session in the church nave. The rector stated that he knew of no canonical basis for refusing entry to anyone and that he had to support the national church's policy of nondiscrimination. Vacillating on the point, however, he turned over to the vestry the final decision. The vestry promptly voted to refuse admittance to any blacks wishing to attend the eleven o'clock service that day. One of the three people who voted against the resolution protested the decision by submitting his resignation, which the vestry refused to accept.[48]

At another special vestry meeting the next evening, Frank Mathews spoke at length about discrimination. The thirty-seven-year-old husky, blond rector had grown up in Montgomery, attended the University of Alabama, and served in the marines. After seminary in Virginia, he served a church in Birmingham before moving to Selma in 1955. He was an exceptional preacher and popular in town as well as in his parish. During the racial crisis, Mathews sought to avoid a split in the congregation and as a result his apparent straddling of the issues frequently left all sides dissatisfied. At the special vestry meeting, however, he reiterated his opposition to discrimination in admitting people to church services. He reminded the vestry of resolutions passed by the national church's General Convention in 1961, a 1962 pastoral letter from the House of Bishops, and a letter in 1963 from the presiding bishop, all of which made clear the church's policy of nondiscrimination. The rector finally advised the vestry not to bar any one from the church on the basis of race or color.[49]

After prolonged discussion, the vestry moved away from its stand prohibiting all blacks from their church. The segregationist views of the majority remained nonetheless obvious in its resolution "that no person, white or colored, who is obviously intent upon gaining admittance to a service in our Church for the purpose of agitating racial strife and discord shall be admitted to such service." It turned over to the ushers "the discretion and authority to deny admittance to any such persons" but carefully pointed out that "family servants" could still attend funerals and weddings. After all the controversy, no blacks sought entry to St. Paul's in 1963 or 1964.[50]

By early March 1965 when Jon Daniels first arrived in Selma, the turmoil and tension at St. Paul's and in Selma generally were extraordinary. Many law-abiding whites did not know what to do when they saw their town invaded by thousands of outsiders. In the "Rector's Word" column in the weekly church bulletin, Mathews had railed against Martin Luther King as "one self-seeking opportunist" and had criticized "the irresponsible tactics" of using youths in the voting rights demonstrations. As he later said, "the white people of Selma . . . had been living for two months in the explosive atmosphere of a city in the throes of the worst turmoil we had ever experienced. People's nerves were frayed. . . . Our city was being ravaged and we were 'shell-shocked.' "[51]

Unknown to Daniels, the day after he and others conferred with Mathews about the church's attitude toward integration, the vestry of St. Paul's met in a special session to review its policy. After the rector again reminded them that no member of the church could be excluded, the vestry voted 12–2 to admit Episcopal clergy at the rear of the church but to leave to the discretion of the ushers whether to permit other visitors. Mathews repeated his objections, and the vestry ordered him to go to Florida for a vacation. Coincidentally, his doctors had also insisted that he get away from the pressures of Selma so he could nurse his ulcer; he had been hospitalized for a bleeding ulcer six months earlier and they worried about a recurrence.[52]

The resistance to admitting blacks to St. Paul's was more intense than Daniels and the other visiting Episcopalians could have known. The adamant segregationists in the parish who fought against an open-door policy included vestryman David McCullough and his wife Annette. Members of the John Birch Society, the McCulloughs believed that the civil rights movement and the National Council of Churches were somehow linked to communism. David McCullough, a prosperous soft drink and wine bottler, was St. Paul's largest financial supporter. He personally paid for Mathews's sudden Florida vacation at a critical time for the church; other parishioners suspected that McCullough wanted Mathews away from Selma because he feared that the rector would cave in to the civil rights demonstrators, whereas the vestry and the ushers would keep them out if left on their own.[53]

On the Sunday after their initial attempt to enter St. Paul's, Daniels and others were turned away from the church a second time. While the rector vacationed in Florida, the vestry met in several special sessions to clarify its admissions policy. On tie votes it failed to agree either to exclude the disorderly or to accept only the orderly who intended to worship. The ushers therefore were allowed to continue to use their discretion and on the next Sunday, March 21, refused admittance to a smaller and more orderly group.[54] By the following Sunday Jon Daniels had returned to Selma from Cambridge and renewed his attempts to integrate the church.

Frank Mathews, who had also returned to Selma, promptly presided over still another special meeting of the vestry. Following the requests of the rector and the bishop, the vestry voted 8–3 to abide by the canons of the church regarding admitting people to church services. In addition, however, it reiterated that the canons gave the ushers the authority to "maintain order and decorum during the time of public worship." Disgusted with the decision, David McCullough immediately resigned from the vestry. In a special letter to the congregation, Mathews praised the "unselfish and dedicated devotion" of the vestry: "Your Vestrymen have displayed a remarkable love for the church by putting their personal feeling aside and acting like Episcopalians, which they are proud to be. I urge you to follow their example." In a second letter he emphasized that he "concur[red] wholeheartedly in what they have done" and relayed the bishop's commendation of the vestry's action.[55] In spite of their setback in the vestry, however, St. Paul's segregationists had not given up.

Another ardent racist at St. Paul's was Judge James A. Hare, the son of a Dallas County planter and a mentor of Sheriff Jim Clark. In 1965 the fifty-nine-year-old circuit judge observed, "Your Negro is a mixture of African types like the Congolite who has a long heel and the blue-gummed Ebo whose I.Q. is about 50 or 55." In 1963 he had declared, "Any form of social or educational integration is not possible within the context of our society." Hare thought that his view was "pretty well like that of the community. This view has prevailed for 300 years. The racial issue is nothing new to this part of the state." An outspoken enemy of the civil rights movement in his community, Hare claimed that federal officials, including the army, had targeted Selma and helped plan the civil rights demonstrations that racked his city. In March 1965, he presented to another special meeting of the vestry a petition from some of St. Paul's communicants. Referring to subversives and militants among the civil rights demonstrators, the group requested that the rector and vestry "limit the regular services to known communicants of this Parish during this emergency." In executive session, the vestry brushed aside Hare's proposal and reaffirmed its decision to conform to the church canons.[56]

McCullough and Hare were certainly not the only parishioners outraged by the admission of Jon Daniels and other civil rights workers to their church. The events in Selma and at St. Paul's so upset Frances H. Hamilton that she complained to her bishop. In her opinion, "Our problem is not a race one but rather one of upholding moral standards as contained in the Ten Commandments." Specifically, she mentioned "the acts of immorality" committed by people who came to Selma for the march — not only interracial sex but also sexual escapades involving clergymen. One white girl, she declared, had died of exhaustion after providing "sexual comfort to the visiting clergy." Hamilton protested the vestry's decision "to let the immoral characters into the church next Sunday" and argued that it made the church appear to condone the immoral behavior. Intimating that the rector had succumbed to bribery, she reported a possible deal to let some demonstrators attend only because civil rights workers had planned to recruit one thousand Negroes to flood St. Paul's on the following Sunday.[57]

Others in the congregation also ardently defended racial segregation and voiced a range of racist views typical of much of the white South. "What's it like to be a Christian in a segregated society? It is sublime," declared one member of St. Paul's. "Segregation keeps Christians of each race separated where each race can develop their special racial qualities at all levels of society without the real possibility of intermarriage." Echoing Frances Hamilton, a Selma Episcopalian opposed integration because the blacks' lower moral standards would corrupt white children. Another argued that blacks should not attend services at St. Paul's "because their religion is different from ours, and they would not understand our way of worship. The Negroes like to sing and shout, and they have a mourners' bench." A number of communicants objected to the "pressures" and "harassments" inflicted by outside agitators who were more interested in publicity and politics than religious worship.[58]

A continual irritant to many parishioners was the National Council of Churches, which St. Paul's indirectly supported through the national Episcopal church. The NCC endorsed the civil rights movement and therefore seemed to be connected with communists and un-American forces. After studying the church's ties to NCC, a committee of St. Paul's vestry discovered that each member of the church contributed only about seven cents indirectly to the organization. The vestry nevertheless adopted a resolution alleging that NCC "is now sponsoring activities in social, inter-racial and political areas, the tendencies of which are to promote and incite civil unrest, discord and even violence." A majority of the vestry particularly objected to NCC's involvement with the Selma-to-Montgomery march, the Mississippi Summer Project, and the opposition to Hammermill Paper's plans to build a new plant in Selma.[59] Though not unusual in the South, the attack on NCC was partly just an indirect way to voice displeasure with the changes occurring in Selma without appearing to be overtly racist.

A minority in St. Paul's congregation disagreed with the strict segregationists, though they might not have welcomed integration. For some Episcopalians, blacks had to be permitted into the services at St. Paul's simply because the church canon required an open door to all. One parishioner, who admitted not liking all the characteristics of black people, asked, "If we ignore them, hate them, despise them, ridicule them, belittle them, exploit them, or embarrass them are we not transgressing the Commandment of God?" The answer was obvious and led at least one church member to ask if it was proper to "seat them, our neighbors,

in an obscure corner where they will not contaminate 'God's elite?' "
While some parishioners thought that Daniels and his co-workers complained unnecessarily about details like where they were seated and when they were served Communion, one Episcopalian understood their position: "perhaps if one has always had to enter a building by a certain door and has always heard his 'white friends' say how devoted they are to Negroes as long as they stay in their places — well, perhaps these trivialities don't seem so trivial."[60] Within the parish, the divisions over race relations were real and in many ways mirrored the disputes in the larger community and the South.

While a few members either sought integration of their services or were at least willing to accept the presence of blacks, most of the congregation wished for things not to change. They saw no reason for the demonstrations in Selma or for the controversy within their own church. Happy with their town and comfortable in their church, they did not like Martin Luther King, Jon Daniels, or anyone else coming in and upsetting things. They understood that any change, even gradual change, would lead to a revolution in their community, so they tenaciously defended the status quo. Daniels, on the other hand, assumed the goodwill of Selma's Episcopalians. He simply believed that as Christians they would respond positively to his peaceful Christian witness for the brotherhood of all, regardless of race, and realize that their faith required action now, not sometime in the distant future. He thought that as educated people they could be convinced by calm and reasonable discussion. If necessary, he would gain their attention by forcing the church to accept integrated groups of worshippers. As Judy Upham later wrote, he thought that "[r]econciliation . . . could best be effected by forcing the local parish to wake up to the necessity of being the Church, the Body of Christ, and not just a social club for middle-class whites."[61] His Christian witness, therefore, collided with the parishioners' determined defense of their way of life; his call for immediate change clashed with their insistence on no change at all.

Though knowing little of the fears and bitter debates within St. Paul's, Jon Daniels quickly learned of the church's decision to abide by the canons and prepared to attend St. Paul's with an integrated group. In preparation, he and Upham had been reading Morning and Evening Prayer with some young blacks who wanted to go with them. On March 28, Daniels, Upham, nine other whites, and five blacks were admitted to St. Paul's eleven o'clock Morning Prayer service "with grace but with obvious reluctance." The ushers greeted them, gave them bulletins, and sat them in the front row, where they listened to Mathews preach on the "Ministry of Reconciliation." Without ever mentioning race relations or the recent troubles in the church, the rector pointed out that "our inability to admit to ourselves . . . [and] to persons from whom we are separated that we are not always right" was a major impediment to reconciliation. "Really, the underlying reason for separation that exists between man and man," he concluded, "is the real separation that exists between man and God." After the service, a number of people greeted the integrated group of visitors, some warmly.[62]

Overjoyed with their successful integration of St. Paul's, Daniels told a friend in New Hampshire that "the local Episcopal Church *welcomed* our mixed group. Glory to God in the highest!" Although his enthusiasm and inexperience led him to misread what had happened, the apparent victory at St. Paul's inspired him. "What a change in three weeks!" he declared, as he prepared to undertake more work with blacks and the white Episcopalians.[63]

Although to Jon Daniels the question of who would be admitted to St. Paul's may have seemed settled on March 28, it was not. Meeting in a special session two days later, vestrymen suggested that the church canons did not require the admission of non-Episcopalians and that some of the blacks attending on Sunday had not been Episcopalians. It was reported that a number of parishioners "objected strongly to their being admitted and felt that the ushers should restrict admissions to the letter" of the canon. The Reverend Frank Mathews nonetheless maintained that the church stood for an open-door policy, whether explicitly required by the canons or not. In addition, on tactical grounds he argued that an open-door policy would avert "more 'scandal' and adverse publicity for our parish and diocese." By consensus the vestry agreed to follow the rector's advice for a few weeks and see what happened.[64]

On April 11, Palm Sunday, Daniels and Judy Upham returned to St. Paul's with some young blacks, but this time to attend a 7:30 A.M. Communion service. The ushers refused to let them enter the church and called the police. Only when Mathews interceded did they finally gain entrance. Mathews told them, "This may cost me my job, but you can go in." The integrated group sat in the back and received Communion last. Daniels exulted in their small victory: "we went to Palm Sunday Communion, by golly!" Later in the morning he returned with other black children who had not wanted to attend the Communion service. As they were entering the church, a white man who was also heading inside called to them: "You goddamned scum!" Mathews, though looking a little chastened by the earlier experience, was friendly to them after the service and talked with Daniels.[65]

To smooth the way for Easter, several meetings took place in the following week. Daniels and Upham acceded to an agreement reached between the Reverend Henri A. Stines, a Haitian who was the southern field director for ESCRU, and Mathews that they would not ruin Easter at St. Paul's by taking the black children to the main service at eleven o'clock. Though Daniels worried that the agreement might disappoint some of their black friends, he recognized that the "concession may be an important guarantee of our good will."[66] On the other side, Bishop Charles Colcock Jones Carpenter arrived in Selma for a special meeting with the vestry.

Sixty-six-years old, Carpenter had served as bishop of the Diocese of Alabama since 1938. He was an impressive man — tall, with a deep voice and commanding presence — and popular throughout the diocese. In the early 1950s he had worked as chairman of an abortive interracial committee in Birmingham and many criticized him for being an integrationist. In fact, he was a conservative remnant of an older generation. His genteel paternalism left him with little patience for the protests and disruptions of 1965. Before the Selma-to-Montgomery march, Bishop Carpenter countered King's call for clergy to join the protest by declaring that he hoped no Episcopalians would participate because it "can serve no useful purpose," would "be detrimental to progress," and was "a foolish business and sad waste of time." He objected to the demonstrations in Selma as "causing much ill-will and unnecessary unhappiness in our state," at least for white Alabamians (he seemed unaware of or unconcerned about the wishes of blacks).[67]

In his afternoon meeting with St. Paul's vestry, Carpenter endorsed the national church's policy of admitting all to the worship services. To rescind the open-door policy would, he feared, cause much unfavorable publicity and lead to even greater demonstrations. In addition, calling for a uniform policy, he said that the church could not let people into Morning Prayer but bar them from the Communion service. In regard to seating, the bishop maintained that ushers had the right to seat visitors wherever they chose, usually in pews normally vacant; a wiser policy, he suggested, might be to allow guests to select their own seats. The vestry took no formal action at the meeting. Mathews thought that the bishop's discussion with the vestry "got us all over a difficult hurdle" and that "we can look for smooth sailing from here on."[68]

That evening, an integrated group attended the Maunday Thursday Communion service at St. Paul's. Without incident they willingly seated themselves in the last pew and thus were the last to receive the Sacrament. "Praise the Lord!" exclaimed a relieved Mathews in sending the bishop the good news.[69] Indeed, the racial problems at St. Paul's seemed nearly settled.

The day before Easter, Jon Daniels and Judy Upham went to confer with Frank Mathews because they had learned that some of the young blacks in the Carver Homes were planning to attend the main Easter service at eleven despite the agreement between Stines and Mathews. To prevent the children from going by themselves, the seminarians told Mathews that they would all be coming to the service. The rector assured them that Bishop Carpenter had informed the vestry that an integrated group could not be barred from Communion and that the ushers could use their discretion in seating visitors. Mathews, pointing to their ecumenical concerns, also suggested that Daniels and Upham ought to stop coming to St. Paul's and instead worship at a local Negro church. After their friendly and frank discussion, the two seminarians left the church office and suddenly came face-to-face with the power of segregationist feeling in the church. The husband of the church organist met them on their way out and proceeded to question them about why they persisted in attending St. Paul's. When they explained that they were merely trying to follow the gospel, he blurted: "You go to hell. You goddamned fucking son-of-a-bitch!" Stunned by the blast, the pair merely said, "We are sorry that you feel that way, sir," and then departed.[70]

The next day Daniels and Upham went with several blacks to St. Paul's for the early Communion Easter service. An usher, who was a conservative vestryman, told them not to bring any Negroes to the eleven o'clock service and then seated the racially mixed group in the rear of the church about six rows behind the nearest worshippers. They, therefore, received Communion after everyone else. Daniels noted the grim irony of the inscription over the altar— "He is not here. For He is risen." He later described it as an existential moment because, while under the hostile glares of many in the church, he had to overcome his own hatred with compassion and charity before he could accept the Sacrament. With sorrow he took Communion and began "to taste joy and perhaps the triumph of the Cross." After the service Daniels and his friends stopped to speak to Mathews, who they thought "studiously ignored" them for five minutes until he could no longer avoid a meeting. For the eleven o'clock Easter service, Daniels and Upham went with some black friends to a black Methodist church, where Jon Daniels participated in the service.[71]

The reaction of St. Paul's on Easter proved so disappointing to Daniels that several days later he and Judy Upham sent a letter of protest to Bishop Carpenter. In reviewing their conversations with Mathews, they explained their understanding of the bishop's instructions to the vestry about the handling of integrated groups. They related how the usher and the rector had treated them at the early church service on Easter, and they suggested that the most recent events were not particularly unusual. On previous occasions, Daniels, Upham, and their black companions had "repeatedly been the objects of obscene remarks and insults by some of the congregation . . . and recipients of hostile glares by others." Though "a small minority [at St. Paul's] have been extremely gracious" and Mathews had usually been "most cordial," they conveyed to the bishop their acute dissatisfaction with their overall reception at the church. (The two seminarians also objected to Mathews about the seating arrangements, and he pledged to do what he could to prevent such treatment in the future.)[72]

Daniels and Upham granted that the bishop's apparent policy and the behavior of the parish "may indeed approximate the letter of the canon," but they believed that the bishop and the Selma church "scarcely fulfill its spirit." "Surely," they argued, "the Gospel, as it is delivered to this Church and proclaimed at her altars and pulpits, calls for a charity, a witness, and a living reconciliation that the racial policy of St. Paul's Church currently negates." They pointed to the "deliberate breach of the conditions cited in the Invitation to Holy Communion — and a compromise of the Gospel, as well." Hoping that Carpenter did not support, and would now oppose, the practices of St. Paul's, they referred to the "policy attributed to you" and "the policy you are represented as having enunciated." In any event, the seminarians implored the bishop to act to correct the injustices at St. Paul's. To rally outside pressure on him, they sent copies of their letter to several other bishops and to two Episcopal publications.[73]

Ignoring the substance of the letter from Daniels and Upham, Carpenter focused instead on their allegations of obscenities and insults coming from members of the St. Paul's congregation. "This is very strong language," he wrote them, "and I cannot imagine the good people of St. Paul's Church, Selma, using obscene language in your presence." The proper and genteel bishop apparently found foul language more offensive than racial discrimination, or perhaps he just wanted to divert attention from the more troubling racial issue. "Please tell me by immediate mail just what these obscene remarks were," he requested. "I would like to know the exact wording so that I may look further into this situation."[74]

On the following Sunday, April 25, Daniels, Upham, and Rev. Henri Stines went to the 7:30 morning service at St. Paul's. The treatment of Easter, however, was not repeated. They were permitted to seat themselves among the other worshippers without the assistance of an usher, and when their turn came, they went to the altar and received Communion with everyone else.[75]

Unsatisfied with the bishop's reaction and unconvinced that St. Paul's policies had really changed, Daniels the next week drove to Birmingham with Upham and Stines to meet with Bishop Carpenter. They wanted to discuss both the situation in the Selma church, which they interpreted as segregation, and the diocese's racial policies, which they believed condoned the actions in St. Paul's. As he had requested, Daniels and Upham told the bishop exactly what obscene remarks had been made to them as they entered and left St. Paul's. The ESCRU workers received little satisfaction from their conference. Daniels thought that the bishop was "sarcastic" and that he "consistently avoided the real issues." Instead, Carpenter tried to place the blame on Daniels and Upham, charging, in effect, that they were destroying the church.[76]

Frustrated by the bishop's attitude, the three returned to Selma to plan their next moves. Daniels and Upham first sent another, more pointed protest to Carpenter. Rejecting the bishop's emphasis on the indecent remarks made by offending parishioners, they declared that "obscenity is only a symptom of the complicated sickness that affects the life and witness of St. Paul's." Their reason for driving to Birmingham was not to discuss the epithets but the more critical issue: "the objective fact of the policy of racial discrimination practiced by St. Paul's, Selma, and endorsed yesterday by the Diocesan of Alabama." The question for Daniels and Upham was not whether someone's feelings had been hurt but that St. Paul's had violated the canons of the church. Though the bishop had suggested that they and their black friends ought to wait humbly and thankfully for Communion, they argued that there was "a difference between humility and humiliation." "The measures you employ to facilitate the 'humility' of our black brothers," they charged, "constitute a clearcut instance of racial discrimination." They closed by pleading that the bishop reconsider his position; they hoped he would accept his responsibility and use his authority to lead the way toward eliminating the discriminatory practices at St. Paul's.[77]

The pace and intensity of protest escalated the next day when ESCRU released a statement signed by Daniels, Upham, and three members of the society's staff. It charged that a "new form of segregation is emerging in the Episcopal Diocese of Alabama." Recounting the April 18 Easter service when an integrated group was ushered to seats at the rear of St. Paul's, ESCRU argued that "it now appears that insidious devices will be employed to circumvent the spirit of the canon and the generally accepted teaching of the church." Referring to Montgomery's old, unconstitutional ordinance requiring blacks to sit in the rear of the bus, the statement suggested that "the church now seeks to use the nefarious method of segregated seating to maintain the old racial patterns." Going further back in history, it termed the segregated seating in St. Paul's a "new expression of the old slave gallery." Calling segregation an "affront to Christ and His Church," Daniels and his colleagues were particularly outraged that the segregated seating seemed to be required at St. Paul's only for Communion services, not for regular Morning Prayer. They further reported that the church was "now seeking to discard the 'common cup' in favor of intinction [which] adds only shame to a grievous situation."[78]

The ESCRU statement, which was sent to every bishop in the nation, also unwisely blasted Bishop Carpenter. It acknowledged that some had praised the bishop for advising the St. Paul's vestry to abide by the canon, but it then indicted him for taking "steps to undercut the spirit of that same canon by telling them that the choice was theirs as to where visitors were seated." According to the ESCRU activists, the bishop sanctioned a "devious maneuver" to segregate worshippers at Communion services. "The Carpenter of Birmingham," they declared, "must not be allowed to forever deny the Carpenter of Nazareth." For them, segregation was simply "a denial of the unity of all men in Christ Jesus." To protest segregated seating in the church and Carpenter's apparent approval of it, the signers of the ESCRU statement announced their intention to picket the diocesan headquarters in Birmingham the next day.[79]

Early on Friday, April 30, Jon Daniels and Judy Upham drove to Birmingham to meet the Reverend John B. Morris (executive director of ESCRU), the Reverend Henri Stines, and the Reverend Albert R. Dreisbach, Jr. (associate director of ESCRU), all of whom had just flown into Birmingham from Atlanta. Late in the morning the five Episcopalians went to the diocesan offices downtown. For fours hours they marched in front of the headquarters with signs condemning racial segregation in the church. One sign charged "Slave Gallery Revived," and another declared that "Bishop Sanctions Segregated Slavery in Selma Church." Daniels carried a sign depicting a cross that was half black and half white divided by a barbed wire fence; on one side was a white person and on the other a black, while below them was the phrase "Segregation . . . Separation."[80]

Coincidentally, the presiding bishop of the Episcopal Church was in Birmingham on the day of the picketing, but he did not see the demonstration because he was taken directly from the airport to a meeting at a church camp. Moreover, Bishop Carpenter did not go to the office that day either, so he missed the protests aimed at him. Workers in the diocesan office tried to ignore the picketers but naturally sneaked glimpses out the windows and encountered them going to and coming from lunch. The picketing received some attention in the newspapers but had no immediate impact on the bishops.[81]

At St. Paul's, Frank Mathews reacted angrily to the ESCRU statement. He declared that ESCRU was "notorious for presenting half truths" in its campaign against the Episcopal church in Selma. Though he acknowledged that on Easter an integrated group had been seated in the rear of the church for the early Communion service, the rector maintained that "the situation was remedied *immediately*" and that the next Sunday an integrated group attended the early morning service and "sat right in the middle of everyone else and received the sacrament along with everyone else." (Mathews failed to note, however, that on the Sunday after Easter the black member of the integrated group was an Episcopal priest.) He claimed that ESCRU reported the earlier episode and ignored the later one "to further blacken the image of St. Paul's . . . [and] to further slander the name and reputation of this parish." Moreover, on the Sunday after the demonstration, Daniels and Upham attended the early service with two black girls and all received Communion without any fuss; ESCRU's failure to mention this episode was for Mathews just another "clear example of false and misleading reporting." Mathews also said that ESCRU's allegation of segregation at the diocese's camp was "a lie!" In fact, at the time of the Birmingham picketing an integrated group was at the camp listening to the presiding bishop's speech.[82]

The continuing controversy at St. Paul's brought considerable stress on Mathews from both within and outside his parish. Among the parishioners, for example, David and Annette McCullough stopped going to church and began holding private services in their home. Their actions put pressure on the rector and the parish to restore their former racial policies, because the McCulloughs' financial support of St. Paul's had amounted to more than $13,000 in the previous three years. The rector resisted their efforts, however. "I'll be damned if I'll be bought," he wrote to his bishop coadjutor. "He can take his money and go to hell before I let him 'take over' this church — though not a few would just as soon follow his leadership." From across the nation Episcopalians, including Bishop James A. Pike, wrote to Mathews, mostly to protest the reported restrictions at St. Paul's. In addition, an article in the summer issue of the Episcopal periodical *Cathedral Age* was particularly critical of Selma and St. Paul's. The ESCRU statement and demonstrations thus only added to Mathews's worries.[83]

In the week after the picketing of diocesan headquarters in Birmingham, Jon Daniels and Judy Upham discussed with Mathews many of the issues involved in their protests. Daniels believed that their conversation was "frank, . . . cordial, and mutually informative," although "there was little fundamental agreement on cultural and racial lines." Mathews objected to the errors and distortions in the ESCRU statement. He particularly disagreed with ESCRU's suggestion regarding St. Paul's plan to replace the common Communion cup with intinction (the practice of dipping the individual piece of bread or wafer into the wine before serving it to the communicant). Mathews maintained that plans to change the administration of Communion had been under way for several months and had nothing to do with the arrival of blacks at Communion services. Accepting his explanation, Daniels and Upham acknowledged that the ESCRU statement had misrepresented the issue. The rector also said that he had intended no discourtesy to them after the Easter service and that he wished they had spoken to him about their impressions before publicizing them. Though still unconvinced about his behavior, Daniels and Upham conceded that they should have discussed the episode with him first and apologized for the misunderstanding.[84]

Daniels continued to attend services at St. Paul's and to take blacks with him, and Mathews remained concerned about the impact on his parish. On May 9, for instance, Daniels and a black person sat with other worshippers during the early service and received Communion without incident. Moreover, the rector was friendly toward them after the service. Later in the summer, Daniels was frequently accompanied by Gloria Larry, a black activist college student from California who had converted from the Baptist to the Episcopal church as a graduate student in Cambridge, England. While pursuing further study in comparative literature at Berkeley, she had become involved in the free speech movement, campus politics, and unionization efforts at the university. At the end of the spring semester in 1965, she left California to join the civil rights movement in the South and went to Selma.[85]

By July, after Jon Daniels brought an integrated group to St. Paul's, Mathews was able to exclaim to the bishop: "No discrimination in any way, shape, or form — praise the Lord!!" Kept fully informed about Jon Daniels's activities at St. Paul's and in Selma, Bishop Carpenter became increasingly annoyed and volunteered to intercede for the local rector. "If he is hanging around causing trouble," the bishop told Mathews, "I think I will just have to write to his bishop and tell him to take him on back to Seminary."[86] But before Carpenter could act, the situation at St. Paul's came to a head.

The prospect of blacks appearing for an eleven o'clock Communion service had especially worried the rector. "It could precipitate a real crisis," he fretted, "and most probably will." To avert more trouble, Mathews worked carefully to select and instruct ushers for the eleven o'clock service on August 1. When Jon Daniels and Gloria Larry arrived at St. Paul's a few minutes before eleven, several parishioners standing outside (including one of the rector's specially chosen ushers) promptly left and went home. Once inside, Daniels and Larry sat with the congregation and received Communion without incident. Mathews was proud that no disturbances occurred and that "everyone in the congregation behaved as Christians should."[87]

The turmoil in the parish persisted, however. Anonymous mimeographed mailings from "concerned Episcopalians" increased dissension. "Wild rumors are continuing to be spread throughout the parish which have no basis in fact," warned Mathews. One allegation was that Jon Daniels was preparing a group of blacks to be confirmed at St. Paul's. According to another rumor, the church choir would soon be integrated. In a note to his parishioners, the rector declared that the accusations "have no basis in fact and are detrimental to the harmony of this congregation." A few families left the church because blacks were allowed to worship there. The church also suffered financially from withheld pledges and in the summer had to borrow money to pay for routine expenses.[88]

The problems at St. Paul's were so great that on August 8 Mathews dispensed with the regular sermon and just talked to the parishioners "about dissension, about money, about affiliations, and about primary loyalties." He defended the vestry's decisions regarding the admission of blacks, criticized individuals seeking to destroy "the Episcopal nature and affiliation of this parish," repeated that St. Paul's contributed no money directly to the National Council of Churches, and emphasized the members' ties not just to the parish but also to the diocese. Mathews called on all Episcopalians in Selma to "put aside our personal grievances which have been fanned by the hate pamphlets and the anonymous articles that fill the mails, and get back to the primary business of religion — namely worshipping Almighty God in His Church, and supporting the work which He is trying to do through this Parish Family."[89]

The integration of services at St. Paul's Episcopal Church in Selma had indeed been, in the rector's words, a "traumatic experience" for him and for the congregation. Though the effects of the integration cannot be measured, the church and its members were changed by the experience and in spite of the ordeal the church survived. Along with others, Jon Daniels had in the spring and summer of 1965 successfully pressed and badgered the congregation into accepting blacks at regular worship services. The changes in St. Paul's had not been easy, but they had occurred. Without Daniels, the parish may have eventually confronted the racial question, but the absence of black Episcopalians in the city made integration unlikely. Jon Daniels made sure that the church faced the issue squarely. In doing so, his witness forced many individuals in the Selma congregation to come to grips with prejudice in a very personal way, in a way more intimate than the demonstrations that had racked their community.

THE BLACK BELT:

REALITY IS A

KALEIDOSCOPE

3

Selma and the South intrigued Jon Daniels. "Reality is a kaleidoscope in the black belt," the New Englander observed in April 1965. "Now you see it; now you don't. The view is never the same." If the racial views and practices within Selma's Episcopal church had in many ways confounded Daniels, he encountered even greater complexities in the wider context of Selma and the Alabama Black Belt, away from the familiarity of the Episcopal church. Southern race relations, he discovered, involved myriad combinations of good people and bad, kindness and cruelty, hope and despair. The surprising complications and contradictions of a seemingly simple, small southern community forced him to reassess his attitudes. In spite of his best efforts, however, Daniels could not quickly comprehend the intricate etiquette of southern race relations. The etiquette that informally governed relations between whites and blacks required that all southerners behave in specific ways that validated white superiority. Blacks, for example, had to yield to whites on sidewalks and to use courtesy titles (Mr., Mrs., and Miss) when addressing whites. Though baffled by southern customs, Daniels knew immediately that he must work for greater civil rights for blacks.[1]

The irrational racial injustice and hatred in Selma that initially bewildered Daniels soon caused him to become frustrated and angry. Agonizing over the best tactics to employ in his civil rights work, he even considered using violence. Though somewhat ashamed of his hostility, he admitted that he sometimes "would like to get a highpowered rifle and take to the woods" so he could "fight the battle as the klansmen do." Unless a miracle happened, he thought, "guerrilla warfare" might be necessary to surmount the intransigence of the local white power structure, including the Episcopal church, and the general "sickness of our civilization." "This is a grim business — it might as well be war," he declared.[2]

Daniels's thoughts about violence were undoubtedly affected by his own apprehensions while working in Alabama. He remembered the death of the Reverend James Reeb in Selma. After the night-rider slaying of Viola Liuzzo as she returned from the Selma-to-Montgomery march, Daniels wisely showed some hesitance about driving Judy Upham's Volkswagen lest its Massachusetts plates attract the wrong kind of attention. He also traveled to Montgomery with a priest just "so he won't have to go alone (which is *not* a good idea)." Like other civil rights workers, he heard disquieting reports of violence in Selma and the surrounding area. In April, for instance, he learned that "a hacked up black body was found today in a nearby county" and that "snipers are still doing their dirty work." One of his white co-workers received death threats from members of Sheriff Jim Clark's posse. On many occasions, Daniels was sure that he was being followed. In May, after a mistrial in the Liuzzo murder case, his fears escalated. He worried that that decision might encourage the Ku Klux Klan to increase its attacks on blacks and civil rights workers. "I wonder," he wrote a friend, "how long the southern white will rule by terror. Sometimes I think this place isn't even civilized . . . sort of like being deep in enemy lines."[3]

On April 6, Jon Daniels traveled farther into "enemy" territory when he, the Reverend Morris Samuel, and several others from Selma drove forty miles south to Camden, the seat of neighboring Wilcox County, to participate in demonstrations. Wilcox was an overwhelmingly rural county in the Black Belt. When the voter registration drive started in Selma, it had ripple effects in Wilcox County; in fact, Martin Luther King targeted Wilcox for voter registration activity. Although about 80 percent of the population was black, no blacks were registered to vote at the beginning of 1965. In February, however, six blacks and four whites —

the sheriff, the probate judge, the superintendent of schools, and the circuit solicitor — started planning for the registration of qualified blacks. The interracial group worked inconspicuously in, according to the *Birmingham News*, "a determined, planned effort to help Negroes . . . win the right to vote." And in the middle of March the first Negro, a blacksmith, registered in Camden.[4]

In spite of their success in registering, blacks protested the discriminatory requirement that they go to the old jail to register while whites went to the courthouse. In support of the voter drive, Wilcox County blacks initially tried a boycott of the public schools, but the principal of Camden Academy, the largest black school, refused to allow his students to participate. In an unusual move against a local black, other blacks then invaded the school and led a walkout, which was cut short by the police. In the first few days of April blacks staged marches on the courthouse in Camden, but Mayor Reg Albritton and the police halted every demonstration. "If you want to vote, come down Monday when the Registrar's Office is open," the forty-two-year-old farmer-businessman-mayor told more than one hundred protesters, "but don't come into the city like a herd of cattle." When one woman pointed out that blacks paid their taxes at the courthouse just like whites but whites did not register at the jail, Albritton replied that he had nothing to do with the procedures. The demonstrations continued, with many of the participants youngsters. When the pressure increased, the mayor and his forces arrested some demonstrators and used tear gas and smoke bombs to break up the marches. Adults were allowed to go to the Registrar's Office, and three-fourths of the applicants were approved.[5]

On their first day in Camden, Daniels and his companions merely observed the protests. On the next day, the eighth day of demonstrations, they participated in a series of attempted marches from Camden Academy and from a local Baptist church. The police stopped the marchers and let them stand in the street for a few hours before once again using half a dozen tear gas canisters to disperse them. Daniels knelt in a nonviolent position and covered his face with a handkerchief. When a canister of tear gas rolled to his feet, he recklessly picked it up and hurled it back. Later Camden police took Daniels and a seminarian from California into protective custody but released them after a few minutes. Daniels returned for more demonstrations during the next two days, but Wilcox County authorities, wanting to avoid another "Selma," allowed blacks to register and did not try to crush the protests.[6]

Camden was a harrowing experience for Jon Daniels, and it did much to change his attitudes about the South. He wrote:

> My hostility lasted really until last week. I think it was when I got teargassed leading a march in Camden that I began to change. I saw that the men who came at me were themselves not free: it was not that cruelty was so sweet to them (though I'm afraid sometimes it is), *but that they didn't know what else to do*. Even though they were white and hateful and my enemy, they were human beings, too. I found myself feeling a kind of grim affection for them, at least a love that was real and "existential" rather than abstract. . . . Last week in Camden I began to discover a new freedom in the Cross: freedom to love the enemy. And in that freedom, the freedom (without hypocrisy) to will and to try to set him free.

Daniels's previous thoughts of violence, abstract and rhetorical as they probably were, no longer influenced him. His commitment to nonviolence had been tested and strengthened by his experience in the "Camden ruckus."[7]

For the next few months Daniels concentrated primarily on Selma and Dallas County. While in Selma he worked on a paper for an ethics course at ETS on Christianity and the question of violence. Within the church he found great "ambiguity" over violence because it went to the heart of the gospel and because it was connected to myriad other unsettled social problems. Daniels believed that "the Christian will know only one motivation in his thinking and dreaming and acting that is ultimately legitimate and unambiguously authentic. That is *agape*." At the same time, the committed Christian "is anguished at the moral dilemma occasioned by all the forms of violence perpetrated in society" and by the possibility of total nuclear war. Presumably referring to his own conflicts, he considered the "intolerable tensions which threaten to disintegrate the sensitive Christian."[8] The problem of violence certainly perplexed and troubled him.

Daniels denied that the Sermon on the Mount was impractical or irrelevant; instead, he suggested that the "question here is not one of effectiveness, nor of immediate practicability, but of obedience to the claims of the gospel." It required nonviolence but not inaction — he pointed to "the lyric of radical upheaval, of social and political and economic revolution, the world-breaking, world-shaping utterance of Amos and his heirs [that] echoes in Mary's glad song." He believed that the Negroes of the Black Belt were "strategically situated . . . to stumble into the way of the Cross." For Daniels, the solution both to the problem of violence generally and to his own situation in particular had become clear:

> Like Him, we seek Jerusalem, "not to destroy men's lives, but to save them." We go to make our witness to the truth that has set us free. We go to stand with the captives and the blind and the op-

pressed. We go in "active nonresistance," not to "confront," but to love and to heal and to free. Our motives must be loving and our methods, chaste. Otherwise, the means of "proclaiming" open to us know no bounds but those of our own imagination and initiative.

Whether the Christian "demonstrates" in a picket line or "boycotts" an oppressor must depend upon whether the action is undertaken vindictively or coercively. If his protest is an act of contrition, he may act with confidence.

. . . Between deliberate provocation and passivity there is a middle course for compassion and truth. To find it, of course, one must be *in* Jerusalem. And one must pray for strength to carry a cross. That done, lo the Presence, and a living sacrifice of praise and thanksgiving.[9]

Based on his own thinking and his experience in Wilcox County, as well as his great respect for Martin Luther King, Daniels dedicated himself to nonviolence. He was, however, also committed to action — to doing something about racism. In his attempt to promote racial justice in Alabama, he hoped that he was motivated by agape and compassion. The reconciliation he sought between the races was a reconciliation based on equality, not the old patterns of black subservience. To many Selmians, his tactics surely must have seemed confrontational and "un-Christian," but only because his ultimate goal was so radical.

In Selma, Daniels and Judy Upham teamed up for several weeks with the Reverend Morris Samuel, the thirty-six-year-old white director of ESCRU in Los Angeles who had arrived in Selma with his wife and three children. Initially, the Episcopalian civil rights volunteers were tied loosely to King's Southern Christian Leadership Conference, whose leaders in Atlanta made most of the early postmarch decisions. Though Daniels continued to regard Martin Luther King as "one of the greatest men I've ever laid eyes on," he found some of the other civil rights workers difficult to bear. In particular, some of the SNCC workers, especially the whites, were "officious . . . immature . . . just a little arrogant from past success, and obviously not indigenous." On the other hand, many of the local blacks in Selma impressed him enormously. "I am so grateful," he wrote, "for the men and women in this beloved community who, despite educational and cultural starvation, are able to think clearly and honestly. And who are brave enough not only to risk life and limb in a moment of flamboyant action, but to give up their jobs and incomes."[10]

Gradually, the ESCRU workers began to operate more independently of other groups in Selma. Judy Upham's red Volkswagen was essential to their independence because it provided mobility around town and elsewhere as well as a means of escape both from danger and from the stresses of their work.[11] Soon after Daniels and Upham returned to Selma, for instance, they drove south to Mobile, on the Alabama coast, for some important shopping. As the only Episcopalians remaining in Selma's black community after Samuel left, they decided to wear clerical collars to make their Christian witness more obvious. As seminarians, however, their collars were not entirely white but had a black vertical bar in the front, and the nearest store selling the seminarian collar was in Mobile. After the trip, Daniels rarely went anywhere without his collar.[12]

During his stay in Selma, Daniels found support and friends in three institutions within Selma's black community — Brown Chapel, the George Washington Carver Homes, and the Society of St. Edmund's mission. Brown Chapel AME Church, started in 1867, was the first AME church in Alabama. In 1908 it moved into the Byzantine-style red-brick building on Sylvan Street that it still occupies. During the winter and spring of 1965 it was the unofficial headquarters of the Selma civil rights movement; King and SCLC held numerous mass meetings in Brown Chapel before the march to Montgomery. After the march, it remained a focus of activity within the black community and the civil rights movement. Jon Daniels did not worship at Brown Chapel, but he did go to innumerable mass meetings and rallies there.[13]

Surrounding Brown Chapel was Selma's black public housing project, the George Washington Carver Homes. Started with federal funds in 1950, the Carver Homes provided desperately needed good low-cost housing for some of the city's poor black residents. The first tenant moved into the housing project in March 1952, and all 216 units were occupied as soon as they were completed. The Selma Housing Authority, which operated the Carver Homes, based the sliding-scale rents on the occupants' earnings and number of children. The units ranged from standard one- and two-bedroom apartments to a few unusually large ones with four or five bedrooms and two bathrooms. The Carver Homes were, of course, strictly segregated — on the other side of town, the housing authority ran the smaller Valley Creek Homes for whites.[14]

When thousands went to Selma for the march to Montgomery, they gravitated to Brown Chapel and the Carver Homes, and the police cordoned the visitors off in that neighborhood. Most of them slept on the grass or in the streets of the housing project, but residents made room in their apartments for some of the visitors. Though hard pressed themselves, they also helped to furnish food for the visitors and assisted them in many other ways, not the least of which was providing bathroom facilities. Jon Daniels rapidly became friends with many of the residents.[15]

Through a third institution in the black community, Daniels met a number of whites, none of whom was a native of Selma. Specializing in work among Negro Catholics, the Society of St. Edmund of the Roman Catholic church had first established a mission for blacks in Selma in 1937. By the 1960s it included a school for grades one through eight (Morris Samuel's two older children were students there in April 1965, for the first school integration in Selma), youth clubs, St. Elizabeth's Catholic Church, and the Good Samaritan Hospital, which cost $1.5 million dollars and opened early in 1965. In the spring of 1965 Father Maurice F. Ouellet was the head of the mission. When he was a boy, working in Selma became his dream after he saw a film about the Edmundite Order's work there. "The film showed the poverty of the people and their needs, and I was intrigued by the work that needed to be done," he later said. "I saw the work of a priest and I wanted to do the work of a priest the same way some boys see an airplane and want to fly one." A native of Vermont, the thirty-nine-year-old priest served in Selma in 1952 before beginning a three-year-stint on Alabama's gulf coast. He returned in 1961 to direct the Society of St. Edmund's mission.[16]

Father Ouellet took an active part in the developing civil rights movement in Selma. By 1962 he regularly attended meetings of the Dallas County Voters' League, which encouraged black registration, and on a number of occasions he spoke at the gatherings. In addition, he frequently visited jailed civil rights workers. Ouellet and the Edmundite Fathers and Brothers used a full-page advertisement in the *Selma Times-Journal* to announce their support for the civil rights demonstrations and to call for calm discussion of Selma's race relations. Ouellet made St. Elizabeth's church available for clinics to teach blacks how to register to vote, and at the time of the Selma-to-Montgomery march, he opened the mission and the hospital to visiting clergy. The only white man active in the Selma movement, Father Ouellet became the target of threats and harassment. His telephone was tapped, his home was monitored, he was threatened with arrest, he was charged with teaching children how to demonstrate and resist the police, and finally he was asked by leading white citizens to leave town.[17]

Selma whites even appealed to Father Ouellet's superior, Archbishop Thomas J. Toolen. Though barring the priest from participating in demonstrations, the bishop initially defended his voter registration work. Clearly not a segregationist, Toolen in 1961 had ordered all Catholic schools in Alabama to integrate by September 1965. In the spring of 1965, however, he opposed the participation of northern clergy in the march to Montgomery. Yielding to growing pressures, he finally ordered Father Ouellet to leave Alabama by July 1. Disappointed and unhappy, the priest was transferred to the Vermont headquarters of the Society of St. Edmund.[18]

Jon Daniels first met Ouellet when a Catholic family in the Carver Homes took him to church at St. Elizabeth's. Attracted to the Roman church, Daniels had a special interest in the Edmundite mission and in Father Ouellet. The Episcopal seminarian and the tall, soft-spoken, courageous priest soon became friends; they frequently discussed religion, their work for civil rights, and the massive problems in Selma. Ouellet, who could remember his own experiences when he first came to Alabama, was also a good source of information and advice for the inexperienced newcomers.[19]

Once, for instance, Daniels told Ouellet about stopping with Judy Upham at a small country store to buy some gas. Daniels was wearing his seminarian's collar and their car had Massachusetts plates — neither of which would endear them to rural Alabama whites. Insensitive to the attitudes of the white men sitting around the store and confident of his own reasonableness, Daniels proceeded to explain civil rights and social justice to them. The story horrified Ouellet, who worried that Daniels's naïveté made him a real threat to himself. Trying to explain to his innocent friend that such behavior could get Daniels and Upham beaten up, or worse, he warned him to be careful and to remember how volatile the racial question was in Alabama.[20] Although Daniels may have listened intently to the priest's advice, it probably had little effect on his activities. He understood that hazards existed but seemed to underestimate their pervasiveness and seriousness. He was also, as he had written for his ethics class, more concerned about "obedience to the claims of the gospel" than about being either practical or effective.

Just as important as Father Ouellet's sensible counsel was his friendship and support. He appreciated the difficulties in adjusting to Selma as well as the demands of seminary studies. Daniels frequently stopped by the Society of St. Edmund's mission to talk with Ouellet and others, and on many occasions he stayed for lunch or supper. The mission had generously provided a peaceful place for the seminarians to pursue their studies, and the priests gladly made a typewriter and other amenities available for their use in preparing papers for the classes at ETS. Daniels also worshipped regularly at St. Elizabeth's Church. Ouellet assumed an important role for Daniels in part because he received no support from the local Episcopal church. After he had been there for several weeks, Daniels considered the Catholic priest to be his real pastor in Selma.[21]

Daniels's efforts to integrate worship services at the Episcopal church were a part of his larger, if less successful, attempt to get white Selmians to recognize their prejudice and overcome it. He worked primarily in the church, where the evils of racial bias seemed most obvious and unavoidable; moreover, he thought that Christians should have been the people most ready to confront the sin of segregation. Daniels did not limit his work to St. Paul's, however. To promote reconciliation between the races and greater civil rights for blacks, he tried to meet individually with Selma's leading citizens — what he called the "white power structure" — to discuss informally the community's racial problems. He believed that "compassion, the attempt to understand, genuine concern for the 'enemy' will accomplish more for real integration of the races than belligerence"; thus his personal witness coupled with reasoned persuasion based on Christian values would convince others to change their racist attitudes.[22]

Conveniently for Daniels, St. Paul's contained many of the city's influential citizens, so his efforts overlapped considerably. The Reverend T. Frank Mathews, for example, was more than just the rector of the Episcopal church; he once described himself as a kind of "parson to the whole community because of my active involvement in community affairs." Daniels tried to get to know as many lawyers, judges, and doctors as he could.[23] Though not all of his contacts bore fruit, he succeeded in meeting a range of whites in Selma.

Two of the very few people at St. Paul's who were overtly friendly to Jon Daniels were Harry and Kate Gamble. A prominent lawyer in his mid-sixties, Harry Gamble had grown up in the parish, where his father had served as rector from 1903 to 1937. Gamble had objected to the vestry decision in 1963 to bar blacks and had resigned from the vestry in protest. He and his wife were known for their liberal views. Kate Gamble, twelve years younger and a native of Montgomery, was one of the rare members of the church to speak to the integrated group that first attempted to enter St. Paul's on March 14; when they were barred from the church, she went home without attending the service. A few weeks later, when the rest of the congregation shunned Daniels after a service, she walked up to him and introduced herself.[24]

After his encounter with Kate Gamble, Daniels, who was finding it difficult to meet local whites, called the Gambles to ask if he could visit them and they readily agreed. Daniels went to their home on several occasions for dinner and to discuss his work and black-white relations generally. While he expressed his frustration with the church, they tried to help him understand the community and to warn him about the way many white Selmians reacted to his behavior. For example, living with a black family and walking down the street with blacks, especially females, offended whites and might provoke them. In fact, Daniels's flagrant violation of the southern racial mores against such interracial contacts between the sexes in public irritated even the enlightened Kate Gamble, who once refused to speak to him when she passed him on the street because he was walking with his arms casually over the shoulders of two black girls.[25] Though the Gambles' advice appears to have had a negligible impact, Daniels undoubtedly appreciated their genuine interest in him and their relative support for his work.

A few days after meeting the Gambles, Jon Daniels and Judy Upham decided to visit Harry Gamble at his law office. At first Gamble had seemed a bit suspicious and defensive and had urged Daniels to leave Selma, but he gradually warmed up to him. On that occasion Gamble, Daniels, and Upham engaged in a cordial discussion about the racial situation, including the relevance of the gospel, the role of a southern moderate, and rumored changes in the local school system. As Daniels wrote, "We left his office in a spirit of something very much like friendship. Something having to do with human hearts, something like the faith of the Church had been explored and shared with a white man in the black belt."[26]

Daniels also got to know B. M. Miller Childers, another local attorney and later a county judge, and Roswell Falkenberry, editor of the *Selma Times-Journal*. Both men belonged to St. Paul's and were among the more moderate whites in town. In early 1965 Childers, a native of Selma and a member of the vestry, had been horrified when he saw Sheriff Clark's possemen preparing to attack schoolteachers who went to the courthouse to register to vote; the incident made him realize that the situation in Selma had gone too far. He later voted to admit blacks to St. Paul's and turned away from the church on the Sunday they were denied admittance. He also refused to join the White Citizens' Council. For his actions Childers endured social and familial hostility. Because he sang in the church choir, he never had to decide whether to speak to Daniels in church. He met the seminarian first in meetings with Mathews at the church and with Kate Gamble. Daniels later gave the lawyer a copy of William Stringfellow's *My People Is the Enemy* and several times dropped by his law office for more extended conversations. He also went to the newspaper office several times to confer with Falkenberry.[27]

His acquaintance with liberal and moderate Selma whites like the Gambles, Childers, and Falkenberry encouraged Daniels to think that change might be possible in the Black Belt city; it also caused him to redefine the terms *liberal* and *moderate* within the context of Selma. He was not overly optimistic because he learned that even the few white liberals were "a rather disappointing lot — liberalism seems to mean *not hating* — and not doing anything to rock the boat." He often despaired that he would "find a Christian who has both imagination and the guts of a saint," but he kept trying.[28]

For white Selmians, on the other hand, Jon Daniels was one of the few civil rights workers they ever met and got to know. As a white, middle-class, well-educated, and clean-cut seminarian, he could approach them more naturally than could many other outside agitators. They found him friendly, bright, and articulate, if also intense and naive.[29] Talking to a handful of congenial whites did little, however, to address the real opposition to civil rights. Ardent segregationists were not hard to find in Selma, especially among the affluent, educated Episcopal parishioners. Jon Daniels met them too.

One of Selma's leading segregationists was Bernard Reynolds, the judge of probate court and a member of St. Paul's. Devoted to racial segregation as well as to the Episcopal church, Reynolds had been one of the ushers who barred Daniels's integrated group of civil rights workers from entering the church at the time of the march to Montgomery. His influence extended considerably beyond the parish. In the early 1960s he considered that Selma's race relations to be the best they had been in his lifetime, and as a judge he had participated in the county's attempt to suppress demonstrations. In the courthouse he had opposed yielding to black demands for ending Jim Crow drinking fountains because he thought one concession would just lead to another demand, and he had steadfastly opposed desegregating restrooms because of what he said was the high incidence of venereal disease among blacks. Reynolds's racism was well known.[30]

Perhaps because they knew of the judge's "notorious" reputation, Jon Daniels and Judy Upham went to his Dallas County Courthouse office to talk with him about the racial situation at St. Paul's and their hopes for change in Selma. He said that the church would always welcome them, "but the nigger trash you bring with you will *never* be accepted in St. Paul's." Taken aback by his unabashed racism, Daniels realized then that his "strategy of love" had failed. Later when the seminarians suggested that the gospel did not support the idea of an all-white Episcopal church, the judge replied that the gospel prohibited them from living with black families "since God made white men and black men separate and if He'd wanted them commingled He'd have made them all alike." When pressed for a scriptural source, he said that he was dealing with reality, not the Bible.[31]

Reynolds maintained that blacks in the Black Belt were treated more kindly than anywhere else and that the real source of Selma's racial problems was outside intervention, particularly by the federal government. Still angry that out-of-town photographers had accompanied the first group trying to integrate St. Paul's, he told Daniels and Upham that, as members of the contingent, they shared in the "guilt" for the presence of cameras. Even though they stated their dissatisfaction with the photographers, Daniels and Upham suggested that Reynolds was similarly responsible for the racial injustice in Dallas County. He bristled at the idea and said that he had lived in Selma all his life. When they noted the inconsistency, he said, "That's not inconsistent. That's the way we think here, those of us who have spent all our lives here and really know the situation." Only white natives of the Black Belt could, in his opinion, really understand its race relations. "I'm not guilty of anything," he concluded. "Only guilty men have trouble sleeping at night. I don't have any trouble sleeping." After suggesting that perhaps he *should* have trouble sleeping, Daniels and Upham shook hands with the judge and left.[32] Though frustrated by their unproductive exchange with a judge they could only despise, they redoubled their efforts to bring about change in the city's race relations.

Daniels's contacts with local whites also extended beyond the Episcopal church, though the ones in the larger community usually were much briefer, less friendly, and often less genteel than his meetings with the parishioners of St. Paul's. Daniels learned something from nearly everyone. He confronted racism and hostility in even his most ordinary daily activities. When he and Upham went to the post office to pick up a registered letter, for example, they encountered the stares of local whites. Noticing Daniels's seminarian's collar and ESCRU button, one redneck asked his buddy, "Know what he is?" When the friend said that he did not, the man declared, "Why, he's a white niggah." Everyone then looked at Daniels. He felt uncomfortable but soon experienced "an affirmation and a tenderness and a joy" because "it is the highest honor, the most precious distinction I have ever received." He realized that his hands were white but his heart was black.[33] Jon Daniels had come to identify with the blacks of Selma more than he did with the whites.

Just walking in downtown Selma, Daniels and his colleagues ran the risk of verbal abuse from antagonistic whites. While they waited on the sidewalk for a traffic light to change, for instance, a man got out of his car and walked up to them. Unlike the man in the post office, he was wearing a business suit and seemed to be a decent member of the white middle class. Checking them out, the man spied their ESCRU buttons and Daniels's seminarian's collar. He asked, "Are you the scum that's been going to the Episcopal church?" They replied, "Scum, sir?" The man said, "S-C-U-M. That's what you are — you and the nigger trash you bring with you." They assured him that they could spell and then told him that they were sorry he felt as he did. After the man left, Daniels and Upham laughed "at the man, at his cruelty, at his stupidity, at our cleverness, at the success with which we had suavely maintained 'the Christian posture.' " Later they realized that as Christians they should have recognized the man's real need, that he "was asking us for something better than a smirk."[34]

One of Daniels's earliest introductions to local white animosity came after he and Upham acquired Alabama license tags that they hoped would draw less attention to their red Volkswagen. At the time they were staying with Rosa Scott and her family in the George Washington Carver Homes and naively listed her address as their home when they filled out the forms for the Alabama plates. Within a day, the Selma Housing Authority told Scott that they were watching her apartment and that she had better not have any civil rights workers staying with her. The operators of the Carver Homes were especially concerned about the presence of "those troublemakers at the Episcopal Church," or even their bags or personal effects. In fact, the rents were fixed by income and number of occupants, and any unauthorized people living in the apartments could constitute grounds for eviction. As a result, Daniels and Upham slipped out of the Scotts' home and into the privately owned home of another black family.[35] The incident illustrated the pervasive power of the local authorities and their relentless opposition to civil rights activists.

Although the opposing sides in Selma seemed obvious, Daniels increasingly recognized that the situation was complex and ambiguous. As he quickly learned, "There are good men here, just as there are bad men." He found good and bad among whites, among blacks, among civil rights workers, and even within himself. He saw himself as some combination of an activist trying to "confront a people with the challenge of freedom" for blacks, a neutralizer who worked carefully to maintain peace, and a reconciler between blacks and whites. His varied roles involved him in activities ranging from demonstrations to boring meetings to conversations with local people, and he confronted whites extending from the polite, upper-middle-class parishioners of St. Paul's to the more numerous rednecks. "Sometimes we confront the posse," he reported, "and sometimes we hold a child."[36]

The variety of Daniels's roles appeared most clearly in his work within the black community: he demonstrated and protested with blacks, worked to improve their daily lives, sought reconciliation between the races, and sometimes actually held children in his arms. After the triumphant march to Montgomery, Selma's black population tried to force further improvements by applying continued economic pressure on the local white merchants. A boycott of white businesses sought better treatment of black customers, more jobs for blacks, and more concessions from the local government. Daniels supported the boycott. Right after the march, when he learned that his sister had just given birth to a boy, he had to drive to Montgomery to buy a gift because "the whites stores here are being boycotted." Several weeks later, he went to Montgomery again to purchase a mother's day card. Daniels and Judy Upham also drove there at least once a week to shop for themselves and to buy shoes, clothing, and other necessities for their new friends.[37]

The blacks in Selma continued their economic boycott throughout the spring and occasionally picketed stores. Daniels helped organize and was always ready to join in the demonstrations against hostile businesses. In one protest, where the police made nearly forty arrests for disorderly conduct, the picketers carried signs saying "Don't Buy Here and Help the Posse," "We Want Our Freedom," and "Don't Buy Here." One well-established grocery store in the black section was boycotted because the owner's son joined Sheriff Jim Clark's posse; after eighteen years in business, the store closed as a result of the boycott. A shoe store down-town experienced a similar fate.[38]

By early April the boycott had induced the mayor and city council to begin meeting weekly with black leaders, but only gradually as white sentiment shifted did officials start responding to the blacks' grievances. The white leaders found the militancy of the blacks frustrating and even infuriating, while the blacks only grew more impatient with the lack of progress and more skeptical of white goodwill. One moderate Selma black warned, "The white man has lied so much over the years, it's hard to believe he wants to do anything now." An observer reported, nonetheless, that the "bi-racial negotiations represent a spectacular progress in a city that was totally segregated when 1965 began."[39]

After more than one thousand white Selmians signed an advertisement in the *Times-Journal* supporting equal protection of the law and the right to vote for all, the city's public safety commissioner pledged to hire two black policemen and the mayor promised to appoint blacks to a committee to administer federal funds from the Office of Economic Opportunity. In addition, local merchants seemed ready to hire black clerks. Voter registration remained slow, however, and the city simply closed the municipal swimming pool instead of integrating it as blacks had wished. Interested in tangible gains for blacks in Selma, Jon Daniels appreciated the advances brought about by the economic boycott; dedicated to a reconciliation between the races, he valued the biracial meetings. Although the slow and limited reforms undoubtedly frustrated him, he continued to support the consumer boycott and demonstrations.[40]

Less public and less dramatic than the demonstrations in Selma and

Wilcox County or his efforts to integrate the local Episcopal church, but probably just as meaningful, was Jon Daniels's work within the black community itself, especially in the George Washington Carver Homes. By staying in Selma, Daniels, Judy Upham, Morris Samuel, and others hoped to prevent a major letdown after the great march. They realized that, although a big battle for equal rights had been won, the victory could easily turn into defeat and the larger war could be lost if people did not keep up the spirit of the civil rights movement. Daniels's purpose was simply to be part of "the presence of the church in the social revolution" occurring in Selma. As a Christian witness, he hoped to demonstrate to blacks and whites his commitment to the movement.[41]

Daniels's closest relationship with blacks was with the West family in the Carver Homes. After living briefly with the Bell family, Daniels and Judy Upham moved across the yard to stay next door to Brown Chapel with Lonzy and Alice West and their children. Natives of Dallas County, Alice and Lonzy had married in 1946 after he returned from World War II; they had eleven children. As a veteran, Lonzy West qualified early for the new apartments in the Carver Homes, and his family was one of the first to enter the project in 1952. From the 1950s Lonzy had been marginally active in the civil rights movement. A painter by trade, he had not joined the NAACP or any other civil rights group because he feared that the whites in Selma would retaliate by not giving him work; he had to be careful. When he began participating in the movement in 1963, he lost painting jobs for whites. By the time of the Selma-to-Montgomery march, Lonzy West could not get work and the Wests' apartment had become a meeting place for the movement, an unofficial second freedom house in Selma. Bernard Lafayette, John Lewis, and other leaders went there frequently.[42]

Daniels met the Wests soon after he arrived in Selma. He first encountered Lonzy West in front of Brown Chapel one evening before the march. After they talked for a while, West took Daniels home and introduced him to his wife. Daniels smiled and shook hands with her, and she was immediately impressed with his warm friendliness, but she did not like or trust any white people. Alice West's attitude changed. Soon feeling they had known him for a long time, the Wests offered Daniels and Upham a place to stay in their home. Poor as they were, the Wests shared what they had. With ten children at home, the West's apartment was crowded even though it had five bedrooms and two bathrooms. They nevertheless gave Upham a room downstairs and Daniels a room upstairs and put all of their children in two bedrooms. Other civil rights workers occasionally slept on sofas or in sleeping bags on the floor.[43]

In an unusual way, religion formed a bond between the Wests and Jon

Daniels. During World War II Lonzy West had been impressed by a Catholic chaplain in the army, and in the early 1950s he had worked as a custodian for the Society of St. Edmund. As a result of his associations, he and his wife, though lifelong Baptists, decided to join the Catholic church. After months of instruction, they became members of St. Elizabeth's Church, the small black parish connected to the Edmundite mission. The West children also attended St. Elizabeth's School at the mission. Daniels, who had moved from the Congregational to the Episcopal church, could appreciate the change made by the Wests, and the high-church Episcopalian was much more comfortable with the West's faith than he would have been with the more common southern Baptists.[44]

Because Lonzy often drank too much, Alice provided the stability that held their family together, and she became a closer friend to Jon Daniels than did her husband. Not long after the seminarians moved into their home, Alice and Lonzy West took them to the black Elks Club. When a militant black questioned the Wests about being with whites, Alice West replied: "Jon and Judy are my friends. They're staying in my home. I'll pick my own friends, and nobody will tell me otherwise." Only a half-dozen years apart in age, Mrs. West and Daniels frequently talked over the kitchen table at breakfast or supper. They swapped stories about growing up in Alabama and New England, and they shared ideas about the South and race relations. He discussed with her, for example, his efforts to integrate St. Paul's; sometimes he showed his frustration with the rector and the congregation by slamming his fist on the table. Drawing on her long experience in Selma, Alice West could help Daniels better understand events in the black community.[45]

Daniels and Judy Upham participated in many of the family's activities. On Sundays, after going to the white Episcopal church downtown, they usually accompanied the Wests to St. Elizabeth's; during the week they often were together at mass meetings in Brown Chapel. Daniels sometimes accompanied Lonzy and Alice West to a local night spot for entertainment and relaxation over a few beers. He also went grocery shopping with Alice, helped in the kitchen, baby-sat with the younger children, and played with the older ones.[46]

The West children particularly enjoyed having Jon Daniels around. "He was never a stranger," recalled Rachel West, who in 1965 was nine years old and called "Bunnie." "I only knew we liked being with him." During demonstrations in the street, Daniels held the children's hands and made sure they were safe while singing the protest songs and marching. At other times he played with them in the yard and told the younger ones stories while they sat on his lap. He let them go with him on errands in town and, when he had a little extra money, took them to local stores for lollipops, soft drinks, or ice cream. Occasionally they went out for hamburgers — but only to integrated restaurants. Two of the older West girls invited Daniels and Upham to a "hullabaloo" at the local high school. They considered the white visitor "a part of our family."[47]

Rachel West, who participated in many demonstrations in 1965, later described one very significant moment with Daniels:

> I remember one day after many of our people had been arrested and there was talk of more trouble before us, I was standing outside in the apartment yard watching some of the other children play. Jonathan saw me and came and knelt down beside me.
>
> "Why aren't you playing with the others?" he asks.
>
> And I had shrugged. "I don't know why."
>
> So he stares at me very seriously and puts an arm around me. "You afraid of something?"
>
> And I told him I was thinking about the sheriff's posse and some of the bad things that had been happening.
>
> "You don't have to be afraid anymore," he said. "I'll watch you and make sure nothing or nobody bothers you. All right?"
>
> But I didn't know. So all of a sudden he picked me up and tossed me up in the air, spinning around and around. "Now are you afraid?" he asked. And I started laughing then. He kept spinning around and throwing me up and catching me. Finally I yelled that I wasn't afraid, and he put me down.[48]

Just by being in the black neighborhoods Daniels made an important contribution. As Rachel West wrote, "He made me feel more secure when he was with me. When Jonathan came to us, I knew for certain that there were really good white folks in this country, and with them on our side we would win our freedom."[49] Adults, though lacking such optimism, must have been encouraged by Daniels's persistent efforts on their behalf.

In the Carver Homes, Daniels seemed a part of the other black families too. He befriended a retarded black girl who was confined to a wheelchair; he visited with her and pushed her around in her wheelchair. He played with other children, too. Once he and Judy Upham packed nine youngsters from the housing project into the Volkswagen and went for ice cream cones. Occasionally young people, especially the Bells and the Wests, accompanied the seminarians to services at St. Paul's. Sometimes the children annoyed Daniels when they crowded around and made it difficult to work or to drive away in their car.[50]

Daniels's keen sense of humor enabled him to help people in the Carver Homes overcome embarrassing moments. At first, for example, the black families who invited the seminarians home for meals wanted their white guests to eat first. Daniels and Upham naturally felt uncomfortable and began to refuse to eat unless the families joined them. To relieve the awkwardness, Daniels joked about living with "segregationists" like his black friends. He also used humor to respond to one friendly black boy who felt close enough to Daniels and Upham to call them "white trash"; he teasingly called him "nigger."[51]

Within the Carver Homes, Daniels worked with adults to improve their daily lives. For example, he tried to increase hygiene in the project by waging a losing war against cockroaches. He was more successful in encouraging the families to learn about nutrition so they would have a more balanced diet. In part, his efforts may have been in self-defense; he ate many meals of peas, beans, greens, rice and gravy, cornbread, assorted fried foods, and koolaid, and he lost weight because "I'm starved most of the time." Daniels also became acquainted with the needs of many other black people in Selma and managed to obtain supplies from the Edmundite mission and from goods sent from the North.[52]

Like a pastor, Daniels assisted the adults in other, more personal ways too. A constant concern was Lonzy West's fondness for gin. Daniels tried to talk to him about his problem but had little success. One night in early May, he struggled to prevent Lonzy from beating his wife and wound up staying up all night to keep the peace. After considerable persuasion, Daniels managed to get West to see a psychiatrist at the local mental health office. Daniels hoped to start a chapter of Alcoholics Anonymous with Lonzy West as a founding member. Both maneuvers failed, however, and West continued to drink.[53]

While Jon Daniels and Judy Upham were becoming more accustomed to Selma, they remained full-time students at ETS. Both seminarians, however, found it very difficult to read and study in Selma. Friends at the seminary forwarded books and information on their courses, and professors sent some tests to be taken in Selma. In April, Daniels lamented that he had not "gotten a cussed lick of work done in ages." A month later he had begun to "panic over papers and exams," but he reported that he and Judy were then trying to get started on some assigned work. In fact, Daniels and Upham did complete much of their academic work before returning to Cambridge.[54]

After nearly two months in Selma, the seminarians prepared to leave in the middle of May. Though he had not firmly made up his mind, Daniels wished to return later in the summer, whereas Judy Upham had plans to go to St. Louis. ESCRU wanted Daniels to go back to Alabama, for he now had valuable experience and contacts in Selma. Deeply convinced that "the Holy Spirit had brought me here" to Selma, Daniels believed that his "life is not my own but His — which means that before anything else I am a servant of Christ." His doubts persisted, however, about whether he should "pursue an academic ministry or . . . be a slum-type priest," and he still felt some attraction to the Roman Catholic church. He nonetheless thought that "the chances are about a thousand to one that I'll decide to come back."[55]

Part of Daniels's inspiration to return came from Father Ouellet. The night before they left Selma, the two seminarians dined at the Society of St. Edmund's mission. After the meal, they had a moving visit with Ouellet, who told them about his long, frustrating experience in Selma and how he had finally stopped hating and lost his bitterness. "We were stunned at the honesty, the integrity, and the beauty of this saintly man . . . . we loved and revered him," Daniels wrote. Before saying good-bye, Daniels and Upham knelt for the priest's blessing. When he placed his hands on their heads, Daniels believed that, "from almost any perspective, a miracle had occurred."[56] Compelled by Ouellet's example and rewarded by his own work, Daniels knew that he would be returning to Selma.

In the third week in May, Daniels and Upham loaded up her car for the trip back to Cambridge. He had been tempted to replace the Alabama plates with the Massachusetts ones but did not because, "in an ambivalent fashion, I had come to love" the blue and orange "Heart of Dixie" tags. Leaving late one day, they drove north through the night. On the highway between Washington and Baltimore the symbolic importance of the Alabama tags became clear. When a black couple passed them and stared, Daniels realized that they thought he was a white Alabamian. He felt like shouting to them, "No, no! I'm *not* an Alabama white. I'm on *your* side." He and Upham felt ashamed. Gradually they began to realize that, if they had become "white niggers" in Selma, they had also become "Alabama whites." Their witness meant they had had to bear the suspicion and hostility of white Selmians, but it also "meant absorbing their guilt as well and suffering the cost which they might not yet know was there to be paid." As part of the Christian atonement, Daniels thought, "[t]heir guilt was ours, and ours, theirs." The recognition of his identity with all of Selma made his return to the Northeast even more meaningful.[57]

At the Episcopal Theological School, Daniels and Upham faced the frenzy of final exams and graduation. Most students and faculty supported their civil rights work and were excited to hear about their adventures in the South. The Selma veterans struggled to catch up with their classmates and finish assignments on time; Daniels managed to take his exams on schedule, but he received extensions on a few papers and continued to work on them during graduation exercises. The day before commencement, during a worship service in the ETS chapel, he became disturbed when a sermon on the civil rights movement attacked southern prejudice. As one who had learned to identify with both whites and blacks, he assumed that the civil rights rhetoric must be upsetting to the family of a friend from the Deep South. "I became so uncomfortable for them," he wrote, "that I stole to their pew to sit with them." After the service he discussed with the southern visitors the relationship of Christianity to the movement. They appreciated his thoughtfulness, and he understood even more the plight of the white southerner.[58]

With his academic life in order, Daniels visited his mother and relaxed in Keene. After he gave an illustrated talk at the annual meeting of the women of St. James Episcopal Church describing his experiences in Alabama, a rather liberal member of the parish complained about his reference to the Selma Episcopalians as "Christians" instead of just "churchmen." Daniels felt defensive for the Selma congregation because he had come to appreciate the "painful ambivalence and anguished perplexity . . . some of them were beginning (belatedly, it is true — for all of us) to feel." Remembering the "self-righteous insanities I permitted myself to indulge in, early in my life in Selma," he paused before delivering "a gentle blast" at the New Hampshire woman.[59] Once again he enjoyed the irony of identifying with white Selmians while in the North.

Jon Daniels stopped to see his maternal grandmother on the way to a church meeting on Lake Winnipesaukee. Near the end of June at the Diocesan Youth Conference in Geneva Point, he spoke movingly about his involvement in the "revolution" called the civil rights movement and about its effect on him. He described the "hate and fear and love and discovery" in the movement, the clubs and tear gas, the jails and Klansmen, the attractive and intelligent young black people. He, however, no longer felt afraid in the Black Belt because he believed that the Holy Spirit had sent him there and that he "had truly been baptized into the Lord's death and Resurrection." His "life got stood on end in Selma, Alabama," he confessed to the young audience, when he experienced personally "the story of the Cross."[60]

On June 28, a few days after addressing the Episcopal youth, Daniels left New England for Selma. Driving Judy Upham's Volkswagen, he followed an indirect route that allowed him to see several friends on the way. Perhaps quieter and more intense, Daniels seemed anxious to get back to Alabama and certain that he was supposed to be there. In St. Louis he enjoyed a more leisurely five-day visit with Upham.[61] By the end of the first week in July, Daniels had returned to Selma where he was freer than he had ever been. Away from home, the rules of VMI, and the ETS faculty, he could make his own decisions about his work.

Although he enjoyed the warm hospitality of the West family, without Judy Upham or Morris Samuel, Daniels was much more alone than he had been in the spring. Soon, however, he began associating with two other civil rights workers. Born in 1934, Eugene McKinley Pritchard grew up in Selma's black community and went to a local Lutheran private school. He joined the army and fought as an airborne infantryman in the Korean War. Pritchard left the army in 1956 and went to Chicago, where he learned several trades before moving back to Selma in 1962. Though he had not previously been involved in the civil rights movement, he soon joined the Student Nonviolent Coordinating Committee. As he became more committed to the movement, he quit his job as a cook and joined the SNCC staff in Selma. He first met Daniels at a mass meeting, and they quickly became friends. Gradually Daniels began to work more closely with Pritchard and other SNCC workers. Daniels frequently went with Pritchard to the SNCC office on Alabama Street across from the Dallas County Courthouse. Daniels sometimes worked in the SNCC office (using the mimeograph machine, for example, to run off leaflets), where SNCC staffers generally kept him informed about the civil rights movement in Selma.[62]

More formally, Marc Oliver joined Daniels in July. A nineteen-year-old Episcopalian from California, Oliver had just completed a training program with the Race Relations Institute at Fisk University (he had been the only white in DuBois dormitory), and the Episcopal Society for Cultural and Racial Unity assigned him to work with Daniels in Selma. His mother had been active in ESCRU for years, and Oliver himself had flown in for the final day of the Selma-to-Montgomery march earlier in the spring. The march experience convinced him to become more deeply involved in the civil rights movement, and his parents supported his decision. Oliver's parents were lifelong liberal Democrats and strong advocates of civil rights, notwithstanding his father's career in the marines and their South Carolina and Texas origins. Working as Daniels's assistant, Oliver ran errands, drove the car, and acted as something of a protector for the smaller man.[63]

Daniels's role in the summer had changed somewhat because he had become the experienced ESCRU worker, whereas Oliver was the raw recruit. The Californian's inexperience was evident upon his arrival in Selma. The bus from Nashville dropped him off too early in the morning to call Daniels. Dressed in a sport coat and tie, he innocently took his two suitcases into the Silver Moon Cafe, the nearest open business but also a "white racist den and the one Selma restaurant the movement had avoided 'testing' " under the public accommodations provisions of the 1964 civil rights law. The Reverend James Reeb had been killed just outside the Silver Moon. The white clientele greeted Oliver with silent stares. After eating breakfast, Oliver asked the man on the next stool for directions to the Carver Homes. According to Oliver, the man looked at him as if he were crazy and said nothing, then left; Oliver later learned that the man was Sheriff Jim Clark. Oliver then decided to call Daniels, who rushed over, quickly pulled him out of the feared café, and then explained to Oliver the dangers in Selma. The incident provided a powerful introduction to Selma.[64]

Daniels's new position as the veteran of the movement in Selma did not make him cautious. He continued to be bold and unafraid in his actions. The seminarian seemed to take pleasure in going to restaurants, movies, and other public places with Pritchard and other blacks. One weekend he, Oliver, and a group of blacks went to a downtown theater to see *The Sandpipers*, a movie about an Episcopal priest. In the theater, Oliver and the blacks instinctively headed for the balcony, where blacks traditionally sat, but Daniels, eager to challenge segregation, suggested they all sit downstairs. The others worried that something might happen but Daniels insisted; he did agree, however, to leave before the lights came on to avoid trouble. When they took their seats, some whites moved, but that was all. Caught up in the film, the integrated group forgot to leave before the end. When the lights came on, they rushed out. In a few tense moments they escaped the crowded theater only to find their car blocked in its parking place. With Oliver at the wheel, the car went over the curb and down the sidewalk. Followed by another car, the group raced back to the Carver Homes through red lights and stop signs. The scary incident prompted Daniels to ditch the red VW in favor of a more powerful and reliable Plymouth, which ESCRU made available to him.[65]

During his second tour in Alabama, not all of the work involved challenging segregation or speeding to elude chasing whites. Daniels resumed some of the projects he and Judy Upham had begun in the spring and tackled a few new ones. The seminarian persevered in his efforts to integrate the local Episcopal church, to open channels of communication with Selma's white residents, and to witness generally in the black community. He also spent time encouraging blacks to register to vote. Daniels worked with Eugene Pritchard and Marc Oliver on several undertakings involving health care, housing, and social services for blacks in Dallas County.

Voter registration continued to occupy some of Daniels's time. Though he did not speak at the large mass meetings in Brown Chapel, he urged blacks individually to register, and he often went door-to-door in the black community and traveled around Selma and Dallas County with Lonzy West promoting registration. In addition, he assisted Eugene Pritchard, who was encouraging blacks in the Third Precinct to attend the voter registration meetings, and he occasionally spoke movingly at smaller precinct gatherings at the Tabernacle Baptist Church. He also helped Alice West and others who were teaching citizenship classes in freedom schools to prepare blacks to pass the registration tests.[66]

Within the black community Daniels attempted to improve the residents' quality of life. He, Pritchard, and Oliver, for example, struggled to get qualified blacks on the welfare rolls and to have reinstated those who had been wrongly dropped from the rolls. A special area of concentration was a slum in east Selma around the city dump. They urged local authorities to improve the water facilities and housing but had little success. Blacks continued to inhabit shacks with no running water or with one toilet used by several families, with only one electric outlet per building, and with five or more people per room. Individual problems in the slum also drew their attention. They were stunned when a mother of eleven refused to stop having children out of wedlock because they were more important to her than any welfare check could be; she would not give up her boyfriends to qualify for assistance. When another woman balked at taking her apparently worm-infested and malnourished children to a doctor, only considerable persuasion by Daniels succeeded in changing her mind.[67]

The doctor who treated the poor black children was Isabel Dumont, a native of Cologne, Germany, who came to the United States in 1929 on an exchange scholarship. After receiving a medical degree and completing residencies in surgery and obstetrics, she interned at St. Vincent's Hospital in Birmingham. She was preparing to go to Africa as a missionary when the bishop of Mobile suggested that she stay in Alabama and work with the Society of St. Edmund. In 1944 Dumont went to Selma and with Joan Mulder, a Dutch nurse, opened a small clinic in a former bar in the middle of a black neighborhood. For four decades the two women, who had met and become friends in Washington, D.C., lived and worked together in the Black Belt city. With Mulder working as anesthetist, X-ray technician, and medical technologist and Dumont as head of the medical staff at Good Samaritan Hospital, the two women served the medical needs of Selma's black community. Dumont charged her patients modest fees if they were able to pay; otherwise, she readily arranged other terms ranging from payment in kind to extended credit. Daniels became friendly with Dumont and Mulder, often visited in their home, and dined with them. At times that summer, they were virtually his only white contacts in Selma. More important, he took many sick blacks to Dumont's clinic.[68]

To reach more people with information that could improve their lives, Daniels decided in July to compile a comprehensive guide to Dallas County's social services, which many blacks did not realize were available to them as citizens. Daniels and Pritchard investigated the resources available from the Dallas County Department of Pensions and Security (welfare department), the county public health office, the state vocational rehabilitation program, the American Red Cross, social security, and other organizations as well as the conditions required for eligibility to receive the various services. They then circulated the data in a four-page mimeographed memorandum. The directory not only gave the location of the welfare office, for instance, but also described it as "a big white building, with columns, which used to be a funeral home" and noted that people should enter "the right-hand side door as you face the building." Also included were a straightforward description of the requirements for aid to dependent children ("even occasional visits by a wandering husband or boyfriend will in most cases disqualify you for support under this program — as, of course, will continued pregnancies") and an explanation of how to appeal a decision of the welfare department.[69]

Much of the information distributed by Daniels and Pritchard pertained to women and children. It included, for example, detailed information about the obstetrics and pediatric clinics, including the hours of the obstetrics clinic and the precise times a doctor would be present. Mentioning birth control pills and the intrauterine contraceptive device (IUD), the guide suggested that women consult with the local Planned Parenthood office to learn how to "limit the size of your family so that you may provide adequate care for the children you already have." It also warned that "V.D is notoriously common in our community, and you should expect a high incidence in your neighborhood, even among your acquaintances and friends." Daniels and Pritchard urged both women and men to take advantage of the local venereal disease clinic for prompt diagnosis and treatment.[70]

Throughout the memorandum, Daniels and Pritchard told black Selmians that individuals had to act on their own to benefit from the services in the community. For example, the memo proclaimed, "*V.D. is easy to treat, but you have to take the first step by bringing it to the attention of the clinic.*" Regarding the dental clinic, it instructed residents to "bring your children for examination, X-ray, and treatment!" Although Daniels and Pritchard listed their addresses and telephone numbers and volunteered to help anyone who contacted them, they recognized that they could not assist everyone individually. The closing lines of the memo restated their belief that individual initiative was essential: "By taking advantage of the resources that are available to you, you can improve the life, health, and well-being of your family — and of the entire community. *IT'S UP TO YOU*. Good Luck!"[71]

Solutions to some problems clearly exceeded the ability and power of most black residents in Selma. The local public hospital, for example, allocated only thirteen beds to black patients. Because seriously ill or injured patients often filled the beds, most black women could not have their babies in the city hospital even if they wanted to. While the Edmundites' Good Samaritan Hospital handled some births, most black mothers depended on midwives. The shortage of hospital beds for blacks, especially babies, dismayed Jon Daniels and Marc Oliver, though Eugene Pritchard was not surprised. Unintimidated by the power of local officials, they appealed to the local hospital administrators for more beds and then carried their protest to federal authorities. They learned about the civil rights requirements of hospitals that received federal funds under the Hill-Burton Act and used their knowledge to threaten local authorities. Partly as a result of their lobbying, they secured a pledge that a new wing for blacks would be added to the hospital.[72]

In surveying the social services available and directly assisting some blacks to obtain help, Daniels met a number of social workers and doctors in Selma. One doctor who got to know Daniels after meeting him at the county health department was Robert Jefferson Henderson, a specialist in obstetrics and gynecology. He first introduced himself to Daniels on July 21 at the clinic and then attempted to learn more about him. From the start, Henderson suspected that civil rights workers like Daniels were being used "as a tool or front to promote the interests of . . . the Communist conspiracy," and he considered it his civic duty to find out if Daniels was a communist agent. The doctor told Daniels that he believed that civil rights workers did not understand Selma's race relations because they remained isolated in the black community and did not get to know local whites. When Daniels countered by naming several whites that he knew, Henderson dismissed them as "liberal" and not "typical, white Southerners." One day he invited Daniels to visit his home and meet his family. The seminarian naturally welcomed the opportunity to discuss the civil rights movement with prominent white residents.[73]

Daniels went to the physician's home the next evening. Henderson later reported that, during their conversation, the seminarian suggested that the civil rights movement was part of a worldwide revolt against the power of whites and that he expected whites would lose in the long run. Until that time, however, he pledged to help blacks combat discrimination and injustice, even if he had to work outside the law. His host, who thought that Daniels was advocating anarchy, asked him if he was a communist. Daniels said he was not a member of the Communist party but, according to Henderson, considered himself something of a Christian-Marxist, which made no sense to the doctor. Daniels tried to explain that Marxism and Christianity were not mutually exclusive and that Marxism could supplement the teachings of Christ. Unconvinced as well as alarmed, Henderson then asked if Daniels and others like him would soon be priests in the Episcopal church, and Daniels assured him that they would. When the doctor revealed that his family had not attended a service at St. Paul's for months to protest the church's support of the National Council of Churches, Daniels stressed the importance of receiving Communion regardless of what the church did. Realizing for the first time that the Hendersons were Episcopalians, Daniels surprised them by saying that he was the one who had been taking blacks to services at St. Paul's.[74]

After their frank and sometimes provocative discussion, Daniels and the Hendersons parted on cordial terms. He agreed to pay another visit for further conversation about race relations. Though he saw Henderson only one more time, briefly in downtown Selma, Daniels came to think of "my segregationist doctor friend and his wife" as two of his better contacts among local whites. Part of the Hendersons' appeal was that they were open and courteous, even if segregationists, but also that many of Daniels's other white contacts seemed to be drying up. Father Ouellet had been transferred to Vermont and other whites were on vacation. Daniels suspected that some local whites were avoiding him because of community pressure.[75]

Daniels, of course, retained strong ties to the black community in Selma, though even some of them were beginning to sour. Especially unpleasant was his relationship with the Wests. "Lonzie is impossible," Daniels informed Judy Upham in early August. "Just can't *abide* Lonzie." His alcoholism remained a serious problem, Daniels reported, despite the seminarian's efforts to assist him. Unhappy at the Wests, Daniels wanted to move out but lacked the nerve to shift to another family in the Carver Homes. Moreover, with the integration of St. Paul's and the completion of the social services survey, his work in Selma had reached a plateau. He had helped achieve many changes in Selma since the march — the violence against blacks had declined, blacks registered to vote more easily, nearly all public accommodations were open to blacks, and the Selma public schools were scheduled to integrate the following September — but he was unsure of what to do next. He had become discouraged by his futile efforts to work with local whites and had grown weary of the increasingly routine nature of his work. As he told Upham:

"It may be too much to say I'm beginning to despair of Selma, but at any rate I am not optimistic." From the SNCC workers he met in Selma, Daniels had learned of civil rights activities in the adjacent county and by the middle of July he decided to shift his energies east to the rural area known as "bloody" Lowndes.[76]

"BLOODY" LOWNDES

A longtime observer of post–World War II race relations in Lowndes County, Alabama, declared that whites had always assumed that "a black man who lived to be twenty-one in Lowndes County was a 'good nigger.' "[1] Any adult black man had learned to accept that he was inferior to whites. Others who refused to conform to the code of white supremacy either had to leave quickly and quietly or face probable physical punishment, including death. The history of actual and threatened violence produced an ingrained fear of whites that intimidated blacks and contributed to their suppression. Violence served to enforce white supremacy, slavery, peonage, disfranchisement, and segregation; it occurred most brutally perhaps in lynchings. White violence against blacks, which was only one form of violence prevalent in the community, made the county notorious as "bloody" Lowndes.[2]

For over a century from the antebellum era to the emergence of the civil rights movement, violence played a key role in the history of

Lowndes race relations, but changes in the county's population, politics, agriculture, and economy also affected race relations. In the antebellum era, for instance, the rapidly developing importance of cotton led to a dependence on black slavery. In the twentieth century, a revolution in agriculture (from once king cotton to cattle and timber) and the concurrent exodus of many blacks who had been sharecroppers influenced relations between the dominant whites and the suppressed blacks.

On January 20, 1830, the Alabama legislature carved Lowndes out of seven hundred square miles of Butler, Dallas, and Montgomery counties.[3] Located about forty miles south of the center of the state, the roughly square county has the Alabama River, winding westward across central Alabama before turning south toward Mobile, as its northern border. The low, swampy land along the Alabama River prevented the development of a river port in the county. Instead, Montgomery, only a dozen miles from Lowndes's northeastern edge, and Selma, a similar distance from the northwestern side, served the county.

The area constituting Lowndes County had first been inhabited by Indians. As white settlers began slowly pushing into the region around 1800, conflicts between whites and Native Americans developed. Lowndes, in the heart of the Creek domain, experienced significant action in the Indian wars. With the expulsion of the Indians and the return of peace, white migration into the area intensified. The influx of blacks and whites in the late 1810s exceeded the capacity of surveyors and the federal government to prepare for land sales, and many settlers just squatted on their newly claimed property. The flood of newcomers strained the state's food supply. The original settlers of Alabama came primarily from the Georgia and South Carolina piedmont and from Tennessee; most of them were men on the make.[4]

Although Georgians and Tennesseeans apparently dominated the settlement of Lowndes, numerous South Carolinians exerted influence. The new county took its name from William Lowndes (1782–1822), a low-county South Carolina aristocrat and planter who was first elected to Congress in 1810. Most settlers of the county seat near the middle of Lowndes also came from South Carolina and named their town for another famous South Carolinian. Robert Y. Hayne (1791–1839), the son of a prominent rice planter, won election to the U.S. Senate in 1822. Advocating low tariffs and state rights in the Hayne-Webster debate of 1830, Hayne defended nullification and the southern position against Yankee arguments favoring the power of the federal union.[5]

In taking the names of Lowndes and Hayne, the settlers of Lowndes County and Hayneville made appropriate choices, because the new Alabama settlement shared many characteristics with the South Carolina politicians. They may have differed over the tariff and the Bank of the United States, but Lowndes and Hayne both represented the wealthy white planter elite in their state. The planters, dependent on the forced labor of black slaves to grow cotton and rice in the Carolina low country, steadfastly defended slavery, first through attempts to nullify threatening federal legislation and finally through secession and civil war. The people of Lowndes County soon resembled the constituents of William Lowndes and Robert Hayne, though they lived several hundred miles west of the Palmetto State and their terrain differed substantially from the Carolina low country.

Instead of lying along the coast, as did the Carolina low country, Lowndes County was situated inland, in the middle of a twelve-county area known as the Alabama Black Belt. According to one scholar of antebellum Alabama, the term *Black Belt* "can be applied with equal truth to the soil, the inhabitants, or that part of the map where the greatest population density is indicated." Whatever the origins of the term, the soil certainly came first, followed by black slaves. The clay soils of the gently rolling northern two-thirds of Lowndes lay within the Black Belt, while the southern hilly section shaded off into the coastal plain, where the soils were sandy loams or loams.[6]

The sticky clay of the Black Belt held surface moisture particularly well and was, therefore, very productive for agriculture, but the same characteristic meant that the clay made a tenacious mud when wet and an extremely hard surface when dry. According to local folklore, a horse could sink a hoof as much as one foot deep into the Black Belt mud, only to lose all the hair from its leg and maybe even the shoe from its hoof when it managed to extract itself from the sticky mud. Farmers, of course, had difficulty working the soil when it was wet and faced nearly insurmountable tasks breaking the clay when it was dry and hard. In spite of these obstacles, the Black Belt lands were quite fertile. One story actually suggested that a peg-legged man ought to walk quickly through Lowndes County to make sure that his wooden leg did not take root in the rich soil.[7]

The Black Belt's sticky soil initially stymied would-be cotton planters, who generally settled elsewhere before 1830. In addition, large sections of the area lacked an adequate supply of drinking water. In 1830, therefore, Lowndes had only 9,410 residents, whereas the population of the entire state had exploded from 125,000 ten years earlier to more than 300,000. Once settlers discovered the suitability of the Black Belt for cotton and figured out how to work its soil and dig adequate wells, more farmers arrived and cotton became the key crop. By 1840 Lowndes had more than doubled its population and had become the seventh most populous county in the state. Cotton soon dominated its economy, as production jumped from 800,000 pounds in 1840 to 21 million pounds on the eve of the Civil War.[8]

If cotton was king in Lowndes County, its benefits accrued unevenly among the people. Not only were many residents slaves, but among whites the ownership of land and slaves varied greatly. In the antebellum period nearly 20 percent of adult white males did not own land, while in 1850 one-fourth of the landowners held five hundred or more acres (an elite owned more than five thousand acres each). Sixty percent of the white residents who engaged in agriculture owned slaves. Half of the slaveholders probably possessed no more than ten slaves, and nearly 80 percent had fewer than thirty slaves. On the other hand, perhaps only seventy-five slaveholders in Lowndes had more than forty slaves and a mere handful of them owned more than one hundred. By 1840 slaves constituted the overwhelming majority of the county's inhabitants. By 1860 the white population numbered 8,362, whereas the slave population had swelled to 19,340.[9] About seven hundred white slave owners thus dominated the county.

Although relations between the white masters and their black slaves were undoubtedly intricate and varied, slavery in Lowndes County essentially involved one white human being owning and dominating another who was black. Establishing a tradition of white supremacy, the slaveholders held the economic, political, and social power — they made the crucial decisions affecting both their own lives and the lives of their slaves. The white owners provided housing, food, clothing, and health care for their slaves, and they organized and directed their work. However resourceful blacks may have been in preserving some autonomy and in maintaining their own culture, the slave system itself depended on white coercion, exploitation, and oppression because, as one historian has aptly put it, the "purpose of slavery was work" by the slaves for their masters. Whites justified slavery on the assumption that blacks were naturally inferior to whites and were better off under slavery than they would have been as free people. They rationalized slavery as necessary for social order, especially in the Black Belt, whether it made economic sense or not.[10]

In controlling their slaves, Lowndes County owners had the backing of an evolving series of state laws known as the slave code. While the slave code guaranteed slaves certain rights, such as a jury trial in capital cases (but not a jury of their peers), it more generally gave power to the owners. For example, the owner had absolute authority over discipline. The code also severely restricted the behavior of blacks: slaves could not own property or obtain it by finding it, could not hire themselves out for pay, and could not rent living quarters other than those provided by their own-ers. A slave could not even possess a dog. Of course, a slave was also pro-hibited from owning a gun or any weapon without the master's permis-sion. Even the physical movement of slaves in Lowndes came under the jurisdiction of the slave code. A slave could not leave his or her owner's plantation without a pass, and anyone who did could be arrested and punished. Authorized by the state, a system of patrols by slave owners regulated slave behavior and enforced the slave code. The dozen free blacks in Lowndes also came under many of the slave code's constraints.[11]

Exploitation of slaves allowed some owners to prosper and live com-fortably. Lowndesboro, a little planter town in northern Lowndes County, became "the jewel of Alabama's planter villages" with a number of sumptuous mansions built in the popular Greek Revival style. Com-monly a two-story, rectangular building, the planter home had spacious, airy halls and rooms; large porches and numerous windows added to its expansiveness and free feeling. At Meadowlawn, which was representa-tive of the finer homes of Black Belt planters in Lowndesboro, thirteen large white columns supported a portico that extended around two sides of the beautiful two-story frame house.[12]

Not all towns in Lowndes resembled Lowndesboro. For example, Hayneville, known successively as Big Swamp, Lowndes Court House, and finally its present name when the county was officially established, lacked majestic mansions with impressive columns and cupolas. Located less than ten miles south of Lowndesboro nearer the center of the county and in the middle of the Black Belt, the small trading center and county seat "boiled and bubbled with life." The town also had a reputation as "the greatest gambling town of its size in the United States." People flocked to Hayneville to place their bets on horses racing at the local track and on cocks fighting in pits on the town square, as well as to enjoy the diversions offered by the town's eight gambling houses.[13]

Antebellum Lowndes County was, therefore, really a rough frontier society. Although most "planters" were just moderately prosperous farmers and even the largest planters often had modest incomes, the small minority who lived in Greek Revival mansions contributed to the later widespread belief that an aristocratic plantation culture existed in Alabama's Black Belt. As one of the region's romantic residents put it in the 1930s, the term Black Belt "represents a civilization" epitomizing the Old South at its pinnacle, with "charm and distinction . . . [and] leisure." Thinking only of whites, the commentator observed that the heat caused people to expend as little effort as possible: "One cannot be energetic in the Black Belt. . . . Therefore the people of the Belt take their leisure, and out of it have evolved the charming philosophy that one should live with a minimum of effort and a maximum of enjoyment." Rejecting the work ethic, they allegedly tried "to make life an art instead of a bread and meat existence." Though hardly in a well-established aristocratic society, the white lady or gentleman of the Black Belt ostensibly had good breeding, education, manners, and taste.[14]

For the county's white population, the Civil War lacked much of the death and destruction experienced by other parts of the South because no major battle occurred in or near the county. It was a nightmare, nonetheless, as the whites' vaunted Black Belt culture was severely damaged, if not completely destroyed. The central institution of slavery came to an end with the Emancipation Proclamation and the later arrival of federal troops in April 1865, and more than 19,000 freedmen gained political power under "radical" Reconstruction; the freedmen's new status profoundly affected Lowndes County, particularly its politics, government, economics, and race relations generally. Nearly everything the white minority valued about its antebellum way of life had been changed or ruined by the intrusion of outsiders. Whites would not forget the experience, including the death of more than eighty soldiers from Lowndes who fought to preserve their society, even as they worked to survive in the postwar South.[15]

During Reconstruction, Lowndes County experienced black political dominance and some violence and corruption. Aided undoubtedly by scalawags, blacks overcame white opposition and gained control of the local government. The county, for example, sent only Republicans to the state legislature from 1870 through 1877, and Republican candidates for governor carried Lowndes in 1870, 1872, and 1874. Blacks and their white allies also dominated the state government until the end of Reconstruction in 1874, and they maintained their grip on Lowndes and other Black Belt counties until about 1880. According to local whites, rampaging freedmen in a "wave of incendiarism" destroyed cotton gins, barns, and fences. At the same time whites believed that graft and financial irresponsibility plagued the black-controlled county government. Exasperated with the misdeeds and encouraged by the end of radical Reconstruction elsewhere, Lowndes whites rallied early in 1880 to throw out the blacks and their supporters. White Democrats soon controlled the county once again and learned to use the remaining black votes to exert power in the state government.[16]

The important changes in Lowndes wrought by the Civil War affected king cotton, which still reigned but over a less impressive domain. Cotton production plummeted during and immediately after the conflict, and it only slowly rebounded. In 1870, Lowndes farmers produced less than half the cotton grown in 1860, and by 1880 production amounted to only about 30,000 bales, far less than the antebellum high of more than 53,000 bales. The cotton kingdom clearly faced serious problems. Near exhaustion plagued much of the Black Belt land, and many farmers had already begun to desert the region for more productive fields in Texas and Kansas.[17] After the war Lowndes farmers faced even more pressing problems involving personal debts and labor.

Landowners often struggled just to hold onto their land because, with wartime interruptions and later declining cotton prices, their debts incurred during the war remained unpaid. In the 1870s many landowners relinquished their property to unpaid lenders or lost land to tax officials, who auctioned it off to pay back taxes. On occasion, farmers lost several hundred acres for a few dollars in unpaid taxes. Most Lowndes landowners nevertheless managed to keep their land, and the white landed elite continued to control the county's economy after the Civil War and Reconstruction.[18]

After the war landowners in Lowndes also had to contend with a drastically different labor force. Landless freed blacks still needed work on the land owned by whites, and whites still needed the labor of their former slaves. The transition in labor relations was not always easy, but planters had to accept the change. One planter bluntly explained the new circumstances to his former slaves:

> Formerly, you were my slaves; you worked for me, and I provided for you. You had no thought of the morrow, for I thought of that for you. If you were sick, I had the doctor come to you. When you needed clothes, clothes were forthcoming; and you never went hungry for lack of meal and pork. You had little more responsibility than my mules.
>
> But now all that is changed. Being free men, you assume the responsibilities of free men. You sell me your labor, I pay you money, and with that money you provide for yourselves. You must look out for your own clothes and food, and the wants of your children. If I advance these things for you, I shall charge them to you, for I cannot give them like I once did, now I pay you wages. Once if you were ugly or lazy, I had you whipped, and that was the end of it. Now if you are ugly and lazy, your wages will be paid to others, and you will be turned off, to go about the country with bundles on your backs, like the miserable low-down niggers you see that nobody will hire. But if you are well-behaved and industrious, you will be prosperous and respected and happy.[19]

Some white planters preferred to pay blacks a set wage for their work in the fields, but a wage labor system never developed in the Black Belt.

Instead, a system of tenancy emerged and soon dominated the South, especially Black Belt areas such as Lowndes County. By 1880, tenants farmed 2,757 of the 3,462 farms in Lowndes. Though many rented land from the owners for a fixed amount of money, most tenants entered into more complicated relationships with the owners. The crucial ingredients involved the landless tenant's labor and the planter's land and capital. At first the agreements between tenants and landowners varied widely, but quickly a common practice prevailed: the planter furnished the land, all the supplies needed for farming, and a house for the tenant; in return, the tenant did all the work to produce the crops. Usually covering just one year, the contract stipulated the amount of financial support the owner would provide, the number of acres to be farmed, the crops to be raised, and the authority of the owner over farming practices. At the end of the year, landlord and tenant split the crop into equal parts. Sharing the crop with the landowner, the tenant became known as a sharecropper. In a variation, when the landowner supplied only the land (and a house for the tenant), the share tenant got to keep three-fourths of the cotton and two-thirds of other crops and paid the remainder to the owner as rent for the land.[20]

Tenants operated almost 90 percent of the farms in Lowndes County, and more than 90 percent of the tenants were black. Tenants found the life of debt and drudgery little better than slavery. The landless tenant, of course, exercised many more personal choices than had the slave, but freedom had considerable limits without real economic independence. The tenant's "independent decision making was limited to the mundane and menial aspects of farming," with the white merchants and landlords holding the power in all other farming matters. The tenant undoubtedly suffered blows to "his pride, his ambition, and his efficiency as a tiller of the soil."[21]

From the time a Lowndes tenant agreed with a landowner on a contract for the year until he sold the crops, the tenant had to borrow to live. Lacking any collateral except the future crop, the tenant gave the creditor a lien on an easily marketable, nonperishable cash crop, usually cotton. The creditor-merchant frequently was the same person as the landlord, or at least in collusion with the landlord. To grow cotton to pay the merchant and the landlord, a tenant turned increasingly away from growing food-stuffs and toward additional acres of cotton. As a result, a tenant bought more and more supplies on credit from the merchant. The merchant charged a high rate of interest (often above 50 percent), and frequently at the end of the crop year the tenant did not have enough cotton in his share to pay the lien on his crop. When creditors compelled the debtor tenant to stay until all debts had been repaid in full, the tenant had to borrow more for the next year and the downwardly spiraling cycle continued. A new form of oppression had soon snared many tenants in Lowndes County and the rest of the South, the system of debt peonage.[22]

In 1903 a U.S. district attorney in Alabama argued that the center of the South's peonage system was Lowndes County. He told his superiors, "This county, it is claimed, is just honeycombed with slavery." As practiced in Lowndes, however, it involved more than just tenants, crop liens, continual debts, and a loss of freedom. Warren S. Reese, Jr., the federal official, described how county authorities not only allowed peonage but also participated in it. Sheriff J. W. Dixon, for example, once paid the fine of a black man and then signed him to a contract to work off the debt. When the black, Dillard Freeman, asked to go visit a sick brother, the sheriff refused permission. Freeman went anyway. Dixon and another man found Freeman and proceeded to beat him nearly to death. Later, when Freeman went to Montgomery to testify about peonage before a federal grand jury, Dixon threatened him in the courthouse before he took the stand. Scared for his future in Lowndes, Freeman at first denied that Dixon had beaten him; only after federal officials promised to protect him did Freeman describe what Dixon had done. In the meantime, Dixon also threatened a Lowndes black who served on the grand jury by suggesting that he had better look out for people in Lowndes if he expected to live in the county.[23]

In spite of the federal investigations, the peonage system continued in Lowndes. Sheriff Dixon was not indicted for his treatment of Freeman and remained free to use his position to support the interests of white creditors against indebted blacks. Local whites succeeded in blocking further federal probes by threatening federal agents with violence. The officials, worried more about their own security than that of local blacks, stayed out of the county.[24]

Peonage was only one form of oppression that Lowndes County blacks experienced around the turn of the century. Supporting white supremacy, racial segregation dominated Lowndes after the Civil War, whether enforced by law or sustained by custom. Blacks and whites remained separated in churches, schools, and places of recreation, even though the two races worked together on farms and black women worked in the homes of white families. Like other southern states, Alabama in the late nineteenth century enacted laws requiring racial segregation, but many of the laws had little relevance for rural counties such as Lowndes. One state law, for example, barred white women nurses from treating black male patients; the rule seldom applied in Lowndes County, which had no hospitals and few doctors or nurses. Similarly, requirements for segregation in hospitals, mental institutions, and prisons had no effect in

Lowndes. In rural areas, racial segregation resulted more from habit than from legislation, but it existed nonetheless. The larger forces advocating racial segregation in Alabama, moreover, reinforced and encouraged the attitudes of Lowndes whites who believed in white supremacy.[25]

Disfranchisement soon joined peonage and segregation as central to white oppression of blacks in Lowndes County. For years after Reconstruction, blacks continued to vote in Alabama's Black Belt. From 1873 to 1875 Lowndes and the other counties in the Second Congressional District even sent a black, James T. Rapier, to Congress. As a result of Democratic violence and fraud and Republican dissension, however, Rapier lost his bid for reelection to a white Democrat. To reduce the impact of black ballots in several congressional districts, the state legislature in the late 1870s gerrymandered a number of Black Belt counties into one district; consequently, blacks in the new Fourth District repeatedly failed to elect another black to Congress.[26]

Whites in the Black Belt had quickly learned to manipulate black ballots and had grown accustomed to using black suffrage to exert exaggerated influence in the state government. After regaining control of the election machinery, white officials in Lowndes permitted blacks to vote for Republicans and then stole the blacks' votes for Democrats, threw out the ballots for technical reasons, or stuffed the ballot boxes for the Democrats. As one white politician openly declared, "[A]ny time it was necessary the black belt could put in ten, fifteen, twenty or thirty thousand Negro votes" into a state election. Observing the positive effects of election corruption, a Montgomery newspaper in 1879 announced that black suffrage "has resulted well for all our people." Dishonesty thus succeeded, at least for a while. The Populist movement in the 1890s threatened conservative white Democratic control and prompted moves to restrict the suffrage. In 1893 the legislature passed a complex voter registration and election law that served to disfranchise many illiterate blacks and whites; the law also allowed conservative Democrats to rebuff the Populist challenge.[27]

Under the new state law, election fraud continued. Frustrated by the Black Belt's persistent manipulation of black votes to control state elections, predominantly white counties began to argue that Alabama should follow other southern states and disfranchise blacks. In areas like Lowndes County, some politicians resisted a constitutional convention because it might deny blacks the right to vote and, through reapportionment, reduce the Black Belt's power in the legislature. As one Black Belt Democrat confessed, "All we want is a small vote and a large count." Reassured on legislative reapportionment, Lowndes County in a 1901 state referendum supported overwhelmingly the call for a constitutional convention. In addition to many other issues, the convention proposed new requirements for voting: a literacy or property test, new residency requirements, and a poll tax. Although the Black Belt as a region voted for the new constitution by a more than six-to-one margin (and again officials counted thousands of black votes in favor of disfranchisement), Lowndes County cast its ballots against the constitution (1,642 to 1,390). Some whites who voted against it may have followed the lead of a native of Lowndes County who was an influential opponent of the constitution and preferred to continue manipulating the black vote instead of disfranchising it. Other opponents of ratification also suggested that blacks might still control the Black Belt because literate Negroes outnumbered literate whites in nine counties. In spite of the resistance in Lowndes County, the state ratified the new constitution.[28]

The voting requirements of the new constitution disfranchised poor, illiterate whites as well as blacks, but the impact was most devastating for blacks. The new rules effectively stripped all blacks in Alabama of any political power. By the beginning of 1903, only 2,980 out of more than 180,000 eligible black voters were registered in the state. In the Black Belt, registration books that had listed over 79,000 blacks in 1900 contained only 1,081 blacks in the year after the new constitution. Lowndes County, which had recorded 5,500 black voters in 1900, had only 44 black registrants after the first registration period.[29] After the constitution of 1901, blacks in Lowndes County had no voice in politics and government — they could not vote for the superintendent of schools, for the board of revenue, or for the sheriff. The white minority had tightened its dominance of Lowndes County.

Whites in Lowndes found that overt violence was an effective technique for controlling blacks. With beatings, white farmers could keep their black tenants in line. One planter, Robert S. Dickson, reportedly had killed fourteen men, black *and* white. Sometimes blacks were forced to ride off with the planter in his car, never to be seen again. According to a native of the county, right after World War I Dickson killed a Negro soldier because he "couldn't stand the sight of a Negro in uniform and shot him." Even the police in Lowndes as well as in nearby Montgomery and Selma feared the violent Dickson; if they discovered that they had arrested any of his tenants, they would release them to avoid trouble.[30]

The more anonymous blacks faced physical retaliation if they did anything to annoy whites. Violence was routine. In the 1930s, a black woman from Lowndesboro admitted that the county "had a terrible reputation" for violence. When she visited in a nearby county, people treated her cautiously because she was from Lowndes. A Negro woman told her, "You are from the place where they don't promise to kill you but do it."

Unable to contradict the charge, the Lowndes woman said, "You can't mess around in Lowndes. Better stand back."[31] Blacks in Lowndes learned early to "stand back" and avoid confrontations or even simple misunderstandings with whites. The racial etiquette established by the powerful white minority required them always to be obsequious. If a black moved outside the boundaries set by whites, or appeared to act in an unacceptable way, whites often responded with violence. The ordinary pummeling and thrashings usually sufficed, but sometimes they seemed to be inadequate or inappropriate punishment. The whites then turned to the ultimate form of violence, lynching.

Though Lowndes County whites probably killed countless blacks in the obscurity of the rural county's fields, forests, and swamps, a few lynchings received publicity. In 1888, for example, a mob of whites lynched a black man who had shot and killed a local white man in a dispute. The black man had subsequently turned himself over to his employer, who notified the sheriff. While the black man waited in Hayneville for his trial, more than one hundred whites seized him from the jail and killed him. The violent suppression of whites did not stop, in this case, with a lynching. Fearing retaliation from blacks, the sheriff rounded up blacks suspected of plotting revenge. In the process he shot one black; as a result white concern escalated. After armed whites rallied to help the sheriff, further conflict between the races brought a call for the state militia. Within a few days, the sheriff, his white supporters, and fifty militiamen suppressed black resistance and restored order.[32]

One week before Christmas, 1914, a mob of whites lynched a black man near Fort Deposit for allegedly attempting to attack a white girl. In the middle of the night Olie Mae Sullivan, a high school girl, had awakened in her bedroom to discover an intruder; frightened by her cries, the stranger fled through an open window. The next morning local whites found prints left by stockinged feet in the red mud outside Olie Mae's room, and they followed the tracks to a house where they found Will Jones and his mud-covered socks. Jones, who had only recently moved to Lowndes County from Rome, Georgia, reportedly confessed to the attempted assault. County authorities then put the suspect in a buggy, under guard of several deputies, for the trip to the county jail in Hayneville. About half a mile from Fort Deposit, a mob of whites overpowered the guards and abducted their prisoner. In broad daylight the unmasked mob hung Jones from a telegraph pole and then "riddled the body with bullets." After a short investigation on the day of the lynching, a coroner's jury reported that Will Jones had died at the hands of a "party or parties unknown."[33]

Jones's alleged attempt to attack a white female was the crime most likely to arouse the passions of a southern white lynch mob, and the Lowndes County jury's verdict typified rulings dealing with the lynching of blacks. In the Jones case, however, the decision of the grand jury failed to satisfy Alabama's governor, who had, according to the *Montgomery Advertiser*, "stood staunchly for the majesty and supremacy of the law" and pursued "a vigorous policy toward the crime of lynching" during his administration. Governor Emmet O'Neal called on the sheriff of Lowndes County to supply details of the lynching. When ten days later O'Neal still had not heard from the sheriff, the governor took the unusual step of ordering a special session of the grand jury in the state's Second Judicial District to investigate the lynching of Will Jones. O'Neal declared, "The people of Alabama must understand that their protection comes not from a mob of cowardly lynchers, influenced by passion or prejudice," but from the law. Early in January the special grand jury in Lowndes County failed to return any indictments in the lynching of Jones.[34] When even the governor of the state could not make local authorities punish lynchers who had committed their crime in full view of law enforcement officials, blacks in Lowndes County certainly recognized their vulnerability to white violence.

All lynchings, of course, did not involve alleged attacks on white women. Less than three years after the killing of Will Jones, two blacks died at the hands of another Lowndes lynch mob ostensibly for threatening a white man. Well liked and respected in Birmingham, where they had lived and worked for a number of years, Will and Sam Powell returned to Lowndes County to visit their seriously ill father, an elderly man well known in his community. After a visit of several days, they rode with their father in a mule-drawn wagon to Letohatchie to catch the train for Montgomery and Birmingham. Outside Letohatchie the blacks had an altercation with a local white man, A. H. Jenkins. Accounts of the incident differed. According to one report, the Powell brothers held up Jenkins at gunpoint; another version said that their mule brushed against Jenkins's horse in the road, the white man protested, and the blacks then drew guns and forced Jenkins to drive away. The Powells, however, claimed that Jenkins struck them first and only then did they threaten him with their guns. Some also suggested that the incident with Jenkins was merely a pretext for killing the brothers because they had enemies in the area — one of them reportedly had escaped death a few years earlier when he ran away from a white man's farm after killing his 200-pound hog.[35]

Whatever happened on the road outside Letohatchie, the Powells continued on to Montgomery. Jenkins, the son of the local justice of the peace, swore out a warrant for their arrest on charges of assault with intent to murder. The next morning Montgomery police arrested Will and

Sam Powell and took their guns without any trouble in the city's Union Railway Station as they waited for a train to Birmingham. In the afternoon two Lowndes County deputy sheriffs took charge of the prisoners for the return trip to Hayneville. Between Letohatchie and Hayneville a mob of one hundred whites overpowered the deputies and lynched the Powell men. News stories reported: "The lynching is shrouded in mystery. Where the mob came from is not known."[36]

Newspapers protested the outrage. The *Montgomery Advertiser* declared that "[n]othing can be said in extenuation of the shocking offense against law and order committed by Lowndes County parties" in lynching the Powells. Granting that the Negroes had been "aggressive and menacing," the paper pointed out that no shots had been fired and that the two men were safely under arrest before the mob attacked. Similarly, the *Mobile Register* charged that the act "must be admitted even by the persons engaged in it as inexcusable." The *Birmingham Age-Herald* condemned the "flagrant disregard of law and justice" and called "for a prompt investigation. The men who composed the mob can be caught and they should be punished."[37] But they were not. No white was ever punished for the murders of Will and Sam Powell, as blacks in Lowndes County were well aware.

As late as 1931, no arrests were made for the lynching of a sixteen-year-old black youth who allegedly accosted an eleven-year-old white girl one morning as she walked from her home to the grocery store. The sheriff had to use state bloodhounds to find the boy's body; it was tied to a tree with rope and dog chains and had thirty-two bullets in it. After an investigation, the sheriff claimed to have no idea who the killers were.[38] Other examples of white mob violence in the county reinforced for blacks the reality of the white minority's unrestrained power over them.

Whites also responded with violence to any black assertiveness that might threaten white dominance. During the Great Depression, for instance, some black sharecroppers in Lowndes County joined the Alabama Sharecroppers' Union and began organizing. In September 1935 they protested their working conditions by striking at a local plantation. Local white officials responded forcefully. To crush the strike, Sheriff R. E. Woodruff and his posse engaged in a campaign of terror in which half a dozen blacks died and a score were beaten; two dozen leaders of the sharecroppers' protest fled the county for safety. Once again white violence had succeeded in maintaining black subservience and white control.[39]

While tenancy, peonage, segregation, and violence oppressed blacks and assured white supremacy, everyday life in Lowndes was rather dreary for most white farmers. Even in the county seat of Hayneville, the unkempt town square displayed weeds in the corners and worn, uneven walks. Hogs rooted in the streets and fences fell down out of neglect. In the summer, men sitting lazily in front of the stores whittled or played checkers; year-round they gathered inside the stores, the courthouse, and offices for games of checkers. According to one historian, "The number of loafers who had time for such pastime at many intervals of the day was quite large." As a result of community lethargy, Hayneville lost its town charter in 1881 (and did not regain it for several decades). In the late nineteenth century Lowndes residents perennially complained about poor roads and mail service. Daily newspapers from Montgomery some-times took more than a week to arrive in Hayneville, which was only twenty-five miles away. The roads were intolerably dusty in summer and muddy in winter; the mud was so bad that once when someone saw a hat lying in the road, he reportedly feared that it was on top of a man riding a horse that had sunk in the mire. Further, constant outbreaks of malaria, smallpox, typhoid, and hookworm plagued whites and blacks alike well into the twentieth century.[40]

Not every aspect of life was bleak for whites. The Hayneville Literary Society, organized in 1873, studied operas, considered matters of govern-ment and politics, and discussed cooking. Hayneville also had a baseball team and a dramatics club, and leading white citizens staged numerous balls in the county courthouse. In addition, a number of homes in Hayne-ville contained pianos, organs, and other musical instruments for the enjoyment of their white families. Less refined and more popular enter-tainment such as horse racing, cockfighting, and gambling continued to attract crowds.[41]

The conditions in Lowndes, however, discouraged many white resi-dents. Though the county's population continued to grow after the Civil War, the number of whites declined from 8,362 in 1860 to 4,762 in 1900; the trend prevailed throughout the Black Belt. Whites left Lowndes for a host of reasons. Outnumbered four to one by blacks, some whites simply feared the newly freed blacks and wanted to be around more whites. Others tired of the inconveniences of rural and small-town life and moved to nearby Montgomery, to burgeoning Birmingham, or to cities outside Alabama. Still other whites wanted better jobs than were available in the rural county; Hayneville had only a few flour mills, a cotton gin, and a few stores, which together employed no more than a few dozen workers. They also sought better schooling for their children; in Lowndes private acade-mies served the small white elite, while the education of most white children suffered.[42]

At the same time, the black population in Lowndes grew from 19,000 in 1860 to more than 30,000 by the turn of the century. Of course, these citizens never participated in the affairs of the Hayneville clubs or went to the balls in the courthouse; they never played dominoes in the courthouse. On Saturday afternoons, blacks went to town to conduct their business and visit with friends, and whites stayed home. The public schools for Lowndes blacks received inadequate and inequitable funding because the dominant whites depended on private schools and allocated a disproportionate share of public funds to the few white public schools. (One exception was the Calhoun School, a private institution founded for blacks in the 1890s by two northern women associated with Booker T. Washington and Tuskegee Institute.) Blacks had a hard life, but they saw little way or reason to escape.[43]

In their struggle to survive during the late nineteenth and early twentieth centuries, blacks and whites in Lowndes did make progress. In addition to a major expansion of the county courthouse in 1905, Hayneville added a cotton mill and a new bank. The most important change came with the completion of a branch railway line from Montgomery. The railroad allowed Hayneville businesses to survive, but the town's pride in its past kept it from achieving the economic growth enjoyed by its more progressive sister community in the southern part of the county. Fort Deposit, according to a student of the Black Belt, "manifested an enterprise not characteristic of the older, more aristocratic communities of the prairie section" such as Hayneville. Long a stop on the railroad from Montgomery to Mobile, the New South town developed several small industries and even had an electric power plant around the turn of the century. One indication of the county's hardships was the relatively slow appearance of the automobile. The first car did not arrive in Lowndes until about 1910, later than in most parts of the state; moreover, Lowndes was one of the last Black Belt counties to join the movement for good roads when it issued its first bonds in 1914.[44]

For their livelihoods blacks and whites who remained in Lowndes continued to depend on cotton, the perennial source of most income and wealth in the Black Belt. The amount of cotton produced lagged, however, behind prewar levels and market prices remained low. By 1900 county fields yielded only 9 million pounds of cotton, almost 12 million under the 1860 total. In 1910, cotton production grew to 14 million pounds but remained far below the antebellum high; the yields in Lowndes County never recovered to their 1860 level. The Lowndes experience was not unusual for the area. Postwar cotton production in the Black Belt peaked in 1900 at about 80 percent of the 1860 crop, and by 1920 the cotton crop had declined to only one-fifth of that in 1900. After commanding more than forty cents a pound immediately after the Civil War, cotton sold for less than ten cents a pound in the 1870s and for only five cents in the 1890s.

The demands of World War I revived receipts to twenty cents a pound and briefly in the postwar period the price hit forty cents, but the higher prices failed to spell higher profits for farmers producing less in Lowndes County. Falling production and low prices crippled landowners and their tenants.[45]

The dramatic decline in cotton had a variety of causes. Generally, the cumulative effects of the relentless growing of cotton, the careless erosion of the land, and the lack of sufficient fertilizers increasingly depleted the once-rich soils and cut productivity. Low cotton prices, resulting in part from increased competition from the Southwest and overseas, also hurt the profit margins of growers. In addition, a flood in 1916 ruined many crops in the Black Belt. Beginning in 1910, a major out-migration of blacks cut the supply of tenants. Many workers left the Lowndes cotton fields for better opportunities in the North (particularly jobs created by the mobilization for World War I) or were pushed off the land because of their difficulty in obtaining credit from struggling landowners and merchants. The black exodus peaked in 1916–17. After having experienced a steadily expanding black population from the antebellum period to 1910, Lowndes lost more than six thousand blacks between 1910 and 1920. As these laborers left, the devastating boll weevil compounded the county's problems by destroying much of the crop. Crossing the Alabama border from Mississippi in 1910, the weevils first entered Lowndes in 1912 and infested all of the county by 1913. The heavy rainfalls and sticky soil in the Black Belt prevented farmers from planting and harvesting their cotton crops early to avoid some of the insects' destructive effects.[46]

The decline in cotton in Lowndes County fit a pattern common to the Black Belt and contributed to a diminution of the region's power in the state. After producing considerably more than half of Alabama's cotton before the Civil War, the Black Belt by 1910 grew less than half of the state's crop. Cotton growing increased in other areas of the state because railroad development allowed previously inaccessible areas to compete in the marketplace and because fertilizers made poorer and older fields profitable. Urbanization and industrialization elsewhere in Alabama also reduced the Black Belt's relative economic importance. In 1872, for example, Lowndes and nine other Black Belt counties paid 34.6 percent of the taxes collected by the state of Alabama, while the three counties in the mineral district around Birmingham paid only 1.7 percent. By 1900 the Black Belt's share had fallen to 20 percent and the mineral region had expanded to nearly 18 percent, and by 1930 the respective shares of state taxes were 11.3 percent and 31.8 percent. Economically, the Black Belt had been surpassed by the dynamic urban areas of the state.[47]

The Black Belt's political clout in the state also weakened, though not as dramatically. The growth of Birmingham and other towns outside the Black Belt, particularly in northern Alabama, lessened the influence of static rural counties such as Lowndes in statewide elections, especially after the virtual disfranchisement of their large black populations. The Black Belt counties nonetheless retained disproportionate power in the Alabama legislature until the second half of the twentieth century because both the legislature after the decennial censuses and the constitutional convention in 1901 failed to reapportion the state legislature to reflect the shifts in population away from the Black Belt and toward the urban areas. The Black Belt also maintained unfair strength in the Democratic party. Its political power had nonetheless become more tenuous, and its white representatives knew that they would have to work even harder to defend their position in the state.[48]

To break the deadening grip of cotton on Black Belt farming and to overcome the area's economic difficulties, agricultural reformers had long encouraged Lowndes County farmers to diversify. In the 1870s, some in Fort Deposit tried raising sheep, but most planters began to diversify only after the cotton industry collapsed. Soon after the introduction of cattle and dairying, especially in the 1910s, Lowndes ranked high among Alabama counties in the number of cattle; between 1910 and 1920 milk production quadrupled. Other farmers entered truck farming. Peanuts first came to Lowndes in 1912, and a peanut oil mill was built in Hayneville in 1915. Additional new agricultural products included pecans, bees and honey, alfalfa, peaches, and tobacco. In spite of diversification, however, king cotton continued to reign, though its decline and eventual dethroning had a devastating effect on an already poor county. Lowndes cotton farmers suffered in the 1910s and, like the larger South, entered an agricultural depression in the 1920s, only to be joined by the rest of the nation during the Great Depression.[49]

Although in some ways life changed little in Lowndes County from 1910 to 1940, agriculture underwent a revolution in its structure, in the crops produced, and in the population of the county. In the three decades after 1910, the number of farms dropped from 6,436 to 3,508 and the number of tenant farmers plunged nearly 50 percent. While the number of acres under cultivation held steady during the 1920s and 1930s, the size of the average farm grew by more than 40 percent. (The lack of alternatives elsewhere in the early 1930s reversed the trend temporarily, leading to a rise in the number of tenants, a decrease in the average farm size, and an increase in the number of farms.)[50]

Government policies under the New Deal and mechanization accelerated these changes. Lowndes farmers continued to devote more than

Table 1 Lowndes County Farms, 1910–1940

	1910	1920	1925	1930	1935	1940
Number of farms	6,436	5,118	3,580	3,993	4,329	3,508
Average number of acres	47.8	57.2	77.3	69.0	63.9	79.1
Number of tenants	5,704	4,482	2,965	3,383	3,664	2,881

Source: U.S. Bureau of the Census, *Thirteenth Census,* 6:36, 43, *Fourteenth Census,* 6:42, *Fifteenth Census,* 2:975, *Sixteenth Census,* 1:293, *United States Census of Agriculture, 1925, The Southern States,* p. 785, and *United States Census of Agriculture, 1935, The Southern States,* p. 637.

Table 2 Lowndes County Population, 1910–1940

	1910	% Change	1920	% Change	1930	% Change	1940
All	31,894	–20.3	25,406	–9.9	22,878	–.9	22,661
Whites	3,769	–10.1	3,390	–4.2	3,246	+6.5	3,457
Blacks	28,125	–21.2	22,016	–10.8	19,632	–2.2	19,204

Source: U.S. Bureau of the Census, *Thirteenth Census,* 2:54, *Fourteenth Census,* 3:63, *Fifteenth Census,* 3:102, and *Sixteenth Census,* 2:238.

50,000 acres to cotton until the New Deal policies of the 1930s led to a reduction to 32,000 acres by 1935. The cutback in cotton acreage helped push even more tenant farmers off the land because they had less work and because most owners did not share the government benefit payments with their tenants. Increasing mechanization of farming reinforced the trend toward further reductions in tenantry and greater consolidation of farms. A small percentage of farmers began to use tractors, trucks, and other farm machinery that reduced their reliance on the manual labor of tenants, though fewer than one hundred farms had tractors and trucks by 1940.[51]

As a result of hard times, the overall population of Lowndes County declined. From 1910 to the eve of World War II, it fell by nearly 29 percent. The fall was not, however, uniform. In the depths of the depression, for example, the population scarcely changed. More significantly, blacks left the county at a considerably higher rate than whites. The consolidation of farms and the elimination of many tenant farmers forced blacks to seek jobs elsewhere.[52]

Table 3   Lowndes County Farms, 1940–1964

	1940	1945	1949	1954	1959	1964
Number of farms	3,508	2,297	2,689	2,132	1,473	1,352
Average number of acres	79.1	145.9	138.2	192.2	243.8	268.9
Number of tenants	2,881	1,675	1,776	1,262	739	569

Source: U.S. Bureau of the Census, *United States Census of Agriculture, 1945*, pp. 27, 39, 48, 59, 73, 87, 97, *United States Census of Agriculture, 1954*, pp. 65, 71, 84, 89, 101, 107, 113, 119, 137, *United States Census of Agriculture, 1959*, pp. 133, 145, 151, 157, 163, 175, 185, 191, 197, 209, 233, and *United States Census of Agriculture, 1964*, pp. 259, 275, 283, 291, 307, 321, 339, 345, 351, 373.

During and after the war the changes in Lowndes County farming accelerated, as did the shifts in population. Landowners increasingly moved away from cotton and other row crops to cattle and timber. Between 1940 and 1960 the acreage devoted to cotton declined by two-thirds and to corn by more than 80 percent. At the same time the number of cattle more than doubled (beef offered a better investment than cotton) and the percentage of farm incomes from forest products tripled. By 1964, cattle yielded 35 percent of the county's farm income and timber provided 20 percent; both exceeded cotton's value to the economy. Mechanization proceeded apace, though still only about half the farms (presumably the larger ones run by white owners) had tractors. By the early 1960s, the number of farms declined to one-third of the prewar level and the average farm size exploded to more than 250 acres. The percentage of Lowndes County farms operated by tenants also dropped from more than eighty in 1940 to less than fifty by 1960, and only about six hundred tenants worked in the entire county. Whites to a smaller degree also succumbed to the lure of prosperity outside of Lowndes. As a result the county's overall population continued its prewar decline in the 1940s and 1950s, with blacks leading the exodus. Accustomed to wielding power in the county and in the state, the white minority in Lowndes undoubtedly worried about the security of its future as the population declined, as cotton lost its central role in agriculture, and as the balance of power in the state swung irretrievably away from the Black Belt to the urban areas.[53]

In the summer of 1945, one visitor to Hayneville noted the results of the county's severe and continuous decline in the first half of the twentieth century. He "found no bank, no cotton mill, no railroad, a dilapi-

Table 4 Lowndes County Population, 1940–1960

	1940	% Change	1950	% Change	1960	% Change 1910–60
All	22,661	–20.4	18,018	–14.4	15,417	–51.7
Whites	3,457	–7.0	3,214	–7.3	2,978	–21.0
Blacks	19,204	–23.0	14,796	–15.9	12,439	–55.8

Source: U.S. Bureau of the Census, *Sixteenth Census*, 2:238, *Seventeenth Census*, 7:2–87, and *Eighteenth Census*, 1:2–193.

dated, ill-kept courthouse, three or four general stores, a few county offices in a frame building, a new brick consolidated school, and a few residences. The town presented an appearance of leisureliness, disrepair, and near desertion." Many smaller communities presented a similarly discouraging picture. Cotton gins and country stores that had once formed the bases for numerous villages had closed and the communities had dried up. With the building of roads and the arrival of automobiles and trucks, farmers turned increasingly to nearby Selma and Montgomery for goods and services. Many inhabitants of Lowndes, especially blacks, found the county both depressed and depressing.[54]

Though adjacent to Selma and Montgomery, Lowndes County in 1960 remained isolated and backward. It was one of the poorest counties in the nation and bore little resemblance to the suburbs common in the postwar prosperity. Fifty-eight percent of Lowndes's 3,414 households had no automobile, so even Selma and Montgomery remained distant to them. Only 20 percent of the houses had telephones, most of which no doubt were owned by whites living in the county's few towns; most residents still depended on face-to-face communication to learn about events in their community. Though the weekly newspaper, the *Lowndes Signal*, boasted a circulation of about one thousand, it carried news pertaining only to whites and ignored the lives of the county's huge black majority. Lowndes had no radio station (though nearly three-quarters of all homes had radios) and no TV station (37 percent of all households owned television sets). It was one of only three counties in Alabama that provided no free public library service to its residents.[55]

By modern standards, the daily lives of most people in Lowndes county were also rather rough in 1960. Seven of ten homes lacked any kind of washing machine, a mere 2 percent had clothes driers, only 8 percent had food freezers, and just 5 percent had any air conditioning to moderate the hot summers of the Black Belt. Without piped water, more than half of all the occupied residences in Lowndes County lacked bath-tubs or showers, flush toilets, and sewers or septic tanks.[56]

Lowndes County residents, particularly blacks, suffered from poor health and insufficient health care. A doctor reported in the mid-1960s that black "adults showed dismal dental health" and that 80 percent of the black children examined suffered from anemia. Children also com-monly had infected insect bites, impetigo, and an unusual number of amputations, which resulted from accidents and burns. In one sample, 90 percent of black children had never seen a doctor and only about 1 percent of the children who needed glasses actually had them. To obtain adequate health care, the residents of Lowndes had to go to Selma or Montgomery. The county had no hospital, nursing home, or ambulance service; two doctors and two dentists practiced in Lowndes, and three of them worked in Fort Deposit. The county health department had an officer present only one day a week.[57]

Especially among blacks, poor nutrition caused many health prob-lems, such as obesity, hypertension, and anemia. Their diet, emphasizing beans and peas, contained little meat, egg, and wheat products. The most commonly used meat was pork. If they had a garden, blacks often added beneficial turnip and collard greens to their meals, but a local physician reported that the typical diet consisted of "fat meat, corn meal, and beans."[58]

The poor living conditions of most people in Lowndes resulted largely from their low incomes. In 1960 the median annual family income was $1,364, the lowest in the Black Belt and also the lowest of all Alabama counties. The comparable figure for neighboring Dallas County (Selma) was $2,846, for Montgomery County $4,777, and for Jefferson County (Birmingham) $5,103. By making no distinction between black and white families, moreover, the median income figure for Lowndes masked the extent of poverty among black families. The median family income for blacks was actually $935, or about two-thirds of the county's median. More significantly, it was only 36 percent of the white median family income of $2,624. Lowndes was a poor county but the poverty fell un-evenly on its citizens. In 1959 four out of five black families had an income of less than $3,000, whereas less than 20 percent of the whites in the county and under 40 percent of the entire state had incomes that low. Only about 4 percent of black families in Lowndes had incomes above $5,000, compared to more than 40 percent of the white families. The overwhelming number of poor blacks in the county resulted in large measure from their heritage of slavery, tenancy, and peonage, just as the

Table 5 Number of Lowndes Families by Income Group, 1959

	All	White	(%)	Black	(%)
Under $1,000	1,220	67	(8.5)	1,153	(50.7)
$1,000 to $1,999	652	81	(10.3)	571	(26.5)
$2,000 to $2,999	250	79	(10.0)	171	(7.9)
$3,000 to $3,999	194	102	(12.9)	92	(4.3)
$4,000 to $4,999	201	122	(15.5)	79	(3.7)
$5,000 to $5,999	147	105	(13.3)	42	(1.9)
$6,000 to $6,999	77	61	(7.7)	16	(0.7)
$7,000 to $7,999	36	18	(2.3)	18	(0.8)
$8,000 to $8,999	64	57	(7.2)	7	(0.3)
$9,000 to $9,999	27	23	(2.9)	4	(0.2)
$10,000 and over	77	73	(9.3)	4	(0.2)
Total	2,945	788		2,157	

Source: U.S. Bureau of the Census, *Eighteenth Census*, 1:2-140-2, 2-233-35.

upper-income levels of the preponderance of whites reflected their long-term landownership and power.[59]

The changes in Lowndes County in the twentieth century were part of a larger revolution in the rural South, "a gigantic yet muted transition from the old cultures to a more rationalized and businesslike way of farming." With farmers increasingly dependent on federal programs, machines and chemicals replaced mules and tenants. Pines, ponds, and pastures also appeared as farmers turned from cotton to timber and cattle. White landowners retained their power and many blacks either left farming or sunk lower into poverty, but the revolution produced much uncertainty and apprehension about the future.[60]

In spite of, and because of, the revolution taking place in Lowndes's rural society, the dominant whites were committed to maintaining their status, often at any cost. They followed, according to one observer, "a century-old Lowndes County tradition — unquestioned, unbending white supremacy." A key to white control was the local sheriff, the leading official in the county. In the 1940s and 1950s, Otto C. Moorer kept the peace. Over six feet tall and close to 250 pounds, he was a tough sheriff who enforced segregation by intimidating blacks. "Big" Otto was assisted by his son, "Little" Otto, who was even meaner and more hot-headed than his father. Sheriff Moorer roughed up blacks whenever they did anything that he did not like. Once he savagely beat a black man for riding a horse with a saddle and for riding double with another man. On another occasion, while taking a troublesome black to jail, he told him to decide whether he wanted to go back dead or alive — and the prisoner knew that Moorer would not hesitate to kill him. Blacks feared the Moor-ers and tried to keep out of their way; in this manner, the sheriff main-tained the racial peace and status quo.[61]

As important as the sheriff's own actions was his toleration of other whites' extralegal violence against blacks. Whites often killed blacks not because they tried to assert their rights or protested discrimination, but merely because they did something to irritate the whites or make them mad. Law enforcement officers ignored such crimes, especially if whites disposed of the body and did not carelessly leave it along the side of a road where it could be discovered. Racial oppression continued even though no lynchings occurred in Lowndes in the 1940s and 1950s. One observer concluded that blacks "are subject to sinister whims and their fears [are] inflated by a folklore of violence."[62]

In 1960 whites controlled Lowndes County as completely as they had in 1860. Not only did whites own most of the land, but they also ran the local government. The board of revenue (county commission), the board of education and the superintendent of education, the sheriff, the probate judge, the tax assessor and the tax collector, the coroner, the circuit solicitor and the circuit clerk, the jury commission, the board of regis-trars, and the county's representatives in the state legislature — all were white. Except for schoolteachers, no black professionals lived or worked in the county. As late as January 1965, not one of the nearly 6,000 eligible blacks was registered to vote in Lowndes. Exclusion from the polls meant that blacks could exert no influence on public officials or the policies they established and that blacks could not serve on local juries. In fact, no Negro had been registered to vote in Lowndes County in the twentieth century. A popular saying among local whites was that the first black who tried to register would be dead by nightfall.[63]

A decade after the *Brown* decision, Lowndes County whites continued to maintain strict racial segregation. Black and white students and teach-ers were completely segregated in the public schools, and the black schools were inferior. The county maintained nearly thirty schools for its four thousand black students and two for the nearly six hundred whites. Most of the black schools had fewer teachers than grades as well as inadequate equipment; in some cases, the black schools actually posed a danger to the students. According to one report, "Elementary schools for

Negroes are shacks in fields. The larger Negro 'training schools' are poorly staffed and equipped, and fall rapidly into dilapidation. In one the 'library' is a cinderblock closet in a drafty auditorium; the washrooms have the appearance and redolence of a Mexican railway station." The segregated schools in Lowndes fell far short of even the outdated separate-but-equal standard, and only recently had some white officials realized that the county needed to provide, whether for pragmatic or idealistic reasons, equal schools for blacks. Segregated schools nonetheless continued to perpetuate the inferior status of blacks by offering them little opportunity for education and advancement.[64]

Segregation in Lowndes County, however, extended far beyond the classroom. As one man said early in 1965, "I was raised in Mississippi and always thought we were segregated there. But it's not like here — we got no integration — and what's more, we won't." Even after passage of the 1964 Civil Rights Act ensuring equal access to public accommodations, blacks faced rigid segregation in Lowndes. In 1965 the courthouse in Hayneville still had three rest rooms — "White Women," "White Men," and "Colored." Though a receptive federal court in Montgomery would have ruled in favor of a black who challenged Lowndes's segregated facilities, a local white explained, "But you don't get the point. He would never make it to Montgomery."[65]

Racism in the 1960s even affected what people could buy in the county's stores. When a journalist stopped at a rural store to buy a pack of Marlboro cigarettes, the clerk told him, "We don't sell them, and I don't know a store in the county that does." The visitor also learned that he could not easily buy Falstaff beer. He finally discovered that whites in Lowndes refused to sell Marlboros, Falstaff beer, and other popular products because of a boycott started in the 1950s by many southern whites after they heard that the manufacturers had reportedly contributed to the NAACP. In other areas the boycott soon petered out, but Lowndes whites continued it for years.[66]

In the early 1960s, then, Lowndes County was widely known among Alabamians and civil rights workers alike as a bastion of white racial prejudice in which whites would readily resort to violence to protect their segregated way of life. Lowndes seemed to symbolize Black Belt resistance to racial change. Some local whites even expected, according to one report, "Congo-like violence," referring to the bloody colonial civil war in the former Belgian Congo. In the spring of 1965 the leaders of the march from Selma to Montgomery worried most about what might happen when their march passed through northern Lowndes County on Highway 80. If violence against the marchers occurred, they believed it would happen in bloody Lowndes. Warning Martin Luther King, Jr., and others in advance, a black Lowndes minister described his county as "worse than hell."[67]

Statements by white residents reinforced the perception that the county remained intransigent in the face of the civil rights movement. For example, Frank Ryals, the forty-two-year-old sheriff of Lowndes, had opposed the march. Though he wanted to get the demonstrators through his county without incident, he said, "I feel like any other good citizen. This march is uncalled for. It's a lot of expense for nothing. It's disrupting people in their homes and on the highway." Claiming that most of the marchers he had seen were "beatniks and screwballs," Ryals argued that the protest would not accomplish anything because "these professional agitators would [not] be satisfied with anything you gave them." Ryals, furthermore, declared that the march was unnecessary because change was not needed; he claimed, "We have been getting along fine here. And we will continue to unless they come in here with a lot of this unlawful stuff and this provocation." Though speaking for himself, the sheriff seemed to reflect the unyielding attitudes of the overwhelming majority of white residents in Lowndes.[68]

The physical characteristics of the march's route through Lowndes intensified their apprehensions about the county. The march to Montgomery passed through rich farmlands that varied from flat cotton fields to gently rolling pastures. It also went through the ominous Big Creek Swamp. Though alerted to watch for water moccasins enjoying the warm sun on the road, the marchers feared even more attacks from white people; snipers worried them more than snakes. In many places the terrain along the highway made an adequate defense of the route difficult. The four-lane Highway 80, named the Jefferson Davis Highway, abruptly shrank to two lanes when it entered Lowndes, and the narrow road continued for twenty miles. Frequently the highway became exceedingly narrow as it passed over swamps, creeks, marshes, and bogs; in some places the shoulder was only four feet wide. The swampy areas with large trees draped in Spanish moss and shrouded in early morning fog could appear especially eerie to strangers. Despite the anxieties of the demonstrators and the hostility of the local white citizenry, King led the procession through Lowndes County to Montgomery after spending an uneventful night in a Lowndes pasture owned by a black woman. Once the march was over, however, the county's heritage of white violence reemerged.[69]

After the march and a massive rally in Montgomery, an incident in Lowndes County illustrated the county's persisting heritage of racial violence. Many marchers promptly returned by automobile to Selma; one of the cars was driven by Viola Liuzzo. A white woman from Detroit and the mother of five children, Liuzzo had worked for a week in Selma preparing for the march; she spent most of her time assisting people who, like herself, had come for the big demonstration. Because she had a car, she had transported many people between the airport in Montgomery and Brown Chapel in Selma. Failing to heed two precautions suggested by the leaders of the march, she had drawn attention to her green Oldsmobile with Michigan plates by driving too fast and by stopping for gasoline in Lowndes County. On the last day of the march, Liuzzo drove to Montgomery and joined the final procession into the capital.[70]

When the rally concluded, Liuzzo took a carful of marchers back to Selma, then returned along Highway 80 to Montgomery for another group. Leroy Moton, a black teenager working with the Southern Christian Leadership Conference, accompanied her on the trips. About eight o'clock that evening, on the edge of Selma, a carload of Ku Klux Klansmen from Birmingham spotted the white woman and the black youth. Realizing immediately that they were civil rights workers, the white men decided to give chase. At speeds up to one hundred miles an hour, the Klansmen pursued Liuzzo's car along Highway 80 into Lowndes County. Finally overtaking the Oldsmobile, the Klansmen fired through the windows at Liuzzo and Moton. Although Moton escaped injury, two bullets struck Viola Liuzzo in the head. Slumping against the steering wheel, she died instantly. Moton tried to gain control of the car, but it zoomed off the road across a ditch and stopped against an embankment. The Klansmen turned around and went back to check their prey; they quickly concluded that they had killed both occupants of the car because Moton pretended to be dead. The Klansmen were arrested early the next morning after the Federal Bureau of Investigation received a call from Gary Thomas Rowe, one of its undercover informants in the KKK. Rowe had been in the car with the Klansmen when they killed Liuzzo.[71]

The Klansmen's trial took place in the county courthouse in Hayneville because Viola Liuzzo was killed in Lowndes. The first defendant, Collie Leroy Wilkins, was brought to trial for first-degree manslaughter early in May. Circuit Judge T. Werth Thagard, a native of Greenville in neighboring Butler County and a former state legislator, presided. The prosecution consisted of county solicitor Carlton L. Perdue, circuit solicitor Arthur E. Gamble, Jr., and an assistant attorney general, Joe Breck Gantt. Wilkins was defended by Matt H. Murphy, Jr., the Imperial Klonsel of the United Klans of America. Imperial Wizard Robert M. Shelton, Jr., attended the trial and sometimes sat at the defendant's table.[72]

Local whites seemed to resent that outside agitators (including Klansmen from Birmingham as well as the slain Liuzzo from Detroit) and the trial had brought so much attention to their community and upset their peaceful lives. Most denied that any racial problems existed in the county. One woman declared, "We grew up with the Negroes and played with them as children. We have never had any trouble getting along. Up until the recent agitation began, there was the best of feeling between the races." Solicitor Perdue said, "I was born and reared in Lowndes County, and I'd say the spiritual kindness that has existed here cannot be surpassed." Most local whites did not expect an all-white jury to convict Wilkins, even though the defendant was from outside the county. Though contradicting his neighbors, a local official admitted that "it can't be a real trial. There has been too much racial conflict, too much hate, too much bitterness."[73]

Wilkins's prosecutors urged their neighbors on the jury to convict the Klansman from Birmingham. Perdue asked them, "How much stronger could the evidence be?" He told them to "meet this issue" and "make a decision" — "Thou shall not . . . kill in Lowndes County . . . from outside or from within." Arthur Gamble, the circuit solicitor, while admitting that he did not agree with Liuzzo's activities, argued even more strongly for a conviction. "But, gentlemen," he told the twelve white male jurors, "she was here, and she had a right to be here on our highways without being shot down in the middle of the night." Imploring them to muster their courage, Gamble said, "Don't put the stamp of approval on chaos, confusion, and anarchy." Like Gamble, the assistant attorney general confessed, "I'm a segregationist but we're talking about murder today." Joe Breck Gantt charged that the night-rider slaying of Liuzzo was "a yellow bellied act of cowardice." In his summation to the jury he contended that an acquittal of Wilkins would mean "blood will spill in Hayneville streets . . . there will be no law . . . justice will be forgotten and there will be no fear of God."[74]

Matt Murphy, the Klan lawyer defending Wilkins, presented only twenty-one minutes of testimony yet talked more than one hour in his closing harangue to the jury. Disregarding contrary evidence presented by the state toxicologist, Murphy appealed to the jury by claiming that Liuzzo had engaged in sexual relations with Leroy Moton shortly before her death. Frequently shouting, Murphy denounced "niggers" and "the black race" and tied the civil rights movement to a worldwide communist conspiracy. "The Communists are taking us over," he cried. "I say never! gentlemen. We shall die before we lay down and see it." Finally, the KKK attorney implored the jurors, "I urge you as patriotic Americans to find this defendant not guilty." Cutting off Murphy's closing argument, Judge Thagard ended the defense's case.[75]

The jurors deliberated for more than ten hours spread over a two-day period. As required by state law, they spent the nights sequestered in

Montgomery because no adequate facilities existed in Lowndes County. The jury finally reported to Thagard that it was deadlocked.[76] As most local whites apparently expected, and as most observers had predicted, the all-white jury refused to convict Wilkins for killing a white civil rights worker. Though the defendant was a known Klansman from outside the county, the jurors would not convict a white man for protecting their way of life. In rendering that decision, they upheld the tradition of bloody Lowndes as a place where whites could brutalize blacks and their white allies without fear of punishment in the halls of justice.

THE LOWNDES COUNTY MOVEMENT: A GENUINE SOCIAL AND POLITICAL REVOLUTION

When Jon Daniels began working in Lowndes County in August 1965, he joined a new, developing movement for civil rights in the Black Belt county.[1] The civil rights movement had come to the rather isolated Lowndes later than to many areas of the South, especially cities like Birmingham and Montgomery. When the movement did make its first, tentative inroads, it faced strong resistance from Lowndes whites, who realized, probably more instinctively than rationally, its revolutionary potential. More significantly, the movement encountered reluctance among many local blacks who only with considerable encouragement could imagine a positive change in the county's race relations and who feared retaliation from powerful whites if they became involved.

Reacting to developments outside the county, a courageous core of indigenous leaders initiated the Lowndes movement. In early 1965 outside organizers associated with the voting rights campaign in Selma went to Lowndes and spurred it forward. The emergent movement in Lowndes grew significantly in the first half of the year, and by the end of the summer it had begun to acquire real power. It had also experienced a major tragedy in the community once described by a northern journalist as "the very heart of darkness."[2]

In the late 1950s and early 1960s half a dozen blacks in Lowndes County had begun to confer quietly about how to pay their poll taxes and register to vote. They met several times in the home of the Reverend J. C. Lawson in Gordonsville but never organized the effort. Though fear immobilized most black residents, two brave individuals did try to register. In 1958 Robert L. Strickland, a black construction worker who had recently moved to Lowndesboro, made an unsuccessful attempt to register in Hayneville. The following year John Hulett, who had just returned after a ten-year absence from Lowndes, went to the courthouse to pay his poll taxes. The county tax collector refused to take his money until he had registered, but the voting registrar would not let him register without proof that he had paid his poll taxes.[3]

In late 1964 another group met secretly in the home of John Arthur Webb and discussed the possibility of registering in Hayneville. Apprehensive but hopeful, they decided to act. As their first meeting ended, they discovered a local white man outside who had been eavesdropping on their meeting. Though they realized that many of their landlords, creditors, and employers would hear of their plans, the men refused to be intimidated. The group soon received much needed support from the Student Nonviolent Coordinating Committee and the Southern Christian Leadership Conference.[4]

In February 1965, as the voting rights campaign began in Selma, James Bevel of the SCLC staff ventured into Lowndes County to recruit blacks for a voter registration effort. Martin Luther King, Jr., had announced that the voter drive would start in Selma and then spread to the surrounding rural counties, including Lowndes. Bevel found "quite a lot of fear among the Negro people in the county, particularly among those who are dependent upon the white people for employment," including just not sharecroppers but also schoolteachers. A few interested blacks drove from Lowndes to the Dallas County seat to confer with representatives of SNCC and SCLC. Emboldened by the activity in Selma, they decided to attempt to register on the next day the registration board would be in session. The local white authorities had announced that they would register blacks as individuals but not as part of any organized campaign. Wary of going singly, the blacks went as a group anyway.[5]

On March 1, thirty-seven blacks went to the Lowndes courthouse on the Hayneville town square. According to county officials, they were the first blacks to try to register to vote in more than thirty years; certainly no black had been registered or had voted in recent memory. The registrars turned all thirty-seven applicants away. Later the same day, Martin Luther King went to Hayneville to protest the complete absence of registered blacks in the county. In the hallway of the courthouse, King confronted Carl Golson, a member of the board of registrars. Tall, husky, and balding, the fifty-nine-year-old Golson was a wealthy landowner, an automobile dealer in Fort Deposit, and a former state senator. "There is a better relationship between the Negroes and whites here than anywhere in the world," Golson told King. "If you folks would stay out of Lowndes County, we can take care of the situation."[6]

When King requested information about registration procedures, Golson refused to provide it. King and his aides were not prospective voters, he angrily told the visitors, and Lowndes regulations were none of their business. King then said they did not understand, and Golson retorted, "You are damned dumb if you don't understand." Shaking his finger in King's face, Golson denounced "agitators." "None of you can help the Negroes of Lowndes County," he asserted. Asked whether he wanted a lawsuit filed against the board, Golson said, "I don't care what you do." He then declared the registrar's office closed and walked away.[7]

In the winter and spring of 1965, Lowndes was not the only Alabama county without any registered black voters. In Camden, the seat of Wilcox County, blacks demonstrated for the right to vote and won some cooperation from local whites; Jon Daniels had joined in the protests. A similar effort apparently occurred in Macon County. But in Lowndes, where the pace of change was much slower than in the two other counties, no interracial cooperation developed.[8]

Two weeks after King's visit, local blacks returned to Hayneville to register. They discovered that black applicants must now go to the old county jail a few blocks away, while whites still registered in the courthouse. In one concession to blacks, the registrars did not require a registered voter (necessarily a white because no blacks were registered) to verify that each black applicant was a resident of the county. Seventeen Negroes completed the registration forms and took the literacy test; two passed and became the first blacks to qualify to vote in the county in the twentieth century. John C. Lawson, a sixty-five-year-old blind man, successfully answered the test questions read to him by Golson. The registrars also accepted John Hulett, even though Golson claimed that Hulett "didn't make a good grade but . . . he had been registered in Jefferson County [Birmingham] and we didn't think it would be fair to turn him down." The board rejected the other candidates, reportedly because three had criminal records and twelve failed the literacy test. "Our policy on the board," Golson announced, "is just this: If they can qualify, we are going to put them on." As a Birmingham journalist commented, the registration of the first black constituted "a social and political revolution" in Lowndes.[9]

Four days later, the civil rights movement in Lowndes County took an unprecedented step. On the evening of March 19, twenty-eight local blacks met with SCLC representatives in an old store in the Trickem community along Highway 80 in northern Lowndes, not far from Selma. Because his property had no mortgage, Frank Haralson could allow his friends to use his store without fear of economic retaliation by whites. The meeting began, like most in the civil rights movement, with prayers and Scripture readings. For further inspiration the group sang popular songs of the movement, including "We Shall Overcome" and "We Shall Not Be Moved." In an open discussion they then considered how they should organize and what they should try to accomplish. Adopting the name Lowndes County Christian Movement for Human Rights (LCCMHR), the group determined to promote black voter registration and generally to voice the grievances of blacks in the county. To lead them they chose John Hulett as the first chairman of the LCCMHR.[10]

In many ways John Hulett already was the leader of the civil rights movement in Lowndes County. Born in 1927 in the Gordonsville community, he was the grandson of a Lowndes County slave. Hulett's grandfather, who must have been a remarkable man, had struggled after slavery and gained ownership of more than one hundred acres, a grist mill, a cotton gin, and a sawmill. Though better off than most blacks, Hulett's family lived in a two-room house without ceilings, glass windows, or indoor plumbing and farmed their land and other rented property with horses and mules.[11]

In a strictly disciplined family, Hulett's life focused on the church, the family farm, and school. He walked to the local black schools, while whites rode buses to theirs. Though physically small, he played on the school basketball team and traveled to other towns in the area for games. After graduating from high school in 1946, Hulett worked with an older brother in Georgia and on the family farm in Lowndes before moving to Birmingham in the fall of 1948. For over six years he worked at a foundry of the Birmingham Stove and Range Company. He also briefly sold insurance and worked as an elevator operator for the Alabama Power Company. After returning to Brunswick for a short time, Hulett moved back to Lowndes County in 1959.[12]

While in Birmingham, Hulett became an activist. As a foundry worker he joined a union and served for a few terms as its president. In his own community of Pratt City, Hulett did local organizing to promote paved streets and playgrounds. More important, he joined the NAACP in 1949 and later its successor, the Alabama Christian Movement for Human Rights. He also participated in the NAACP the second time he was in Georgia. One of Hulett's inspirations was the association's state leader, W. C. Patton; he also knew Fred Shuttlesworth, founder of the Alabama Christian Movement for Human Rights, and had met Martin Luther King in the 1950s. Though Hulett did not picket or march while in Birmingham, he did register to vote and encouraged others to do so. By the time he returned home, largely to help care for his ailing father, he was prepared to lead civil rights efforts in his native county. He was a tireless, determined worker with unusual intensity and a powerful personality.[13]

Though Hulett was a major force, other blacks in the county also exerted significant leadership in the early days of the Lowndes movement. Charles Smith and Robert Strickland, for example, were active in the LCCMHR, and their backgrounds, like Hulett's, hinted at their later participation in the struggle for equal rights in Lowndes. Smith was born in 1914 in the Calhoun area of Lowndes County. His father was a tenant farmer until he managed to buy some land when Smith was still a boy. The Calhoun School, a private industrial school modeled after Hampton and Tuskegee institutes, helped the father purchase his first land. Started in 1892 by a Connecticut white woman with the help of Booker T. Washington, the Calhoun School had received two years later over four thousand acres in Lowndes from George Washington Carver and used the land to start a land bank to help blacks buy tracts of forty to sixty acres. Landownership provided Smith's family and other blacks in the Calhoun area a crucial, and unusual, measure of independence from landlords and creditors.[14]

Charles Smith started school late and attended irregularly because he had to work on his father's farm. As an older teenager and young adult, he attended Calhoun School for three years before dropping out after the ninth grade to get married. After farming for a few years, he moved to the Gulf coast for a better job in the shipyards as the nation prepared for World War II. Though a small man, he helped construct the shipyard in Pascagoula, Mississippi, and later worked as a hull erector for Alabama Dry Docks in Mobile. During the war Smith found life unlike anything he had known in rural Lowndes County; for example, on a visit to Hayneville, he saw a black uniformed soldier beaten by the sheriff for using the restroom in the courthouse. In Mobile, however, Smith realized for the first time his ability to defend his own interests by joining an affiliate of the Congress of Industrial Organizations (CIO) and the NAACP, organizations that did not exist back home. Prospering at his job in wartime industry, he and his wife bought a home and more than forty acres in Calhoun.[15]

After the war Smith farmed in Lowndes briefly before returning to the shipyards for a few years. In 1948 he moved back to Calhoun, bought a truck, and entered the logging business. When the Montgomery bus boycott started the civil rights movement in Alabama in the mid-1950s, white landowners in Lowndes County often forced black loggers out of business by refusing to buy their timber. The whites especially pressured blacks who gave any indication that they supported the civil rights activists. Because Charles Smith had driven occasionally to Montgomery to keep informed about the boycott, he had to stop logging and resume independent farming. He also worked in construction when it was available. In 1965, therefore, Smith was ready to join the civil rights movement when it came to Lowndes County.[16]

Another local activist, Robert Strickland, had long refused to be cowed by whites. In 1940, at age seventeen, he had shot and killed one of four white boys who had hit and chased him. Convicted of premeditated murder, he served five years of a life sentence before gaining parole and eventually a pardon. A big, powerful man, Strickland became a construction worker in Montgomery. He and his wife had participated in the bus boycott: they attended many meetings of the Montgomery Improvement Association and used their vehicles to transport others boycotting the municipal bus system. The following year the Stricklands, wanting to raise their children in the more wholesome atmosphere of a small rural community, bought a house on a one-acre lot in Lowndesboro, his wife's home. Continuing to work for a Montgomery construction company, Strickland escaped economic dependence on Lowndes whites, but he soon encountered their racial prejudice. Especially threatening to his safety were whites who retaliated against any black who failed to be properly subservient and accommodating. Once, for example, a white man became incensed when Strickland passed his slow-moving car. After passing Strickland, the white man blocked the road with his car and confronted Strickland when he stopped. But Strickland remained calm and, using common sense, avoided a violent clash.[17]

Strickland also believed that the white Lowndesboro policeman harassed him and other blacks by giving them unwarranted tickets for speeding; they were tried in a local court, whose judge and jury had been elected by white voters. The lack of political power irritated Strickland. He was especially frustrated because he had signed a document supporting the recent incorporation of Lowndesboro yet had not been allowed to participate in the selection of the town's officials. When he tried to register to vote, the county registrars rejected his application. Strickland therefore also embraced the civil rights movement on its arrival in Lowndes.[18]

From the beginning the Lowndes County movement also involved women. Two were Sarah B. Logan and Lillian McGill. Born in 1915 in the Gordonsville section, Logan was the only child of a woman who farmed on a plantation owned by whites; she never knew her father. Lacking transportation to school, she boarded with a family near the Lowndes County Training School. As they walked to school she and the other black children made good targets for rocks thrown by whites from passing school buses. Logan graduated in 1934. After teaching one year on an emergency teacher certificate, she married and began a family. Her husband farmed first as a renter, but in the 1940s he began to achieve some independence by buying land. Sarah Logan had six children before attending college irregularly for a number of years while teaching in the county, usually in a one-room school. She received a college degree from Alabama State University in Montgomery in 1958, the same year her oldest daughter finished her studies at Tuskegee.[19]

Logan experienced firsthand white harassment and discrimination. She witnessed white resentment when blacks achieved any success, such as her husband's owning a car. She watched the physical abuse of blacks, such as a white man hitting a black boy for carrying a soft drink from a local store. Even more, she had known the gross inequality of the public school system. Educated, aware, and resolute, Logan joined the NAACP and later attended the first civil rights meetings in the county. As the movement coalesced she became a leading force in the push to integrate the public schools and at the mass meetings urged blacks to send their children to white schools. Eventually Logan lost her teaching job (because of her activism, she believed), and her husband was threatened by a planter from whom he rented land; the planter became the principal of the county's new all-white private school.[20]

Eighteen years younger than Sarah Logan, Lillian McGill she grew up in the White Hall section of Lowndes County. Her family had more independence than blacks who were croppers and tenants because her father worked for the Western Alabama Railroad. In 1943 he quit his job and bought a small farm near White Hall before entering the armed forces. McGill attended the local black school, the boarding high school of Selma University, and Alabama State in Montgomery. By the mid-1950s she was married and still living in Montgomery, where she worked as a domestic for white families and in a commercial laundry; her husband was employed in a local industry. The couple took part in the Montgomery bus boycott of 1955–56 and got to know its leader, Martin Luther King.[21]

After her mother's death in 1964, McGill moved back to Lowndes to help care for her father and manage his farm. She was present when the Lowndes County Christian Movement for Human Rights was organized and was elected its first secretary. Among the first blacks in Lowndes to register in the early summer of 1965, she devoted much of her time to voter registration. As the mother of several young children, she also took an interest in school integration. Her son was the only black student on the first integrated school bus in the county when the schools were finally integrated at the beginning of the 1965–66 school year.[22]

John Hulett, Charles Smith, Robert Strickland, Sarah Logan, and Lillian McGill were only five of more than a score of local activists — including William J. Cosby, Jesse Favors, Frank Haralson, Matthew Jackson, and Sidney Logan, Jr. — who ignited the county's Christian Movement for Human Rights and civil rights movement. Though they had never voted or held public office, many of them had earlier gained significant political experience in local black organizations. The skills that they developed in church groups and fraternal lodges were valuable in organizing the civil rights campaign in Lowndes. In addition, they shared important characteristics common to a number of the early participants in the Lowndes movement. Their parents had been strong, resourceful, and determined individuals who had succeeded in buying their own property and who had encouraged their children to be independent. By the 1960s they owned their own homes and could not be evicted by a white landlord for their activism.[23]

Hulett, Smith, Strickland, and McGill also could draw on their experience outside the repressive atmosphere of Lowndes County. While working in Montgomery, Mobile, or Birmingham, they had learned about organizing to protect and promote their rights. In particular, as members of civil rights organizations they had come to realize the possibilities for social change and racial justice that had seemed unthinkable in Lowndes. They were prepared when the Selma-to-Montgomery march gave momentum to the civil rights movement in their county.[24]

On March 22, the second day of the march, Martin Luther King led the demonstrators into Lowndes County. James McShane, the head of the U.S. marshals protecting them, described Lowndes as "a no man's land and I'm afraid of it." But Hosea Williams of SCLC corrected him: "You mean it's a no-black-man's land." One of the county's state legislators had predicted that there would be violence. Instead, they were welcomed by jubilant black tenant farmers and laborers who had waited patiently for four hours to greet them. When she saw King, Mattie Lee Moorer, a fifty-year-old woman from Hayneville, screamed, "It's him! It's him!" With tears running down her face, she ran to hug and kiss him.[25]

The courage of the three hundred marchers inspired Lowndes County blacks, only to have the slaying of Viola Liuzzo later in the week shock them. On the Sunday night following Liuzzo's death, activists in the

Lowndes County Christian Movement held a mass meeting at the Mount Gillard Baptist Church in Trickem; more than 150 people attended to protest the murder. Speakers also urged blacks to register to vote. The gathering reinforced the confidence of local blacks in challenging the power of the whites.[26] By the time of the mass meeting, however, they had been joined by a leader of the Student Nonviolent Coordinating Committee.

Stokely Carmichael, a full-time organizer with SNCC, came to Lowndes County the day after the shooting of Liuzzo. Born in Trinidad, the West Indies, in 1941, Carmichael moved to New York with his parents when he was eleven. After elementary school, he attended the highly competitive Bronx High School of Science, where he became friends with students already active in leftist politics. As a high school student, he participated in protests and demonstrations, met black members of the Communist party, became a socialist, and learned much from Bayard Rustin, a black pacifist and democratic socialist who later became an adviser to Martin Luther King. Inspired by the sit-ins by Howard University students in 1960, he decided to continue his education there. He soon became a leader in the Nonviolent Action Group, an affiliate of SNCC. Carmichael was beaten and arrested in the 1961 freedom rides, worked in voter registration in McComb, Mississippi, and demonstrated against the police in Cambridge, Maryland. After graduating from Howard, he joined SNCC and became the highly effective director of Freedom Summer in Mississippi's Second Congressional District.[27]

Carmichael resigned his Mississippi post to work in the rural areas of Alabama but had not selected a site. During the protests in Selma in the early spring of 1965, he learned of the racial situation in Lowndes County and decided to work there. Though he opposed the Selma campaign (he thought it would fail), Carmichael joined King in the Selma-to-Montgomery march because it passed directly through Lowndes, where Carmichael wanted to gain credibility with the blacks who held King in great esteem. On Saturday, March 27, after the march and Liuzzo's death, he arrived in Lowndes with only a small amount of cash and a sleeping bag; he contacted a person he had been told he could stay with and set to work. A charismatic figure, Carmichael possessed remarkable skills that were especially appropriate for organizing blacks in Lowndes. According to one scholar, he "combined astute political awareness with an ability to communicate with less-educated people on their own terms."[28]

Though King and SCLC had turned their attention increasingly northward after the Selma-to Montgomery march, Carmichael did not labor alone in Lowndes for long. In the late spring and early summer, other SNCC workers joined him — Bob Mants, Judy Richardson, Jimmy

Rogers, Ruby Sales, Scott B. Smith, Willie Vaughn, and others. Most were black college students from the South and experienced civil rights workers, but they had never encountered an area as difficult to organize as bloody Lowndes. For example, Bob Mants, the son of a custodian, had became involved in the civil rights movement while a high school student in Atlanta. In 1963, at age nineteen, Mants left Atlanta and his studies at Morris Brown College to work with SNCC in southwestern Georgia. Jimmy Rogers, Ruby Sales, and Willie Vaughn were all students at Tuskegee Institute when they joined SNCC.[29]

Viewing Lowndes as "a truly totalitarian society — the epitome of the tight, insulated police state," Carmichael and SNCC knew that if they could succeed in Lowndes then working in other counties would become far easier; Carmichael later dubbed the plan "a kind of SNCC Domino Theory." Though critical of both SNCC and SCLC, Carmichael refused to let his disagreements with them, or the competition between the organizations, interfere with the work in Lowndes. Supporting the Lowndes County Christian Movement, SNCC first had to overcome the fears that kept the local black population from doing anything to fight racism in Lowndes. The LCCMHR and SNCC wanted to persuade blacks to register to vote and then help them qualify. Finally, Carmichael hoped that blacks in the county would form their own independent political movement.[30]

The campaign was a quintessential grass-roots effort, and progress in Lowndes came slowly. Even with the assistance of LCCMHR, Carmichael and his SNCC co-workers had to move about the county carefully, frequently at night, because they knew that local whites would forcibly resist their efforts to organize blacks and might resort to violence. In particular, they avoided the small towns of Hayneville, Fort Deposit, and Lowndesboro during daylight and hence worked primarily along the unpaved rural roads in the county. SNCC could depend, of course, on the members of the Lowndes Christian Movement for support, but many other leaders in the black communities hesitated to join or assist the committee.[31]

Respected schoolteachers and principals, for example, felt constrained from helping because they depended on the white school superintendent and board of education for their jobs. Similarly, black ministers, who had considerable influence over their congregations, also hesitated to aid SNCC and LCCMHR. Their churches could not provide them with full-time positions, so the preachers worked elsewhere during the week in jobs that often depended on whites. In addition, clergymen worried that if they became identified as supporters of the civil rights movement, whites would retaliate against their churches, either by bombing them or by forcing them to move off white-owned land.[32]

Without the assistance of teachers or ministers, SNCC activists walked in the backcountry from door to door and from field to field to introduce themselves to black housewives, pulpwood loggers, sharecroppers, farmers, and laborers, as well as to workers who commuted to Selma and Montgomery. Trying to replicate the voting rights campaigns occurring in Selma and other parts of the South, they encouraged the fearful local blacks to assert their latent political power by registering to vote. The activists told them, "Political power is the first step to independence and freedom" and "You can control this county politically" — but their arguments persuaded few people. As one organizer later commented, blacks in Lowndes "did not even feel that they had the *right* to fight."[33]

Frustrated by the initial lack of success, Carmichael sought some way to arouse interest in the voter registration effort. Though LCCMHR continued to function, its meetings remained rather small and the movement had difficulty finding places to gather. Finally, it received permission to meet in the Mount Gillard Baptist Church at Trickem. In April the Ramer Baptist Church in Calhoun also allowed the group to use its building, and by summer LCCMHR could meet in the Bogahoma Church in Gordonsville as well. Located in strong black communities, the churches seemed safer than other places in Lowndes, and the ministers and members showed considerable courage in allowing the movement into their facilities. Of course, no possibility existed that the Lowndes Christian Movement could use public buildings like the county courthouse in Hayneville.[34]

The SNCC workers finally decided to hold a mass meeting in Lowndes County. They hoped that a gathering of fifty to seventy-five people would raise the morale of blacks interested in the civil rights movement and increase their commitment to voting. More important, Carmichael and the others hoped that the strength displayed by a large meeting would inspire others to join the cause. Simply publicizing the event presented a special set of problems — organizers could not contact people by telephone because very few blacks had them, and the only newspaper in the county certainly would not announce the meeting; even if the newspaper did cooperate, blacks tried to keep the location of their meetings secret from whites to avoid attack.[35]

After the SNCC activists first tried to pass out leaflets around the county, Carmichael decided to take them to the Lowndes County Training School and ask the students to distribute them. As school was ending for the day, Carmichael handed out the fliers. Alarmed by his tactics, someone called the county sheriff. When the police arrived and tried to stop the school buses from leaving the grounds, a confrontation ensued.

The sheriff's men warned Carmichael that he should not be there, that whites did not like what he was doing, and that he could be arrested. Refusing to be intimidated, the activist dared the officers to arrest him. After considerable talking and shouting back and forth, the police told Carmichael to wait while they investigated, but he said he was leaving and if they wanted to arrest him they could come and get him anytime. The students who had watched the encounter then went home to spread word not just of the pending mass meeting but also of how SNCC had clashed with the police and not backed down.[36]

The planned mass meeting on April 3 drew about two hundred people, far more than the organizers expected. Probably held at the Trickem church in one of the new movement's strongholds, the Sunday evening assembly included hymns, prayers, Scripture readings, and exhortations to register to vote. For the first time the SNCC workers were all introduced, and the local blacks and the activists became acquainted. The mass meeting had two significant results. First, Matthew Jackson, a farmer who owned land near the Trickem church, offered Stokely Carmichael and the other SNCC members a house on his property to use as their headquarters. Just north of Highway 80 toward Selma, the house became SNCC's permanent base throughout the voter registration drive. Second, plans were made for a group to go to the courthouse in Hayneville on the following day and attempt to register to vote.[37]

The next day was the first Monday in April, one of two days that month when the Lowndes County Board of Registrars regularly convened. Fifty blacks went to Hayneville to register at the old county jail. The registrars — a chicken farmer, a retired railroad worker, and the car dealer Carl Golson — administered tests to the applicants two at a time. Two weeks later more than sixty blacks filled out applications and took the tests. On the first Monday in May, the registrars finally announced the results of the tests. Only three of the more than one hundred applications received in April had been accepted. Out of 5,922 blacks of voting age in the county, therefore, only 5 had been registered. Comparable figures for the white population revealed the extent of corruption and discrimination in the registration process: the voter rolls included the names of 2,314 whites, even though fewer than 2,000 whites of voting age lived in the county.[38]

Though they made progress very slowly, blacks had finally broken what one observer called "the stalemate of fear"[39] in Lowndes County. After years of white opposition to any suggestion of change in the status quo, they had in the spring of 1965 at last mustered the courage to join the civil rights movement. Though still apprehensive, even scared, they had begun to push for change.

Throughout the early summer of 1965, the county's black residents continued to appear before the registrars. As was true throughout Alabama, applicants in Lowndes had to complete a three-part registration form administered by white officials. The form included (1) a request for basic biographical information, (2) two pages of detailed biographical questions to be read by the applicant and answered in his or her own handwriting, and (3) answers to the literacy test. A typical literacy test contained four questions based on general knowledge and four more based on a reading from the U.S. Constitution. The questions on the Constitution frequently came from its most difficult sections, and the Constitution itself was therefore employed as an obstacle to registration. Typical questions were, What document contains the Bill of Rights? Does the Senate choose the vice-president if no candidate receives a majority in the general election? And, How many congressional districts are there in North Carolina? Applicants had to answer five of the questions correctly, and the white registrars were the sole judges of the accuracy and adequacy of the responses.[40]

In addition, Lowndes, like many other counties in Alabama, required that a registered voter vouch that each applicant had lived in the state for at least one year, in the county for six months, and in the precinct for ninety days. Blacks, of course, objected that the voucher rule kept blacks from registering because only whites were registered and they refused to vouch for blacks. Although it had proved effective in preventing blacks from registering, Lowndes officials dropped the voucher requirement in the spring of 1965.[41]

Blacks also protested that the literacy test was administered unfairly to prevent blacks from voting. One often-told story in the Black Belt vividly illustrates the practice. A Negro with a doctor's degree went to register in Lowndes. After he finished the lengthy questionnaire, the registrar said, "Recite the Gettysburg Address," and the applicant did just that. The official then asked, "What is the number of congressional districts in each state?" The black man listed them flawlessly. When requested, he also recited the preamble to the Constitution. Finally, the registrar asked, "What does the Ninth Amendment mean?" The black man smiled and said, "It means no Negro is goin' to vote in Lowndes County."[42]

On May 3, the opening day of the trial of Collie Leroy Wilkins for killing Viola Liuzzo, 150 blacks went to the old jail in Hayneville to register during the board's regular session. Organized by the SNCC workers in the county, they stood in line in the hot sun as they waited their turn to be examined by the registrars. Of the first 15 applicants processed by the board, 11 were unable to fill out the required forms and 1 failed the literacy test. During the five-hour session, the board approved only 9 of the 60 applicants examined, for a total of 11 registered black voters in the county.[43]

The chief obstacle to registration in Lowndes remained the literacy test, which, blacks contended, was administered unfairly. In May a New York lawyer working with SNCC began to collect information in preparation for filing a suit against the test. Under pressure from the pending lawsuit, the Lowndes County Board of Registrars on July 6 reached an agreement with representatives from the U.S. Justice Department to suspend the use of the literacy test for forty-five days. In addition, the registrars agreed to keep their office open every day that week so blacks could take advantage of the new rule and procedure. The changes elated SNCC workers. "We've fought for the removal of this test for so long that it's hard to believe it's really gone," declared Stokely Carmichael. "Our next step must be to urge all of the people to flock to Hayneville . . . to register before 4 o'clock Friday." In an unusual move, civil rights activists held mass meetings every night to organize the enormous registration drive. Hundreds appeared before the registrars, and although the acceptance rate continued to be lower than for whites, hundreds of Lowndes County blacks registered for the first time.[44]

The work of Stokely Carmichael and others in the hostile, dangerous Black Belt county appealed to Jon Daniels. Whereas Selma in the spring had been an exciting vortex, Lowndes County in the summer offered him the greatest challenge for Christian witness and the best opportunity for existential action and meaning.[45]

The first white volunteer to join the civil rights campaign in Lowndes, Daniels encountered some opposition among SNCC workers when he arrived in late July. In 1965 the Student Nonviolent Coordinating Committee was on the verge of abandoning interracialism, and Stokely Carmichael was moving toward his later position advocating black separatism and black power. Less than a year later, in fact, Carmichael would be quoted as having said that if white civil rights workers "want to organize, they can organize white people. Negroes will organize Negroes." The SNCC staff in Lowndes County believed that a white might not work effectively with local blacks and that the presence of whites could be generally disruptive; more specifically, it feared that blacks might respond to Daniels's encouragement to register simply out of an ingrained deference to white people. Carmichael also worried that the appearance of a white civil rights worker might provoke violence, which could directly endanger Daniels, and he tried to persuade him to stay out of Lowndes. He nonetheless liked Daniels's humility and found him cooperative and particularly willing to listen to blacks. After considerable, and sometimes heated, debate among themselves, the SNCC workers agreed to allow Daniels to work with them unofficially.[46]

When he started going into Lowndes (Daniels continued to sleep in the Wests' apartment in Selma), he had no specific goal other than to help the civil rights movement any way he could. As he had in Selma the previous spring after the momentous march to Montgomery, he hoped to provide a Christian witness just by being present in the black community and thereby to give moral support to the emerging black movement. His experiences in Lowndes, however, differed in a number of important ways from those in Selma. The county had no Episcopal rector to introduce him to other whites. Throughout his few weeks in Lowndes, Daniels therefore never got to know any local whites; he worked exclusively with blacks. His main contacts were civil rights organizers from SNCC, not local blacks like the residents of the Carver Homes in Selma, and consequently he wound up working on SNCC projects instead of starting his own. Perhaps the greatest difference, however, was the omnipresent threat of violence in Lowndes. In the rural county Daniels had to be even more concerned for his personal safety because he could not depend on the presence of others to prevent an attack. Moreover, Lowndes's law enforcement officers were even less friendly than Selma's. Whereas Selma differed in dramatic ways from Keene, New Hampshire, Lowndes County was foreign territory even compared to Selma, with a severe, pervasive racism unlike anything Daniels had ever experienced.[47]

At first, one of Daniels's main functions in Lowndes was to provide transportation for the SNCC field workers. With the financial assistance of the Episcopal Society for Cultural and Racial Unity, he had rented a speedy and dependable Plymouth. The SNCC staff, most of whom lacked access to automobiles (Carmichael often rode about the county on a mule), welcomed Daniels's help. For example, he used his car to ferry the SNCC workers back and forth between Lowndes and Selma. Even committee veterans who were native southern blacks often could not endure the stress, danger, isolation, poor diet, and unpleasant living conditions in Lowndes for long stretches; periodically, they needed time in Selma for rest and recuperation. Daniels and his car also made it easier for some of the activists to move around the countryside.[48]

Daniels's involvement in Lowndes soon expanded. Early in August, for instance, he accompanied a SNCC lawyer to the Dan River Mills textile factory in the northwestern corner of the county. The new, modern mill, which paid no local taxes because it had received a tax waiver to locate in Lowndes, was the only significant industry in Lowndes; nevertheless, it employed a few blacks only in menial jobs. Most of the employees came from Selma. Daniels and the attorney wanted to investigate Dan River employment practices and to attempt to persuade plant officials to hire more blacks. They achieved little during the visit.[49]

In Lowndes, unlike in Selma, Daniels had few other opportunities to work for better jobs, health care, social services, and access to public accommodations for blacks simply because the county had few non-agricultural employers, no hospital, virtually no welfare system, and no theater, public library, motels, golf courses, swimming pools, or other public facilities. As a result of the limited options available to Daniels and SNCC's focus on voting rights, he quickly joined the campaign to register blacks.

Traveling with other young civil rights volunteers for security and support, Daniels helped in the laborious task of canvassing the county's black population. As another white activist described the voter registration campaigns common throughout much of the South:

> The work is long and hot. We drive from farmhouse to farmhouse. . . . The roads are in despicable condition . . . where the pavement stops the Negro sections are likely to begin. And if there is not even gravel on the roads, we can be reasonably sure that we are in a "safe" neighborhood. . . .
>
> When we walk up to a house there are always children out front. They look up and see [a white man] in the car, and fear and caution cover their expressions. Those terrified eyes are never quite out of my mind. Children who have hardly learned to talk are well-taught in the arts of avoiding whites. They learn "yassuh" as almost their first words. If they did not, they could not survive. The children run to their parents, hide behind them. We walk up, smile, saw howdy, and hold out our hands. As we shake hands I tell them my name. They tell me their names and I say Mr. — —, how do you do. It is likely the first time in the life of this farmer or housewife a white man has ever shaken hands with them, or even called them "with a handle to their names." . . . The news [of the voter registration effort in the county] is usually greeted with mingled fear, excitement, enthusiasm and gratitude. But the confrontation is more serious and more threatening. They think, if Mr. Charlie knew . . ., and they are afraid. They have good reason to be. . . . [As share-croppers t]hey may be evicted, and have often been for less serious offenses. . . . The threat of suspended credit and foreclosure is a tremendous burden.[50]

In addition to encouraging blacks to register to vote in general elections, Daniels supported efforts to get black farmers involved in the local

elections held by the U.S. Department of Agriculture's Agricultural Stabilization and Conservation Service (ASCS). Organized in 1961 to replace agencies created during the New Deal, the ASCS played a central
role in administering three large federal programs involving billions of
dollars each year. First, under the Agricultural Conservation Program,
ASCS reimbursed farmers for part of the cost of soil and water conservation programs, including planting trees and grasses to control erosion.
Second, the ASCS oversaw acreage allotments of many major crops,
including cotton, and paid farmers who agreed to reduce their acreage
devoted to the crops. Third, the ASCS sought to protect farmers' incomes
and guarantee stable commodity prices by making loans to farmers,
buying some crops, and supporting prices through additional payments
to farmers. The ASCS programs, according to one analysis, were "decisive factors in the livelihoods of farm operators and the communities in
which they live."[51]

For all farmers, but especially for black farmers in Lowndes County
and the rest of the South, the organization and staffing of ASCS directly
affected them. In addition to a national administrator, six regional offices,
and fifty state offices, ASCS had more than three thousand county offices,
including sixty-seven in Alabama and one in Lowndes. The key to the
operation of ASCS was the use of farmer committees at the state and
county levels to make the important decisions about crop allotments,
price supports, and payments for conservation programs. ASCS committees could, in effect, determine how much money a farmer made in a
year. The state commissioner of agriculture named the state farmer committee, and in 1965 no black had ever been appointed to the Alabama
state committee. That spring, the national ASCS administrator directed
that each southern state establish a committee of blacks to advise the state
ASCS committees. In Alabama, the state advisory committee had only
one black who was actually a farmer, and black farmers in Lowndes
continued to lack adequate representation.[52]

The farmers in each community first elected a three-person community committee, which in turn named the three-person county committee.
The county committee was "the primary point of control in local ASCS
programs" because it set policy goals, implemented the county program,
supervised elections, and hired personnel. As late as 1965 the Lowndes
County committee, like all other committees in the South, had never had
a black member. The local committee nominated its own candidates and
tended, as one civil rights worker put it, "to keep it in the family." "It's
not a matter of black and white," according to one SNCC worker, "but of
economics."[53]

Though democratic in intent, the committee system actually represented the large, white landowners. One SNCC worker claimed that the big landowners in Lowndes regularly channeled ASCS resources and benefits to their own plantations. Black farmers in the county knew very little about the ASCS programs, in part because they had no role in the committee system. As a result they received few benefits from the ASCS programs, and many of the crop reduction programs had the effect of pushing more blacks tenants off the land. Although some black farmers may have received ballots for a number of years, many did not vote for fear of economic reprisals by whites. Other blacks wound up voting for whites because their landlords collected the ballots to make sure they voted "correctly." One black farmer in Lowndes considered the election process futile because "it was always the same kind of people on the ballot."[54]

Under growing pressure to improve the committee system, ASCS officials in Washington directed in March 1965 that the Lowndes County committee (as well as all others in the South) should include on the November ASCS ballot the same percentage of black nominees as of black farmers in the county.[55] At the same time, the Lowndes County Christian Movement for Human Rights became interested in the ASCS elections and civil rights organizers from outside the county started urging blacks to participate in them.

Jon Daniels joined in the effort to stimulate interest in the fall ASCS elections as well as general voter registration. In the summer of 1965, the ASCS elections provided blacks an immediate, tangible, and powerful reason to become involved in the civil rights movement. In agricultural Lowndes County, whereas general voter registration promised distant and rather abstract benefits, the results of the ASCS elections could have a direct economic impact on thousands of black farmers. Daniels and the SNCC workers canvassed the county to tell farmers that they could not only vote in the election but also nominate themselves for the committee by getting six eligible voters to sign a nominating petition. They also held meetings to discuss the upcoming elections. A few local blacks reacted with enthusiasm. One young farmer became particularly excited when he realized that he could be nominated for the county committee. SNCC workers, however, worried that white farmers would engineer the nomination of so many black candidates that the black vote would be splintered. "Then if the white folks stick together," one volunteer suggested, "they can still elect an all white committee in spite of the Negro nominees."[56]

In the hottest part of the summer, Daniels traversed the isolated sections of rural Lowndes County and saw firsthand the poverty of most black residents — the shacks without windows or plumbing, the goats and mules wandering in fields near the houses, the discarded cars littering yards, and the malnutrition and ill health of many of the people. His ever-present seminarian's collar helped reassure the fearful that the white stranger posed no threat to them; he could then begin to overcome their suspicions about voting by talking with them as a friend. Rarely did he or the other canvassers immediately win a loyal supporter and potential voter. At best, they persuaded an individual to join other blacks at one of the weekly mass meetings.[57]

Held in a friendly church on Sunday evening, the mass meetings provided a chance for interested local blacks to come together for mutual support and to meet the SNCC organizers. Resembling a church service, each gathering opened with a prayer, hymns, and biblical allusions. A local leader often gave an inspirational talk. As one observer reported, "An old man in shirtsleeves, he communicated with the soul of the crowd, arousing their enthusiasm, laughter, or indignation. . . . Biblical verse was stirred in liberally." The crowd responded to the emotion and logic. On one occasion a speaker ended by threatening, "If you don' register to vote you goin' to hell, that's all they is to it!" More hymns and civil rights songs reinforced the message.[58]

Others joined in the proceedings by recounting their experiences, explaining the voter registration process or ASCS elections, exhorting their fellows to work hard, inspiring them to further bravery, and leading in prayers and singing. Though local leaders were in charge, SNCC workers often spoke too. One evening Stokely Carmichael addressed the gathering, "grabbing the tension already built up and manipulating it to give them courage," according to one observer. "He urged, cajoled, and ordered them" to go to Hayneville to register to vote. "What do we have to do?" Carmichael asked. They responded by shouting, "REGISTER!"[59]

Jon Daniels attended several mass meetings in Lowndes County and usually participated unobtrusively as a member of the audience. He impressed the people around him with his quiet but intense commitment to civil rights, with his personal warmth and friendliness toward strangers, and with his courageous presence as an unusually supportive white. Even though the style of the meetings was foreign to his high-church preferences, and despite the summer heat, Daniels relished the enthusiastic, spiritual atmosphere and joined readily in the singing. No doubt his experiences were similar to the ones described by another northern white civil rights worker, who vividly recalled "the sweat. It was . . . so therapeutic. I was literally thawing out . . . loosening up, letting go. It was just so different from the way I had been raised . . . to be proper and demure. . . . It was just a great feeling."[60]

At a few mass meetings Daniels spoke briefly. On the evening of

August 8, he attended the first one ever held at the Mount Carmel Baptist Church in the Gordonsville community west of Hayneville. The pastor had opposed opening his church to the movement because he feared retaliation, but area residents insisted on meeting there. Presiding over the gathering somewhat reluctantly, the cautious and worried minister tried to divert the people from voter registration and other civil rights issues by emphasizing the life hereafter. Toward the end of the meeting he asked if anyone had anything to say, and Jon Daniels volunteered to speak.[61]

The Yankee seminarian went to the front of the rural Alabama church and tried to explain his involvement in the civil rights movement. He told the blacks assembled that his freedom depended on their freedom. Holding up the Bible, he told them the story about the children of Israel and how Moses had led them out of bondage. He repeated several times, "Let my people go," and each time the crowd responded, "Amen." When he had completed his short talk, Daniels, at the minister's request, gave the benediction. He so impressed the members of Mount Carmel's congregation who were present that they immediately invited him to return in several weeks to speak at their revival.[62]

After the final prayer, each mass meeting ended with the traditional singing of "We Shall Overcome." With their arms crossed and hands clasped, everyone "sang out all fatigue and fear, each connected by this bond of hands to each other, communicating an infinite love and sadness," according to one participant. They sang "with all the voice, emotion, hope, and strength that each contained. Together they were an army."[63] Daniels and his colleagues needed the inspiration provided by the mass meetings, for the opposition of the local whites, the timidity and fears of many blacks, and the lack of governmental support at any level made it difficult for them to sustain their efforts.

While Daniels and the other activists held mass meetings, canvassed the county for voters, and prepared for the ASCS elections to be held that summer, they also encouraged and counseled local blacks about ending racial segregation in the county's public schools. Following the wishes of the local whites who considered the *Brown* decision unconstitutional, the superintendent and the school board made no effort to comply with the 1954 decision. Only in the spring of 1965, under pressure from the federal government, did the school board finally submit to the U.S. Office of Education a plan to desegregate grades nine through twelve at the two white schools. If the board did not comply with the plan, the county schools would lose all federal funding. The board decided that its poor county could not afford to lose any financial support.[64]

The Lowndes desegregation plan involved what was called "freedom of choice" for all students. Under freedom of choice, an individual student could ask the school board for permission to switch to another school. By putting the responsibility on black students to move to the white schools, the freedom of choice approach meant that, if no black students requested a transfer, then blacks would continue to attend all-black institutions and no desegregation would occur. The plan also gave final authority to the local, all-white school board to approve or deny the transfers. Blacks disliked the freedom-of-choice plan because of the burden it placed on them to achieve what should have been their right. Though the requirements of freedom of choice undoubtedly frightened off many applicants, thirty-five black students did apply in July for a transfer from the Lowndes County Training School to the white Hayneville School.[65]

The county's white community reacted hostilely to the attempt to end school segregation. After the black students submitted their applications for a transfer, a group of half a dozen white men — merchants and landlords who held considerable power over blacks — visited the parents of the applicants and threatened retaliation if their children actually attended the white schools. One merchant who regularly sold seed and fertilizer on credit to a black farmer went with the group of whites to talk to him after his daughter had applied for a transfer to Hayneville School. The storekeeper said to the farmer, "Don't ask me for no damn help for nothing." Another white told black parents that the Ku Klux Klan would come after them.[66]

Despite such intimidation, few black children withdrew their applications to transfer, and the white community chose other ways to retaliate. To avoid any mixing of the races, a group of whites in the spring of 1965 had formed the Lowndes County Private School Foundation and planned to open a private white high school in the fall. By the middle of the summer, the head of the foundation reported that 150 whites had paid the foundation's ten-dollar membership fee.[67]

Even more effective in preventing school desegregation was the action of the Lowndes school board. The board rejected almost forty applications to transfer and finally approved only five; in letters to the applicants, it gave no reason for its decisions. Unlike their response in the past, blacks refused to accept the board's actions. Frustrated and outraged, many of the parents of the rejected students boldly went to the office of the superintendent of schools to demand an explanation. The superintendent told them that the board based its decision on either the students' poor attendance records or their low California Achievement Test scores in the eighth and eleventh grades. The reasoning dumfounded the parents. One black teacher, whose son had applied to the Hayneville

School, said she had never heard of using the achievement test to make a judgment about integration. The disappointed parents had little alternative but to accept the verdict and then redouble their organizing efforts.[68]

During the summer of 1965, while blacks campaigned to desegregate schools and register voters in Lowndes County, important events were occurring in Washington, D.C., that would affect the civil rights movement in the small Black Belt county. Voting rights legislation had become a prime objective in the nation's capital. Previously, the national administrations had preferred litigation to achieve equal voting rights for southern blacks. Late in 1964 the Johnson administration moved gradually toward proposing tough legislation for that purpose, and events in Selma in the winter and spring of 1965 accelerated its plans. After the bloody attack on the Selma demonstrators but before the climactic march to Montgomery, President Lyndon B. Johnson addressed a joint session of Congress and a live television audience about the need for voting rights legislation. "I speak tonight for the dignity of man and the destiny of democracy," he declared. "Every American must have an equal right to vote. There is no reason that can excuse the denial of that right." He outlined the bill that he planned to send Congress in a few days and demanded prompt action: "This time, on this issue, there must be no delay, or no hesitation or no compromise with our purpose." Aligning himself with the civil rights movement, Johnson vowed: "Their cause must be our cause too. Because it is not just Negroes, but really it is all of us, who must overcome the crippling legacy of bigotry and injustice. And we shall overcome."[69]

Johnson's voting rights bill would automatically suspend literacy tests in states where less than 50 percent of the potential voters had voted in the last presidential election. The bill would thus apply to Alabama, Georgia, Louisiana, Mississippi, South Carolina, and Virginia, and part of North Carolina. In addition, the U.S. attorney general could send federal registrars into the affected areas when he concluded that they were needed. Martin Luther King and some civil rights leaders wanted the bill to apply to several southern states that did not have literacy tests, while SNCC thought that new elections should be held after the federal registrars finished their work. Most liberals believed that the legislation should include a ban on poll taxes in state elections, which Alabama and three other southern states still required. The bill nonetheless generally satisfied civil rights activists and promised to bring about tremendous change in southern politics.[70]

Congress immediately took up the voting rights bill, with southern congressmen realizing the growing futility of their opposition. In the Senate, debate focused on repeal of the poll tax and on a provision to weaken the bill by freeing a state from its requirements if the state registered 60 percent of its eligible voters and did not block black registrants. The Senate rejected both changes and on May 25 invoked cloture, which halted extended debate on the bill. The next day the Senate passed the legislation. Meanwhile, the House of Representatives moved more slowly. Finally, the House rejected weaker Republican alternatives, which southerners favored, and on July 9 passed a bill containing a repeal of poll taxes in state elections. Negotiations between the House and the Senate over the differences in their bills dragged on for another month.[71]

While watching the hopeful progress of the voting rights measure in Washington, the Lowndes County civil rights movement persisted in its efforts to register voters. Scores of blacks appeared before the board of registrars during its regular sessions on the first and third Monday in July and August. Even though they expected federal registrars to be in the county within a week or two, more than 100 blacks filed applications to vote on August 2; notification of acceptance, of course, would be transmitted by mail. By early August perhaps as many as 1,200 blacks had attempted to register, but only 200 had succeeded.[72]

With increased black voter registration and with the submission of applications by black students to attend white schools, the pressure for change in Lowndes mounted rapidly and white resistance intensified. Though the campaign to register blacks voters had a low success rate and though it appeared that school desegregation in the fall would be limited to a few token blacks, whites understood that the eventual outcome would mean an end to the way of life they had always known. As one sympathetic Birmingham newspaperman remarked, "[T]he white people in Lowndes County have been living with and under a set of guidelines handed down from grandfathers and great-grandfathers. It has been an accepted way of life. And when things have 'always' been one way it does not come easy to have a stranger come in to disrupt things."[73]

The threat of racial change alarmed white citizens and many became fearful and angry. Their fears were, as one observer put it, "real fears, not imagined ones." Whites, realizing instinctively that the civil rights movement sought genuine social and political changes in their community, resisted the revolution. They stoutly opposed school desegregation because, as one resident argued, "Niggers in our schools will ruin my children morally, scholastically, spiritually, and every other way if the number [of blacks in the schools] is too high." Another white insisted that the racially desegregated students must be segregated by sex to ensure "absolutely no social contact in between" the races. When it appeared likely that only five blacks would be allowed in the white schools in the fall, one man who had threatened the black applicants became more tolerant. "If it is the law, I guess we'll have to stomach it," he conceded.[74]

More ominous to whites than school desegregation was the prospect of black political power. If blacks could freely register and vote, then whites would soon lose control of county politics. Blacks would become sheriff, superintendent of schools, probate judge, voter registrars, and other public officials. The idea that blacks could assume political power frightened white citizens in Lowndes. "It's just inconceivable," declared a store owner, "that white landowners are going to surrender control of the county to the non landowners — you know what I mean?" Everyone knew what he meant. Whites were willing to take extreme measures to prevent such an occurrence. A number of them considered two possible solutions: either the blacks must leave the county or the whites would. The landowning whites could exert their economic power to take jobs from blacks and to force blacks off the land. If blacks did not leave and gained control of the local government, many whites said they would go elsewhere. The Lowndes County solicitor admitted that he would move. "I would if I was living," said Carlton Perdue. "I wouldn't live here under no Negro."[75]

Not all whites considered black political power to be imminent. Betraying a profound lack of understanding of the civil rights movement taking place on their doorstep, some whites still believed that blacks would continue to defer to whites in politics. According to registrar Carl Golson, a leader in the White Citizens' Council, "A lot of Negroes feel like they'd be more or less an ingrate now [to seize power from whites]. They've been dependent on the white man for a long time."[76]

Most whites in Lowndes, however, probably did not share Golson's sanguine outlook. Their worries and apprehensions came out in their humor. Their targets included the federal government, which, in their opinion, was responsible for much of the turmoil. In a local restaurant, one woman said, "I hear that if anything happens to Martin Luther King, Johnson might become the President." A compatriot responded that he had heard "old Martin Luther King is going to be the next State Highway Commissioner." When someone asked him to explain, he said, "Well, he black-topped the road from Selma to Montgomery, didn't he?"[77]

Behind the humor lay deep resentment and suspicion of the people and forces behind the civil rights movement. Many Lowndes whites believed that communists were plotting the civil rights movement, and they could not understand how the rest of the country could be duped by the obviously sinister forces. The report of a special state legislative committee confirmed their suspicions. In the report, issued in late June, the Commission to Preserve the Peace declared that SNCC, the civil rights group most active in Lowndes, was "extensively Communist dominated" and "an extremely dangerous, irresponsible group which tends to promote acts of violence to gain support for their own goals." SNCC "substantially follows the Communist Party line" and was "an agent for the Communist conspiracy." The commission also concluded that the Southern Christian Leadership Conference, headed by Martin Luther King, "actively engaged in promoting the Communist line" and was "substantially under control of Communists."[78] With the implicit sanction of the legislative committee, therefore, white segregationists in Alabama could console themselves with the notion that they were indeed fighting for true American principles when they opposed the civil rights movement.

Suspicions extended beyond organizations to particular individuals involved in the movement. At the time of the Selma-to-Montgomery march, for example, many Alabamians doubted that all the clergy who joined the march were really ministers and priests. On March 30, in a joint resolution asking people to "refrain from any future ungodly demonstrations," the Alabama legislature warned people of "supposedly religious leaders" and "so-called preachers." Less than six weeks later, it enacted legislation to "outlaw impersonation of the clergy and religious orders. . . . Whoever being in a public place fraudulently pretends by garb or outward array to be a minister of any religion, or nun, priest, or rabbi or other member of the clergy, is guilty of a misdemeanor."[79] Like many white Alabamians, state legislators could not comprehend that *their* God supported the civil rights movement. Even to consider the possibility that God opposed racial segregation would mean that whites had to question their own faith and personal relationship with the Lord. To guard their consciences, therefore, any suggestion that the outside agitators had God on their side had to be discredited immediately. The acts of the legislature and its special committee reinforced the beliefs of many whites in Lowndes that the civil rights movement should be opposed at all costs as un-American and un-Christian. As the momentum behind the movement grew, therefore, whites stiffened their resistance.

Published in Montgomery during the summer of 1965, *Sex and Civil Rights: The True Selma Story* buttressed some of the worst fears of whites about sex between the races and the sexual indecencies of white civil rights activists, including the "so-called" clergy. The book was prominent at many newsstands and truck stops in Alabama. Claiming to be an exposé of what really happened during the Selma-to-Montgomery march, it reported many lurid details in an attempt to inflame whites against the movement. For example, a Catholic priest had been seen having sexual intercourse with a black girl, and a black male civil rights worker had been observed in "several unnatural acts with a red-haired white girl." Even more sensational was the allegation that "half the women in the Selma march wore no underpants." As portrayed by *Sex and Civil Rights*, the civil rights movement posed a serious threat to white southern sexual standards and to the purity of the white race. Therefore, white supremacists should do all they could to fight the movement.[80]

The White Citizens' Council and the Ku Klux Klan had long led the defense of white supremacy and the opposition to integration in Lowndes County. The Citizens' Council continued to hold regular public meetings in the courthouse in Hayneville, but the Klan was more secretive. Even state investigators had little success in obtaining information about the organization, although the Alabama attorney general believed that it was very active in Lowndes. On July 10 about two hundred people attended a KKK rally in Hayneville to bolster white supremacist resistance to the civil rights movement. Later in the month, the Klan held a major rally in Fort Deposit on a Friday night and one in Hayneville the next evening. In addition, Klansmen reportedly burned crosses and threatened blacks involved in the movement. In July SNCC workers finally realized that their difficulty in organizing in Fort Deposit was due to the Klan's effectiveness in intimidating local blacks. Whites, presumably affiliated with either the KKK or the Citizens' Council, frequently harassed the movement's mass meetings too; nevertheless, the gatherings continued to draw as many as three hundred black residents by the first of August, and one meeting was planned for Fort Deposit early in the month.[81]

Any social and political revolution in Lowndes faced intense opposition among the white minority. White residents intuitively understood that the civil rights movement threatened their way of life. An end to racial segregation would, they believed, inevitably threaten not just their economic and political power but every aspect of their lives — including their religion, morality, and family. It had to be stopped.

Jon Daniels at VMI. (Courtesy of Virginia Military Institute)

Judith Upham in Selma, with the George Washington Carver Homes in the background. (Courtesy of Judith Upham)

Jon Daniels and Rachel West in Selma. (Courtesy of Judith Upham)

The Reverend T. Frank Mathews. (Courtesy of T. Frank Mathews)

Jon Daniels speaking at a mass meeting in Gordonsville community on
August 8, 1965. (Courtesy of UPI/Bettmann)

John Hulett. (Courtesy of John Hulett)

The Reverend Richard Morrisroe. (Courtesy of Richard Morrisroe)

Ruby Sales as a high school senior. (Courtesy of Ruby Sales)

The Cash Store in Hayneville. (Courtesy of the Federal Bureau of Investigation)

Tom Coleman at home after his arraignment for manslaughter. (Courtesy of AP/ Wide World Photos)

Tom and Coralie Coleman leaving the Lowndes County courthouse after the first day of his trial. (Courtesy of UPI/Bettmann)

The Lowndes County courthouse in Hayneville. (Courtesy of UPI/Bettmann)

Judge T. Werth Thagard (*right foreground*) and prosecutor Arthur Gamble
(*right background*) outside the courthouse before Tom Coleman's trial.
(Courtesy of UPI/Bettmann)

The clerk of court carrying the shotgun that Tom Coleman used to kill Jon Daniels. (Courtesy of AP/Wide World Photos)

158

Oliphant cartoon of the Coleman trial. (Courtesy of the *Denver Post*)

"Manslaughter"

Hugh Haynie
cartoon of the
Coleman trial.
(Courtesy of
the Louisville
Courier-Journal)

Jurors relaxing in front of the Confederate monument in the Hayneville town square during a recess in the trial. (Courtesy of UPI/Bettmann)

'*Gentlemen of the jury, let's have a little decorum until after you've reached your not guilty verdict*'

John Fawcett cartoon of the Coleman trial. (Courtesy of the *Providence Journal-Bulletin*)

We'uns Got Us a Huntin' License!

Arthur Poinier cartoon of the Coleman trial. (Courtesy of the *Detroit News*)

DEMONSTRATION

AND DEATH

6

As racial strains in Lowndes County continued mounting in the late summer, events in Washington, D.C., and California compounded the tension and brought the situation in the Black Belt county closer to a climax. Congress passed the momentous voting rights bill, and on Friday, August 6, President Johnson signed the bill into law and pledged speedy action in implementing the new legislation. On the following Monday the attorney general announced that he was sending federal voting registrars to nine southern counties, and on Tuesday, August 10, Lowndes County was one of four in Alabama to receive federal examiners. The Justice Department selected Lowndes because only 3.8 percent of the blacks of voting age were registered, and all of them had registered since March. The department found, moreover, that 80 percent of the 112 blacks rejected by the local registrars during the special registration in the first week of July "should have been accepted" "according to standards already set by the courts." In spite of what the Justice Department interpreted as flagrant errors by the local registrars, registrar Carl Golson said that he was "just sick" over the arrival of the federal agents. He thought that Washington had agreed not to send in registrars after the county dropped its literacy tests. "We bowed, we gave in," he commented angrily, "but their agreement was not worth a damn."[1]

When Richmond Flowers, the state attorney general, visited Lowndes to observe the federal registrars on their first day of work, he learned that others were also upset. The attorney general had broken with Governor George C. Wallace over the race question and had in the last few years begun to take a more moderate stance. Unlike the new governor, who stood squarely for segregation in 1962, Flowers had called for "calm deliberation and cool calculation" in defending "our southern tradition." He urged Alabamians to "discern and distinguish between a fighting chance and a chance to fight." Though he continued to call himself a segregationist and opposed civil rights legislation, Flowers also denounced violence and conducted a widely publicized probe of the Ku Klux Klan. In the spring of 1965, he predicted an integrated state in his lifetime. To many whites in Alabama, especially those in the Black Belt, Flowers had begun to sound suspiciously like a traitor to his race.[2]

Attorney General Flowers had some difficulty checking on the federal registrars because they had been sent to Fort Deposit rather than to the county seat. Starting at 8:30 A.M., the three officials were ready to register voters at the Fort Deposit post office, but the first black applicants did not arrive until after 11:00. Apparently most of them, like Flowers, thought that the registrars would be in Hayneville. In spite of Golson's disgust and the initial confusion over the location, black voter registration proceeded. Though only forty-eight blacks registered on August 10 (the lowest in the nine southern counties affected) and sixty more on the following day, registration rose sharply under the federal registrars. As the Associated Press reported, "The balance of power could soon be in the hands of Negro voters. . . . [and in some] counties, heavy registration of Negroes could even give them a voting majority by next year's election."[3] Whites in Lowndes readily understood that possibility.

Just as the federal registrars got to work in Lowndes County, some of their worst fears seemed to be confirmed by events in California. For the first time since World War II, a major race riot occurred in the United States. On August 11, the Watts section of Los Angeles exploded as mobs in the black ghetto clashed with police and later National Guardsmen in rioting that lasted six days and spread over forty square miles. Thirty-four people were killed, more than nine hundred were injured, and about four thousand were arrested during the violence. In the days following the outbreak in Watts, blacks rioted in Chicago and in Springfield, Massachusetts.[4]

The whites in Lowndes County, like the rest of the nation, read in their newspapers about the racial violence and, more significantly, watched it on television where the pictures and sounds intensified their awareness of the ensuing destruction. As William Bradford Huie, an Alabama reporter, observed, in mid-August "the talk in the community was of the Los Angeles riot, outsiders inciting Negroes to vote, 'Sex and Civil Rights,' priests in the arms of Negro girls, and the dead body of Viola Liuzzo without underpants." The threat posed by the civil rights movement in their community seemed more ominous to Lowndes whites in the wake of the Watts uprising because they had now seen that blacks could easily turn to violence, just as they had always suspected. Whites who for generations had with impunity used violence against blacks could only expect that the blacks would return the violence if they ever tried to seize power. At the same time, according to Huie, the nation's response to the Watts riots convinced Lowndes white supremacists that they had widespread public support in combating black insurrection.[5]

As the federal registrars arrived in Lowndes and violence erupted in the Watts ghetto, Jon Daniels left Lowndes temporarily to attend the annual convention of the Southern Christian Leadership Conference in Birmingham. Though most of his recent work had been with SNCC, Daniels felt a kinship with SCLC because of his respect for Martin Luther King and their common religious commitment. He had never attended a conference of a civil rights organization, and the five-day meeting of one thousand delegates — including King, Constance Baker Motley, James and Diane Bevel, John Lewis, Ella Baker, Bayard Rustin, and Rosa Parks — held great promise.[6] For Daniels, the SCLC convention also provided a few days of relief from his intense work in Lowndes County.

In sessions held at the Sixteenth Street Baptist Church, where four black girls had died in a 1963 bombing, the conference speakers considered the future of the civil rights movement. They urged blacks to become responsible citizens by exercising their new right to vote, and they called for the movement to develop a broader conception of civil rights that would encompass economic problems as well. The theme of the meeting was the need to create a "Grand Alliance" of SCLC and liberals, labor unions, and religious groups. Harvard University professor Harvey Cox and a spokesman for the AFL-CIO joined King in endorsing the idea.[7]

In addition to listening to speeches, Jon Daniels talked with many people. He saw a fellow ETS student and told him about his work in Lowndes — the difficulties of seeking reconciliation while whites chased him down the highway but also the rewards he derived from his work. On Thursday afternoon he met Richard Morrisroe, a twenty-seven-year-old Roman Catholic priest. Morrisroe had lived all of his life in Chicago, except for seven years at St. Mary of the Lake Seminary in Mundelein, about forty miles northwest of the city. The son of Irish immigrants, Morrisroe grew up in an ethnically diverse, working-class neighborhood eight miles from the downtown area. He went to parochial schools and then, thinking about becoming a priest, continued his education in one of the Chicago Archdiocese's preparatory high schools to prepare for the seminary and graduated in 1957. After completing the seminary program at Mundelein, he was ordained a priest in April 1964.[8]

Father Morrisroe had requested assignment to a parish in a Chicago black community. In June 1964 the handsome young priest began work at the South Side's two-thousand-member St. Columbanus Church, the home parish of some of his seminary friends before it shifted from a white to a black neighborhood. At Columbanus, he made his first significant contacts with blacks and with people active in politics and civil rights. Particularly influential was Sam Rayner, the proprietor of a funeral home across from the church and an unsuccessful congressional candidate in 1964. Rayner took the priest to hear Martin Luther King speak at an Catholic Interracial Council dinner and to listen to veterans of the Mississippi Freedom Summer project at a meeting of the Council of Catholic Men. Later Morrisroe talked with activists who had been in the South and learned more about the civil rights movement.[9]

When Martin Luther King summoned clergy to Selma in March 1965, Morrisroe flew south with a group from the Catholic Interracial Council. During his week in Selma, he lodged with a family in the Carver Homes, visited with black families and with other clergy, marched to the county courthouse, and spent a few days in the Good Samaritan Hospital with a strep throat. He did not meet Jon Daniels or anyone else later involved in Lowndes County, and he left before the historic march to Montgomery. The experience deepened Morrisroe's interest in the movement. Back in Chicago, he became more directly active in civil rights protests. In June, during a lie-down demonstration at State and Madison streets to oppose the racial policies of the city school superintendent, he was arrested and charged with disorderly conduct and obstructing traffic. With the charges still pending, he went to Birmingham in August with Sam Rayner and a carload of Chicagoans for the SCLC convention. Morrisroe joined the expedition in part because he wanted to get to know Selma better under more normal circumstances. From Chicago friends in SNCC, Morrisroe had learned of the organizing efforts in Lowndes County.[10]

When they first met Jon Daniels struck Morrisroe as not very "street smart." The priest was also a little suspicious of Episcopalians generally; his parochial school and seminary training had taught him that in many ways the Church of England was the enemy of the Roman church. Talking with Daniels overcame much of his initial skepticism. The seminarian's high-church orientation and his attraction to the Catholic church undoubtedly eased some of Morrisroe's apprehensions, and their interest in the civil rights movement gave them a common bond. When Morrisroe discovered where Daniels was staying and that he would be returning there that night, he knew that he had found a way to go back to Selma and to see Lowndes County.[11]

Daniels and Morrisroe spent the night at the Carver Homes in Selma, then headed for Lowndes the next morning. In addition to driving around the county and visiting, they assisted in the preparations for a demonstration in Fort Deposit on Saturday.[12]

On the previous Sunday, SNCC workers had finally staged a major mass meeting in Fort Deposit. More than four hundred people attended the first civil rights rally in the Klan stronghold. During the following week, while Daniels was in Birmingham, SNCC activists had helped young Lowndes blacks who wanted to organize the demonstration to be held on Saturday morning. It would be the first demonstration of its kind ever held in the county and would signal a more aggressive approach to attaining civil rights. Nonviolent protests by young people would supplement the voter registration efforts by adults. Though the largest town in the county, Fort Deposit had fewer than fifteen hundred residents. The farthest town from both Montgomery and Selma, it was the most commercially developed, with two automobile dealerships, a dozen stores and businesses, a city hall, and its own police department. The area around Fort Deposit also had the highest percentage of whites in the county. Whereas the northern and western sections of Lowndes were about 90 percent black and Hayneville was over 75 percent black, the vicinity of Fort Deposit was less than 70 percent black; it also had the most dense population in the sparsely populated county.[13]

For several months Jimmy Rogers, a SNCC field worker, had been working primarily with young blacks in the Fort Deposit area because most older blacks were too fearful to join the movement. The twenty-eight-year-old native of Brooklyn, New York, had served in the air force for four years, worked for the New York State Commission Against Discrimination, and studied at Tuskegee Institute before becoming directly involved with the civil rights movement. After participating in the Selma march and in demonstrations in Montgomery, he joined the SNCC effort in Lowndes in the late spring of 1965. At the urging of young blacks in the area, Rogers had helped plan the demonstration in Fort Deposit.[14]

The demonstration aimed to protest the discriminatory and allegedly dishonest treatment of black customers by white storekeepers. Some businesses, for instance, still had separate entrances for blacks, and the white restaurant served them only in the rear. Perhaps most offensive and irritating to blacks were the constant indignities shown them by whites. Stores refused to hire blacks, even though most of the their business came from the black community. Blacks believed that the white-run businesses charged them more than whites for the same products. A grocery store, for example, allowed blacks to charge purchases by signing a receipt but kept all the records; when the black customer came back at payday to settle the account, the bill was always larger than the customer thought it should be. Black adults were too dependent on whites for jobs and housing to protest, but the young activists hoped to give their elders the courage to protest the discrimination they experienced in the local stores.[15]

The organizers of the demonstration clearly recognized the danger in Fort Deposit, especially that posed by the Klan. And they knew they could not depend on the town's small police force for protection if trouble developed. The SNCC workers on the scene informed their headquarters in Atlanta that they were "REALLY AFRAID OF VIOLENCE" and asked for help in obtaining press coverage and security from state and federal authorities. Two days before the event John Lewis, the national chairman of SNCC, sent a telegram to Governor Wallace to alert him about the protest and to "demand protection of demonstrators." The governor's office, however, took no action.[16]

On Friday evening, while Richard Morrisroe attended a religious revival in Lowndes County, Daniels ate supper and visited with a black family in Gordonsville. He returned late that night to Selma. After talking with SNCC workers and watching television news reports of the Watts rioting until nearly midnight, Morrisroe spent the night with other civil rights workers at a SNCC freedom house in Lowndes. As he left the Wests' apartment on Saturday morning, Jon Daniels said good-bye to Alice West, then returned from his car to tell her good-bye a second time and to ask her to save some supper for him in case he returned that evening. Daniels met Morrisroe at the freedom house and the two men discussed whether they should participate in the demonstration; Daniels was more willing to do so than the newly arrived priest. After consulting with Stokely Carmichael and others, they decided to meet the marchers at a church just north of Fort Deposit and to accompany them downtown. Although Daniels and Morrisroe did not plan to get directly involved in the protest, they gave several blacks rides to the demonstration.[17]

The white community of Fort Deposit had heard that a protest was scheduled and expected trouble. On an otherwise typical Saturday morning, many whites had mobilized in the downtown area to resist any demonstration. According to reporters, "The town looked like it was getting ready for war. Crowds of whites lined the sidewalks, filling the air with the buzz of tense whispering." Rumors circulated among the bewildered, fearful white residents that freedom riders had come to Fort Deposit. Armed whites patrolled the town in angry anticipation. Guns and clubs were evident everywhere. The police and their special deputies could not easily be distinguished from other whites planning to resist the demonstration. Golson Motor Company, operated by Carl Golson, seemed to serve as the headquarters of the white activists.[18]

Whites became apprehensive as they watched the arrival of groups of blacks. More than one hundred lined up outside the post office to register to vote, and others were coming to participate in the demonstration. Seeing their numbers swell, an alarmed Carl Golson called the supervisor of the federal registrars in Montgomery before nine o'clock to alert him to the rising tensions; an FBI agent on the scene, on the other hand, thought that the number of blacks in Fort Deposit was not unusually large for a Saturday morning.[19]

As planned, the protesters gathered at the black Methodist church north of town. The night before some older local blacks had tried to discourage the demonstration by arguing that it would be counterproductive to voter registration, and they repeated their concerns the next day. Rejecting their warnings, the assembling protesters spent more than two hours discussing tactics and targets. Initially many of the young people balked at the instructions in nonviolence; they argued the merits of nonviolence if attacked. The protesters decided to split into three groups to picket the three businesses thought to be the most discriminatory toward blacks. Even though FBI agents warned them that the local police would arrest them and that white mobs might assault them, the activists refused to call off the demonstration.[20]

While the young people made final plans, a few menacing whites at the post office tried to stare down the blacks waiting to register and to dissuade them from meeting with the federal registrars inside. FBI agents returned to the church to warn Jimmy Rogers and the waiting demonstrators of an armed white mob gathering downtown. Pointing out that they were present only to observe and not to protect the demonstrators, the

FBI agents asked them to call off the protest to avoid bloodshed. The federal officials also cautioned that local police would undoubtedly arrest them as soon as they began to demonstrate. For more than an hour the group reviewed its strategy and reconsidered the possibility of violence and arrest. One young woman said of the FBI, "They're trying to intimidate us — that's all they're doing." A man declared, "I don't want to scare the older people away from voter registration, but I think we need this." When a few people reiterated an interest in violence, John McMeans, a local black, responded sharply, "If you can't participate peacefully, stay out." In the end, the demonstrators rejected any suggestion that they cancel the protest but agreed to proceed nonviolently.[21]

About fifteen minutes before noon on the hot and humid August morning, Jon Daniels, Richard Morrisroe, and about two dozen protesters proceeded in cars and on foot from the church to downtown Fort Deposit. To encourage the local youth in their first demonstration, Daniels and Morrisroe had decided to join the protest; Daniels seemed relaxed and happy as he marched downtown. When they arrived in the center of town, representatives from *Life* magazine, the *National Guardian* (a socialist weekly in New York), and the *Southern Courier* (a weekly on the civil rights movement published in Montgomery by northern college students) were present to observe the demonstration. Out of fear for their own safety, the journalists habitually traveled in Lowndes at least in pairs — the *Life* reporter drove to Fort Deposit with two men from the *Southern Courier* and two reporters came from the *Guardian*.[22]

In three groups of eight to ten, the young people began to picket McGruder's Grocery Store, Waters Dry Goods Store, and the Community Grill. Most of the demonstrators carried signs that urged blacks to stop shopping in the stores: "Wake Up! This Is Not Primitive Time," "Equal Treatment for All, and No Back Doors," and "No More Back Doors." The protesters were orderly, did not block customers from entering the businesses, and allowed pedestrian and vehicular traffic to proceed without interruption.[23]

The first group of six black males arrived by car in front of McGruder's Grocery Store and were arrested by the chief of police and his auxiliary force after demonstrating for about one minute. The two other groups marched up the street to their targets. As a hostile mob of whites armed with clubs, bottles, and guns approached the protesters, the Fort Deposit police and their special deputies arrested the demonstrators, among them, Jon Daniels and Richard Morrisroe. Daniels pointed out their constitutional right to picket, but to no avail. Violence seemed imminent. Except for some pushing and shoving, however, the authorities made the arrests without physical abuse. One white who held a gun while helping the police told a protester from Fort Deposit that he hoped the demonstrator had a gun because he would then have an excuse to blow his brains out. Across the railroad tracks a block away, a crowd of blacks waiting to register watched "with fear written on their faces" as the police marched their detainees to the town jail. The protesters were charged with violating a city ordinance, passed in November 1963, that prohibited "any parade, procession or other public demonstration on the streets or other public ways . . . unless a permit has been secured from the Town Council." The entire demonstration had lasted less than five minutes.[24]

In the tense atmosphere, only one violent incident occurred, but it did not involve the demonstrators. Eight white men armed with clubs threatened four newsmen in an automobile and told them to get out of town. In their own way, the journalists were also outside agitators because they intended to publicize the actions of the protesters, the reactions of the whites, and the general racial situation in Fort Deposit. When the reporters started to drive away, one white man — later identified as Carl Golson — smashed the car's windshield. Flying shards of glass struck the passengers, and one required hospital treatment for cuts on his head.[25]

While the demonstrators were being arrested, the men searched, and all of them taken to the local jail, another incident occurred involving Stokely Carmichael. After driving some of the demonstrators downtown and letting them out of the car, Carmichael and Christopher Wylie, another SNCC worker, were blocked on the street by a carload of armed white men. When they tried to extricate their car, the two cars bumped; only Carmichael and Wylie's vehicle suffered damage. To prevent any violence, the two black men agreed to go with the whites to the police station and let the authorities settle the dispute. At police headquarters, Carmichael (a passenger) and Wylie (the driver) suddenly were both charged with reckless driving and with leaving the scene of an accident. Arrested by Lowndes County deputies, Carmichael and Wylie joined the demonstrators at the town jail.[26]

The police quickly realized that the two-room facility in Fort Deposit was too small to hold all the demonstrators. While they deliberated about what to do and a crowd of armed whites milled around outside, the prisoners started singing freedom songs. Scared blacks continued to observe events from across the railroad tracks. After holding the demonstrators for an hour, the police decided to transport them to the larger county jail in Hayneville. The only vehicle big enough to carry the two dozen protesters was a flatbed truck used by the county to collect garbage. Daniels, Morrisroe, Carmichael, and the other prisoners piled on the truck for the twenty-mile ride to the county seat. Daniels appeared calm, but some of the younger people were worried in the face of jeering whites. To pass the time and relieve the stress, they sang "We Shall Overcome" and other freedom songs on their way through bloody Lowndes to Hayneville.[27]

In Hayneville the sheriff's department, which maintained the jail facilities two blocks from the courthouse, received the new prisoners early Saturday afternoon. Twenty-one blacks plus Jon Daniels and Richard Morrisroe faced the misdemeanor charges, and Carmichael and Wylie were booked for the more serious traffic violations. Within hours the Fort Deposit police authorized the release of five of the protesters who were under eighteen. (Some of the remaining prisoners were juveniles but had given false ages to the police. Ruby Sales, for example, said that she was twenty instead of seventeen.) The police apparently refused to believe that Daniels was a seminarian and Morrisroe a priest and assumed that they had lied about their names because the jail's register noted the admission of "Richard Morrison w[hite]m[ale] 26 (alias Morrisroe)" and "Jonathan Vaniels w[hite] m[ale] 26 (alias Daniels)." Lying whites posing as churchmen would be given no special consideration in the jail. Though racial segregation always extended to prisoners in the Hayneville facility, the sheriff's men put Daniels and Morrisroe with the black males in cells on the second floor. The women were given a cell on the first floor.[28]

Unprepared for the sudden activity and unaccustomed to inquiring reporters, the jailers refused to let anyone speak with their prisoners and barred everyone from asking officials about the arrests or the charges against the civil rights activists. When representatives from the Medical Committee for Human Rights arrived to check on the condition of the jailed activists, an armed group of whites surrounded their car, told them to get out of town, and chased their car to the county line. Anxiety and the expectation of violence permeated Hayneville. When one county official spotted a newsman with a camera outside the jail, he tossed his gun aside and charged the reporter with a billy club. In response to quick reminders of a journalist's rights, the official shouted, "Civil rights or not, I gonna bust you right between the eyes." He failed to follow through on his threat when the reporter stood up to him, but the reporter did not get into the jail or take any pictures.[29]

The SNCC offices in Selma and Atlanta, of course, soon learned of the arrests in Fort Deposit. Immediately workers began trying to raise bail money for their colleagues and to secure a lawyer to represent them. Initial attempts to communicate with the mayor of Fort Deposit, the county sheriff, and the chief of police failed because all reportedly were "out of town." When SNCC representatives managed to contact the mayor, he told them that the demonstrators could be released if someone posted one hundred dollars for each of them. In the meantime SNCC learned that Stokely Carmichael, Chris Wylie, and several juveniles had been taken briefly back to Fort Deposit, where, according to other reports, an angry mob had formed.[30]

Worried about the welfare of the demonstrators, SNCC promptly dispatched representatives to Lowndes County. On Saturday evening Scott B. Smith, a SNCC field worker, went to Hayneville with a small group including a reporter for the *Chicago Defender*. At the county jail, he spoke briefly through the bars with his friends inside. Later Smith saw people he understood to be Klansmen talking with local authorities about which frequencies they could use on the two-way radios they had recently installed in their cars. In addition to local whites, a number of men from Selma and Montgomery were armed in Hayneville. In the middle of the night Smith surreptitiously observed groups of white men as they milled around the jail and the courthouse square and talked about the new prisoners. Outside the sheriff's courthouse office, he overheard a deputy sheriff and other whites discussing what they should do the next time there was a demonstration. The white men agreed that if they did not act, the blacks in Lowndes County would become like the ones in Watts.[31]

Inside the Hayneville jail, the sheriff's deputies locked Jon Daniels, Richard Morrisroe, and their eighteen black compatriots in cells. The prisoners did not know how long they would be held. Except for Daniels, Morrisroe, and the four SNCC workers, all of the jailed protesters were between eighteen and twenty-four years old. The four black women shared a single cell on the first floor near the office and kitchen, while the sixteen men occupied several cells upstairs; Daniels shared a space with Stokely Carmichael and Chris Wylie. In the succeeding days, the men and women could communicate only by shouting or by persuading the black trusty in the jail to carry notes back and forth.[32]

The women included Ruby Sales, a Tuskegee student, and Gloria Larry, the SNCC worker from California who had helped Jon Daniels integrate the Episcopal church in Selma earlier in the summer. Two local women were also arrested in Fort Deposit. Geraldine Logan, who was active in civil rights at Alabama State University in Montgomery, worked with SNCC when she returned home to Gordonsville in the summer. The daughter of a college-educated schoolteacher and an independent farmer, she spent only one night in jail before her father obtained her release. The other woman was Joyce Bailey from Fort Deposit. Her father worked for the Louisville and Nashville Railroad, which passed through Fort Deposit; his job gave him a measure of independence that was unusual for blacks and allowed his daughter to join the civil rights movement with little fear of economic retaliation. Bailey was arrested on her nineteenth birthday.[33]

Ten of the male prisoners were also natives of Lowndes. A number of them, however, did not have the family support and economic security enjoyed by Logan and Bailey. Wilbur Jenkins's parents, for instance, agreed with the aims of the movement but wanted their son to stay out of trouble so their white landlord would not evict them. Willie Jenkins's father, a parttime police officer for the town of Fort Deposit, was also vulnerable to white pressure in his job. A few of the men, such as Joe Frank Bailey, came from families that owned their own homes and consequently faced fewer threats from whites. Others were on their own and could act without direct risk to their families.[34]

Before their incarceration in Hayneville, Jon Daniels and most of the others had never been in jail. After a few days they found conditions in the Lowndes facility deplorable. Crammed four or more to a cell, they had no privacy and little room to move about. Even more distressing, the jail lacked air conditioning or fans to shield them from the August heat and humidity. Each cell had a toilet and a lavatory, but the toilets were totally inadequate. When the commodes clogged, the jailers made no attempt to fix them; on several occasions, the toilets backed up and spilled sewage on the floor. The cells had no shower and the prisoners were not allowed to bathe elsewhere. Further, they could not wash in the lavatories because someone frequently turned off the water to the sinks. After a few days, the cells and their occupants, still wearing the clothes they had on when they were arrested, were miserably dirty.[35] The filth must have especially disconcerted the usually fastidious Daniels, who had become accustomed to order at the Virginia Military Institute.

The civil rights workers considered the food to be even worse than the physical conditions of the jail. Undoubtedly feeding such a large group presented great difficulties, and the sheriff and his deputies would not have gone to much trouble for the first civil rights protesters arrested in the county. Although Daniels and Morrisroe might have been expected to balk at a diet heavy in corn bread, pork and beans, fatback, greens, grits, and biscuits and gravy, the southerners objected too. Balogna sandwiches for breakfast pleased nobody, and the prisoners complained that the food was cold, poorly prepared, and even bug-infested.[36]

Family and friends in the county managed to keep in contact with the jailed demonstrators. Though somewhat relieved by news of their condition, well-wishers still worried about their safety. On Sunday afternoon, about fifty blacks met at Trickem and drove to Hayneville to check on their friends before attending a mass meeting nearby. Though none of them could get in, the prisoners knew they were outside. On Monday doctors with the Medical Committee for Human Rights visited the protesters and reported that their morale was high. In addition, the mothers of Geraldine Logan and Joyce Bailey cooked them food, which John Hulett and others took to the jail. They also received chewing gum and cigarettes. Someone brought several books — Richard Wright's *Native Son*, *The Life and Times of Frederick Douglass*, John J. Considine's *The Church in the New Latin America*, and *The Fanatic* by Meyer Levin. Most visitors were not permitted in the jail but stood outside and talked with the prisoners through the cell windows.[37]

On Wednesday morning, August 18, the prisoners had an important visitor. Bob Mants, a SNCC staffer in Lowndes, had obtained the release of Stokely Carmichael and Chris Wylie, who had been charged only with motor vehicle violations. By paying the premium of $120 to the Alabama Bonding Company of Montgomery, Mants posted bonds totaling $1,200. Carmichael and Wylie left the county jail with Mants that morning but were ordered to return to the Fort Deposit justice of the peace court on the following Saturday for a hearing. Their departure left Jon Daniels alone in a cell.[38]

The next day two representatives of the Episcopal Society for Cultural and Racial Unity arrived in Hayneville to check on Jon Daniels. Rev. Henri Stines, the dark-skinned associate director of ESCRU who had known Daniels in Selma, brought with him the Reverend Francis X. Walters, whom ESCRU had assigned to replace Daniels when he returned to seminary in the fall. Walters, a thirty-two-year-old white native of Mobile, had alienated Bishop Carpenter by his association with the civil rights movement. After a disagreement involving race relations at his first pastorate in Eufaula, the bishop had refused to allow Walters to move to another parish in his diocese, so Walters in 1959 accepted a position in Savannah, Georgia. Later he had served a church in Jersey City, New Jersey, before returning to Alabama in 1965.[39]

Stines met Walters in Selma. On the drive to Hayneville, they were stopped by the police and Stines was given a speeding ticket; they regarded the episode as just more harassment of outside agitators. The experienced priest always carried enough money to pay a traffic fine because he never wanted to be taken to a remote southern jail. When they reached Hayneville, a worker at the county jail refused to let Stines and Walters see the prisoners until the two ministers obtained permission from Sheriff Frank Ryals, who was not present. When they finally located him in the courthouse, Ryals showed great irritation that Stines, the apparently black priest (he was wearing a clerical collar), seemed to be in charge. Noticing a Free Mason ring on the sheriff's finger, Stines gave him a secret signal indicating that he too was a Mason. Suddenly, the sheriff became more cooperative and authorized their visit. The ESCRU representatives met with Daniels in his cell. They found the seminarian in good physical condition, even if somewhat unkempt, and in remarkably good spirits. Being locked in an isolated jail in bloody Lowndes appeared not to bother the seminarian; the inhumanity and cruelty experienced at VMI apparently had prepared him to deal with the jail's discomfort. In fact, he seemed exhilarated. Perhaps he did not comprehend the danger inherent in being held by unfriendly whites in bloody Lowndes and instead was thrilled by the opportunity to continue his Christian witness in jail in the thick of the civil rights movement. Stines and Walters worried that Daniels and the others were not safe because anyone who wanted to harm them could easily enter the jail. They left to call John Morris in Atlanta for bail money. Morris quickly telegraphed sufficient funds to bail out Daniels and Morrisroe. The seminarian, however, refused to be released until the demonstrators could go too. ESCRU lacked that much money, so Daniels and Morrisroe remained in jail.[40]

In the county facility, Daniels and the others spent a lot of time discussing their predicament, the civil rights movement, and the tactics of nonviolence. In considering the ineffectiveness of their aborted demonstration in Fort Deposit, some suggested that nonviolence had been a mistake and that the next time they should not hesitate to employ violent methods. When not talking among themselves, they frequently sang and prayed. Called "Reverend" by some of the blacks, Daniels led them in hymn singing and prayers, and he generally helped boost morale, which fluctuated from day to day. The prisoners also sang freedom songs — as loudly as they could. Luck and Joe Jackson, the sheriff's deputies who lived in the jail, repeatedly told them to be quiet because all the hubbub was annoying them. Knowing that their boisterous singing could be heard all over Hayneville gave them a lot of pleasure. Additional commotion came from the repeated banging of knotted trousers against the metal interior walls of the cells; the booming reverberated in the jail and out into the town.[41]

The racket coming from the jail at all hours disturbed the peace and quiet of Hayneville. With the jail just two blocks away, the noise easily reached the courthouse and the businesses on the square. More significant, at night the disturbances could be heard in many residences. Perhaps even more than the actual sounds, the noise bothered local whites because it constantly reminded them of the presence of the civil rights movement and the threat that it posed to their way of life. As a result of the commotion, tension increased in Hayneville.

Daniels and the other prisoners were, of course, helpless to do anything about their situation, but their friends were active in their behalf. For several days after the arrests, efforts concentrated on getting the leader, Stokely Carmichael, out of jail. Once Carmichael gained his freedom, attention turned to the demonstrators. Peter Hall, a black lawyer from Birmingham who frequently defended civil rights activists, wanted to have their cases moved from the justice of the peace court in Fort Deposit to federal court. Claiming that the defendants had been wrongly arrested in violation of their civil rights and that they could not receive equal protection of the laws in the state courts, he hoped to persuade U.S. District Judge Frank M. Johnson to hear their cases in Montgomery.[42]

On Friday morning, August 20, Peter Hall filed a petition in Montgomery to transfer the cases to federal court. A hearing to act on the request was scheduled for September 21. When Fort Deposit officials learned of the maneuver, they feared that the civil rights lawyer had taken a rather simple misdemeanor and was literally trying to make a federal case out of it. In reaction to the surprising legal development, Mayor O. P. Edwards called the town's attorney, William Hamilton, to ask for his advice. Concerned that the little town of Fort Deposit would be held in violation of federal civil rights laws if it continued to hold the demonstrators, Hamilton advised the mayor to release them without requiring any bonds. "I don't understand all of the act but I didn't want us to run afoul of it," declared Hamilton. To avoid legal complications, Mayor Edwards contacted the sheriff's office in Hayneville, but he could not reach Sheriff Ryals because he had gone to Montgomery for a doctor's appointment. The mayor then called the Hayneville jail and instructed the sheriff's deputies to release the demonstrators.[43]

I n the courthouse that Friday morning, Tom Coleman, a local employee of the state highway department, played his usual game of dominoes in the county clerk's office with his buddies. About noon, accompanied by a couple of friends, he drove around Hayneville to make sure everything was peaceful, then returned to the courthouse. Soon after the mayor called the sheriff's office, Coleman and the other people hanging around the building learned that the civil rights demonstrators were going to be turned out of jail that afternoon. Rumors that the freed protesters would cause a major disturbance in the small town put Tom Coleman and other whites on their guard.[44]

Around two in the afternoon, the sheriff's deputies opened the cells and told their prisoners that, after signing personal recognizance bonds, they were free to go. They were told to appear in the Fort Deposit court on September 11. While happy to be leaving jail, the activists expressed surprise at the sudden turn of events and asked who had paid their bond and why they were being released. The deputies had no explanation. Alarmed by the lack of information, they feared that they might be entering a trap. In spite of their apprehensions, Jon Daniels and his friends walked out of the county jail for the first time since their arrest six days earlier.[45]

Outside, in the heat of the August afternoon, the civil rights workers greeted each other warmly. They were excited to be reunited and chatted about their predicament. The men were especially relieved to see that the women were all right. They realized immediately, however, that Hayneville was not a friendly place for an integrated group of activists. Their lack of transportation to safety compounded their concerns; not only did they have no cars, but also no friends had been notified to meet them and they could not easily call for help because few blacks in the area had telephones. Considering the county jail the safest place in town, they milled about in the yard as they considered what to do. When deputy Luck Jackson came out about fifteen minutes later and said to "get the hell off county property," someone suggested that it was federal property. The deputy insisted that it was county property and told them to leave immediately. Reluctantly, they walked down the street toward the town square. Willie Vaughn and a few others then left the group to find a telephone and call for rides.[46]

Daniels, Morrisroe, and the remaining activists walked a more than a hundred yards down the road, past a cotton gin and a warehouse, to the intersection with state Highway 97. While they waited at the corner under a mimosa tree for Vaughn to return, one of the activists, Robert Bailey, left to buy a package of cigarettes and a box of matches at the Cash Store, about fifty yards away. A very small, one-story, wood-frame rural grocery with a beauty parlor in a back room, the Cash Store was one of the few places in Hayneville where blacks shopped freely. About ten minutes after Bailey returned, four others decided to go to the store for cold soft drinks. Unmindful, if not unaware, of the southern taboos involving interracial sexual relationships, and in any case more concerned with following the dictates of the gospel, the two white men — Jon Daniels and Richard Morrisroe — and two of the black women — Ruby Sales and Joyce Bailey — set off south along the highway away from the town square toward the Cash Store.[47]

Willie Vaughn failed to reach anyone on the telephone. As he walked back to rejoin the group, he passed by the reddish brown, weather-beaten store. Outside, Vaughn noticed a white man wearing a pistol and a shotgun nearby. The man was Tom Coleman. In response to a call to the sheriff's office about possible dangers posed by the released civil rights workers, Coleman had interrupted his dominoes game and driven to the Cash Store. He had known Virginia Varner, the owner, for a quarter century but had very seldom gone to the store. Reportedly fearing for Varner's safety, Coleman had parked his car, entered the store, and asked her if she had a "Closed" sign to put on the front door. When she said no, he had stayed in case she might need his protection.[48]

Calling to the four civil rights workers as they walked toward the store, Willie Vaughn tried to tell them of the man with the guns. Either they did not hear him or they ignored his warning, because they continued their stroll to the store. A Coca-Cola sign hung over the double front doors and Pepsi signs were on either side. Like in many little country stores, cigarette advertisements were displayed in the front windows and "Colonial is good bread" was emblazoned on the screen doors. Outside, to the right of the doors, a wooden bench sat on a concrete apron that went across the front of the store.[49]

When the two white men and two black women approached, Ruby Sales went first as Jon Daniels, wearing his seminarian's collar, reached to open the screen door for her. Richard Morrisroe and Joyce Bailey were several feet behind them. As Daniels opened the screen door, Tom Coleman suddenly appeared at the door with his shotgun. He shouted that the store was closed and ordered them "to get off this property, or I'll blow your goddamn heads off, you sons of bitches." In an instant, Daniels asked if he was threatening them and pushed Ruby Sales out of the way and to the ground as Coleman, standing only a few feet from Daniels, abruptly fired his twelve-gauge shotgun at the seminarian. At point-blank range, a load of buckshot tore a hole in the right side of Daniels's chest. He fell backward onto the concrete apron and died instantly.[50]

At the first shot, Morrisroe grabbed Joyce Bailey's hand and turned to flee. Coleman, however, lifted his shotgun and fired again. Buckshot struck the priest in the lower right back and side, and he fell to the ground. Sales then got up and ran with Bailey for cover. Coleman saw the other blacks standing on the corner in the distance and threatened to shoot them. He then left his shotgun at the store and drove off to the county courthouse.[51]

From the corner Willie Vaughn, Jimmy Rogers, and several other civil rights workers watched the shootings. As soon as Coleman left, they approached the motionless Daniels and heard Morrisroe asking for water. Before they could help either of their fallen friends, the sheriff's deputies and other whites hurried to the scene and the scared blacks ran for safety. Vaughn rushed to call the SNCC office in Selma, and someone there dispatched an ambulance to the store. Later the frightened group of civil rights workers in Hayneville obtained rides to Fort Deposit and Selma.[52]

Minutes after the shooting a dozen cars and many whites converged on the scene. When Deputy Joe Jackson saw that two white men had been shot, he sent Harvey Lancaster, the local Alcohol Beverage Control

(ABC) agent, to the courthouse to summon an ambulance from Fort Deposit, but someone there had already called. When he looked at Daniels, lying with his feet at the steps of the store and his head hanging over the edge of the concrete slab, Jackson easily determined that he was dead. Meanwhile, several men pulled Richard Morrisroe out of the hot summer sun into the shade of a nearby old seed barn used as a warehouse, where a local doctor assisted the priest.[53]

Dr. William L. Staggard, an elderly physician from Benton who worked in Hayneville two afternoons each week, was in his office in the county seat when notified of the emergency that afternoon. In great pain, Morrisroe told the doctor that his spine must have been injured because he could not move his legs. After quickly examining the priest to determine the extent of his injuries, Staggard gave him some medication to calm him and placed several pieces of gauze over the wounds on his right hip and side. When the priest asked for water, the doctor asked someone to bring him some. The doctor also verified that Daniels was dead.[54]

Within half an hour of the shootings, Jack Golson, the coroner for Lowndes, arrived from Fort Deposit in the county ambulance. With Harvey Lancaster's help, he lifted Morrisroe and Daniels's body into the ambulance and sped to Montgomery. They took the priest to the emergency room of Baptist Hospital on the southern edge of the city. As soon as doctors could X-ray Morrisroe's wounds and get him blood transfusions, they wheeled him into surgery. Two teams of surgeons operated on the priest for eleven hours, removing nine or ten large buckshot from his flank and back; he remained in critical condition for several days. After leaving the hospital, Golson and Lancaster took Daniels's body to White Chapel Funeral Home in Montgomery, where the director of Alabama's crime laboratory performed a postmortem examination early that evening.[55]

August 20 was Constance Daniels's birthday. To celebrate, she went out to dinner with a friend, Theresa Roberts, and then to Roberts's home for a game of bridge with two other women. About the time they started playing cards, Roberts's daughter called and told her mother she had heard that a Jon Daniels had been killed in Alabama, but she did not know if it was Keene's Jon Daniels. Only after several more calls from her daughter, who confirmed the reports with the local police, did Roberts tell Connie Daniels that her son was dead.[56]

Condemnations of Daniels's death came from across the nation and even from Alabama. The *Gadsden Times* called the shooting a "mad and damnable deed" and demanded "swift and unrelenting punishment." Comparing the situation in Lowndes County to that in Watts, the *Birmingham News* argued that "in neither set of circumstances do the fears and frustrations of people justify resort to violence." From the Alabama state capital, the *Advertiser-Journal* concluded, "A killing such as that in Hayneville is indefensible in the mind of anyone who truly subscribes to our moral law and our statutory law." But the Montgomery newspaper also pointed to "the folly and fanaticism of the provocation by priestly incendiaries."[57]

In the days after Daniels's death, the seminarian was honored at several memorial services and meetings. On the next Sunday the Reverend Malcolm Boyd spoke at a requiem mass in Washington's Church of the Atonement. The Episcopal chaplain and member of ESCRU said, "Jonathan Daniels was the most alive young man in the church I have met . . . he was one person who was not afraid of getting involved." Churches in St. Louis, Chicago, Atlanta, and Boston conducted memorial services for the slain activist. Also in Chicago, the Coordinating Council of Community Organizations held a rally in Grant Park and then marched to the new federal building as a memorial to Daniels and as a prayer vigil for Richard Morrisroe.[58]

At a mass meeting in Lowndes County that same night, Stokely Carmichael said, "We ain't going to shed a tear for John 'cause John is going to live in this county. . . . We ain't going to resurrect John, we're going to resurrect ourselves." Daniels's death made blacks in the Lowndes movement even more dedicated to change. "We're going to tear this county up. We're going to build it back, until it's a fit place for human beings," Carmichael exhorted the crowd of one hundred people. The blacks in Lowndes held a formal memorial service the following Tuesday evening at the First Baptist Church in Hayneville, but no similar service occurred in Selma's Episcopal parish.[59]

In the words of the Reverend T. Frank Mathews, "Episcopalians in Selma were shocked by the tragic slaying of Jonathan Daniels," and St. Paul's Episcopal Church offered special prayers for Daniels and his family at both Sunday services. When civil rights workers requested permission to hold a memorial service at St. Paul's, however, Mathews turned them down because "tensions were 'at the breaking point' in both the Negro and white communities of Selma." He suggested that "the atmosphere in Selma is still potentially explosive and any small 'spark' could set off a dangerous 'conflagration.' " In explaining his position, the rector denied any disrespect for Daniels, any disagreement with the civil rights movement, or any lack of grief over his death. The head of ESCRU quickly denounced Mathews's decision as "denying all that Jonathan Daniels gave his life for." The rector's stand received prompt endorsements from the church vestry; Roswell Falkenberry who edited the local paper; and Wilson Baker, the director of public safety in Selma.[60]

A memorial service for Jon Daniels was held in Selma the following week. On that occasion the Right Reverend Charles F. Hall, the Episcopal bishop of New Hampshire, led a delegation of prominent Episcopalians to the Cash Store in Hayneville, where the young seminarian had died exactly one week earlier. They also went to see Richard Morrisroe at Baptist Hospital in Montgomery. On Friday, August 27, Bishop Hall delivered a sermon at the memorial service at Selma's Brown Chapel AME Church, where an empty casket covered with white lilies and carnations had been placed at the front of the sanctuary. The service also included talks by the Reverend Henri Stines of ESCRU, Lillian McGill of the Lowndes County Christian Movement for Human Rights, and the Reverend John B. Coburn of the Episcopal Theological School. Nearly three hundred people, including many of Daniels's friends from Selma and Lowndes County, attended. Neither the rector of St. Paul's Episcopal Church nor any of its parishioners were present.[61]

The primary service for Jon Daniels, however, took place in his hometown on the Tuesday after the shooting. A major obstacle to the Keene observance was returning his remains to New Hampshire. The ordinarily simple task became difficult because of the circumstances surrounding Daniels's death. The Reverend John B. Morris of ESCRU had contacted various air service companies in the area about transporting the body back to Keene, but all refused the assignment because of the publicity. Finally, on Sunday, Morris enlisted the help of an Atlanta lawyer who had a small airplane, and his friend flew with Morris to Montgomery to pick up the body and then took it to Washington. From the nation's capital, Morris rented another plane for the trip to Boston; prevented by inclement weather from flying to Keene, Morris and Daniels's remains traveled in a hearse sent from Keene. They arrived shortly after midnight.[62]

Daniels's body lay in state at St. James Episcopal Church in Keene for most of Monday and on Tuesday morning before the one o'clock funeral. More than a thousand mourners filed past the casket. In just two hours on Tuesday morning, more than four hundred people paid their respects. Stokely Carmichael, Ruby Sales, Alice West, Jimmy Rogers, and Willie Vaughn traveled to Keene from Selma and Lowndes County, while Judith Upham and a number of other seminarians and faculty went from the Episcopal Theological School in Cambridge. John Morris, Malcolm Boyd, and Malcolm Peabody led a delegation from ESCRU. The Right Reverend Arthur Lichtenberger, the former presiding bishop who had offered the benediction before Daniels and his classmates left ETS to participate in the Selma-to-Montgomery march the previous spring, represented the presiding bishop.[63]

The Tuesday afternoon service included the reading of a message from President Lyndon B. Johnson to Constance Daniels. All the officiating clergy had known Jon Daniels well. The Reverend Chandler Mc-Carty, the rector of St. James, headed the procession of the casket and other participants into the church as he repeated, "I am the resurrection and the life, saith the Lord; he that believeth in me, though he were dead, yet shall he live: and whosoever liveth and believeth in me, shall never die." Following the Book of Common Prayer, the service proceeded along the standard Episcopal form. McCarty, the minister who had supported Jon Daniels's decision to enter the seminary, led the memorial service. The dean of ETS, the Reverend John B. Coburn, read from the Scriptures, including verses from Paul's letter to the Romans: "Who shall separate us from the love of Christ? shall tribulation, or distress, or persecution, or famine, or nakedness, or peril, or sword? Nay, in all these things we are more than conquerors through him that loved us."[64]

After reciting the Nicene Creed, Dean Coburn's colleague, Professor William J. Wolf, presented the main address at the one-and-a-half-hour service. Instead of offering a eulogy or even his own remarks, Wolf read a paper Daniels had prepared that summer for Wolf's course in theology. Daniels had sent "Theological Reflections on My Experience in Selma" to Wolf on June 22. In trying "to tell a story, to sing 'a song of myself,' " Daniels wrote of his decision to go to Selma, his participation in the demonstrations, and the integration of St. Paul's church:

> All of this is the raw material for living theology. And yet in as deep a sense, from my point of view, it is the *product* of living theology. The doctrines of the creeds, the enacted faith of the sacraments, were the essential preconditions of the experience itself. The faith with which I went to Selma has not *changed*: it has grown. Darkening coals have kindled. Faith has taken wing and flown with a song in its wings. "My soul doth magnify the Lord, and my spirit hath rejoiced in God my Savior. . . . "
>
> I lost fear in the black belt when I began to know in my bones and sinews that I had truly been baptized into the Lord's Death and Resurrection, that in the only sense that really matters I am already dead, and my life is hid with Christ in God. I began to lose self-righteousness when I discovered the extent to which my behavior was motivated by worldly desires and by the self-seeking messianism of Yankee deliverance! The point is simply, of course, that one's motives are usually mixed — and one had better know it. It occurred to me that though I was reasonably certain that I was in Selma because the Holy Spirit had sent me there, there nevertheless remained a fundamental distinction between my will and His.

"... And *Holy* is His Name." I was reminded by the Eucharist, by the daily offices, by the words of confession, by the healing judgment of the Spirit, that I am called *first* to holiness. Every impulse, every motive, every will under heaven must attend to that if it is to be healthy and free within the ambiguities and tilted structures of a truly fallen Creation. . . . Of the ubiquitous Kingship of the eternal Word, through Whom all things were made, I found very real if ambiguous confirmation in that beloved community who ate and slept and cursed and prayed in the rain-soaked streets of the Negro "compound" that first week in Selma.[65]

Eight hundred people at the funeral more than filled the church; many sat in the parish hall and stood outside. They listened as Professor Wolf concluded his reading from Daniels's paper:

Another kind of organicity has dawned upon me more gradually. As Judy and I said the daily offices day by day, we became more and more aware of the living reality of the invisible "communion of saints" — of the beloved community in Cambridge who were saying the offices, too, and sending us carbon copies of their notes (and a thousand other things as well!), of the ones gathered around a near-distant throne in Heaven — who blend with their our faltering songs of prayer and praise. With them, with black men and white men, with all of life, in Him Whose Name is above all the names the races and nations shout, whose Name is Itself the Song Which fulfills and "ends" all songs, we are indelibly, unspeakably *one*.[66]

After prayers and confessions, the Right Reverend Charles F. Hall, who had sponsored Daniels at ETS, celebrated Holy Communion, which only family members received. The church service closed with prayers and two hymns, after which many of the mourners then accompanied the casket to a nearby cemetery for the committal service. At the graveside, McCarty and Dean Coburn read prayers. Jon Daniels was buried next to his father. At the conclusion of the service, as people drifted away, a small group of whites and blacks gathered around the grave. Joining hands, a tearful Stokely Carmichael and others softly sang "We Shall Overcome."[67]

PREPARING FOR TRIAL: FRIENDS MEET IN HAYNEVILLE

7

Leaving Jon Daniels and Richard Morrisroe lying in front of the Cash Store, Tom Coleman drove his black and white Chevrolet the block and a half back to the Lowndes County Courthouse. For Coleman, the courthouse was a friendly, comfortable place where he could feel safe. Law enforcement officials did not intimidate or worry him; his father had served as sheriff in the 1910s, and Tom had always been on good terms with succeeding sheriffs and their deputies. Nearly every day he played dominoes with friends in the courthouse, just as his father had for decades before him. In addition, Coleman's father had had an office in the courthouse when he was county superintendent of schools, and Tom's sister held the same position in 1965. At the courthouse, therefore, Coleman knew that he would be among people he had known and trusted all his life.

Coleman was a native of Lowndes County and in many ways a product of its rural, poor, isolated, segregated, and violent culture. Like others growing up in Lowndes, particularly whites, he absorbed its customs without questioning them because he had had little contact with other ways of living by which to judge his community. White supremacy, for example, must have seemed natural to whites who condoned the use of violence as necessary to control the black population. Manifested in a lack of libraries and other amenities, the county's poverty and backwardness similarly would not have appeared unusual. Tom Coleman in many ways typified the whites of Lowndes in his unsophistication, his acceptance of racial segregation and discrimination, and his acquiescence in the county's stagnant economy and social life.

Coleman's ancestors arrived in Alabama in the mid-nineteenth century and settled in the Black Belt. His paternal great grandparents lived south of Lowndes in the Manningham community of adjacent Butler County. His grandfather, Thomas Livingston Coleman, was born in 1847 and married Mary Ray of Mount Willing. He farmed near Mount Willing, in the south-central part of Lowndes County about twelve miles from Hayneville. Their first child and Tom's father, Jesse Albert, was born in Mount Willing in 1872. Jesse attended county schools and then took a five-and-a-half-month business course at Howard College. At age twenty-one he went into the mercantile business in Mount Willing. In 1898 he married twenty-year-old Mary Hinson, from the same town, and soon after he left business and started farming. Jesse and Mary Coleman had eight children.[1]

Jesse Coleman was active in the civic life of his rural community. In addition to serving as an officer in the Masons and as a deacon in his Baptist church, he was, as he put it, "an organized Democrat without any prefixes or suffixes." After one unsuccessful campaign for state representative, Coleman won election in 1907 and served one term. Later he moved to Hayneville and was the county sheriff for six years. Though apparently not as brutal as some sheriffs of bloody Lowndes, Jesse Coleman did not oppose the racial status quo. In 1914, for instance, he was the sheriff who failed to arrest a local mob for seizing Will Jones from the authorities and lynching him in broad daylight; when pressed by the governor, Sheriff Coleman refused to provide any details about the crime.[2] Though a small boy at the time, Tom Coleman no doubt absorbed the values behind his father's failure to cooperate in bringing the lynchers to justice.

In 1918 white voters elected Jesse Coleman superintendent of the county schools, a post he continued to hold until his retirement in 1939.[3] As superintendent Coleman, like his counterparts throughout the state, operated a thoroughly segregated and discriminatory school system in Lowndes County. He thus achieved prominence in the county even though he did not own a large plantation, employ many tenants, or have professional skills. With his steady but modest income as superintendent, Jesse Coleman was better off than most whites in Lowndes. He owned his own home, enjoyed political influence in the county, and had a healthy family.

His sixth child and third son, Tom Lemuel Coleman, was born on November 26, 1910, in the family home in Hayneville. Named for his grandfathers — Thomas Coleman and Joseph Lemuel Hinson — Tom grew up in the family's one-story frame house, located a block from the courthouse and the town square. By contemporary standards the Coleman home was comfortable even though, throughout Tom's childhood, it lacked indoor plumbing and electricity; only the homes of a few wealthy people in Hayneville had plumbing and a motorized pump to draw water. The Colemans cooked on a wood stove in the kitchen, heated with a coal stove, read by kerosene lamps, and drew water from a well. Ice for their icebox came from a local ice plant or from Montgomery.[4]

Like most other whites, the Colemans could easily afford to pay blacks the minimal wage necessary to have them do many tasks around the house; however, they did not own enough property to make use of tenants and just hired blacks. For example, they always had a black cook to prepare all the meals and a black nurse to care for the young children. Other help did washing, carried water, and tended the family's buggy. Although Jesse kept cows, hogs, and mules behind the house, young Tom did not feed the animals and never learned to milk cows or work with mules — hired blacks did all the labor. Tom also did not help much with his father's garden, which always included a few watermelons, corn to feed the stock, and some years a little cotton. Once as punishment, Jesse Coleman ordered him to go plow with the mules, but Tom did not know how to handle a plow. He could work only about twenty feet before he quit in frustration and told his father to get someone else to plow.[5]

As a child, Tom devoted his time to play. When he was small his playmates included white and black children. They went fishing and swimming and played ball, with the black children chasing the balls for the whites. Approaching adolescence, black and white children in Hayneville stopped playing together, but Tom Coleman continued to have fun. When he was old enough to handle a shotgun, he started hunting quail, turkeys, and doves, along with ordinary birds and squirrels. He had his own horse and rode it out into the country to hunt and fish. More quiet entertainment came when court was in session, because he often walked to the courthouse to watch the proceedings. He also enjoyed dances in the courthouse, where there was frequently an orchestra, good food, and bootleg whiskey during Prohibition.[6] From an early age, therefore, Coleman was indoctrinated in the rural culture's intricate race relations, guns and hunting, and hard drinking. Segregation, shotguns, and whiskey came naturally to him.

Despite his father's position as school superintendent, Tom Coleman was never a good student and he received a limited education. Math was his favorite subject, but he really did not like any of his studies; with barely passing grades, he managed to finish high school in 1928. Most of his activities at school did not involve academics and often got him into trouble. One time, for example, he managed to lock the classroom door after the teacher arrived, and he then put red pepper on the stove that heated the room. While everyone sneezed, Tom threw the door key out the window. The teacher and class could not leave the room until the janitor came and unlocked the door.[7]

On another occasion Coleman bolted from his high school class when he heard gunfire from the courthouse. Precipitated by the castration of a bull, a feud between two Lowndes white families had resulted in the shooting deaths of two men. During the trial of the second assailant, when the accused encountered a relative of his victim in the courthouse, another shootout occurred. On hearing the gunfire, young Tom Coleman suspected what had happened; running the short block to the courthouse, he arrived just in time to see the latest victim lying dead on a table in the clerk of court's office. His father's post did not prevent teachers and principals from punishing him for such conduct, and he often received whippings. Because of his mischief, teachers often blamed Tom for things he did not do.[8]

Coleman also participated in sports. The Hayneville school, which did not have a gymnasium in the 1920s, fielded baseball and football teams. The practice and playing fields at the school were less than a block from Coleman's house. Though interested in football, Tom, who weighed only one hundred and twenty-five pounds in high school, was too small to compete. Baseball was his sport, and he played catcher on the local team. Even more than athletics, however, hunting and fishing remained his favorite activities.[9]

With no preparation for or interest in college, Coleman had to find a job when he finished high school. Unlike many of their white acquaintances, the Colemans had no land for Tom to farm or supervise. Except for a few trips to Montgomery by buggy and then by automobile after his father got a car in 1925, his world had been limited to Hayneville and the surrounding countryside. He had never worked on a farm or even had a summer job, and as a high school graduate he had no clear idea of what he wanted to do for a living. Coleman decided to move to Montgomery, where he lived with an older sister and worked with his brother for the Louisville and Nashville Railroad. His job was to help service the trains in the rail yards by making sure that the engines had sufficient water and grease. Later he was employed by a sporting goods store before returning to Hayneville in the early 1930s.[10]

In 1933, in the depths of the depression, Jesse Coleman helped his son secure a job with the state highway department. Tom's initial assignments were in the northern Alabama towns of Decatur and Gurley, where as a rodman he assisted engineers and surveyors by clearing bushes and trees for survey parties, by holding a rod for surveying, by driving stakes in the ground for grading, and by helping to measure roadways for some of the state's first highways paved with asphalt.[11]

In 1937 Coleman married eighteen-year-old Coralie Caruthers, the daughter of a Presbyterian minister who was superintendent of the public schools in Marion, Alabama, and a former president of the Marion Female Seminary. Her father had known Jesse Coleman professionally, but the children of the two superintendents met through mutual friends when Tom visited Marion. When they married, Coralie Coleman, a devout Presbyterian, volunteered to join Tom's Baptist church, but instead he switched to her denomination. She was always much more active in the church than her husband, who attended services irregularly. In the late 1930s Coleman brought his wife to the Black Belt and began working on the construction of Highway 80 between Montgomery and Selma. Their first child, Tom, Jr., was born in 1939 in Montgomery, and a daughter Hulda arrived two years later.[12]

Coleman's return to Hayneville coincided with his father's final illness. Because of poor health, Jesse resigned in 1939 after twenty-one years as superintendent of the Lowndes County school system. The board of education named his twenty-five-year-old unmarried daughter, Hulda, to succeed him. A graduate of Huntingdon College in Montgomery, Hulda had worked in her father's office before he retired. She was elected to a full term as superintendent in 1940 and thereafter won reelection every four years until her own retirement in 1975.[13]

Tom and Coralie Coleman rented an apartment in a large house just west of the town square. His sister Hulda, their mother who lived with Hulda, and another sister, Mattie Haigler, also lived in the small town. In 1950 Tom and Coralie moved into their permanent home on the northeastern edge of town less than half a mile from the courthouse. Tom Coleman knew everyone in town and most of the whites and many blacks in the county. One of Hayneville's main gathering spots for white men was the clerk's office in the courthouse, where for generations men had met to play dominoes every day after lunch and at least once a week in the evening. The participants drew for partners, with the winners playing the challengers who had been watching. The rather tame but serious entertainment included no drinking and involved only modest bets — in later years, up to fifty cents a game. During and between games there was plenty of gossiping, joking, and storytelling.[14]

As an adult, Tom Coleman continued to enjoy fishing and hunting. Occasionally he went deep-sea fishing in the Gulf of Mexico, but mostly he frequented the nearby ponds. His wife and son also enjoyed the sport, and the family often fished from their boat equipped with a small electric motor. Tom, however, enjoyed hunting the most. Owning a number of guns, he knew how to handle pistols, rifles, and shotguns. He particularly liked hunting deer and, with his dogs, doves and quail. For safety he never hunted with people who drank in the fields, though sometimes they had a nip while waiting for doves to fly over. On hunting trips, he drank with his buddies in the evening at their camps.[15]

Drinking liquor was, in fact, one of Coleman's favorite pastimes. Though he consumed corn whiskey when liquor was unavailable in the county, he preferred good liquor. In the fifties and sixties, he drank often and a lot — at home, at friends' homes, at Carl Golson's car dealership in Fort Deposit on the way home, at a café in Hayneville, and anywhere else he could get a drink. He took Jack Daniels straight followed by a chaser, but he favored Old Forrester's bourbon. He did not especially like the taste of liquor but enjoyed how it made him feel; drinking helped him relax from the pressures of dealing with people on the job and overcome his tiredness at the end of the day. At his worst, one quart would not last him two days. Though Coleman frequently drove while drunk, the police never caught him. Nevertheless, in the community he was well known as a hard-drinking man.[16]

Living in Hayneville and working most of the time out of an office in Greenville, Coleman in the 1940s and 1950s gradually moved up the ranks in the state highway department. With two children to support and a friendly draft board, World War II did not interrupt his work. Trained on the job, he moved from rodman to inspector to project engineer and finally to resident engineer. As an inspector, Coleman ensured that contractors built roads and bridges properly by inspecting their work as it progressed. Project engineers supervised an entire project, which included roads, bridges, and culverts. In that post, for example, he directed the construction of state roads from Hayneville to Lowndesboro and from Hayneville to Letohatchie. Coleman's last position as resident engineer gave him responsibility for all road construction and maintenance in his district, which at times included Lowndes and neighboring Butler counties. From his headquarters in Greenville, Coleman regularly drove the roads in his district; he often arranged his schedule so he could stop by the Hayneville courthouse for a game of dominoes and conversation.[17]

As resident engineer, Coleman supervised work crews doing everything from repairing roads to cutting the grass on the rights of way. Numbering about forty-five, his employees were all white, but he also used chained gangs of convict labor from a state highway department prison camp in Greenville. The labor camp customarily had at least sixty prisoners, most of whom were black. To control the convicts working for him, Coleman always carried a pistol and he frequently had a shotgun in his car.[18]

On the evening of August 21, 1959, the guards at the Greenville camp called Coleman and told him about trouble with one of the prisoners. Coleman hurried to the camp. When he arrived, he found Richard Lee Jones, a twenty-seven-year-old illiterate black man, in the recreation hall. Jones had refused to cooperate with the guards and to leave the recreation area. Carrying a shotgun, Coleman entered the hall with two of the guards and tried to persuade Jones to leave peacefully. Jones, who was serving a twenty-year term for robbery and grand larceny, told Coleman that a shotgun did not scare him. Armed with a broken drink bottle in each hand and a guard's nightstick, the convict took a few steps toward Coleman. When he kept advancing, Coleman fired one shot and killed Jones. An investigation that was completed before Jones's body was taken to a funeral home accepted Coleman's claim of self-defense and cleared him of any wrongdoing.[19]

As a result of Coleman's responsibility for state convicts, he got to know many of the law enforcement officials who helped when convicts escaped. In Lowndes County, of course, he knew the sheriff and his deputies well; he also became acquainted with police officers and sheriffs in the surrounding counties and towns. Coleman liked them, respected them, and enjoyed working with them. He spent considerable time in and around the sheriff's office in the Lowndes courthouse and occasionally assisted him. In 1961 his own son became a state trooper. Coleman's friends also included Sheriff Jim Clark of Dallas County and Colonel Al Lingo, Alabama's public safety commissioner and head of the state highway patrol, both of whom became notorious for their opposition to the civil rights movement. Observing from Hayneville, Coleman approved the way they protected southern customs and the methods they used to handle the civil rights disturbances.[20]

When the civil rights movement came to Lowndes County, Tom Coleman responded with implacable opposition. Early in the summer of 1965, for example, when two reporters visited the courthouse, Coleman got up from his dominoes game to chat with them about the history of the county and to show them proudly around the old building. He may have warmed to the reporters for New York and Chicago newspapers because one of them, Roy Reed of the *New York Times*, was clearly a native southerner. When their discussion turned to race relations and the civil rights movement, however, his mood abruptly shifted as he employed the usual rhetoric of white segregationist resistance.[21]

Coleman especially objected to outsiders, including the federal government, who, he said, came to stir up what he thought was an otherwise peaceful and happy relationship between the races. Though Coleman denied ever belonging to the Ku Klux Klan, the Student Nonviolent Coordinating Committee early in the summer regarded him as "a known Klansman," which indicated that SNCC considered him to be a serious opponent of the civil rights movement. Coleman did acknowledge belonging to the White Citizens' Council. Particularly powerful in the Black Belt, the Citizens' Council rejected any equality between blacks and whites and fought to preserve states' rights and white supremacy. Coleman subscribed to the precepts of the Citizens' Council, knew many of the state leaders, including Sam Englehardt of the central Alabama group, and often went to Council meetings in the Hayneville courthouse.[22]

Tom Coleman may have felt the challenge of the civil rights movement even more keenly than other whites in Lowndes. He did not own a large tract of land and had no great wealth, so he could not easily sell his property or become an absentee landlord; his job and his home were right there in the county. Even more important, the arrival of blacks at the ballot box would imperil his sister's job as superintendent of schools, a position that had been held by Colemans for decades and was the source of the family's respect and influence. He could not tolerate any threat to the established order in Lowndes County. Coleman, moreover, may have needed to prove his importance to himself, his family, and his community. After all, his son had become a successful state trooper in Montgomery, his daughter had gone to college and married a popular football coach, and one of his sisters had an important job in Hayneville. In his middle fifties, Coleman may have felt a need to accomplish something noteworthy before his career ended and he reached old age. He saw his world threatened by the civil rights movement and recognized that in an integrated society he would be far from the top. Strong action in defense of his white community would have been in the best interests of himself and his family, would have solidified his status by thrusting him into a position of leadership, and would have brought him considerable attention beyond Hayneville.

Late in June, Coleman received encouragement for his unyielding stance in an ominous warning from his friend Sheriff Jim Clark. After the demonstrations in Selma, Clark urged Coleman and many other whites to defend their communities against the civil rights movement. He wrote:

> [This is] about an assassination. This is about a murder. You might say it is a lynching. It is about the assassination of a peaceful town, Selma, Alabama. . . .
>
> [Y]ou think your town is safe from this type of persecution. You think there will never be a situation where an all-powerful central government can turn its terrible vindictive fury, persecution, criminals, and propaganda on your comparatively peaceful town.
>
> A similar situation may be blowing its breath of destruction down your back right now. . . . God help you if these bunch of race baiters and criminals, with the blessing of the federal government, descend upon you, your family, your block, your city. It will be an experience that you can never erase from your mind.[23]

Clark's warning helped prepare Coleman for the arrival of federal voting registrars in August after the enactment of the Voting Rights Act. Perhaps wary of federal power, Coleman did not challenge the registrars. When the Alabama attorney general arrived in Hayneville to check on the registrars, he went to the post office on the town square to ask their whereabouts. Tom Coleman, who happened to be at the post office, did not hesitate to accost Attorney General Flowers, who was well known for his friendliness toward the civil rights movement. "Ain't nobody down here gonna tell you anything, Richmond. . . . Ain't none of these folks down here gonna tell you a damn thing," he said. Angry and agitated, Coleman told the attorney general to "get off the Ku Klux Klan and get on these outfits down here trying to get these niggers registered." He then threatened, "If you don't get off this Klan investigation, we'll get you off."[24]

Coleman's encounter with Flowers surprised few because, according to one observer, he was known for his hot temper and for being "maddened by the prospect of Negroes voting in Lowndes County." Coleman detested outside agitators, especially white members of the clergy who challenged white solidarity and tried to put the imprint of Christianity on the movement for black rights. Undoubtedly the presence of two white churchmen and black civil rights protesters in the Hayneville jail provoked Coleman for many reasons. Living just two blocks from the jail, Hulda Coleman and Mattie Haigler could not escape the commotion caused by the prisoners, and they had trouble sleeping because of the singing and banging on the walls. Already concerned with the imminent desegregation of the county schools, Hulda Coleman especially found the clamor nerve-racking. Tom Coleman, like other whites, resented the raucous intrusion into his tranquil little community; he was especially angered that it bothered his sisters.[25]

When about noon on August 20, Coleman sensed a disturbance brewing in Hayneville, he acted to maintain law and order as he saw it, to resist the threat posed by unruly civil rights activists, to protect defenseless white women, and to challenge fraudulent clergy causing trouble in Lowndes. Quick-tempered and accustomed to taking action, even with a gun when necessary, Coleman drove to the Cash Store and shot Jon Daniels and Richard Morrisroe.

Armed violence was not uncommon in Lowndes, even in the post–World War II era, and whites frequently took the law into their own hands. In one well-known incident, a white man in a Hayneville barbershop took exception to another man's profanity in the presence of his young daughter. The offended man announced that he intended to settle the matter after he went home to get his gun. Shortly thereafter, the two men confronted one another in a downtown street and engaged in an old-fashioned shoot-out. Both men died. Though he did not actually witness the shootings, Coleman hustled to town and saw both men in the doctor's office before they died.[26] In such a violent context, Coleman's actions on August 20, 1965, must have seemed to him appropriate and not extraordinary.

When Coleman returned to the courthouse, he went directly to the sheriff's office and called his son, a state highway patrolman in Montgomery, and Al Lingo, the public safety director, to tell them what had happened and ask them to come to Hayneville. He also telephoned his wife. Lingo called his driver and bodyguard, Tom Coleman, Jr. The younger Coleman contacted Robert Black, Tom's nephew and a Montgomery attorney, and asked him to find a lawyer and go to the courthouse in Hayneville where his father was awaiting arrest. Later in the afternoon Captain E. J. Dixon, an investigator from the Alabama Department of Public Safety, arrived and questioned Coleman. Dixon had once been stationed in Lowndes County and had known Coleman for more than a dozen years. Coleman admitted to Dixon that he had shot the two white civil rights workers but did not sign a formal confession. He then waited in the courthouse for the authorities to arrest him and for the arrival of help from Montgomery.[27]

By late Friday afternoon, the courthouse in Hayneville buzzed with activity. Blacks were noticeably absent from town, but dozens of white residents gathered quietly in small groups outside the courthouse. Other, happier whites arrived in Hayneville that evening for the Second Annual

Lowndes County Quarterhorse Show, only to find a tense community. At her husband's suggestion, Coralie Coleman went to his sister Hulda's home to be with his mother — Hulda had gone to Montgomery. The elderly Mrs. Coleman, whose cataracts prevented her from reading the daily newspaper, liked to listen to the evening news on television, but that day her daughter-in-law read the afternoon newspaper to her so she would not hear the disturbing news. Meanwhile, newsmen began arriving in Hayneville to cover the developing story.[28]

Three lawyers came from Montgomery to advise Coleman. Al Lingo also arrived from the capital, and Sheriff Clark drove over from Selma. Additional state investigators were in Hayneville to help gather evidence. Sheriff Ryals, who returned late in the evening, told newsmen that, in response to a call to the sheriff's office about a disturbance at the grocery store, Coleman had acted as a special deputy sheriff. For the most part, however, officials remained silent about the facts in the case. When one reporter asked a question, Al Lingo barked, "It's none of your damned business."[29]

By Friday evening agents of the Federal Bureau of Investigation had joined the inquiry. The Mobile office had learned about the shootings by 4:30 that afternoon and had immediately contacted FBI headquarters in Washington. At the request of the Civil Rights Division of the Justice Department, the FBI gave the case "continuous and preferred investigative attention" to determine whether federal civil rights laws had been violated in the attack on Jon Daniels and Richard Morrisroe. If Coleman had acted in an official capacity as a special deputy sheriff, his actions may have violated federal law. Agents from Mobile attempted to interview Coleman and to locate witnesses to the shootings. But Coleman's lawyer refused to permit the FBI to talk with his client, and the Student Nonviolent Coordinating Committee kept their workers incommunicado and asked for FBI protection.[30]

About midnight on Friday evening, after five hours of deliberation, Carlton L. Perdue, the Lowndes County solicitor, decided to charge Tom Coleman with first-degree murder. Sheriff Ryals swore out the arrest warrant and Coleman was immediately taken into custody. Perdue told the press that Coleman was being held without bond until an arraignment, when bond might be set, but otherwise he refused to discuss the case. "We're not going to pre-try this man," the solicitor explained. "We got our stomach full of that when the President tried to pre-try those other men" — a reference to the Klansmen charged with killing Viola Liuzzo earlier in the year. Nonetheless, Perdue observed that if Daniels and Morrisroe "had been tending to their own business like I tend to mine, they'd be living and enjoying themselves today."[31]

Attorney General Richmond Flowers took a very different approach to the case. On Friday evening he dispatched his assistant, Joe Breck Gantt, and several investigators to Lowndes County. From the state capital, Flowers charged that the killing of Daniels was "another Ku Klux Klan murder." "Everything points to another Klan killing as the accused is strongly believed to be a Ku Klux Klan member," Flowers said. A bitter foe of Al Lingo, Flowers accused the public safety commissioner of trying to whitewash the case and of having driven to Hayneville with a known Klansmen. From Hayneville, Lingo countered that state investigators would not give the attorney general's office any information "until I'm ready." He did, however, promise to provide information to the local prosecutor.[32]

At eleven o'clock on Saturday morning, after spending eleven hours in the county jail, Tom Coleman was arraigned before J. B. Julian, the local justice of the peace. In proceedings that lasted only fifteen minutes, Coleman was charged with first-degree murder (that he "unlawfully and with malice aforethought killed Jonathan M. Daniels by shooting with a gun") and with assault with intent to murder the Reverend Richard Morrisroe. Julian set bond at $10,000 for the murder and $2,300 for the assault. Coleman's chief lawyer, Vaughan Hill Robison of Montgomery, objected that the bonds were excessive; nevertheless, William Haigler, Coleman's brother-in-law who operated a garage, immediately posted the bonds that allowed Coleman to leave police custody. The accused then hurried from the courthouse to a waiting car driven by his son. Speaking to reporters at the courthouse, Robison declared, "We have no statement for news media at this time. We are confident that if this case is tried by legal process, Mr. Coleman will be acquitted and exonerated. We do not propose to try this case in the newspapers, but in the courts." The attorney refused to let FBI agents interview his client; he and Coleman would wait for the scheduled meeting of the county grand jury on September 13.[33]

Although reluctant to speak in public, white people in Lowndes County supported Tom Coleman. Ones who knew Coleman spoke well of him. A deputy sheriff said that he was "respected in the community . . . a friendly person" who "laughs and jokes a lot." Others called the accused murderer "mild mannered," "even tempered, calm, and not easily upset," and a "hell of a nice guy." The county solicitor, Carlton Perdue, conceded, however, that Coleman was "like the rest of us. He's strong in his feelings." According to Sheriff Ryals, local whites were upset by the killing — "They hate it mighty bad" — in part because everybody knew Coleman and he was "from one of our oldest and best families." They also resented the fact that their community would once more be in the national spotlight, as it had been after the Viola Liuzzo murder and during the subsequent trial in May. With Tom Coleman, however, the situation was markedly different. As one service station operator pointed out, the trial of a man accused of killing Liuzzo "was a show, but this involves one of us."[34]

In Hayneville, whites rallied to defend their friend and neighbor. In the courthouse the day after the shooting, one deputy sheriff agreed with the shooting. Referring to Father Morrisroe, he said, "I hope the son of a bitch dies. That'll give us two of them instead of just one." Other whites, who may not have endorsed Coleman's actions, nevertheless understood them. They too opposed advances by the civil rights forces and had been particularly upset by the commotion caused by the demonstrators during their week in jail. One Hayneville man observed, "This [violent retaliation by whites] has been expected for a good while. If they continue this thing it will happen again — maybe not here, but somewhere." Another prominent white resident declared, "Fever is at a high pitch" because whites felt "pushed in a corner and stepped on. I think it is a strong resentment of those outside people, combined with a lot of frustration over the encroachments of the federal government." A fellow townsman added, "I know the white people are really worked up. I haven't seen any sign of anyone backing off since the shooting."[35]

White resistance to the civil rights movement continued because the activists in Lowndes County did not retreat. In the weeks before Coleman's indictment and trial, however, no organized protests occurred, and as a result the FBI stopped monitoring the racial situation in the county. In fact, however, the challenges to white dominance mounted and the tensions between whites and blacks escalated. During the night between Coleman's arrest and arraignment, someone burned a cross into the grass of the town square across from the front door to the courthouse. In spite of the intimidation, Lowndes blacks persisted in their efforts to register to vote. Though seventy-one blacks had registered on the day Jon Daniels died, in succeeding days the numbers declined until in September, an average of only twenty people registered each day. The fewer applicants allowed the federal registrars to cut back their hours to Saturdays only. The diminished numbers still alarmed many Lowndes whites, who opposed any black suffrage and realized small increases could soon add up to a majority for blacks. By the middle of September, the federal registrars had accepted 1,328 black voters in the county whereas local officials had registered none; potential white voters totaled only 1,900. With the assistance of the federal registrars, Lowndes County blacks indeed seemed on the verge of becoming an electoral majority. For the first time black political power would threaten white dominance. As one Alabama journalist reported, "In Lowndes County, a Negro trying to vote is equated as an insurrectionist with the Los Angeles Negro who is looting and setting fires."[36]

With county and state elections still a year off, Lowndes blacks posed no immediate threat to white control of local government. In the fall of 1965, white dominance of the local Agricultural Stabilization and Conservation Service committees would face challenges from blacks, who constituted nearly two-thirds of the farm operators eligible to vote. After the slaying of Jon Daniels, SNCC workers continued to encourage blacks to participate in the ASCS elections by nominating blacks and then voting for them in the mail balloting.[37]

A more imminent worry for Lowndes County whites appeared in black attempts to integrate the public school in Hayneville, and blacks did not back off after Tom Coleman's attack on the two civil rights workers. Under the county's "freedom of choice" plan, five black students had been accepted to Hayneville School for the fall term. Ten days after Jon Daniels died, the Hayneville School opened its doors to black students for the first time. The sheriff's deputies and a corps of armed volunteer deputies (including four blacks) guarded the entrance to the school, and four FBI agents observed the scene. In the tense atmosphere, a small crowd of whites gathered on the square in front of the courthouse to watch blacks enter the school less than a block away. Like blacks desegregating schools elsewhere for the first time, the black students had conferred with the superintendent, Hulda Coleman, and decided not to appear at the Hayneville School on the first day. Although Superintendent Coleman was not surprised, the absence of the blacks students puzzled most observers.[38]

The next day four black students did go to Hayneville School without incident. Under the watchful eyes of the sheriff's deputies, several newsmen, and a few local whites, one student rode on the school bus with whites while the others arrived in a car. Arthalise Hulett, the fifteen-year-old son of civil rights activist John Hulett, entered the tenth grade at the Hayneville School. "No one spoke to me the whole day," he reported. When the black students walked down the halls, the white students gasped and jumped aside or just turned their heads the other way. Unaware of the law, the white students segregated the blacks at every opportunity. "They asked us to sit by ourselves at lunch," Hulett said, "and they asked me to sit at the back of the bus on the way home." Whatever their treatment by whites, the black students had finally desegregated the county school system and breached a major white stronghold.[39]

Unhappy with the desegregation of their schools, whites could only fear for the future. Plans for a segregated private school in Lowndes

County depended on the level of white concern. "We just don't know how many parents are interested," commented Ray D. Bass, president of the school foundation, "because we are all waiting to see how extensive integration of the public schools will be." A survey revealed considerable support but no demands for immediate action, so preparations continued to start a white school the next year. The segregationists received little help from the county school superintendent. As Hulda Coleman put it, "They have their little red wagon to pull, and I have mine." By the fall of 1966, whites had organized Lowndes Academy in Lowndesboro and most white students had deserted the public schools.[40]

As the civil rights movement made whites more apprehensive, three cases related to the slaying of Jon Daniels made their way through the courts. First, *McMeans v. Mayor's Court, Fort Deposit, Alabama*, challenged the original arrests of the civil rights demonstrators in Fort Deposit. Second, *White v. Crook* attempted to stop all jury trials in the Black Belt county because women and blacks were systematically excluded from serving on juries. And third, *State of Alabama v. Tom L. Coleman* brought Daniels's killer to trial. In addition, federal officials considered bringing federal charges against Coleman.

Filed in U.S. district court in Montgomery the morning before Daniels died, *McMeans* sought to have the case against the seminarian and the other demonstrators transferred from the Fort Deposit court to federal court. Representing the demonstrators, including John McMeans, a twenty-two-year-old Lowndes black, Peter Hall argued that the defendants could not get a fair trial in Fort Deposit. Although the case could have no effect on Tom Coleman, it could establish whether Daniels and the others had been treated properly in Fort Deposit. At a hearing held by Judge Frank M. Johnson, Jr., in the state capital on the morning of September 21, the representatives of Fort Deposit did not object to having the case removed from their jurisdiction. Johnson, therefore, accepted the case and proceeded to prepare his decision.[41]

The case of *White v. Crook* had more relevance to the prosecution of Tom Coleman. Five days after Coleman killed Daniels, Charles Morgan, representing five Lowndes blacks, filed a suit against the county jury commission. Morgan, a white native of Birmingham who directed the activities of the American Civil Liberties Union (ACLU) in the South, had for three years wanted to challenge the exclusion of blacks from southern juries. "There are only two instrumentalities of power—the vote and jury," he believed. "The jury system stands behind the power to vote. How easy is it to cast a ballot when you are afraid someone, from the sheriff on down, might shoot you and nobody will do anything about it?" Morgan's Atlanta office was just down the hall from the offices of the

Episcopal Society for Cultural and Racial Unity; further, he was an Episcopalian and a friend of John Morris, the director of ESCRU. When Morgan heard of Daniels's death, he immediately thought of preparing a challenge to jury discrimination. He cleverly listed the plaintiffs and defendants so that the case would be deliciously entitled *White v. Crook.* White was actually Gardenia White, a black woman in Lowndes, and Crook, the white defendant, was Bruce Crook, a forty-four-year-old farmer and one of the county's jury commissioners.[42]

The plaintiffs in *White v. Crook* argued in federal court in Montgomery that the defendants "have failed to select or summon plaintiffs and the class they represent for jury service solely because they are members of the Negro race, either by excluding them from the rolls of names placed in the jury boxes, drawn and summoned for jury duty, or by keeping the number so included, drawn and summoned so small that only a token number of Negroes may serve on grand and petit juries and, in the case of petit juries, can be systematically and uniformly challenged and prevented from serving in the trial of any cases." According to the complaint, the exclusion of blacks from jury service violated their rights under the due process and equal protection clauses of the Fourteenth Amendment. In addition to $15,000 each in damages, the plaintiffs called for a speedy hearing, an injunction against the defendants, and an injunction against further systematic exclusion of blacks from Lowndes County juries. The case was placed on the docket of the U.S. district court in Montgomery, where a panel of three judges (Clarence W. Allgood, Richard T. Rives, and Frank M. Johnson) would hear the case.[43]

The state's case in *State of Alabama v. Tom L. Coleman* was prepared by circuit solicitor Arthur E. Gamble, Jr., with the assistance of Lowndes County prosecutor Carlton Perdue; Colonel Al Lingo of the state highway patrol directed the investigation. Some questioned the quality of the state's preparation. Not only did Richmond Flowers challenge the thoroughness and fairness of Lingo's investigation, but also the county prosecutor's fitness to prosecute Coleman came under attack. Based on Perdue's statements on the day of the shooting, a group called the Concerned White Citizens of Alabama declared "that he could not possibly execute justice impartially" and that "there is no doubt about the immaturity and incapability of a county solicitor who implies that emotional outrage is justification for killing." When the head of the Concerned White Citizens asked Flowers to remove Perdue, the attorney general refused because he believed that the removal of the county prosecutor "would ruin any chance you might have for conviction." Furthermore, Flowers hopefully maintained that even though Perdue was "a strict segregationist whose sympathies would not be with any civil rights group, he would not let his personal beliefs interfere with his prosecution of the case."[44]

Al Lingo declined to cooperate with the Federal Bureau of Investigation's efforts to determine whether a fourth case based on federal charges could be brought against Coleman for the slaying of Daniels. On orders from J. Edgar Hoover, the bureau's Mobile office gave the case "top priority" immediately after the shooting. FBI agents continued interviewing witnesses and gathering evidence about Daniels, Coleman, and the shootings, including reconstructing the crime scene. The FBI stressed three issues. Its prime concern involved Tom Coleman's official status as a representative of the Lowndes County sheriff's department. Second, the FBI sought to determine if the killing had resulted from a conspiracy, especially one involving the Ku Klux Klan. Third, the bureau checked reports that the four civil rights workers who approached the Cash Store had been armed.[45]

Soon after Coleman shot Daniels and Morrisroe, Colonel Lingo, Sheriff Frank Ryals, and other Lowndes authorities had identified Coleman as a special deputy and had implied that Coleman had acted in his official capacity as a special deputy sheriff. Naive about civil rights law, they failed to realize that if Coleman had acted in an official capacity, his actions fell under federal jurisdiction. The FBI's inquiries determined that Coleman had given others the impression that he served as a special deputy, that he was frequently in the sheriff's office, that he had assisted officers of the sheriff's department when they made arrests, and that he carried a card designating him a special deputy sheriff. The card carried by Coleman said that the bearer had been appointed and had the power of a deputy sheriff in the county. Ryals, however, had quickly been informed about the legal implications of Coleman's actions. The sheriff explained to the FBI that he used the card in lieu of a gun permit because he had no clerical help and that he told Coleman and every other cardholder that they were not deputies and could not enforce the law. Indeed, two hundred other Lowndes citizens (including several blacks and a few white women) also carried the cards. Ryals also denied that Coleman had been asked to assist the sheriff's department and that he had been sent to the Cash Store by the department. The FBI concluded that Coleman had not acted in any official capacity in going to the Cash Store or in shooting Daniels and Morrisroe.[46]

Within days of the crime, the FBI agents working in Hayneville also determined to the bureau's satisfaction that Tom Coleman had acted alone in killing Daniels. It uncovered no conspiracy involving the Ku Klux Klan or any other organization or individual. Agents of the FBI in

Mobile who knew Coleman personally conceded that he was an ardent segregationist but said that they had never seen any evidence that he belonged to the Klan.[47] The FBI pursued reports that the victims had carried a knife and gun but never found any weapons or evidence that Daniels and Morrisroe had ever had them. The FBI did not share its findings with local prosecutors who conducted their own investigations.

In the weeks following the shootings, the prosecutors refused to comment on the case against Tom Coleman before their presentation to the Lowndes County grand jury at its regular meeting. The attorney general, however, had vowed to seek a first-degree murder indictment if the prosecutors did not. With the regular circuit court judge ill, a special judge, William F. Thetford of Montgomery, went to Hayneville to organize the grand jury on September 13. One black man, a farmer and storekeeper from Hayneville, sat on the grand jury with seventeen white men.[48]

In presenting the state's case to the grand jury, Carlton Perdue called more than a score of witnesses. Several of them later claimed that he had asked them irrelevant and silly questions. Jimmy Rogers, for example, said that he had been asked if whites lived at the SNCC freedom house and if civil rights workers had threatened to blow up the homes of blacks who did not try to register to vote. A young black man from Fort Deposit reported that he had been asked if Jon Daniels preached to them in the jail on Sunday. Other blacks present at the time of the shooting thought that they should have been asked to testify, but they were not subpoenaed. Joe Bell Coker and Leon Crocker, two local whites who witnessed the crimes and were friends of Tom Coleman, did testify.[49]

Coleman had originally been arrested under a warrant charging him with first-degree murder and with assault to commit murder, but the Lowndes County grand jury returned indictments that reduced the charges to first-degree manslaughter for killing Daniels and to assault and battery for wounding Morrisroe. Instead of the death penalty, the maximum penalty for the first-degree manslaughter charge was ten years in prison. Assault and battery carried a maximum penalty of one year in prison and a $500 fine. As soon as the indictments were returned, Coleman voluntarily appeared in court for arraignment. After he declared his innocence to the charges, the court freed him under the same bond posted after his arrest. His trial in the Hayneville courthouse was scheduled to begin in less than three weeks.[50]

In a prepared statement the defense attorneys expressed confidence that Coleman would be "acquitted and completely exonerated of all charges." Declaring the defense ready for trial, Vaughan Hill Robison said that his client "has confidence that the court and the jury in Lowndes

County will do justice and justice will demand his acquittal by a jury verdict." He further emphasized, "We want this case tried by the court and on the facts, not by the out-of-state news media or on the streets."[51]

The indictments "shocked and amazed" Attorney General Flowers. His hopes that the local prosecutors would handle the case fairly despite their personal opinions had been dashed. "If this is not murder," he charged in reference to the slaying of Daniels, "it is no case at all." The prosecution's failure to obtain the essential testimony of Richard Morrisroe before appearing before the grand jury particularly distressed Flowers. Though he had never criticized any jury's decision, the attorney general considered the grand jury's failure to bring a first-degree murder indictment against Coleman "an abdication of grand jury responsibility." Unwilling to accept the lesser indictment, he pledged to "take all necessary steps to see that the accused is correctly and properly charged with first-degree murder."[52]

In Hayneville, Flowers's criticism drew fire not just from the defense but also from the prosecution. Vaughan Hill Robison, obviously pleased with the reduced charges against his client, admonished Flowers for criticizing the grand jury: "To criticize a legally constituted grand jury cannot be justified, in my judgment." Solicitor Perdue more explicitly expressed his satisfaction with the grand jury's action. "We had all parties represented," he maintained, and "we had all the evidence." He rejected the attorney general's contention that Morrisroe's testimony was necessary. "I don't see how that so-called priest from Chicago would have had influence one way or the other," he observed. Referring to two local white men who testified about what they witnessed from the bench in front of the Cash Store, the solicitor declared, "These are high class Christian men who have a lot more influence and sayso in this place than a person from Chicago." He speculated that the grand jury concluded that Coleman had acted "spasmodically" in trying to protect the woman who owned the Cash Store.[53]

The attorney general refused to accept the prosecutor's explanations and soon became deeply involved in the case. The grandson of two Confederate veterans, Richmond Flowers was born in Dothan, Alabama, the day World War I ended. After graduating from Auburn University and starting law school, he served in the army during World War II; he finished law school at the University of Alabama in 1948. Flowers practiced law and worked in the insurance business in Dothan before winning election to the state senate in 1954. Defeated in his first race for attorney general in 1958, the tall redhead was elected in 1962 at the same time George Wallace won the governorship.[54]

As attorney general Flowers disagreed with Governor Wallace by counseling moderation in dealing with the civil rights movement. Though he objected to the civil rights bill of 1964, Flowers also sternly opposed white violence. He confessed to being a segregationist but denounced demagogues like Wallace who used the race issue for political purposes; he considered Martin Luther King an extremist but urged whites to accept inevitable changes in race relations. Though opposed to social equality between the races, he believed public places should be open to all: "It is up to the person who doesn't want integration to leave an integrated facility." In his speeches Flowers frequently told Alabamians that "the good old days," which he admitted were not really so good, "are gone forever." Instead of opposing change, he wanted to accept and adjust to it. Forces, such as the Ku Klux Klan, that preached and practiced resistance came under the attorney general's relentless attack. His office strenuously investigated the Klan and even assisted probes by the despised Justice Department. For his stands, Flowers became known as a traitor to his race.[55]

As a politician, Flowers had ambitions for higher office in his state. Although he believed in the possibility of a coalition of blacks and whites in Alabama, he recognized that an insufficient number of blacks had registered to make such an alliance potent. Flowers, therefore, doubted that he would run again in 1966 because the coalition would still be weak, but by 1968 or 1970 he thought enough blacks would have registered to forge an effective union with some whites. In the meantime, in a state wracked by the civil rights movement, his unusual but moderate course struck many Alabamians as "freewheeling, unpredictable, agrarian Populist."[56]

With the trial of Tom Coleman set to start on September 28, the day after the second trial in the Liuzzo murder case, the attorney general had to move quickly if he wished to try Coleman for first-degree murder. If Coleman were tried for manslaughter in Daniels's death, he could not later be tried for murder. Flowers apparently had two options. He could ask the circuit solicitor and judge to reconvene the grand jury and then try to persuade the grand jury to change its indictment to murder. Or he could have the criminal division of the attorney general's office supercede the local solicitor in the Coleman case, and his representatives could then, after securing a delay in the trial, resubmit the case to a new grand jury for a murder indictment.[57]

Flowers chose the second option. Two days after Coleman's indictment for manslaughter he made his first move. "If this case was presented properly — and I have to assume that it was — the members of that grand jury are just as guilty as the man who pulled the trigger," he declared. Calling the manslaughter charge "a dark day in Alabama judicial history," he tried to place the responsibility on the grand jury and maintain a positive relationship with the local prosecutors. He further stated, "I do not intend to go to trial on a manslaughter indictment. It is my duty to get a murder indictment, and I'm going to try to do it." To obtain the new indictment, Flowers planned to ask for a postponement of Coleman's trial because Richard Morrisroe, who was still hospitalized in Montgomery, would be unable to testify; he then wanted Arthur Gamble to call a special grand jury to rehear the evidence against Coleman. Claims that presenting the same case to another grand jury might be tantamount to subjecting Coleman to double jeopardy failed to worry the attorney general. If Gamble resisted, Flowers said he was prepared to supersede the prosecutor and take over the case himself.[58]

Gamble balked. Although he refused to comment on the case, Flowers reported that Gamble said he accepted the grand jury's manslaughter indictment because he thought he could not do even that well before another Lowndes County grand jury. Flowers disagreed and, less than a week after the original indictment, took over the prosecution of Coleman. After his investigators briefly interviewed Morrisroe in Montgomery before he was moved to a Chicago hospital for further convalescence, the attorney general believed even more strongly that the priest's testimony should have been — and would be — vital to any proper grand jury proceeding. Flowers announced his intention to seek a continuance of the case so he could go before another grand jury. Also influencing his decision was the progress of *White v. Crook* in federal court; he hoped to delay Coleman's trial until the jury discrimination case had been settled. Flowers realized that the equitable inclusion of blacks on both the grand and trial juries could have a dramatic effect on the outcome of the Coleman case. The attorney general's office kept informed about *White v. Crook* because Flowers's assistant, Joe Breck Gantt, was an old friend of ACLU lawyer Charles Morgan from their days in law school together at the University of Alabama.[59]

While Flowers struggled with the local prosecutors, the defense team quietly prepared for trial. The attorneys continued to bar the FBI from interviewing their client and refused to talk publicly about the case. Soon after the shooting, however, a key part of their strategy became known. They planned to present witnesses who would testify that Jon Daniels and Richard Morrisroe were armed when they approached the Cash Store. Even though no weapons had been recovered, they expected the jury to conclude that Coleman had acted in self-defense, and in defense of the white female store owner, when he shot the seminarian and the priest.

In Hayneville, meanwhile, Tom Coleman continued his life, though it was hardly as peaceful as it had been before August 20. Receiving many threatening letters and telephone calls, Coleman feared for his own safety and that of his family. Supportive whites from the community protected his home in the evenings, but he nonetheless kept all windows tightly closed during the hot September nights even though his house was not air conditioned. Coleman's lawyers urged him to stay at home and out of trouble, but he did not consistently follow their advice. Just before the desegregation of the public school in Hayneville, for example, Vaughan Hill Robison encouraged him to avoid any possible confrontation with blacks and civil rights supporters by coming temporarily to Montgomery. The lawyers apparently worried that demonstrations at Coleman's house might provoke their client to further violence. Still wanting to believe that he and other whites were in control of their community, Coleman told his lawyer not to worry. If any demonstrators came into his yard, he could handle the situation: he would make sure they never made it downtown to the school.[60]

The night before his scheduled trial, Coleman defied his lawyers and took an even greater risk. With his buddy George Dansby, he drove to a Montgomery hotel to attend a party honoring Al Lingo, who was getting ready to retire as public safety commissioner. Just going to the city, of course, violated his lawyers' advice to stay at home. As he usually did, Coleman carried a gun for protection in spite of the instructions of his attorneys. Fortunately for Coleman, the excursion was uneventful. His seemingly reckless behavior may have indicated that he had learned little from his experience, but it also demonstrated his confidence that, regardless of his behavior before the trial, a Lowndes County jury would find him innocent.[61]

On Monday, September 27, case number 174, *The State of Alabama v. Tom L. Coleman*, was scheduled to be heard by Alabama's Second Judicial Circuit Court in the Lowndes County Courthouse. Built by slave labor in 1856, the two-story, Greek Revival building faced west on the shady town square that contained a ten-foot statue memorializing the county's eighty-five soldiers who died in the Civil War. Originally the courthouse had twin curving staircases that led to a raised portico outside a second-floor courtroom, but a 1905 remodeling of the structure added a domed cupola on top, built wings on the northern and southern sides, and enclosed the staircases leading to the courtroom. On each side of the spacious, high-ceilinged courtroom several ten-foot, green-shuttered windows brightened the room and allowed in the occasional breezes that provided the only relief from the summer heat. In a rear corner of the room stood a triangular, barred cage to hold prisoners. Just across the hall were rest rooms for "White Women," "White Men," and "Colored."

Downstairs were several county offices, including the sheriff's chamber, where Tom Coleman regularly played dominoes.[62]

Behind the courthouse, several additional telephone lines were installed before Coleman's trial to handle stories filed by visiting newsmen from across the nation. In addition to representatives from the Associated Press and the United Press, reporters for the *New York Times*, *Newsweek*, *Time*, the *Washington Post*, the *Los Angeles Times*, the *New York Herald-Tribune*, the *Birmingham News*, and other print media came to the small Alabama town. The major television networks also had correspondents and film crews in Hayneville. Even though a newspaper strike against seven major New York City daily newspapers prevented extensive coverage in the media capital, the events in Hayneville still received wide publicity.[63]

If the trial focused on Tom Coleman, the judge and seven lawyers became its key actors. A headline in the *Alabama Journal* described the gathering of lawyers for the trial as "friends meet in Hayneville."[64] Judge T. Werth Thagard, Arthur Gamble, Carlton Perdue, Richmond Flowers, Joe Breck Gantt, Robert C. Black, Joseph Phelps, and Vaughan Hill Robison were not strangers to one another. Although certainly not all personal friends, most of them surely had known and worked with each other on various occasions, some for many years, and in many cases they had known and worked with the defendant too. The major exceptions were Flowers and Gantt, who came from the attorney general's office and had no personal connections with Lowndes County or that part of the Black Belt.

The sixty-three-year-old judge had been born in Greenville, in adjacent Butler County, and had served as solicitor for the circuit for sixteen years during the thirties and forties. After a few years in the state legislature, Thagard in 1952 was named judge for the Second Judicial Circuit, which included Lowndes County. He succeeded Arthur E. Gamble, Sr., who had died of a stroke after forty-two years in office. Tom Coleman later claimed to have helped secure the judicial appointment for Thagard by working through his brother, who was close to the governor. In the early fifties, Coleman also had given one of Thagard's relatives a job with his highway crew.[65]

Arthur E. Gamble, Jr., and Carlton Perdue had worked together many times, most conspicuously as prosecutors in the first trial before Judge Thagard of Collie Leroy Wilkins for shooting Viola Liuzzo. Like Thagard, Gamble was a native of Greenville and he had known the judge for years. One summer while a student at the University of Alabama, he worked for Tom Coleman on a highway engineering party. After serving as a navy pilot during World War II, Gamble practiced law in his hometown and then entered politics. While he was a candidate for the state house of representatives, his father died; he withdrew from the race when nominated to take Thagard's place in the state senate after Thagard took Gamble's father's position as judge. Later he left the legislature and became solicitor for the Second Judicial Circuit, where he frequently practiced before Judge Thagard. Carlton Perdue was born in Lowndes County in 1905 and was raised there. He first became the county solicitor in 1947. Virtually all of his adult life, Perdue had known Tom Coleman, and at the time of Coleman's arrest the solicitor had caused some controversy by appearing to justify Coleman's actions.[66]

The other prosecutors were not from Lowndes but were well known to the other participants. Thirty-six-year-old Joseph Breckinridge Gantt knew the local lawyers and the judge because earlier in the spring, in his third year as assistant attorney general, he had worked closely with Gamble and Perdue in prosecuting Collie Leroy Wilkins. Before joining the attorney general's office, he had attended the University of Alabama, served in the judge advocate general's corps in the army, and practiced law and served as district attorney in his native Covington County in southern Alabama, where his father had been a longtime sheriff. He had first met Richmond Flowers in the late 1940s at the university.[67] Flowers was not popular in the county, in part because he and the people there knew each other well.

The defense lawyers all came from Montgomery yet were familiar with Loundes County and the other participants. Robert Coleman Black was Tom Coleman's nephew; his mother was Coleman's sister. The thirty-one-year-old lawyer had been born in Greenville and had grown up in Fort Deposit where his father served variously as justice of the peace, city clerk, mayor, and, before his family moved from Lowndes, county probate judge. After completing high school in Montgomery, Black served with the marines in Korea before attending the University of Alabama and its law school. He clerked briefly for an associate justice of the state supreme court and then joined Hill, Hill, Stovall, and Carter in the general practice of civil law. The firm was state counsel for Humble Oil and Refining and had as other clients a number of banks and insurance companies. Black had a good friend, Joe Phelps, who practiced law in the firm of Hill, Robison, and Belser. When Tom Coleman called his nephew and asked him to find him a lawyer, Black naturally turned to his friend's firm and asked Vaughan Hill Robison to help represent his uncle.[68]

A leading lawyer and politician in Montgomery, Robison came from a prominent family in the capital. When his parents married in 1913, the *Montgomery Advertiser* described it as "[o]ne of the most brilliant nuptial events of the spring and a marriage of much interest throughout the State owing to the prominence of both bride and bridegroom." Born and raised in Montgomery, Robison made his first public speech at the age of three and won the state oratorical contest on the Constitution when he was fifteen. "I tell you the doggone truth," he later explained, "I think I developed my voice hunt'n and hollerin' behind the dogs." In spite of his "hunt'n and hollerin'," Robison grew up very comfortably as part of Montgomery's elite. He attended the local public schools and for one semester as a high school student also went to Huntingdon College in Montgomery. He graduated from the University of Alabama law school in 1938 and had to obtain special permission to practice law before he was twenty-one.[69]

Drafted in 1941, Robison rose to the rank of captain and served as a military lawyer and judge during World War II. After the war he resumed his law practice and entered politics as reading clerk of the Alabama House of Representatives during the 1947 and 1949 sessions. Through his mother, Laura Croom Hill, Robison was a first cousin of Senator Lister Hill, who had first been elected to Congress in 1923, and his family ties made him seem a natural for politics. Elected to the state senate in 1950 in a "close, bitterly fought election," Robison demonstrated in the campaign, according to a local newspaper, that the Hill family had "not lost their stinger." Senator Robison quickly became a powerful legislator. In the senate he served with T. Werth Thagard, Arthur Gamble, and Richmond Flowers. In 1955, newspapermen covering the legislature voted Robison the best debater and Richmond Flowers the top orator in the senate. Four years later Robison was elected president pro tempore. Robison was an active Presbyterian and a member of numerous fraternal organizations in Montgomery; in the early 1950s he served as president of the county bar association.[70]

When the lawyers arrived in Hayneville on Monday morning for preliminary arguments in the Coleman case, tension abounded despite their previous friendly relations. Angry exchanges marked the proceedings. The attorney general, who had taken over the prosecution, asked for a hearing before Judge Thagard to request postponements of the trial of Tom Coleman and of the retrial of Collie Leroy Wilkins. Neither of the accused was present. Assistant Attorney General Joe Breck Gantt presented the motion to the judge in a thirty-minute hearing. In arguing for a continuance of the cases, Gantt told the court that he and Flowers feared for their own safety while prosecuting the cases in Lowndes County. "I have received and the attorney general has received threats on our lives," said Gantt, who had come to the court with Flowers under an armed escort. Defense attorney Robison promptly dismissed their worries by countering, "I have been threatened, too, and so has Mr. Coleman, and so has Carlton Perdue." Gantt's argument rested primarily on the inability of Richard Morrisroe to testify in Hayneville for another few months. During his presentation, Gantt twice said that Morrisroe "was shot in the back while running from the defendant." In response, Robison testily shot back that the defense would prove "these are not the facts in this case" and claimed that Morrisroe's testimony was not essential because there were other eyewitnesses to the shootings.[71]

Gantt and Flowers also asked for a delay because of the lack of cooperation given them by other state officials, especially Al Lingo. They called his report on the Coleman case inadequate, improper, and "heavily slanted." They further complained that some witnesses had been too afraid to appear before the Lowndes County grand jury and would not come forward now for the trial. More damning was their charge that they had "strong evidence that several witnesses intend to commit perjury." Robison heatedly challenged the prosecutor, "Is this man charging perjury? If so, I demand that he name names." He also decried as "utterly ridiculous" the prosecution's argument that it had insufficient resources and time to prepare the case.[72]

In concluding the prosecution's presentation to Judge Thagard, Flowers declared, "The state is not ready for trial. We cannot be ready without Father Morrisroe. And we cannot be ready until we have had further time to find witnesses who will risk their lives to stand up in this courtroom and tell the truth." Arguing that his client had a right to a speedy trial, Robison rejected the "frivolous grounds" presented for postponement. He then attacked the attorney general. "I question his motive," said the defense attorney. "I question his sincerity. I question his honesty with this court." When the lawyers completed their arguments, Thagard, without explaining his reasons, denied a delay in the trials of Coleman and Wilkins.[73]

Thagard's decision outraged Richmond Flowers. The attorney general told Tom Jarrell of ABC News that Morrisroe's presence "is an absolute necessity" to the prosecution because his wound in the back while running from Coleman would provide evidence of Coleman's clear intent to commit murder. He noted that Morrisroe was willing to return to Alabama to testify but that, according to his doctors, the priest would be unable to travel for at least sixty days. In addition, Flowers argued, "to go to trial at this time with the attitude of the people of Lowndes County . . . would assure an acquittal."[74] Despite the attorney general's protestations, the trial of Coleman was set to begin the next morning unless a federal judge approved a new motion by the plaintiffs in *White v. Crook*.

While the attorney general argued for a delay in Coleman's trial, the plaintiffs in *White v. Crook* gained a hearing in federal court. On the previous Thursday, Charles Morgan of the ACLU, Orzell Billingsley, and Melvin Wulf had asked the U.S. district court to issue a temporary restraining order or a permanent injunction to block all criminal proceedings in Lowndes County until the issues concerning jury discrimination raised in *White v. Crook* were settled. The plaintiffs' motion also sought to add to the list of defendants the Lowndes County sheriff, probate judge, and prosecutor as well as Judge Thagard and Arthur Gamble of the circuit court. Billingsley, a black lawyer from Birmingham, asserted that verdicts of courts in Lowndes "will be subject to suspicion and attack" if the court later agrees that the county systematically excluded blacks and women from its juries. The brief contained affidavits from the Reverend Henri Stines of ESCRU and others urging that the trial of Tom Coleman be delayed until blacks were included on the jury rolls. Stines declared, "To allow any jury trials in Lowndes County, Alabama to take place until the names of Negroes have been placed on the jury roll and in the jury box without racial discrimination will have a chilling effect upon free speech, subject other persons to killings without equal recourse to law and irreparably hamper our efforts and the efforts of others in Negro voter registration and other efforts."[75]

Lawyers for the defendants, as well as Richmond Flowers acting officially as attorney general, asked the federal judges to strike the affidavits submitted by the plaintiffs because they came from people who did not reside in Lowndes County or Alabama and because they contained "irrelevant and immaterial matters," "scandalous . . . matters which have no bearing on the issue," and "statements, averments and information which attempt to inject into the case before this court highly inflammatory and emotional questions which do not bear on the issues before this court." In response to the plaintiffs' motion itself, the defense argued that the addition of Thagard, Ryals, Perdue, Gamble, and Harrell Hammonds, the probate judge, was unjustified because the plaintiffs "did not allege any misconduct on the part of these defendants" but simply accused them of doing their jobs according to state law. Furthermore, the defense maintained, the plaintiffs were in no danger of being injured by trials pending in the county and had no cases awaiting trial there. For their side, the defense attorneys included affidavits from blacks who were awaiting trial in Lowndes County and who claimed that they would "suffer irreparable injury and damage" by delays in their cases. The plaintiffs' motion, the defense concluded, was "based in part on hearsay, surmise and speculation" and should be dismissed.[76]

Soon after Judge Thagard rejected requests to delay Coleman's trial, Judge Richard T. Rives of the U.S. Fifth Circuit Court of Appeals denied the ACLU's motion for a court order restraining all trials in Lowndes County. In Montgomery, Rives said that to intervene would be "an [almost] unprecedented step"; the court, therefore, was unwilling to grant the ACLU's request.[77] The case of *White v. Crook* would continue in the federal court, and the trial of Tom Coleman would proceed as scheduled in Hayneville.

TRIAL IN A TEMPLE

OF JUSTICE

The next morning, Coralie Coleman prepared to attend her husband's trial. The weeks since the shootings had been especially distressing for her. Like other whites in the county, she believed that the civil rights activity had to be stopped, but she did not know what to do. Tom and Coralie Coleman had never fully discussed the events that occurred outside the Cash Store or the preparation of his defense. If her husband's actions that day had surprised her, she readily accepted his explanation that he had only done what was necessary. She nonetheless did resent that he, instead of the sheriff's deputies who were also at the courthouse, had been the one to go to the Cash Store to protect Virginia Varner. A devout Christian, Mrs. Coleman found her strength and solace in prayer, and in the support of family and friends in the community. Several of her brothers went to Hayneville to be with the Colemans during his trial. Early on the morning of the trial they gathered at the Coleman home on the eastern edge of Hayneville and joined in a short prayer meeting. After Coralie

Coleman read from the Bible, they all said silent prayers in preparation for the day's events. Then they waited to be called to the courthouse.[1]

Before the actual trial commenced, more legal skirmishing between the assistant state attorney general and the judge occurred in the morning. Tom Coleman attended the preliminary arguments but his wife stayed at home. Wearing a dark suit, a light blue shirt, and a blue tie, Coleman paced in front of the courtroom before the proceedings began. Occasionally speaking to friends and well-wishers who crowded the room, he chain-smoked cigarettes during the wait. Several prospective jurors displayed their sympathy for the defendant in racist remarks outside the courtroom, and the reactions of other whites signaled their support for Coleman. Judge Thagard opened the trial by first announcing that jurors and members of the court would have priority in using the upstairs bathrooms. A deputy sheriff, whose dog had accompanied him into the courtroom and strolled around as the trial progressed, then raised a window and hollered down to the courtyard for all witnesses in the Coleman case to come upstairs. When the witnesses entered, the thirty or so blacks sat by themselves in the segregated pattern typical of the Black Belt county.[2]

Judge Thagard then began qualifying the jury. When the clerk of court called the list of potential jurors, Tom Coleman's name was among those called to hear his own case. After a brief pause, someone whispered, "Might as well strike him." The judge next asked the potential jurors if any of them had a "fixed opinion as to the guilt, or innocence, of the accused." A mechanic in Hayneville admitted his prejudice in favor of finding Coleman not guilty. "Judge," the assistant attorney general quickly asserted, "the statement of this juror in open court so prejudices the state's case at this time that we ask — we repeat our request and make a motion at this time for a continuance of this case." After Thagard denied the motion, Vaughan Hill Robison for the defense challenged the man for cause and he was removed from the jury list.[3]

Before the court could continue examining the prospective jurors, Joe Breck Gantt told the judge that "it's impossible for the state to obtain a fair trial before this jury." Referring to the Liuzzo trial, to the reduced manslaughter charge against Tom Coleman, and to the hostility toward the attorney general, Gantt stated, "I think the climate is so bad in Hayneville right now, in Lowndes County, that it's impossible for the state to get a fair trial." When Thagard again refused to grant a delay in the trial, Gantt asked for a continuance because Richard Morrisroe, "the Catholic priest who was shot in the back," was the state's key witness and was not yet well enough to travel to testify. Gantt thought that his request was unexceptional and should be granted. Robert Black and Robison interrupted Gantt to object to his claim that Morrisroe had been shot in the back and to his suggestion that Coleman should have been charged with murder. Robison said that the assistant attorney general was trying to prejudice the jury. When the judge reminded Gantt that Morrisroe was not in Alabama and could not be forced to return to testify, Gantt assured him that the priest would in fact come to Alabama to testify when he was physically able. The judge rejected the prosecutor's argument.[4]

Gantt then moved that the case be nolle prosequi, that it not be prosecuted. Robison requested that the jury be removed from the courtroom before discussion of the motion. After Thagard ordered the jurors to leave, the lawyers continued their heated arguments. Joe Phelps for the defense contended that Gantt's request was just a continuation of the previous day's dilatory tactics; he said that Tom Coleman was ready for trial and asked the court to proceed. Gantt repeated his request and argued that it was customary for the court to concur when the state claimed that it could not go to trial. To the defense's call for a speedy trial, Gantt replied somewhat disingenuously, "I can't see where the defendant can squawk very much, we are not only offering them a speedy trial, we are offering to do away with the trial altogether. No trial at all, we are saying — we won't prosecute, we don't want to prosecute, we can't prosecute, and that should make the defense very happy." Gantt actually hoped to stop the manslaughter trial so that the attorney general could later seek a murder indictment from another grand jury.[5]

Judge Thagard, however, reminded Gantt that the attorney general had intervened in the case specifically to prosecute Coleman, not to dismiss the case. Gantt explained that he did not want to be part of a case that involved perjured testimony and, furthermore, that the state's "case will make out a defense for them. I don't have a case, that's what I'm telling the court." When Thagard denied a motion of nolle prosequi, Gantt said, "Well, the state in good conscience cannot proceed any further." Thagard ordered the assistant attorney general to proceed, but Gantt refused and referred once again to expected perjured testimony. He also declined to surrender the case to the circuit solicitor even when the judge threatened him with a charge of contempt of court.[6]

To get on with the trial, Thagard called Arthur Gamble to the front and questioned him about his role in the case. Gamble explained that, except for a few conversations with Gantt in Hayneville, he had presented all the available evidence to the grand jury without any assistance or offers of help from the attorney general's office. When Richmond Flowers announced that he would take over the case, Gamble turned over everything in his files to Gantt. The tall, handsome, square-jawed circuit solicitor had been ready to proceed with a trial and thought he could make a good case for conviction. Perceiving no advantage to the prosecution in a delay, Gamble observed, "I don't see anything wrong with the atmosphere now, as far as the trial of this case, or any other criminal case." He repeated his willingness to prosecute the case.[7]

When Thagard completed his colloquy with Gamble, Gantt received the court's permission to ask Gamble some questions. Gamble acknowledged that Colonel Lingo had refused to give the attorney general any information about the case, but Gamble declared that he had volunteered to pass on to Gantt and Flowers any information he obtained from Lingo. "Did you not make a statement to me," asked Gantt, "that it was impossible for us to get a jury conviction in this case?" Gamble demurred, "I don't know that I made that statement, no sir." He also denied that he had told Gantt that he would try to get a first-degree murder indictment or that the grand jury would probably return one. Trying to show that the prosecution really had no case, and knew it, Gantt also asked if the eyewitnesses called before the grand jury were not really witnesses for the defense instead of the prosecution. Gamble simply responded that he felt "it's the duty of the prosecution to put on whatever witnesses are available, not just witnesses that are prejudiced in favor of the state or the defense."[8]

When the assistant attorney general had finished questioning Gamble, Thagard asked, "Mr. Gantt, do you still refuse to go further with this case?" When he answered that he did, the judge removed him and the attorney general from the case and instructed the circuit solicitor and the county solicitor to proceed with the prosecution. In a parting shot, Gantt declared, "We object to this proceeding"; then he gathered his papers and walked out of the courtroom. He was surprised that the judge who had been so fair in the first trial of Collie Leroy Wilkins had now behaved so improperly.[9] Arthur Gamble and Carlton Perdue thus became the official prosecutors of the case against Tom Coleman.

With the new prosecutors and the original defense lawyers, Judge Thagard began the process of selecting jurors to hear the manslaughter case. The procedure had actually started long before the judge and lawyers met in the courtroom. In Lowndes County, and throughout Alabama, each governor appointed a three-person jury commission to supervise the creation of the roll of potential jurors. The jury roll excluded, of course, residents under twenty-one, drunks, people physically unfit, illiterates (except for property owners), and individuals convicted of crimes involving moral turpitude. Exemptions would be granted to people over sixty-five, judges, lawyers, physicians and dentists, teachers, and members of several other professions. In addition, Alabama forbade women on juries. Otherwise, the jury roll ostensibly included all honest and intelligent men of integrity, good character, and sound judgment. The clerk of the jury commission was charged to use all available sources of information — registration lists, tax lists, telephone directories, city directories — to gather names for the roll. Each name went on a card and was placed in the jury box. Before every term of court, the judge drew out a predetermined number of cards, usually fifty, and the sheriff summoned the individuals to appear in court. It seemed to be a simple, straightforward method.[10]

In Lowndes County, however, not all male residents had an equal chance to serve on juries. From 1953 to 1965, only seven blacks had appeared a total of twenty-six times on jury lists that contained 2,748 names. In other words, blacks made up only about 1 percent of the persons summoned for jury duty even though they constituted more than 70 percent of the county's population. No black had ever served on a criminal or civil petit jury in the county. Ninety-eight percent of the names of prospective jurors came from the voter lists, and no blacks voted in Lowndes County before 1965. The jury commissioners did include a few blacks whom they knew and considered to have good judgment. Moreover, after the filing of *White v. Crook* and before the trial of Tom Coleman, jury commissioner Bruce Crook, in the absence of the commission clerk, added the names of nineteen blacks and fifty whites to the jury roll.[11]

The discrimination was not just against blacks; a limited number of whites also served on juries. From 1953 to 1965, the names of only 670 whites had been in the jury box, and 211 appeared on jury lists six times or more. The 211 whites actually made up 66.5 percent of the 2,748 names called for jury service. Eight white men had been called thirteen or more times since 1957. Many served during several successive terms of court. Tom Coleman himself had been called a dozen times in the previous twelve years.[12]

Opponents of the Lowndes County jury system claimed that it had great potential for injustice. They believed that over the years prosecutors and jury commissioners could learn how various whites who had served repeatedly would behave as jurors. People who systematically excluded blacks could just as easily select only whites who shared the jury commissioners' or the prosecutors' prejudices. The absence of minutes for jury commission meetings or any record of who had actually served on juries further raised the suspicions of people who objected to the system.[13]

In spite of the alleged inequities in the Lowndes jury system, the lawyers in the Coleman trial readily examined the potential jurors. Of the sixty-five in the pool, forty had served at least six times in the previous twelve years. Including the Coleman trial, they had been called an average of more than eight times each. The odds were great that Tom Coleman had served on juries with many of them. The prosecution and defense quickly agreed on a group of twelve white males to hear the case. Dressed in business suits, the jurors included three farmers, three mechanics, two county employees, one state employee, one federal employee, one brick mason, and one lumberman. It was, in more ways than one, truly a jury of Tom Coleman's peers. After Judge Thagard impaneled and swore in the jurors, the court heard opening arguments from the prosecution and the defense.[14]

Arthur Gamble declared that the prosecution would prove that Tom Coleman shot and killed Jon Daniels on the afternoon of August 20. The prosecution, therefore, expected a guilty verdict on the manslaughter charge. For the defense, Robert Black spoke to the jury. He introduced himself as Robert Coleman Black and emphasized the middle name. "I'm glad to be in a case with 'Bubba' Gamble," said the young lawyer using the prosecutor's nickname. "I can learn something from it. I'm just a young lawyer not long out of law school," he continued in southern good-old-boy fashion. "I'm not a criminal lawyer and I don't represent a criminal here." Reassuring the jury that "my uncle" will be acquitted, he implied that the prosecution would show that Coleman acted in self-defense because the victims were armed and threatened him when they approached the Cash Store. When Black said that the defense was "anxious to get to trial — the first opportunity to tell Tom's side of the story," the white spectators showed their approval and enthusiasm. After the initial presentations, Thagard recessed the court for lunch.[15]

Shortly before one o'clock, when Coralie Coleman and her family went to the trial for the first time, they found state troopers and members of the sheriff's newly formed auxiliary, which included several blacks, guarding the outside of building. Dressed in black, Mrs. Coleman sat in the second row of the courtroom with her tall, crew-cut state trooper son and her daughter, who taught school in Georgia. Scores of their friends filled seats that included some folding chairs in the aisles. Also in the courtroom as observers were Collie Leroy Wilkins, Eugene Thomas, and William Orville Eaton, three Ku Klux Klansmen charged with the murder of Viola Liuzzo. The Reverends John B. Morris and Henri A. Stines of the Episcopal Society for Cultural and Racial Unity also attended.[16]

As people arrived for the afternoon session, the tensions of the morning had disappeared with the assistant attorney general. Though state troopers stood at the doors of the courtroom, everyone seemed more calm and cordial with the case left in the hands of the local prosecutors. White spectators talked freely of how the jury would surely acquit Coleman. In the courtroom, one man leaned forward to a friend sitting in front of him and said, "One thing for sure, gonna be a little bit of twine running from everybody in that box to that chair where Tom's sitting." In the jury's presence, the prosecutors chatted amiably with the defense lawyers. Tom Coleman also appeared more relaxed. The tranquil, informal atmosphere was more typical of Thagard's court than the contentiousness of the morning session. The small, white-haired judge spoke softly from the bench but maintained stern control. He allowed smoking in the courtroom during recesses and permitted reporters to come and go freely. In a concession, he also reserved the first three rows on the right of the court for visiting journalists.[17]

During a recess on the first day, a reporter lucky enough to have found a folding chair on the right side of the room stood up to stretch a minute and quickly discovered that a white woman behind him was taking his seat away. "You can't have my chair," the newsman protested. Still pulling on the chair, the woman replied, "I need it for a lady." The journalist glanced around and remarked, "But I don't see any ladies." A more serious struggle over a seat occurred between an elderly white man and a black civil rights worker. The white told the black to move his foot and, when the activist remained motionless, the white man kicked him. A deputy sheriff swiftly grabbed the black man and hustled him roughly out of the courtroom; soon returning, the friendly deputy assisted the white man out of the room too.[18]

After about fifty witnesses had been sworn in and directed to leave the courtroom, Judge Thagard told the prosecution to present its case. The whites witnesses trooped downstairs to wait in the sheriff's office; the blacks walked outside to mark time behind the courthouse or, during rainstorms, in their cars. And the trial began. As the first witness the circuit solicitor called Joe Jackson, a longtime Lowndes County deputy sheriff. Jackson's testimony hit on points crucial to both the prosecution and the defense. Under examination by Arthur Gamble, Jackson described what he found when he went to the Cash Store about three o'clock in the afternoon, shortly after the shootings: "Well, this Daniels, he was lying right in front of the door, with his feet right on the steps, and his head hanging off a little platform. He was dead, and the other boy was between the store and that old seedhouse." The short, beefy, red-faced deputy with a graying crew cut explained that Dr. William L. Staggard showed up promptly and treated Morrisroe and that Jack Golson came and took the victims to Montgomery. Jackson did not remember seeing Tom Coleman at the scene. When Gamble pressed him about who else was there, Jackson, addressing the prosecutor by his nickname, said, "Bubba, I just don't know who was there, to tell you the honest truth."[19]

Under cross-examination by Robert Black, the sheriff's deputy testified that Tom Coleman had occasionally been called on to help the sheriff enforce the law. Over the prosecution's objection, Black asked Joe Jackson about the situation in Hayneville on the day of the shooting. Although he maintained that he had not expected any particular trouble, Jackson said that Coleman had gone to Montgomery earlier that day to pick up some riot equipment in order "to maintain peace and order" in the county. The prosecution also objected unsuccessfully to questions suggesting that the civil rights workers might have had or obtained weapons while in jail. Jackson explained that the prisoners had been searched when admitted to the jail but that their many visitors had not. Leaving open the possibility that visitors had brought the seminarian and the priest a gun and a knife, Jackson testified that he did not know what they had in their possession when they were released because they were not searched before they left.[20]

Defense attorney Black then asked Jackson about Jon Daniels's actions immediately after his release. "What, if anything, did he do that attracted your attention?" inquired Coleman's nephew. Laughingly the deputy replied, "One thing, he kissed that *nigger* girl." When Black asked whether Daniels had kissed her on the cheek or the mouth, the prosecution objected to the questioning as irrelevant and potentially inflammatory, but Jackson quickly responded, "He kissed her right in the mouth." The white spectators, and a number of the jurors, laughed. The judge could only lamely comment, "He has already answered. I think the objection to that comes too late."[21] The defense had cleverly raised the suggestion of interracial sex, which could only horrify the white jurors. That Daniels had displayed friendship and affection for the black women outside the jail seems likely, even if he had not actually kissed any of them; after all, earlier in Selma he had demonstrated his ignorance of southern racial mores by walking with his arms casually around black women. By August his warm greeting of the women showed his reckless disregard for southern sensibilities, and to whites it may well have been as offensive as an actual kiss. Whether Jon Daniels did or did not kiss any of the black women when they were released from jail — and all accompanying Daniels denied it — the defense had suggested that the white northerner had publicly violated southern taboos against interracial sex, and the clear implication was that Daniels's alleged egregious actions somehow might justify Coleman's deadly deed.

Continuing the cross-examination, Black asked the deputy sheriff what he found near Richard Morrisroe. Jackson recalled that he noticed some books and identified the ones held by Black as the same ones. On redirect examination, Gamble asked if Joe Jackson had seen anything else near Daniels or Morrisroe. When Jackson said that he did not, Gamble specifically inquired about whether there had been a knife or a pistol, and the witness gave the same response. The prosecutor, knowing that the defense would argue that the victims had been armed, wanted to verify that the police had discovered no weapons near them. At the same time, however, his question first raised the issue of a gun and a knife and may thereby have played into the defense's plan by appearing to give credibility to the contention that Daniels and Morrisroe had been armed. Black then proceeded to turn the topic around to help the defense by asking Jackson, "Some of the civil rights workers had been in and out of the area [near the victims] before you got there?" Judge Thagard refused the prosecution's objection, and Jackson replied, "They had been there prior to that time, yes."[22] The clear implication was that the other civil rights workers could have removed the weapons. The defense had effectively used the prosecution's lead witness.

The next witnesses for the prosecution testified to the physical condition of Daniels's body after the shooting. Coroner Jack Golson told of going in the county ambulance to the Cash Store about 3:30 P.M. and finding one man dead and another wounded. On an emergency run to Montgomery, he took the wounded man to Baptist Hospital and Daniels's body to a funeral home. Golson left the funeral home after the arrival of the state toxicologist but before he had started an autopsy. When the defense declined to cross-examine the coroner, the prosecution called Dr. C. J. Rehling, the toxicologist.[23]

Rehling testified that as director of the state's crime laboratory, he had performed postmortems and conducted scientific examinations of physical evidence in criminal investigations for twenty years. On the evening of August 20, he photographed and examined Jon Daniels's corpse. He found "a ragged hole, one and one-eighth inch in diameter . . . one and one-half inches to the right of the middle line of the body, and it was one and a quarter inches below the common nipple line, and its range was acutely downward, and slightly to the left." The wound caused considerable bleeding, which soaked part of the shirt. The doctor concluded that the cause of death was the "obstruction and copious hemorrhage, from the destruction of major blood vessels, due to a shotgun wound of the chest that ranged downward through the liver, and destroyed the great vessels of the spine."

From the body Rehling recovered nine lead buckshot and two waddings from a twelve-gauge shotgun. He told the prosecutor that he had test-fired the Savage twelve-gauge shotgun turned over to him by the state troopers and, after comparing the fired cartridges with two cartridges provided by the troopers, decided that the gun had been used to kill Daniels. The shotgun had a polychoke attachment that allowed for adjusting the spray of buckshot coming out of the barrel. When given to

Rehling, the shotgun's choke had been set on "modified," which caused a rather tight bunching of the buckshot. Firing the shotgun into targets at various ranges proved to his satisfaction that Daniels had been standing only six to eight feet from the weapon when it was fired with the choke set on modified. Rehling left the witness stand momentarily to get the gun and buckshot, which the prosecution then introduced as evidence. Throughout Rehling's testimony and the introduction of his shotgun as evidence, Tom Coleman remained passive.[24]

Under questioning from Gamble, Rehling pulled out of a large cardboard box at his feet, described, and presented to the court the clothing that he had removed from Daniels's body. In addition to khaki trousers, it included a "black clerical shirt, with the hole in the right chest," and a white seminarian's collar, which attached to the shirt. The articles were placed on the rail in front of the jury box in clear view of everyone in the courtroom. Coleman was not fazed by Daniels's bloodstained shirt — he stared blankly across the room and continued chewing his gum — but the shirt clearly perturbed his wife and even more so their daughter. Rehling also turned over Daniels's trousers, undershorts, a belt with the initials "J. M. D.," and a ring from the seminarian's left ring finger.[25]

On cross-examination, Vaughan Hill Robison did his best to transform the doctor's testimony into support for the defense. His first question concerned the victim's shoes. Rehling presented the shoes to Robison, who, according to one observer, "brandished them, smirked and insisted they were indeed relevant" because they "were such as no man of God in Lowndes County ever wears. They were rough, heavy, high-topped, bleached-leather shoes with old-fashioned loops at the top with which to pull them on." The defense introduced the boots as evidence that Jon Daniels was not one of them. The same held true for a book that had been in his trouser pocket. Rehling handed over to Robison *The Fanatic* by Meyer Levin. Robison loudly repeated the menacing title twice while shaking the book at the newsmen seated in the front rows.[26]

Robison next asked Rehling about notes or letters found on Daniels, but the doctor corrected him by saying that an officer had given him some writings at the funeral home. He passed the papers to Robison who started to read from one of them. The prosecution objected. Judge Thagard agreed that the letters were irrelevant and sustained the objection, but Robison just went to another letter and started to read from it, "Love, Joyce [Bailey]" to "Jonathan Daniels." Thagard sustained another objection. Joe Phelps then claimed that the letters were important evidence that "the litigants had communication in jail," and Black started to raise again the fact that they had not been searched before their release, but Thagard cut him off. "Do you have anything here," the judge demanded, "that shows that somebody brought them a weapon, or anything of that sort?" Though admitting that it could not produce such evidence, the defense insisted that the letters proved "they were passing things back and forth" and that it was "going to show that there was a weapon there." Sustaining the prosecution's objection, Thagard nevertheless allowed the defense to make the letters part of the record. Robison then read from yet another letter to "Jon" and signed "Joyce [Bailey]" and "Ruby Nell [Sales]," the prosecution objected, and the judge sustained the objection.[27] In spite of the successful objections, the defense had managed to present to the jury letters between Jon Daniels and black women.

Without explaining the significance, Robison also quizzed the state toxicologist about Jon Daniels's underpants. While waving the red underwear around so everyone in the court could see them, Robison asked if they had smelled of urine when the doctor examined them, and Rehling said yes. "There had not been any post mortem urination?" queried the defense counsel. The physician stated that there had been none and the trunks were dry. A few other questions completed Robison's cross-examination, which had effectively made points for the defense with a prosecution witness. As one white Alabamian who understood the defense's sordid tactics observed, "[T]he white citizens of Lowndes County want to believe that any Christian clergyman who wants Negroes to vote is likely to wear red underpants and yellow shoes, to read books called *The Fanatic* and to carry switchblade knives and .38 revolvers."[28] And, he might have added, kiss black women on the mouth.

After briefly questioning the surgeon who operated on Richard Morrisroe, the prosecution called to the witness stand Mrs. Virginia Varner, the owner of the Cash Store in Hayneville. An attractive dark-haired woman dressed in blue with black gloves, Varner told Arthur Gamble that she had been at her store when Jon Daniels was killed. According to her testimony, Tom Coleman came to the store without her calling him. He brought in a shotgun, leaned it against the wall, and walked outside. In the store with her was a black woman customer accompanied by two of her small grandchildren. Sometime later Coleman came back in, got the shotgun, asked if she had a closed sign, and went to the front door with his gun. She heard him say a couple of times that the store was closed, and then she heard a shot. Though she knew someone had been shot, she just continued making change and did not go to see what had happened.[29]

Under friendly cross-examination by Robison, Virginia Varner smiled at the defendant and said that Tom Coleman was her friend; the previous year she had called him for help when she had a robber in her store. The implication seemed to be that it was natural for her friend to come again to her defense. On the day of the shootings, she had called her daughter at home and told her to lock all the doors in the house because she had heard the civil rights workers had been released from the county jail. In the following few minutes she waited on several customers "as fast as I could, so I could" close the store. Robison's questions emphasized that, except for the women who worked in a beauty shop located in a room in the back of the store, Varner was working alone in the store. When Varner completed her testimony, Robison gallantly helped her from the stand.[30]

The next witness, Abell Hardy, an elderly, heavy black woman who used a walking stick to climb slowly into the stand, acknowledged that she had been in the Cash Store at the time Daniels was killed. She recalled that she heard someone say, "Get out, get out. Don't you know this place is closed?" Realizing that something bad was about to happen, she laid her head down on the counter and did not see the two shots fired. The shooting upset her so much that she had to sit down in the store and Mrs. Varner gave her "a nerve tablet." Later she went outside to her car, saw one dead body on the ground, and then drove away. In his few questions of the witness, defense attorney Joe Phelps again stressed that only women and two children were in the store when the shootings occurred.[31]

After hearing from six witnesses in the afternoon, Arthur Gamble requested a recess until the following morning. When newsmen and others suddenly rushed to leave, Leon W. Crocker, the armed bailiff who sat on a windowsill toward the front of the courtroom throughout the proceedings called out, "Order in the court." He then said, "Shut the door. You all sit down, and stay there." Granting the prosecution's request, Judge Thagard told the jurors to go with the bailiff to a motel in Montgomery, where they would be guests of the county for the evening.[32]

Around the courthouse the first day of the trial, almost no one, including the visiting journalists, thought that Tom Coleman would actually be convicted. A young newsman covering his first civil rights trial for the *Southern Courier* may have been the only one holding out hope for a conviction. Richard Valeriani of NBC News in the late afternoon went to the network's affiliate in Montgomery where he reported for the Huntley-Brinkley Report that everybody in Hayneville was certain that Coleman would be acquitted. Outraged workers at the station objected to Valeriani's "editorializing" and threatened not to transmit his taped or filmed story to New York. Valeriani insisted that it was not his opinion or even his analysis but the readily apparent belief of people in the community that he wanted to report accurately and objectively. Only through the intervention of station management did his report reach NBC News headquarters.[33]

In Montgomery, Attorney General Richmond Flowers agreed with Valeriani and continued to fulminate against the proceedings in Hayneville. He charged, "To try Tom Coleman in Lowndes County today or at this time when passions are so inflamed and when hatred is absolutely ruling the hearts of a majority of the people of that area in racial matters is a travesty that our system of law and order cannot permit." The defense knew, according to Flowers, that Coleman was guilty of first-degree murder and that a dismissal of the charge of manslaughter would lead to first-degree murder charges. His trial for manslaughter instead of murder was "a violation of our judicial processes." The shooting of Richard Morrisroe in the back convinced Flowers of Coleman's intent, and intent constituted the essential difference between murder and manslaughter. In predicting that the jury would acquit Coleman, the attorney general said, "My only hope is that . . . I may goad that jury into a conviction. But I must admit that is indeed far-fetched." The hasty trial of Coleman was an attempt to "whitewash a cold-blooded premeditated murder," "an ugly plot to condone murder in Lowndes," and a "mockery of justice."[34]

Observers from afar also had little doubt about the outcome of the trial. Comparing the proceedings in Hayneville to a kangaroo court, the *Memphis Commercial-Appeal* carried a cartoon depicting an Alabama judge in a kangaroo's pouch calling for "Order in this court!" "The Hayneville court and the citizens of that community," the Tennessee paper charged, "may feel that this is their matter, to be dealt with as they see fit. But justice cannot be cut to fit the whims or the prejudices of the individual or the community. Justice to be effective must be universal." The editorial suspected something other than real justice would result from the trial of Tom Coleman. Similarly, assailing the "judicial crime in Alabama," the *New York Post* assumed that "the defendant had a restful night's sleep" in spite of the "new judicial horror story [that] is unfolding in Alabama." In Congress, Representative Leonard Farbstein of New York deplored "the prostitution of justice that is currently being perpetrated in Hayneville, Alabama." Claiming that "southern courts are not even going through the motions of dispensing justice fairly," the congressman argued that the courts "have flung down defiance at the Nation in order to protect the most vicious agents of the white supremacy system," and he "implore[d] the Justice Department to seek out the power to prevent this outrageous judicial approval of racial murder."[35]

Scheduled to begin at nine A.M., the second day of the trial was delayed by Arthur Gamble's interest in conferring with witnesses and by

Judge Thagard's need to hear a motion in another case. When the Coleman case did reconvene, the defendant's family again sat in the courtroom in clear view of the jury, except that his son stood in the back of the room with other state troopers. In addition, Robert Shelton, Imperial Wizard of the United Klans, and Robert Creel, the Alabama Grand Dragon, arrived with a large contingent of Klansmen, including one man called the chief of the KBI (Klan Bureau of Investigation). The Klansmen showed an interest in the Coleman trial, but their special concern involved the retrial expected later in the day of fellow Klansmen for murdering Viola Liuzzo.[36]

On Wednesday morning prosecution called eight more witnesses. Dr. Staggard briefly testified about the condition of Daniels and Morrisroe when he found them at the scene soon after the shootings. The prosecutor then called court bailiff Leon Crocker, a longtime dominoes-playing friend of Coleman, who had been at the Cash Store when Coleman shot Daniels. The retired U.S. Department of Agriculture employee said that he arrived at the store a few minutes before Coleman appeared with a shotgun. Coleman put the shotgun inside, and then Coleman, Crocker, and Joe Bell Coker, another friend, sat on the bench outside until the four civil rights workers approached the store. Coleman, who had gone back inside, declared that the store was closed. According to Crocker, Daniels asked, "Are you threatening me?" and Coleman replied that he was just trying to get them to leave. When Daniels opened the left door of the double screen doors and started to enter the store, he was shot. Crocker testified that from his vantage point he could not see either the gun or who fired it. After the first shot, Morrisroe "made a break like he was going right in to his [Daniels's] assistance" and then twisted to his left and was himself shot.[37]

After the second shot, Crocker continued, Coleman came out of the store, gave the shotgun to Crocker, and told him, "You take the shotgun, you may need it. I'm going to the sheriff's office." Crocker put the gun in his car and later turned it over to a deputy sheriff. When Gamble handed him a shotgun for identification, Judge Thagard looked worried and said, "Gentlemen, I assume that someone has seen to it that the gun is not loaded?" Laughter rippled across the courtroom and in the jury box. Crocker confirmed that it was the same weapon. He had found two empty hulls on the step into the store and tossed them into his car; he later rescued them from his trash can and turned them over to a state investigator. Finally, the bailiff testified that he and two deputies had moved Daniels's body to some grass in the shade beside the store.[38]

On cross-examination, the defense immediately asked, "Did you see anything, Mr. Crocker, in Daniels's right hand?" The man who had known Tom Coleman for nearly fifty years replied, "There was a bright shiny object that resembled a knife blade. I didn't see the handle and I don't know what kind of knife it was, but it was a knife of some kind." He said that he had seen a three-inch knife blade just when Daniels asked if Coleman was threatening him. Joe Phelps then asked the same question about Morrisroe, and an emotionless Crocker said that he had seen in the priest's hand something he took "to be a pistol. It was a round object that looked like a gun barrel, in his hand. . . . I saw the barrel, I didn't see the handle. . . . He had it in his right hand." The defense could not produce the knife and pistol, but Phelps elicited from Crocker an explanation for their disappearance. As soon as Coleman had driven away, several civil rights workers arrived. "There were three, or four, at least," Crocker stated, "that stood around the dead man first and then left and went to the wounded one."[39] The prosecution's own witness had, therefore, provided crucial testimony for the defense. The prosecution did not immediately challenge his damaging testimony in redirect questioning but reserved the right to recall him at a later time. Thagard excused the witness and declared a short recess.

Twenty minutes later the trial resumed with Gamble recalling Crocker to the stand. Realizing the implications of the bailiff's testimony under cross-examination, Gamble asked, "Did you see him [the black civil rights worker who went to Daniels after he had been shot] pick up, or take away from there, any sort of knife or gun?" "No," said Crocker, "I didn't." The same question about Morrisroe drew another "I did not." Finally, Gamble asked Crocker whether he had seen a knife or gun on Daniels's body when he helped move it to the shade, and Crocker said simply, "No, sir. I did not."[40]

Intent on making his point for the defense, Phelps cross-examined the witness one last time. "Mr. Crocker," asked the attorney, "it's not your testimony to this jury that there was not the opportunity for these Negroes who went to the body to pick up a knife, or a gun, or both of them?" After Phelps rephrased his query, Crocker answered, "Oh, there was an opportunity. They went to the body." He agreed that several blacks had the chance to remove a knife or gun from Daniels's body or from the fallen Morrisroe.[41] Phelps had thus succeeded in getting Crocker to say that, after Daniels and Morrisroe had been shot, the black civil rights workers could easily have taken the weapons that the witness testified he saw in the hands of the victims.

The prosecution next called a succession of five black civil rights workers who had been released from jail with Daniels and Morrisroe on the afternoon of August 20. The first was Joyce Bailey. The attractive nineteen-year-old native of Fort Deposit had graduated from high school in 1964 and started working in a pajama factory in her hometown. She became a civil rights activist and joined SNCC in 1965.[42]

The bailiff shouted out an open window and across the lawn for Joyce Bailey to come up to the courtroom. Wearing a blue dress and red tennis shoes, she climbed the stairs to the courtroom, but before she took the stand, Judge Thagard suggested that "it might be a good idea to throw your chewing gum out. Just throw it out the window, there," he said. Prompted by Gamble, she then told about going to the Cash Store with Daniels, Morrisroe, and Ruby Sales to buy something to eat and a cold drink: "When we got to the door, Jonathan Daniels held the door open, and Ruby Sales stepped up to the door, and this unknown man in the store had a gun and started shouting 'to get out, the store is closed. I'll blow your God damned heads off, you son-of-a-bitches.' When he said that we stopped, and Ruby Sales and I started backing back. Jonathan Daniels was still standing at the door, then the man fired a shot." In reaction to her quoting Coleman, many in the courtroom laughed. Bailey continued to explain that at the first shot, as Daniels caught his stomach and fell backward, Morrisroe jerked her away and they started running. When the second shot hit Morrisroe, Bailey continued to run. The spectators and jury laughed again at the description of her running. To Gamble's last question she testified that neither Daniels nor Morrisroe had had a gun or a knife.[43]

In cross-examining Bailey, Robison again emphasized points favorable to the defense. He stressed that visitors brought things to the jailed civil rights workers. "Who delivered the stuff to you that stopped up all the toilets?" he asked. The judge sustained the prosecution's objection and had the question struck from the record, but Robison had sent his message to the jury. Just as he had with an earlier witness, Coleman's lawyer also asked about communication among the prisoners and quoted from a note to "Dear Jon" that was signed "Love, Joyce." Thagard sustained Gamble's objection. Robison then tried to bring up the prisoners' behavior during their week in jail, but it too was rejected by the court. Returning to his most emotional issue, interracial sex, Robison asked Bailey if she had kissed Jon Daniels when they got out of jail. She said no.[44] Nevertheless, the mere mention of a white man possibly kissing a black woman undoubtedly had the intended effect of creating disgust for Daniels among the all-white, all-male jury.

Robison proceeded to interrogate Bailey closely about events preceding the shootings. One provocatively phrased question suggested that Jon Daniels had told "Jimmie Rogers or Willie Vaughn at the time, that he would go down there, that store was supposed to be open to everybody and he [Daniels] would go down there and show the people about it."

Bailey denied ever having heard Daniels make such a statement, but Robison had again ably communicated to the all-white jury the threatening implication of his question. Under persistent pressure from Robison, she admitted that she had not heard Daniels ask Tom Coleman at the door to the store, "Are you threatening me?" Apparently to discredit her testimony, Robison also challenged Bailey about exactly where she and the other three activists were standing when the shots were fired. He wanted to know, for example, which door Daniels opened and where his feet were, where Ruby Sales was standing, and how far she and Morrisroe ran after the first shot. Several times Bailey had to admit that she simply had not noticed such details or could not recall them precisely. According to one observer, Robison's badgering left the witness "helpless and bewildered" as she floundered for responses.[45]

When Bailey told Robison that neither Daniels nor Morrisroe had anything in their hands as they approached the store, Robison immediately shifted from the threatening knife and gun to the perhaps more worrisome (at least to the provincial inhabitants of Hayneville) books found at the scene and asked if the two men had books with them. Bailey stated that she had not seen any books. Undeterred, Robison took the opportunity to repeat the sinister-sounding titles — *The Fanatic, The Church in the New Latin America, The Life and Times of Frederick Douglass*, and *Native Son*. He also made sure that he mentioned in front of the jury the George Washington Carver Homes in Selma, the black public housing project where Daniels had lived.[46]

Following Joyce Bailey to the witness stand was James Lee Bailey, an eighteen-year-old black from Fort Deposit. The scared young man could barely be heard when he started answering Gamble's questions, so Robison twice asked the court to have Bailey speak up. Bailey said that he had been standing near a fireplug at the street corner when the group of four approached the store; he never saw a knife, a gun, or any weapon in the hands of Daniels or Morrisroe. Bailey heard the shot that struck Jon Daniels and saw Daniels's arms fly up in the air; at the sound of a second shot, he started running for cover and did not see Morrisroe fall.[47]

After a brief examination by the prosecution, Robison returned to ground that he had covered with earlier witnesses. James Bailey admitted that the activists had had visitors while in jail. After he heard Bailey repeat that Daniels and Morrisroe had nothing in their hands as they walked to the store, Robison wanted to know if he had seen them carrying any books. Though Bailey replied in the negative, once again the defense counsel called out the titles. The experienced lawyer and state legislator gave Bailey a map of the area near the jail and the Cash Store and asked him to locate where he had been standing. The fearful youth looked nervously around the courtroom until Robison commanded, "Now, look here!" A moment later Robison asked Bailey if he had been present when someone warned Daniels and the others not to go to the store, and Bailey apparently replied in a near whisper, "Yes, sir." Not hearing the answer completely and suspecting a slight, Robison glared at the black teenager and challenged him, "You said 'Yes, *sir*,' didn't you?" Bailey revised his answer by saying that he had not heard anyone warn Daniels and the others not to go to the store.[48]

John Colvin, Jr., a sixteen-year-old from Fort Deposit, was the third black to testify for the prosecution on Wednesday morning. In a very low voice, Colvin, who had been standing with James Bailey when the shootings occurred, corroborated previous testimony on many points. He had occupied a jail cell with Father Morrisroe all week, and he never saw or heard about a knife or a gun. He also did not hear anyone warn Jon Daniels and the others not to go to the Cash Store. Under tough cross-examination by Joe Phelps, however, the eighth grader did finally say that he had seen Daniels kiss Joyce Bailey and that he had heard three shots. Following the example of Robison, Phelps used the cross-examination as an opportunity to mention the Carver Homes in Selma, to emphasize that many visitors went to the jail, to suggest that someone had warned Daniels not to go to the store, and to demonstrate the witness's inability to recall a number of details about the location of cars at the store and what happened just before the shootings.[49]

After John Colvin left the stand, the court took a brief recess. Most of the approximately two hundred spectators filling the courtroom walked around, went to the rest room, chatted, and smoked cigarettes. Local whites, openly confident of an acquittal and disparaging of the civil rights movement, commented about the interloping journalists, especially television crews from the "Colored Broadcasting System" and the "Nigger Broadcasting Company" who had set up their cameras outside the courthouse. Reporters for the Associated Press and United Press International took advantage of the break to call in their stories while other newsmen reworked their notes and visited among themselves and with people in town. During the recesses in his trial, Tom Coleman often stood and gazed out the window at Coleman Field, the school athletic field named for his father, or toward the home a block away where he had grown up and where his sister Hulda now lived. The jurors either went to the nearby jury room or, if the rain showers had stopped, strolled outside near the Confederate monument in the courthouse square.[50]

When the court reconvened, Arthur Gamble called Robert Earl Bailey to testify. The twenty-four-year-old native of Fort Deposit had bought a pack of cigarettes at the Cash Store a few minutes before the shootings, but he could add little new information about the incident. When the shots were fired, he was standing with the others at the corner and like the others he ran for safety. He testified that he had not seen a weapon of any kind in the hands of either Daniels or Morrisroe. In his cross-examination Robert Black brought out no new facts but tried to create many suspicions in the jurors' minds, especially about the alleged gun and knife. Although Robert Bailey told Black that visitors brought only food and books to the jail, he had to concede that he could not be certain that was all they brought. He also could not explain where the books found at the scene had come from because, just as several other witnesses, Bailey maintained that none of the four people who approached the store had had anything with them. Pressed by Black, Robert Bailey admitted that, except for the seminarian's small Bible, he did not know what Daniels or Morrisroe had carried in their pockets. In a final sarcastic question, Black asked, "Is this the Bible he had, called *The Fanatics*?" Bailey did not respond.[51]

After a recess for lunch, attorneys for each side announced their agreements on evidence that had been introduced in the trial. The defense granted that the gun and shells produced by C. J. Rehling were the same objects that Leon Crocker had found at the scene. On the other side, the prosecution accepted the four books brought to court by Dr. Rehling and Vaughan Hill Robison as the ones deputy sheriff Joe Jackson had found near Morrisroe.[52] After clearing up details concerning some of the physical evidence, the prosecution on Wednesday afternoon called its final and most dramatic witness.

Ruby Sales, the seventeen-year-old daughter of a career army man, had been born in Alabama but grew up in Columbus, Georgia, graduating from high school at age sixteen. She became involved in the civil rights movement at Tuskegee Institute. Working as a SNCC field secretary, she went to Lowndes County in the summer of 1965 where she and Jon Daniels promoted voter registration before participating in the Fort Deposit demonstration. Small, bright, and feisty, Sales made a formidable witness.[53]

Questioned by Arthur Gamble, Sales quickly and precisely told of going to the Cash Store and being confronted by Tom Coleman. He had cursed them and threatened them with a gun, and almost immediately thereafter he shot Jon Daniels. Sales was the only witness to say directly that Coleman fired the fatal shot. Just before the deadly blast, she had felt someone pull her back and she stumbled to the side of the door. When Gamble asked where Daniels fell, Sales, taking care to say only what she knew and could remember, acknowledged that she could not recall because she had been more concerned about his lying there than exactly where he fell. She also refused to speculate on just how far Richard Morrisroe had run from the store before being shot. To a question about a gun, knife, or any other weapon in the hands of Daniels or Morrisroe, Sales forcefully declared, "I did not see a knife or pistol in either of the gentlemen's hands."[54]

Under exhaustive cross-examination the young black girl refused to be intimidated by Vaughan Hill Robison, who was known for his "bullfrog voice box" and "iron-lunged" oratory in courtroom presentations and legislative debates. On several occasions, she even had the courage to correct him. She insisted, for example, that Morrisroe was "Father Morrisroe" because he was a Catholic priest. When the white lawyer referred to SNCC as "Snick," she pointed out that the "proper name" was the Student Nonviolent Coordinating Committee. When Robison wanted to know what kind of work Sales had been doing in Lowndes, she confidently explained, "We had been working in Lowndes County with the Lowndes County Christian Association for Human Rights to rid the racial barriers in this area, and that's [ignoring Robison's attempted interruption] our right under the Constitution of the United States. That's exactly what we were doing." Robison asked if that was "what you were doing in Hayneville when you were arrested?" and Sales declared, "We were down in Fort Deposit picketing for our constitutional rights." Unlike other witnesses who could not recall what appeared on their protest signs, Sales told her skeptical interrogator exactly what the signs had said: "Equal treatment for all, and no back doors" and "No more back doors." Moreover, she reminded the court that others involved in the demonstration "were local people of Fort Deposit and Lowndes County, [who] felt they had certain rights, and they were exercising their rights."[55]

To Robison's suggestion that she had written off for money from the county jail, Sales replied that she had not sent any letters while confined in Hayneville. Under further questioning, however, she acknowledged that she had written to Jon Daniels, "a personal friend of mine." Apparently appalled that a black woman would publicly refer to a white man that way, but also pleased because such an admission would surely offend the jury, Robison repeated, "A personal friend of yours?" Undaunted, Sales reasserted, "Right. He was a friend. We worked together. He was a friend of mine, right." Her response elicited so much laughter and murmuring in the room that the bailiff called out, "Order in the court."[56]

Resuming the questioning on a completely different tack, Robison quizzed Ruby Sales about her statements to the press soon after Daniels's death. "You made a statement for *Time* magazine, didn't you?" he asked. A bit disconcerted but also somewhat defiant, Sales said, "I don't know who I made a statement to. It might have been *Time, Life, Look,* I don't know." But she insisted, "I told the truth about what happened." Robison persisted: "Made statements to UP and AP about it too?" Now annoyed, Sales sarcastically replied, "I told you a moment ago, I made statements and all the people — I don't know who — UP, it could have been IP, I don't know." Coleman's lawyer then read from a statement she had made to the United Press, the Associated Press, and *Time* magazine. It started, "The white man came out and told us the store was closed."

At the end of the long quotation, Robison asked, "Is that true?" When Sales started to answer, the lawyer interrupted, repeating "Is that true?"

"Wait," she asked. "Let me . . ."

"I want you to answer the question," demanded Robison, raising his voice, "is that true?"

"You can answer that yes or no," interjected Judge Thagard.

"Okay, well, thank you," said Sales.

"Is that true?" the lawyer persisted.

"In order for me to tell you . . . ," the black woman tried to explain.

"Is that true?" shouted Robison.

". . . on the grounds — that is — because he — I didn't — he is hollering at me," protested the witness in a shaky voice.

"Is it true?" Robison thundered.

"Yes, some of those things are true," answered Sales.

"Some of those things are true?" Robison repeated.

"Because you know how . . . ," Sales began.

"Never mind," interrupted Robison, "you have answered the question.

Ruby Sales turned toward Thagard and said, "May I say something?"

"I can't let you do that," the judge declared.[57]

Pursuing another line of questioning, one the defense had emphasized with other witnesses, Robison asked Sales what objects the prisoners had in their possession while in jail. She said that she had not had a Bible but did not know if others did. He then repeated the titles of the four, by then, notorious books and asked if the civil rights workers had them in the jail. Like her colleagues, Sales conceded that they did. When she stated that she did not know who brought them to the jail, Robison took the opportunity to establish that the women had not been searched either on entering or leaving the jail. He also got Sales to admit that she did not know where everyone went after they were released.[58] The implications for the jury clearly were that the women could have brought the books into and out of the jail, and they, therefore, also could have secreted into and out of the jail a knife and a gun, and that the male activists who left the main group once they were released from jail also could have obtained a gun and a knife somewhere before going to the Cash Store.

Robison tried to impeach the witness by finding holes in her recollections. He attempted, for instance, to tie her into verbal knots over whether the door to the store was open when they walked up to it. Sales maintained that Coleman had opened the door, yet other witnesses had said that Daniels *reached* to open the door. She tried to clarify the point by telling the court, "Do you think he was standing behind closed doors, in the door? He was standing in the door and the door had to be opened." When Robison sarcastically called her statement "very enlightening," laughter burst out in the courtroom and the bailiff again called for order.[59] The lawyer did not, however, try to resolve the discrepancy by distinguishing between the screen door and the wooden door.

Instead, to discredit the witness, Robison asked about more details surrounding the shooting of Daniels. He wanted to know, for example, precisely where everyone was standing. In describing how far Morrisroe and Bailey had been behind her and Daniels, Sales could be no more exact than "pretty close." Robison was dissatisfied. When he caught her looking elsewhere in the courtroom, he commanded her to look at him and answer his question about the distance. She merely said, "In relationship to feet, inches, mileage, I cannot say." When Robison asked how many cars had been parked in front of the store, Sales replied defiantly, "I didn't pay any attention. . . . I cannot truthfully say and I'm not going to say."[60]

In his final questioning of Ruby Sales, Robison returned to the defense contention that someone had removed the mysterious weapons from Daniels and Morrisroe while they lay on the ground outside the Cash Store after the shootings. Sales stated that she had not seen anyone approach the two white men during the ten or fifteen minutes she remained at the scene. For the first time Robison asked specifically about the whereabouts of SNCC worker Jimmy Rogers. Sales said that Rogers had comforted her and quieted her down immediately after the shootings because she was in shock. The defense lawyer pointed out that she did not know where Rogers went after she left the vicinity of the store.[61] Robison did not accuse Rogers of taking the weapons but obviously tried to suggest that he had the opportunity to do so.

In the most heated exchanges of the trial, Ruby Sales had withstood what one observer called Robison's "scathing cross examination." She had been shaken several times but she had not been afraid and had stuck to her story. In a "loud and clear account," she had accused Tom Coleman of shooting Jon Daniels and Richard Morrisroe.[62]

The prosecution called one more witness. E. J. Dixon, a plainclothes captain with the Alabama Department of Public Safety and longtime acquaintance of Tom Coleman, testified that Coleman told him late in the afternoon of August 20 what had happened earlier at the Cash Store. According to Dixon, Coleman admitted shooting two men with a shotgun — he shot one when he reached into his pocket for what he thought was a knife, and he shot the other when he ran toward Coleman. During his cross-examination of Dixon, Robert Black emphasized that Coleman had signed no confession and that he had made his statement before his lawyers arrived in Hayneville. When the defense lawyer asked about Father Morrisroe and a gun, the state trooper said, "Well, now, a gun was mentioned, but I don't remember the exact statement that was made about the gun at that time." Black then asked, "Could Tom have made the statement that it appeared that Morrisroe had a gun?" Dixon accepted the possibility.[63]

The final element in the prosecution's case came in the form of a showing, or a statement, from the Reverend Richard Morrisroe, who was still in Chicago recuperating from his gunshot wounds. The prosecution and the defense agreed that the statement reflected what Morrisroe would have said if he had testified in court. Arthur Gamble read the declaration to the court. Morrisroe contended that the group of four had gone to the Cash Store to get something to drink, and when Jon Daniels reached the door a man told them that the store was closed and ordered them to leave. Daniels asked if the man were threatening them, and the man "answered in effect, you damn right I am." "Almost instantly after the statement was made one shot was fired at Daniels. I did not want to play hero," admitted Morrisroe. "Another shot was fired, and I was struck by that shot in my lower spine, and I fell to the ground." Aware of the defense's plan to assert that he and Daniels had been armed, Morrisroe stated, "To my knowledge, at the time of the threat and the first shot, Daniels did not have a knife, gun, stick, or other weapon in his hand. The only thing I had in my hand was a dime."[64]

After presenting Morrisroe's brief account, Gamble rested the state's case. Vaughan Hill Robison, refusing to acknowledge the honesty and accuracy of the priest's statement, insisted that Judge Thagard reiterate fully to the jury its limited significance. The judge instructed the jury, "You should take that as if the witness Morrisroe had appeared and so testified. . . . [The defense's agreeing to accept the statement] doesn't mean that the defendant admits that is true. . . . It will be up to this jury, weighing that along with all the other testimony in the case, to determine how much weight he will give to that statement."[65]

The absence of Richard Morrisroe made the victims seem even more invisible and nonexistent and Tom Coleman's deeds less real and important. Not only was the priest not in court, but also Daniels had been reduced to a box of inert clothing and a few books that the defense portrayed as sinister. The white jurors, who heard only rebellious young blacks defend Daniels and Morrisroe, could easily dismiss their testimony as unreliable. Coleman's lawyers created for the jury an image of Daniels as somehow deserving his fate; the slain seminarian became something unworthy of the court's concern. And the prosecution acquiesced in the process. It could not offer contrary evidence in the form of witnesses who had known Daniels well and could describe his humanity — his complex personality, character, motivations, and actions. A reporter for *Newsweek* characterized the proceedings as "like a second, formal, larger crime of extinction and effacement — in a sense, in that courtroom, Daniels died a second and more final time."[66]

The defense obtained a ten-minute recess before presenting its side of the case. In what one observer called "a calm choreography of perjury," four witnesses for the defense testified about the events of August 20, followed by ten character witnesses. The first defense witness was Harvey Lancaster, the local agent of the Alcohol Beverage Control Board. Present when the demonstrators were jailed in Hayneville, Lancaster had searched all of the male prisoners but had found no books or money. He was also at the county jail six days later when they were released and testified that none of the prisoners was searched at that time. After the civil rights workers left the jail, Lancaster drove to the courthouse, and then, with several other men, including two deputies, drove around town to see whether the newly freed people were dispersing or getting ready to start trouble. When he got back to the courthouse, he heard Tom Coleman say that he was going down to the Cash Store.[67]

Under cross-examination by the prosecution, the ABC agent said that no one found any knives or guns on the arrested demonstrators when they were searched. He had gone to the Cash Store after the shooting, had returned briefly to the courthouse to call an ambulance, and then drove back to the store, where he helped load Daniels and Morrisroe into the ambulance. He also rode in the ambulance to the hospital and the mortuary. At no time had he seen a knife, a pistol, or any other weapon. Lancaster conceded to the defense, however, that he arrived at the scene about ten minutes after the shootings.[68]

The second witness for the defense was Tom Coleman's first cousin, Joe Bell Coker. A small man with a nervous tic on the left side of his face, Coker was a lifelong resident of Hayneville. On August 20, he had gone to the Cash Store to buy a Coca-Cola and stayed to visit with Leon Crocker. They sat down on the bench outside and were chatting when Coleman drove up, took a shotgun into the store, and then joined them on the bench. By the time Daniels and "some *nigger* women" walked up to

the store, Coleman had gone back inside. As other witnesses had testified, Coker said that Coleman declared the store closed, that Daniels
asked if Coleman were threatening him, and that Coleman said he was
not and repeated his declaration that the store was closed. To Vaughan
Hill Robison's question, "Did you see anything in Daniels's hand at the
time?" Coker answered, "He had an open pocket knife in his hand."
According to Coker, Daniels tried to enter the store and Coleman shot
him; Morrisroe kept coming forward, even though Coleman told him to
leave. The priest "had something in his hand, an object — shiny object
that looked like a pistol to me." Coleman then fired a blast of buckshot at
Morrisroe too.[69]

Coker's descriptions of the knife and gun became more graphic under
cross-examination. The knife "looked like a switch-blade knife to me,"
and the gun was "[s]ilver colored." Perhaps more significantly, he maintained that Daniels still clutched the knife when he fell to the porch with a
load of buckshot in his chest and Morrisroe held onto his gun as he
collapsed; neither weapon was dropped to the ground, where Coker
might have obtained a better view of them. After the second shot, Coker
went into the store and exited through a side door toward the back. He
never saw either weapon again.[70]

The third defense witness, a construction worker with long sideburns,
had lived in Lowndes County for six years. While driving a gravel truck
home from work on the afternoon of August 20, Edward Mims had
noticed a "bunch of Negroes and two white boys standing beside the
road" near the Cash Store. By the time he returned to town in his pickup
truck, the shootings had already taken place. He parked his pickup next to
the store, got out, and walked around to the front of the store. "Well,
when I got out of the pick-up and walked — started around the store
there," he told defense attorney Joe Phelps, "I met a Negro boy coming
around there, around the store then. . . . He seemed to be putting something in his pocket, when I met him. It looked like a knife." When Phelps
pressed, Mims declared, "It was about the size of a knife . . . it looked like
the back of a knife." Mims went on to the front of the store and saw Billy
Bevis. Together they watched another "colored boy" kneeling and talking with the wounded priest; the black "picked up something from the
ground" and "stuck it in his, ah, britches, or pockets."[71]

On cross-examination Arthur Gamble made Ed Mims repeat that he
did not know for certain what the two black youths put in their pockets.
The prosecutor failed to challenge Mim's testimony on the important
issue of whether the blacks actually removed objects from Daniels and
Morrisroe. Instead, Gamble seemed to concede that Mims had indeed

seen something. For example, he asked him, "Now, Ed, do you know where he got that object from?"[72] The implicit concession constituted a major victory for the defense.

The last defense witness to testify about the fatal events of August 20 was William Lamont Bevis. Billy Bevis had lived nearly all his twenty-five years in Hayneville and currently worked at a local stockyard. In court he said that, as he drove away from another store in town that afternoon, he saw several blacks running toward the square. He parked down the street from Cash Store and walked back to the front of the store. "And, I saw this white man lying on the ground — on this little concrete step on the front of the store," he told an inquiring Robison, "and I saw this Negro, kind of slim, dark looking Negro. It looked like he had been leaning down over him, and he was straightening up and moving off, and I could see the blade of a knife protruding out of his hand, and he run around the corner of the building." Bevis had not yet figured out exactly what had happened. After glancing inside the store, he turned and saw Morrisroe. More important, Bevis

> saw another Negro down on his hands and knees between me and this other white man, and it looked like he was trying to pick up something off the ground, and I hollered at him and told him to get away from that boy because I knew he did not have business being around him. So, I started over there towards him and he started straightening up and it looked like he had a pistol in his hand, and he turned his back to me and stepped across the boy and started going up towards that seedhouse right next to Cash Store, and I walked over to him, the boy on the ground, to see what was the matter with him, and I could see that he was bleeding a little bit. I heard him say something about, "Where is the gun?" He seemed to be in a dazed condition.[74]

In cross-examining Billy Bevis, Gamble again appeared to accept the contention that the victims had been armed. For instance, he asked for a better description of the knife blade. The witness retreated somewhat when he conceded, "Well, I couldn't see the handle. It happened so fast, I couldn't tell if it was a switch-blade. I know it was some kind of pocket knife, though." Unlike Robison, Gamble did not aggressively challenge the wavering witness. He did remind Bevis that one week after the shootings he had told a state investigator that the object looked like a knife. "But now you say it didn't appear to be a knife, it was a knife?" asked Gamble. When Bevis replied, "Yes, sir," the prosecutor let the matter drop. Similarly, he did not try to corner the witness over his vague description of the gun removed from Morrisroe. Claiming to have seen only the handle and the trigger guard, Bevis described them respectively as "walnut, or something like that" and "kind of bright and shiny." Rather than demanding more information about the weapons, Gamble moved on to question Bevis about his help in moving Daniels's body into the shade.[75]

After Billy Bevis left the witness stand, the defense called a succession of friendly witnesses who testified as to Coleman's excellent standing in the community. A Methodist minister from Pine Hill, Alabama, stated that the defendant's reputation "was very good." The Hayneville Presbyterian minister, who had known Coleman for more than thirty years, also said that he had a good reputation. The pastor of the local Christian church agreed. Two employees of the state highway department, including a former director, observed that Coleman performed well on the job. Further, the probate judge of Lowndes County, the sheriff of Butler County, and a judge from Greenville all swore to Coleman's fine reputation.[76]

After hearing from fourteen witnesses in fifty-three minutes, the defense rested. The prosecution did not cross-examine any of the character witnesses, except for a question to clarify the affiliation of one of the ministers. Arthur Gamble did not offer in rebuttal witnesses to raise questions about Coleman's reputation. He did not try to elicit from witnesses information or opinions critical of the defendant, even though people in the community knew that Coleman's character was not pristine. On September 29, the day the last witnesses appeared, an account in the *New York Herald-Tribune* reported that Coleman was "known as a violent, heavy-drinking man, maddened by the prospect of Negroes voting in Lowndes County."[77] The prosecutors also surely knew Coleman's real reputation and remembered that several years before he had killed a man, yet the prosecution neither mentioned the earlier shooting nor offered any explanation for his slaying of Jon Daniels to counter his attorneys' notion of self-defense.

In the middle of a rainy Wednesday afternoon, the lawyers summed up their respective cases for the jury. After one prosecutor spoke, two defense lawyers presented their side and a final prosecutor ended the summations. County solicitor Carlton Perdue declared that Tom Coleman should be convicted because he "voluntarily deprived a human being of his life and this is manslaughter in the first degree." In arguing for conviction, however, Perdue conceded important points that not even defense witnesses had made. He said, for example, that Virginia Varner had authorized Coleman to close her store and that Jon Daniels was "attempting to force his way" into the Cash Store when Coleman shot him. Perdue also said that Richard Morrisroe had been moving forward toward the door when Coleman shot him, even though Morrisroe had been shot in the flank.[78] Prosecutor Perdue's summation, whether careless or deliberate, reinforced Tom Coleman's defense.

For the defense, Joe Phelps spoke first. Noting that he was honored to be associated with the defendant, he reminded the twelve members of the all-white jury that Coleman was one of them, that they had known his parents, that they knew his wife and children. Phelps stated his case simply: "You know Tom Coleman and you know he had to do what he did. . . . Tom Coleman did as anyone of you would have had to do." Although he did not dispute the prosecution's contention that Coleman had fired the shot that killed Daniels, Phelps attacked Perdue's claim that Coleman was guilty of manslaughter. Arguing that his client was "protecting all of us" on the afternoon of August 20, the attorney proclaimed, "I think we ought to thank Almighty God that we have got a man such as Tom Coleman in our midst." He unequivocally stated that Daniels and Morrisroe had been armed and that unidentified blacks had removed the weapons from them after they had been shot; Coleman, therefore, fired in self-defense.[79]

Discounting Daniels's clerical clothing, Phelps quoted scripture to describe the seminarian and the priest: "Beware of false prophets which come to you in sheep's clothing, for inwardly they are ravening wolves." "It is not new in history," he contended, "for people to hide their evil motives behind the cloth of the church. These were not men of God as we know them here in Alabama." Quite the contrary, they were agitators and terrorists. Phelps reminded the jury that witnesses had said that Daniels kissed a black woman after he was released from jail, and interracial kissing seemed to represent the worst kind of attack on the southern way of life. Kissing seemed, in the southern white view of racial etiquette, to warrant shooting. Tom Coleman had, therefore, acted wisely and bravely when he in effect said, according to Phelps, "This far shall they come and no further — here all evil must cease."[80] If the jurors did not accept that the seminarian and priest had been armed, they would surely abhor the slightest form of interracial sex.

Vaughan Hill Robison followed Phelps. Employing his great oratorical skills, he pleaded for his client in "the most unusual case I have ever tried." Addressing the jurors first in a low voice, he said, "You are men, you are *not* IBM machines, you're not computers, but you are men, and as men, you have a mind, you have a heart. You . . . have . . . a . . . *soul!*" Aiming directly for their emotions, Robison stressed, "We got a right to protect ourselves." Daniels and Morrisroe had gone to the Cash Store "looking for trouble." "If a man says to me, 'Are you threatening me?,' " the lawyer confided, "I would say he was looking for trouble. And he found it." Coleman, on the other hand, went to the store simply to keep down violence.[81]

Although Robison repeatedly suggested that visitors to the jail had smuggled weapons to Daniels and Morrisroe and that they were thereby armed when they approached the store, he maintained that the jurors "can believe that knife was there or not. . . . But when those folks came down there and started in on Mrs. Varner, Tom Coleman did no more under this threat to him and to her and to the community than we would." Drawing on a ritual used at rallies of the Ku Klux Klan, Robison, shouted, "God give us such men! Men with great hearts, strong minds, pure souls — and ready hands! *Tall men.* . . ." By shooting Daniels, Coleman was defending the southern white way of life, and in particular its most cherished ingredient, southern womanhood (though Robison failed to explain how a white seminarian, a white priest, and two young black women posed a threat to Virginia Varner). Robison called for an acquittal to show that "a man has a right to defend himself and his lady." Anything other than setting Coleman free would be "a mockery of justice."[82]

The defense strategy involved providing the jury with a legally acceptable justification for Coleman's actions. His attorneys in effect made Daniels the offender and Coleman the defender by claiming that the seminarian was armed. Coleman only responded to Daniels's threat of violence, so the homicide was excusable. Perhaps more significant, the defense also appealed to the jury's meaner instincts. The Jon Daniels presented to the jurors by Robison, Phelps, and Black was offensive to white southern sensibilities. Not only was Daniels working for civil rights for blacks, but he was an outsider, wore strange shoes and underpants, read wicked books, and kissed black girls. If it worked, the defense's emotional appeal would make the all-white jury want to convict Daniels instead of Coleman, and it certainly would ensure Coleman's acquittal.

To conclude the arguments before the jury, the circuit solicitor began his final summation for the prosecution. A number of spectators, assuming anything of importance had already been said, were already leaving the courtroom. At the outset, Arthur Gamble declared, "I feel like I have to apologize to you for the way this case was presented by the state," yet the statement referred not to any weakness in the state's case but rather to bothering the jury with the case itself. With a noticeable lack of passion and commitment, Gamble called for a conviction. Urging the jury to discount Coleman's supposedly good reputation, he reminded the twelve white men that "the cemeteries are filled with people killed by men of good character." Gamble asked the jurors to pay attention to the testimony and to the facts.[83]

In response to the opposition's claim of self-defense, Gamble stated, "The defense would have produced these weapons if they were actually there." Gamble nevertheless played into the defense's hand by twice mentioning "that knife," even though his own witnesses had testified that neither Daniels nor Morrisroe had been armed. He simply accepted a vital element of the defense. "There is no evidence here at all," the solicitor reminded the jury, "that Jonathan Daniels was making any attempt to actually cut him with that knife."[84]

The prosecutor also argued on a higher ground for the conviction of Tom Coleman. "I ask you to remember one thing," he said to the jurors. "This country was built on the theory that this is a country of laws, not men. When we turn to men, when we forsake the law we have not long to survive. . . . It is your responsibility whether we have a government of laws or a government of men." He believed their conclusion should be clear because in "Lowndes County we are still a government of laws, not of men."[85] The significance of Gamble's theoretical position may have been missed by those who believed that the entire civil rights movement demonstrated that the nation was a government of men, such as Martin Luther King and Lyndon Johnson, and not of laws, such as the ones requiring segregation that they supported.

Following the summations, Judge Thagard charged the jury. Tom Coleman had been charged with first-degree manslaughter, he noted. In response, the defendant had pled not guilty. The prosecution, therefore, had to prove "beyond a reasonable doubt, and to a moral certainty" that Coleman was guilty as charged. Thagard explained the charge as "the unlawful killing of a human being without malice. That is an un-premeditated result of a passion-heated blood, caused by sudden sufficient provocation." He defined "sufficient provocation" as nothing less than actual or impending assault; verbal abuse would not be enough. The defendant's plea of self-defense meant the defense had to prove that Tom Coleman "could not have retreated without apparently increasing his peril. If the defendant, by attempting to retreat, would not have exposed himself to greater peril than was involved in his standing his ground and fighting it would have been his duty to retreat." The judge instructed the jurors to "look to the evidence." They should weigh the testimony and use their common sense in evaluating its truthfulness.[86]

Thagard also tried to help the jury understand the relevance of the character witnesses produced by the defense. He said, "[I]f that testimony of good character is sufficient to raise a reasonable doubt in your minds of the guilt of the defendant even though you might not have had such a reasonable doubt without the character testimony, or without the testimony of his good character, then it would be your duty to give the defendant the benefit of that reasonable doubt and to acquit him." In a clear and logical fashion, the judge led the jurors through the issues in the case. First, they had to decide if Daniels had been killed by a gun. Second, they had to figure out if Coleman had fired the fatal shot. Third, the jurors had to determine the circumstances surrounding the shooting. The circumstances would determine if Coleman had killed Daniels unlawfully, which would produce a guilty verdict, or lawfully, which would yield an acquittal. Any reasonable doubt about the lawful nature of Coleman's deed or about his intention to shoot Daniels should cause the jury to return an acquittal.[87]

The case went to the jury a few minutes before five on Wednesday afternoon. The twelve white males met in the jury room just off the courtroom, where the judge made available the indictment and all the exhibits in the case. The lawyers, newsmen, and many spectators milled about the courtroom while the jurymen considered the evidence. Tom Coleman paced around the room before sitting quietly with his family. After deliberating for one hour and three minutes, the jurors returned. They reported that they had not reached a verdict and that they needed more time to confer and consider the charges. Judge Thagard ordered the bailiff to lock them up for the night in a Montgomery motel. "I know you are tired and worn out," he told the jurymen, "and I'm going to let you go back to Montgomery and get a good night's sleep and a good dinner. Be back in the box at nine o'clock in the morning, and I will let you go back in and resume your deliberations." As the men filed by Tom Coleman, who was sitting at the defense table near the jury box, the last juror looked over at him and winked. That wink summed up the sentiment in the courtroom. No one thought that the jury would convict Tom Coleman. Coleman too was confident.[88]

The court convened the next morning at nine o'clock and the jury resumed its deliberations. Few townspeople bothered to go to the courthouse on that dreary, rainy late summer day to hang around for the jury's verdict. The judge and sheriff's deputies sat and drank Cokes as they waited. At 9:28 the jury announced that it had reached a verdict; it had deliberated for a total of one hour and thirty-one minutes. When the jurors returned to the courtroom, Judge Thagard asked, "Gentlemen, have you reached a verdict?" The foreman, Chris E. Gates, a county highway employee, responded, "We have, your honor." He then handed the verdict to the circuit clerk, who was the wife of Tom Coleman's cousin. Mrs. Kelly D. Coleman slowly and soberly read it to the quiet courtroom: "We, the jury, find the defendant, Tom Coleman, not guilty."[89]

"Oh, God, I knew it all the time," Coralie Coleman cried out, then rushed to the front of the courtroom toward her husband, followed by their daughter and son. The gum-chewing Coleman, like most people in the courtroom, listened to the verdict without any show of emotion. The jurors, dismissed by Thagard, filed out of the jury box, and each shook hands with the defendant. One juror called to him, "We gonna be able to make that dove shoot now, ain't we?" Coleman then embraced his wife as other friends and relatives crowded around him. Four white women, who earlier had loudly discussed how they thought Jon Daniels "got what he deserved," joined the group congratulating Coleman and shaking his hand. One woman took Coleman's face between her hands and told him, "Good ole boy. See? Didn't I tell you not to worry?" He said, "Yes, ma'am. Yes, ma'am. Thank you." When a newsman asked for his reaction to the verdict, an unsmiling Tom Coleman remarked between drags on a cigarette, "I'm just happy."[90]

The twelve white jurors went downstairs to the clerk's office, where bailiff Leon Crocker, Coleman's friend and a key witness for the defense, paid each juror twenty-four dollars for his four days of service to the county. It was a happy scene until out-of-town journalists intruded and they suddenly became serious and silent. When one reporter asked how much they were being paid, a juror merrily answered, "Not enough!" The reporters also, of course, wanted to know about the jury's deliberations. One juror teasingly said, "I'll tell you the dog story that fellow over there told us, if you want." Otherwise the twelve men refused to talk about their discussion of the case. One said, "You are wasting your time." The foreman even more emphatically told the newsmen, "No comment, ever." In a drizzling rain, Tom Coleman and his family quickly left the courthouse, and the other participants soon dispersed. The trial was over.[91]

Newsmen covering the trial also rushed from the courthouse to write their stories, with the wire service reporters using the phone bank behind the courthouse to telephone their editors. As word of Coleman's acquittal spread across the country, many people responded quickly. Nearly all of them condemned the verdict. In Washington, D.C., that morning, Senator Thomas McIntyre of New Hampshire informed his colleagues on the floor that he had just seen a report of the jury's verdict on the teletype in the lobby. The communists, McIntyre declared,

> at their very worst, in kangaroo court after kangaroo court, have never mangled justice worse than the court in Lowndes County.
>
> Justice, Lowndes County style, seems to result in the same sort of disregard for the truth and the same sort of distortion of the law for political purposes as any form of communism or nazism ever known in history.

Justice, Lowndes County style, is very simple. Murder is no crime in Lowndes County so long as the victim is engaged in furthering the law of the land by working for equal justice for all men. . . .

Jonathan Daniels was killed in cold blood in Lowndes County, Ala. There is no dispute about this fact. The man who killed him is known. There is no dispute about that. His killer was guilty of murder. There is little dispute about this. But his killer walks the streets today a free man. Mr. President, when the judge and jury which condoned a killer stand before their Maker on judgment day, they shall stand convicted.[92]

Other observers who had wanted a conviction blasted the verdict. In one of the more restrained statements, the Reverend Richard Morrisroe declared from his hospital bed in Chicago that the "judgment does not at all square with the facts in the case." A spokesman for Morrisroe labeled "pure fiction" the idea that Morrisroe and Daniels had been armed. "It sounds like a comic strip to say that they were armed," declared the Reverend Thomas McDonough. Though Morrisroe expected the verdict, Father McDonough stated, "It is so out of keeping with the facts that I could not imagine such a verdict being given by any court of law, any jury of real Americans." The mayor of Jon Daniels's hometown said that the verdict was "beyond my comprehension" and a "miscarriage of justice." New Hampshire's governor damned the acquittal as "a travesty of justice." An official of the NAACP called the jury's decision "a monstrous farce" that gave "a blanket license to kill . . . to every Alabama bigot who declares open season on Negroes and their white friends."[93]

Appalled by the outcome of the trial, Alabama Attorney General Richmond Flowers called the verdict "shameful" and said that it "places the good name of Alabama and her people on the bigoted stake of racism." He perceived in the Coleman trial the "democratic process going down the drain of irrationality, bigotry and improper enforcement of the law." The attorney general worried, "Now those who feel they have a license to kill, destroy and cripple have been issued that license. It is our duty to do what we can to retrieve it." Speaking to newsmen in Montgomery with pictures of the state capitol and President Lyndon B. Johnson in the background, Flowers contended that "the great majority of Alabamians are outraged by this callous disregard for taking of human life and enforcement of the law."[94]

Religious leaders who knew Jon Daniels also criticized the verdict. To Dean John B. Coburn of the Episcopal Theological School in Cambridge, the jury's conclusion was an "utterly shocking travesty of justice" and "a flagrant denial of justice." The Right Reverend John E. Hines, the presiding bishop of the Episcopal Church, also thought it "a travesty of justice"; he was particularly angered by the "studied care with which the defense assassinated the character of a man already dead. . . . Fortunately, Jonathan Daniels's integrity survived such despicable action." The bishop of New Hampshire expressed his grievance more specifically: "Those of us who knew Jonathan Daniels and who know Fr. Morrisroe are absolutely certain that the testimony regarding their possession of knives and guns is false testimony. It is deeply disturbing that the course of justice can be so easily thwarted."[95]

Not all comment, however, was critical. When the trial ended, Coleman's chief lawyer, Vaughan Hill Robison, told newsmen outside the courthouse that he was "gratified by the verdict," which had been rendered in "a fair and just trial in accord with the demands of justice." Robison also gave the press a written statement: "Tom Coleman has been tried in a temple of justice where he should have been tried and where all the facts were presented. The verdict of the jury was the only one that could have been rendered based on the facts. It was a fair and just verdict. Tom Coleman has been exonerated."[96]

Similarly, the Lowndes County solicitor showed no displeasure with the result, even though he had not gained a conviction. Carlton Perdue said, "I wasn't surprised at all. What could you expect in this county?" A few days later Perdue defended the prosecution of Coleman and, in effect, the outcome of the trial. "Mr. Gamble and I," said Perdue, "did the very best we could and presented the case in its most thorough manner." He responded to critics of the manslaughter charge by pointing out that it "was rendered by a true and honorable and a well represented cosmopolitan jury of Lowndes County and with nothing swept under any rug and nothing covered up." In the trial, according to the solicitor, "the matter was handled in the most judicial manner it could be humanly possible in this county or any other county. . . . Everything was done that humanly could be done in fairness to everybody concerned." Gamble was "proud of the actions we took. . . . I have done this case to the very best of my ability."[97]

Newspapers outside the South heaped condemnation on the Hayneville court. Calling it "the shame of Hayneville," the *New York Post* declared, "The Hayneville verdict is an affront to the nation, and to human decency. Contempt for justice has rarely been more brazenly exhibited. . . . there was no serious pretense in this fake trial." The *St. Louis Post-Dispatch* commented, "The notion that men of the cloth, active in a non-violent cause, go about threatening armed deputy sheriffs with knives is one that could only be advanced in the darkest reaches of an area darkened to justice." National columnist William S. White stressed "the absolute, the desperate, necessity that justice must not only be done but that justice must be seen by reasonable men to have been done." The southern-born White contended that "Hayneville has thrown out before all the world an irredeemably soiled suggestion of injustice done." In his newspaper column James Farmer, the national director of the Congress of Racial Equality, excoriated "the monkey logic of the old South" that set Tom Coleman free. Farmer was "outraged that this nation takes the Hayneville charade in its stride, outraged that we still consider the state of Alabama as a sovereign part of our country, outraged that we . . . wink at the scum who make their case through the business end of a shotgun."[98]

Art Buchwald took the acquittal of Tom Coleman as an opportunity to wonder "how Jack the Ripper would have fared if he had been a citizen of Alabama and had been caught and tried in Lowndes County." He speculated that "the grand jury would indict him [Jack the Ripper] for manslaughter instead of murder on the grounds that, although he killed five women, it was done without malice." Before a jury "made up of friends of the Ripper family," the prosecution would then "reluctantly" charge Jack with the crimes while spectators chuckled and applauded. A defense witness would explain to Jack's lawyer, "Rip was walking down the street late at night when this here woman pulls a switchblade on him, and he had no choice but to slash out at her first. It was quick thinking on his part, because that woman meant to do him harm." Another witness, Zeke Ripper, would tell how another woman pulled a pistol on Jack the Ripper, so he slit her throat. When asked about the pistol, Zeke Ripper explained, "Some nigra rushed up and took it away 'fore the police came." The defense then discounted two other of Jack's slayings because "Jack saw both these women kissing nigras and he went up to them and told them to stop it and when they didn't Jack did what any Hayneville gentleman would do and stabbed them both in the abdomen." Finally, Buchwald supposed that the judge in Ripper's case would send the case to the jury for deliberation, but the foreman would say, "No need for that, judge. We find the defendant not guilty and wish to take this opportunity to nominate Jack the Ripper for sheriff of this God-fearing community."[99]

The *Nashville Tennessean* argued that "those who hope for decency to prevail — in Alabama and across the land — weep for the cause of justice." From the western edge of Tennessee, the *Memphis Commercial-Appeal* chastised the participants in the trial. "But if the perpetrator of that crime thinks that he walks free," an editorial warned, "if those people of Lowndes County who condone this decision think their consciences are now free, they are mistaken. They are caught now in the confines of moral judgment which will weigh more heavily each day as time passes for by their failures they have violated more than mere laws of man." A columnist for the *Atlanta Constitution* observed that "press reports say a trial was held this week in Hayneville, Ala., but this was in error. No trial was held there within the accepted meaning of the word." The southern "double standard of justice" had been, according to a *Constitution* editorial, "never more dramatically demonstrated than in the Hayneville episode." And, it maintained, "The nation cannot survive unless standards of justice apply equally to all."[100]

Perhaps the most insightful evaluations of the Coleman trial came from two observers of the proceedings in Hayneville. In a story filed soon after the verdict, the usually detached Jack Nelson of the *Los Angeles Times* criticized the misguided course of the trial. "In the trial, the villain was clearly the victim — not the killer," he concluded. "Coleman was the hero, the defender of Southern womanhood, which is to say white women." The Reverend John B. Morris of the Episcopal Society for Cultural and Racial Unity, left Hayneville shaken and stunned by the verdict after attending the entire proceedings. "We have witnessed an almost total conspiracy of the civil and religious leadership of Lowndes County to exonerate one of their own," Morris said in a statement. "Above all else, the most depressing part of this charade was the manner in which the church was trotted out in the person of local clergy, both on the stand and in the audience, to bless and announce absolution over the whole ritual of absolution."[101]

Notwithstanding the censure by political and religious leaders, the press, and Jon Daniels's friends, the jury's verdict stood. Although Tom Coleman still faced charges of assault and battery in the shooting of Father Morrisroe, he was free in the slaying of Daniels.

In an ironic development just hours after the Hayneville jury returned its decision, the federal court in Montgomery ruled in *McMeans v. Mayor's Court, Fort Deposit, Alabama.* Judge Frank M. Johnson, Jr., dismissed the charges against Daniels and the other demonstrators arrested on August 14. The ruling stated, "The manner in which the petitioners were protesting the alleged discrimination against members of their race was an allowable and constitutionally recognized exercise of their right of free speech and assembly to protest what they considered to be racial discrimination on the part of the establishments involved." Johnson declared that the "ordinance is unconstitutional as applied to the petitioners arrested for its violation." In other words, the civil rights demonstrators had the right to picket stores in Fort Deposit; they should not have been arrested and incarcerated in Hayneville. As *Time* concluded, "Jon Daniels' life might never have been lost if his own civil rights had not been violated in the first place."[102]

THE MAKING
OF A MARTYR

Soon after his acquittal, Tom Coleman returned to his job with the highway department. He still faced an assault and battery charge for shooting Richard Morrisroe, who recovered slowly in a Chicago hospital from his critical wounds. While Morrisroe convalesced, the U.S. Department of Justice considered ways to bring further charges against Coleman for killing Jon Daniels.[1]

Under laws passed during Reconstruction, federal authorities could prosecute Coleman if his actions had involved a conspiracy to kill a person exercising a constitutional right or if he had acted officially as a law enforcement officer. At the request of Assistant Attorney General John Doar, the Federal Bureau of Investigation continued to pursue the case by interviewing many people again, by rechecking any authority Coleman may have had as a special deputy sheriff or as state highway engineer, and by conducting "a complete background investigation of the subject." The FBI probe developed no new evidence that Coleman had acted in a conspiracy or as an officer of the law, and in mid-November the bureau placed the case on a "pending inactive" status.[2]

The state's assault and battery case against Coleman appeared on the circuit court's spring docket in Hayneville for May 16, 1966, but a week before the trial Judge Thagard ordered a postponement until the fall term because the priest remained unable to travel to Alabama. In September, the state attorney general's office asked a Lowndes County grand jury to indict Coleman for assault with intent to murder, a far more serious charge than assault and battery, which carried maximum penalties of a $500 fine and a six-month jail sentence. After hearing testimony from Morrisroe, the Lowndes grand jury, though made up of eleven blacks as well as seven whites, took only five minutes to refuse the request for a new indictment. "I felt from the beginning that this would be the outcome," declared Richmond Flowers. "However, in the name of law and justice, I had to try." One Alabama journalist also found the result understandable: "Even illiterate Negroes in Lowndes County are speed readers of handwriting on the wall. They know that the Klan is 'riding' in Alabama today."[3]

Attorney General Flowers then reverted to the tactic that had proved unsuccessful in the Daniels case — he asked Judge Thagard to nol-pros the indictment, that is, to dismiss it because the prosecution lacked a case. Flowers hoped that he could later convince another grand jury to return a more serious indictment. On September 26, the day the court considered his request, Flowers, Vaughn Hill Robison, and Thagard conferred. "When the conference was over," one reporter observed, "Flowers looked grim and Robison appeared jubilant." Rather than nol-pros the indictment, Thagard dismissed the charge against Coleman "with prejudice," which meant that Coleman could never be tried in the circuit court for shooting Morrisroe.[4]

As the state's case against Coleman ended, the *New York Times* contended that there "is no basis for prosecuting him [Coleman] under federal law" but used the occasion to call for passage of another civil rights bill. A pending measure, which provided federal protection against what the newspaper called "Jim Crow justice," particularly appealed to the *Times*. The editorial enraged John B. Morris, the executive director of ESCRU. Increasingly bitter and cynical, Morris maintained that the Justice Department had failed in its investigation and that it should have brought federal charges against Coleman. Though he too supported more civil rights legislation, he thought the paper's conclusion that Coleman was not involved in a conspiracy was "unwarranted."[5]

Civil rights activists in Lowndes County agreed with Morris's conspiracy theory. They believed that Coleman had been part of a plot to release the jailed civil rights workers abruptly and have them attacked in Hayneville. Though conspiracies against the civil rights movement did occur, one seemed improbable in the Daniels case. Not only did the FBI uncover no evidence pointing to a conspiracy, but also the unexpected release of Daniels and the other demonstrators appeared to be a sudden, simple reaction to the possible federal implications of the arrests. The Fort Deposit authorities merely wanted to avoid an imbroglio with the federal courts over such a minor matter. In any case, even a well-planned conspiracy could not have predicted that after their release from jail the two white men — the obvious targets of white resentment — would have gone to the Cash Store, where Coleman waited with his shotgun. Moreover, Coleman's volatile personality, including his drinking and his temper, made him an unlikely conspirator; more plausibly, he was an impetuous individual acting alone.

Although the Justice Department would not finally rule out prosecution of Coleman until early 1967, Tom Coleman left the Lowndes County Courthouse on September 26, 1966, a free man, confident that the legal system would never punish him for killing Daniels and shooting Morrisroe. He could not, however, easily forget what he had done. He continued to get harassing letters and telephone calls, and reporters often appeared in Hayneville to try, usually unsuccessfully, to interview him about the shootings.[6]

The ramifications of Coleman's deeds did not stop with the closing of the case against him. For example, *White v. Crook*, the suit brought by ESCRU and the ACLU challenging the exclusion of women and blacks from Lowndes County juries, proceeded through the federal courts. In October 1965 the Justice Department intervened on the side of the plaintiffs with a motion asking that all the county's jury records since 1915 be opened, and a few days later Judge Richard T. Rives granted the request. Justice Department lawyers promptly began an extensive examination of the records. Reconstruction of the jury venires for over a decade demonstrated the systematic exclusion of blacks and women; it also revealed that a very few white men had been called repeatedly for jury service.[7]

On February 7, 1966, a three-judge federal panel in Montgomery handed down a decision in *White v. Crook*. Speaking for the court, Judge Frank M. Johnson, Jr., declared unconstitutional both the state law prohibiting women from jury service and the actual jury rolls used in Lowndes County. The court ordered the jury commission to refrain from "any act or practice which involves or results in discrimination by reason of race or color in the selection of jurors for jury service."[8] Ensuring that 80 percent of the population would no longer be excluded, the decision revolutionized the jury system in the county; indirectly it also promised greater protection for civil rights workers by guaranteeing that blacks would serve on the juries that indicted and tried people like Tom Coleman.

Though winning court cases and registering to vote with the help of federal registrars, many black citizens in Lowndes gave up any hope that they could work with local whites. Disappointment for blacks came when white juries acquitted Tom Coleman and found Collie Leroy Wilkins not guilty in his second trial for killing Viola Liuzzo. Even more discouraging for blacks were their losses in the fall's local Agricultural and Stabilization and Conservation Service election. Shortly before the voting, white officials had confused the unsophisticated black voters and diffused their new power by nominating more than seventy blacks for the ASCS positions. Black candidates won only three out of eighteen seats on community committees, and the powerful county ASCS committee remained all white. The white chicanery angered many blacks. Commenting on the elections, Stokely Carmichael said, "We did it fair and square. We believed in them, and they cheated us." Agreeing, John Hulett claimed that blacks "were tricked at the ballot box."[9] Blacks, however, did not give up.

In time, Jon Daniels's death, instead of slowing the movement in Lowndes, inspired and emboldened it; blacks, aware of Daniels's courage and his ultimate sacrifice for their cause, redoubled their efforts to obtain their equal rights in the Black Belt county. Similarly, Tom Coleman's acquittal did not frighten local activists and only temporarily heartened whites. The all-white jury's verdict represented the last stand of white supremacists in Lowndes as their old way of life died; blacks and whites alike seemed to sense that their county would never return to racial segregation, black disfranchisement, and total white dominance. In Lowndes County as across the South, progress might be slow and incomplete, with economic problems remaining the most intransigent, but at least the great fear of the old days was now gone.

Increasingly, Lowndes blacks challenged white political dominance directly. In December 1965, with the help of the Student Nonviolent Coordinating Committee, the Lowndes County Christian Movement for Human Rights began to form its own political party, based in part on the Mississippi Freedom Democratic party established the previous year. The independent black party, which would be known as the Lowndes County Freedom Organization (LCFO), expected to nominate candidates in May 1966 for tax assessor, sheriff, tax collector, and two seats on the county school board.[10]

Early in January 1966, blacks brought suit in federal court to invalidate the election of all officials in Lowndes County because the constitutional rights of blacks had been violated in their selection. Recognizing the connections between economic and political power, they also sued white landowners for evicting black tenants who participated in the civil rights movement; black activists also started a tent city for homeless blacks. Additional impetus for a new party came in February, when the local Democratic executive committee suddenly raised the qualifying fees from fifty to five hundred dollars for individuals running for sheriff, tax assessor, and tax collector. Candidates for the county board of education faced increases in filing fees ranging from ten to one hundred dollars. Poor blacks who could least afford the higher fees found their own independent party even more attractive.[11]

While blacks in Lowndes County began to organize politically, the federal government provided support for the broader movement. Not only did a federal court rule in their favor in *White v. Crook*, but also the Justice Department brought suit against the county schools for failing to create and implement a desegregation plan. In February 1966, Judge Johnson ordered Lowndes to eliminate its segregated public school system over the next two years. A few weeks later, however, joined by two other judges, Johnson dismissed the challenge to all of the county's elected officials. Blacks also lost their suit against white landowners for evicting black tenants.[12]

On April 2, 1966, blacks officially organized the Lowndes County Freedom Organization. The LCFO elected John Hulett as president and, as required by state law, selected a party symbol — the black panther. It became known as the Black Panther party, after which Bobby Seale, Huey Newton, and others soon named their party in California. The Black Panthers of Lowndes County frightened many whites, for the party and its panther symbolized the militant determination of blacks to change their community on their own. As Hulett said in May 1966, the "black panther is a vicious animal" but it "never bothers anything" unless it is cornered. Blacks in Lowndes had long been pushed into a corner, and in 1966 they prepared to act. "Too long Negroes have been begging . . . for things they should be working for," said Hulett. "So the people in Lowndes County decided to organize themselves — to go out and work for the things we wanted in life." "We've decided to stop begging," he explained. "We aren't asking any longer for protection — we won't need it — or for anyone to come from the outside to speak for us, because we are going to speak for ourselves now and from now on." The Black Panther party did not advocate violence but blacks would no longer accept nonviolence either. One elderly black farmer summed up the situation in the Black Belt county: "We been walkin' with dropped down heads, with a scrunched-up heart, and a timid body in the bushes. But *we ain't scared any more.* Don't meddle, don't pick a fight, but fight back! If you have to die, die for something, and take somebody before you." Black residents planned to take over the county through the electoral process.[13]

In keeping with Alabama's requirement that an independent party seeking to nominate candidates had to meet "in or around a public polling place on the day of the [Democratic] primary," LCFO leaders announced plans for a mass meeting on the Hayneville square on primary day, because the courthouse was the only public building in the county used as a polling place (all other polling places were in private homes or businesses). The sheriff, however, denied the LCFO permission to gather on the square because he could not guarantee their safety. Eventually, LCFO obtained permission from the state attorney general and the county probate judge to meet at a local church. Despite their fear of violence, about fourteen hundred blacks boycotted the May 3 Democratic primary and attended the mass meeting at a Hayneville church. Almost nine hundred black voters nominated candidates for tax assessor, tax collector, coroner, the school board, and sheriff, all the offices that were open in the fall election. Although its friend Stokely Carmichael had moved beyond Lowndes and was becoming increasingly controversial as the new president of SNCC and as the leading advocate of "black power," the LCFO pursued black power by continuing its grass-roots work to elect black candidates. All LCFO candidates nevertheless lost in 1966. Their margins of defeat ranged from 273 to 677 votes out of fewer than 3,900 cast. Two years later the LCFO ran three candidates in county elections and again failed by at least 500 votes to elect any of them.[14]

In 1969 the nearly collapsed LCFO or Black Panther party became part of the National Democratic Party of Alabama (NDPA), a statewide black political organization formed the year before. In the 1970 elections, the NDPA in Lowndes County won several crucial victories. Most important, John Hulett, one of the movement's early leaders, was elected sheriff. Two other blacks were elected coroner and circuit clerk.[15]

Barely five years after the first blacks registered to vote in Lowndes, they had succeeded in electing a black sheriff. Taking the control of law enforcement away from oppressive whites signaled a significant shift in the security of black citizens. Without a friendly sheriff to condone their violence, whites could no longer freely harass and beat their black neighbors. The election of a black sheriff also led to a new pattern in race relations. Sheriff Hulett saw concrete evidence of change when he looked at the gun racks in pickup trucks. Before his election, a white man's gun rack usually carried an intimidating shotgun visible in his truck's rear window, while fearful blacks seldom carried a weapon. After Hulett became sheriff, he noticed that some blacks began to keep shotguns in their trucks just as whites did. Gradually, as more blacks put shotguns in their trucks, whites displayed fewer in their trucks. Eventually, the number of shotguns in pickup gun racks began to decline among both races, to be replaced by fishing rods and umbrellas. For Hulett, the shift from shotguns to fishing rods symbolized a major change in power and in community peace in Lowndes County.[16] Initially afraid of a black sheriff, whites rapidly adjusted to Hulett because they discovered that he did a good job.

By the end of the 1970s, blacks effectively controlled the Lowndes County government, but their civil rights movement involved more than just political action. For example, organized blacks sought federal funds to build better housing, pave streets, install water and sewer systems, and upgrade schools. In 1966, the Lowndes County Christian Movement for Human Rights received a $240,000 antipoverty grant to fund literacy programs and vocational training in Lowndes. The largest project began in 1969, when the Office of Economic Opportunity established a million-dollar community health center next to the county jail. The public schools also acquired a Head Start program.[17]

Local community action and federal spending produced impressive changes in the lives of blacks. The more visible improvements included restoration of the antebellum courthouse and miles of new paved roads, including many in Hayneville. By 1980 more than 70 percent of the county's residences had full bathrooms (compared to less than half in 1960), four out of five residences had a motor vehicle (compared to 42 percent twenty years earlier), and most homes had telephones (compared to 20 percent in 1960). Many blacks benefited. In part, the improvements resulted from higher income levels in the county. The median black family income jumped from $935 in 1960 to $7,493 in 1980, while comparable white incomes rose from $2,624 to $18,350. The median black income in Lowndes increased from 36 percent to 41 percent of the median white income.[18]

The small comparative gain in black income over two decades betrayed the persisting economic problems in Lowndes County. In 1980 Lowndes continued to be the fifth poorest county in the nation. As the staff of the U.S. Civil Rights Commission concluded in 1983, "Political gains have yet to translate into economic gains. Blacks in Lowndes County have little reason for optimism." Even the arrival of major industry could not alleviate problems of unemployment and poverty. In the late 1980s, the General Electric Company (GE) opened a $350 million plastics plant in the northeastern part of the county near Montgomery, but its impact on the county was slight. Few employees moved to Lowndes, in part because the almost totally segregated schools were inferior; nearly all of its employees instead commuted each day from places outside of Lowndes. In addition, tax waivers meant that GE paid no county taxes. Even after the company's arrival, a solution to Lowndes County's economic woes seemed as distant as ever. Bleak prospects caused many simply to move away, and the population declined from 15,417 in 1960 to 13,253 in 1980.[19]

Although progress had been limited, the civil rights movement in Lowndes, like the larger movement across the South, had wrought remarkable changes. Blacks voted freely without restrictions, held elective office, attended the public schools freely, served on juries, and lived free of the repressive violence of earlier years. Without the struggle and sacrifices of the civil rights movement, life for blacks in Lowndes County would not have improved. Jon Daniels followed his conscience to the Black Belt, worked in his own way to improve the lives of blacks, and died for his efforts.

The man who killed Daniels continued to live his normal life in Hayneville. In the years after his trial Tom Coleman began to attend church more regularly, and in 1971 he stopped drinking and smoking. He retired from the state highway department in 1977 and, in spite of bouts with bladder and skin cancer, enjoyed a peaceful retirement in Hayneville. Failing eyesight prevented him from hunting, but every afternoon he played dominoes with friends in the new city hall building located just behind the courthouse. He enjoyed watching television, especially sports, and visiting with family and friends. The events of 1965 rarely came up in Coleman's conversations.[20]

That Tom Coleman killed Jon Daniels was beyond dispute. That the legal system of Lowndes County found Coleman not guilty of manslaughter was undeniable. That Coleman should have been convicted remains, of course, problematic and controversial. Whites in Lowndes agreed with the verdict in 1965 and do not discuss it much now. Friends and supporters of Daniels thought then and have continued to believe that Coleman's trial was an outrageous injustice.

Officially, Coleman was acquitted because a jury believed the testimony of two men who claimed under oath that Daniels and Morrisroe had been armed with a knife and a gun when they approached the Cash Store shortly after their release from the local jail. No weapons were ever produced. Richard Morrisroe and the other civil rights workers who were with Daniels have consistently maintained that the two churchmen carried no weapons and that any shiny objects in their hands were only coins to pay for the soft drinks they intended to buy in the store.

The presence of weapons was extremely improbable and implausible. For civil rights workers in "bloody" Lowndes to have obtained a gun and a knife while in the county jail would have been foolhardy. Any weapons, if discovered by the jailers, would have prompted retaliation, either more serious charges against them or bodily harm, which could have been justified as self-defense. For Daniels and Morrisroe to have secured a gun and a knife immediately after their release from jail would have been difficult in the tense and frightened atmosphere of Hayneville. For the two white men in a strange and hostile town to have threatened an armed and belligerent local white man would have been even more foolish. Most significant, for a seminarian and a priest ever to have carried weapons of violence would have been antithetical to their commitment to nonviolence in the civil rights movement and even more to their Christian callings.

More than arguments over weapons or over Coleman's guilt or innocence, however, the trial of Tom Coleman involved a conflict of basic cultures.[21] The Yankee seminarian went south to help bring about racial justice, to agitate for change because he thought that blacks as human beings deserved dignity and respect, that they should have equal rights in jobs, education, politics, the courts, and every other facet of life. Obeying the teachings of his faith, Daniels believed that his Christian duty required him personally to lend a hand in their struggle for freedom and equality in Selma and Lowndes County. In the Alabama Black Belt, however, Daniels encountered a world very different from his native New England. Southern whites had controlled blacks for generations: the deeply embedded traditions of racial oppression, segregation, and discrimination dominated the culture. Few southerners had considered the possibility of racial change — blacks because of their powerlessness and whites because of their comforts. What seemed reasonable to Jon Daniels was unthinkable to Tom Coleman.

Like most whites in Lowndes County, Coleman opposed any suggestion of change in the community's way of life, the core of which was white supremacy. He simply saw no need for any alteration in his society's race relations. He was sure that many blacks liked him and were happy in their lives. Believing that white superiority just made common sense, Coleman was, as one of the dominant whites, satisfied with the racial status quo. His resistance was not philosophical or rational; it was reactive, almost involuntary. He had been raised in that culture and knew of no other acceptable way for blacks and whites to live in the Black Belt. Though he probably could not comprehend the changes posed by the civil rights movement, he knew that the insurrection must be stopped before outside agitators, aided and abetted by the federal government, ruined his way of life by stirring up local blacks and fomenting a real rebellion. He also accepted the obligation of all southern whites to maintain social order, and like his peers he was ready to resort to the traditional ways of maintaining white control — force and violence. Coleman's spontaneous, violent reactions demonstrated the depth of white resistance to racial change represented by Daniels and Morrisroe. Certain that Lowndes whites would support him, he used violence in a desperate attempt to halt the civil rights revolution threatening him and his community. At a moment of crisis for the county, when forces beyond the whites' control threatened to transform it irrevocably, shooting Daniels and Morrisroe seemed to Coleman the right and honorable thing to do, and the jurors at his trial agreed.

In court, not only Coleman but all white residents were on trial because they opposed civil rights and wanted to maintain racial segregation. As the defendant, Coleman represented the white community, and the witnesses who vouched for his character, in effect, defended their own as well. When his two friends testified before an all-white male jury of Coleman's acquaintances that Daniels and Morrisroe carried weapons, they all recognized that the civil rights movement posed a serious threat to their society, and they closed ranks behind Coleman. What Coleman did may have been against the law but it was not a crime in the eyes of his community. Symbolically armed, Daniels and Morrisroe represented forces that were attacking the basic way of life in Lowndes. In the minds of local whites, the menace of civil rights justified Coleman's action, especially because the movement involved *whites* like Jon Daniels and Richard Morrisroe. To acquit Coleman was to absolve not only Coleman but also themselves of the evils of which others in the nation accused them.

Coleman did not shoot Ruby Sales or Joyce Bailey. Although he probably could not have fired at any woman, white or black, Coleman also knew that the two whites posed a much greater threat. He shot Daniels and Morrisroe because they were white men. They offended him the most. In Coleman's view, not only were they outsiders impersonating ministers, but also they had grievously betrayed their race doubly by siding with the blacks and by associating publicly with black women. Traitorous whites threatened white dominance more than insubordinate blacks because they represented a breach in white solidarity. The seminarian's collar, which might have been expected to afford Daniels some protection, only marked him as a fraud and a traitor of the worst kind. Coleman did not have to stop and analyze the situation outside the Cash Store; he could act instinctively and impulsively according to the well-established code in Lowndes County. He did not shoot any blacks because his targets had been white civil rights workers who tried to upset the social order.

Jon Daniels was also on trial in the Lowndes County courtroom, in some ways even more than Coleman. The charge against him in absentia was in effect that he was an outside agitator. The New Englander had come to Lowndes County to help blacks register to vote and thereby obtain their rights and freedoms as American citizens. Just being involved in the civil rights movement proved sufficient to convict any white troublemaker; Jon Daniels, however, affronted southern white sensibilities in many other ways. His peculiar yellow boots and red underwear and his books with ominous titles branded him unmistakably as an alien.

Daniels's friendship with blacks constituted an even more egregious violation of southern customs, and Coleman's lawyers took every opportunity to remind the jury of his repugnant behavior. Daniels had associated closely with blacks as equals before his arrest in Fort Deposit, and he had without hesitation shared their jail cell. More incriminating were the friendly notes he exchanged with the black activists while in the jail, particularly because his correspondents were female; white people in Lowndes regarded letters between blacks and whites that closed with "love" totally improper. By accompanying two young black women to the Cash Store, the northerner further transgressed southern norms. Finally, Daniels's alleged kissing of one of the black women violated southern racial taboos in ways that Lowndes whites found intolerable and unforgivable.

In the Hayneville courtroom, nobody offered any explanation of the seminarian's behavior or any defense in his behalf. Tom Coleman's prosecutors, themselves a part of the local white community, actually seemed to acquiesce in the impeachment of Daniels. But it did not matter because no counterarguments would have been effective. The jury, both in the jury box and in the community at large, readily convicted Daniels of being a menace to their way of life and thereby sanctioned Coleman's action. The outside agitator had to be destroyed, so Coleman was justified in killing him.

The larger meaning of what happened in Hayneville remained under dispute long after the trial ended. Each side struggled to define the slaying, either as a justified homicide or as the creation of a martyr. Despite the improbability that the seminarian and priest were armed, Tom Coleman relied on his friends' testimony about a gun and a knife on the rare occasions when he reminisced about the shootings. In discussing what he sometimes euphemistically referred to as "the time I got in trouble," Coleman continued to maintain that he shot Daniels and Morrisroe in self-defense. Over the years he may even have come to believe it. Without boasting, but also without much self-doubt, Coleman declared that he would do the same thing again in similar circumstances.[22]

Not a philosophical or particularly introspective person, Coleman apparently spent little time questioning his actions on the afternoon of August 20, 1965. He coped with the experience in a variety of ways. One year after his acquittal, Coleman admitted to John Hart of CBS News that the "trial has been on my mind most of the year." He said that before the trial he believed that he should and would be "exonerated," and he claimed that Richmond Flowers "persecuted" him for political gain. When asked why the shootings had occurred, he initially said, "I would rather not comment on that," but then he declared, "They were down here promoting, antagonizing things, promoting trouble." Stern-faced and unblinking, Coleman told Hart that he had no regrets: "I wouldn't change a bit. If the same things happens in the morning that happened that day, I would shoot them both tomorrow." Though conceding that his actions did not solve the community's racial problems, he blamed the difficulties on "outsiders from up North" and claimed, "We still have a lot of good niggers in this county." He also suggested that the shootings "might have solved some problems that would have come up later and," he added almost as an afterthought, "it kept me from getting hurt."[23]

Whenever questioned, Coleman maintained that he did what he had to do: someone had to stand up to the so-called priests who were trying to destroy his community, especially when they were ready to resort to violence. He demonstrated little remorse for killing another man and treated Jon Daniels more as an object than as a real person by displaying no interest in who he really was, what his background was, what he thought about the South or blacks, or how his death affected his family and friends. Coleman's unwaivering belief that he acted in self-defense and his virtual denial of Daniels's humanity undoubtedly were essential for his emotional survival. To have contemplated the possibility that he may have senselessly and needlessly killed another person — especially one as bright and sensitive and dedicated as Jon Daniels — might have been psychologically devastating for Coleman. It was simpler and easier for him to accept the testimony of his friends and the verdict of his community that his actions were proper and honorable.

Tom Coleman did not, however, remained unaffected by the racial changes occurring around him. For example, he developed a complicated and contradictory relationship with John Hulett. Coleman accepted the fact that Lowndes County had a black sheriff; in the evening in the years after Hulett's election, he often listened to the police scanner in his home and contacted Sheriff Hulett when he heard reports of trouble on the radio. Coleman saw Hulett frequently in town and in fact considered him to be a good man and one of his friends. Nonetheless, in spite of his respect for Hulett, Coleman conceded that he could never bring himself to address the sheriff as "Mister" Hulett even though whites of a younger generation did.[24]

By recognizing the limitations of his own capacity for reformation, Coleman symbolically acknowledged that race relations had changed and that he too probably should have adapted more than he had. In reconciling himself to the sweeping changes in his community while refusing to admit that killing Daniels was wrong, he revealed his own complex and ambivalent ways of adjusting to the civil rights movement. His past — both as an individual and as a white southerner — kept him from accepting the new ways completely. Coleman's reactions since 1965 typified the responses of many southern whites who cannot repudiate their prejudiced past even though they accept, however reluctantly, many of the changes in southern race relations brought on by the movement that they once resisted, sometimes violently.

While Coleman tried to ignore the reality of Jon Daniels and thereby minimized the significance of his deed, others have recognized Daniels as a Christian martyr in the cause of human rights.[25] These individuals have realized the importance of Daniels's sacrifice as he bore witness in the struggle for equal rights for blacks. Compelled only by his faith to live according to the teachings of Christian love and by an existential need to act, Daniels went to Alabama to stand beside the weak and support their protests; he stayed in the Black Belt to champion their cause for freedom in the face of resistance from the dominant white population. He willingly joined the cause for equal rights in Lowndes County, risked arrest in Fort Deposit, stayed in the county jail, and stood up to the threat posed by Tom Coleman and other whites. Without calculating the possible danger to himself, Daniels followed the demands of his faith, even to death.

In life and in death Jon Daniels helped lift the great fear in the Alabama Black Belt. No monument indicates the place where he died, and no marker in Lowndes County bears his name. Lowndes blacks remember him nonetheless, and they and his friends elsewhere have kept his memory alive. Soon after his death, St. James Episcopal Church in Keene called a newly acquired structure the Jonathan M. Daniels Building. Later his hometown named an elementary school after him, as did a day care center for black children in Selma. Early in 1966, the Chicago chapter of the Episcopal Society for Cultural and Racial Unity posthumously honored Jon Daniels with its annual award for outstanding achievements. At the Episcopal Theological School in Cambridge, friends created a Jonathan

Daniels Fellowship fund to support "the work of seminarians in areas of social concern." Shortly after his death, William J. Schneider, an Episcopal priest who had met him in Cambridge, wrote a brief tribute to Daniels, entitled *The Jon Daniels Story*, which included a selection of the seminarian's writings. Boyhood friends Gene Felch and Robert Perry perpetuated Daniels's name by each calling a son Jonathan. Richard Morrisroe — who later left the priesthood, became a lawyer, and married — also named a son after Jonathan Daniels.[26]

More public recognition of Daniels's life and witness came from the church. In England, fifteen years after his death, Canterbury Cathedral, where in 1170 Thomas Beckett, the fortieth archbishop of Canterbury, had been martyred, created a Chapel of Saints and Martyrs of Our Own Time. It honored the people "from all the traditions of Christendom" who sacrificed their lives "for the faith of Christ, under many different tyrannies and in the face of many different oppressions." Among the twelve twentieth-century martyrs listed at Canterbury were Dietrich Bonhoeffer, Martin Luther King, Jr., Archbishop Oscar Romero, and Jonathan Daniels. The inscription for Daniels recognized that he had been "[s]hot in Hayneville, Alabama, while helping in the civil rights campaign." A number of his acquaintances have speculated about whether Daniels actually wanted to become a martyr during his work in Alabama. The explanation of martyrdom included at Canterbury no doubt helps to answer their question. Quoting T. S. Eliot, it reads: "A Christian martyrdom is never an accident, for saints are not made by accident. Still less is a Christian martyrdom the effect of a man's will to become a saint, as a man by willing and contriving may become a ruler of men. A martyrdom is always the design of God, for his love of men, to warn them and to lead them, to bring them back to his ways."[27]

A decade later John B. Morris, the former head of the Episcopal Society for Cultural and Racial Unity, led a movement to remember Daniels within the Episcopal Church in the United States. The bishops of Alabama and New Hampshire cosponsored a resolution in the House of Bishops to add Daniels as a martyr to the church's Calendar of Lesser Feasts and Fasts. At the General Convention of the Episcopal Church in July 1991, the Standing Liturgical Commission held a hearing on the proposal at which Morris, Henri Stines, and others testified. With a positive recommendation from the commission, the House of Bishops adopted the resolution unanimously. When, soon afterward, the House of Delegates also unanimously approved it, the delegates rose and sang the "Doxology" and "We Shall Overcome." Daniels's martyrdom will be remembered by his church on August 14, the day of his arrest in Fort Deposit, Alabama.[28]

NOTES

PREFACE

1. Coleman's full name was Tom Lemuel Coleman, not Thomas Lemuel Coleman as press accounts reported at the time.

2. Calling the shooting of Daniels the "last atrocity" of the first phase of the movement in no way diminishes the horror of later deaths; it highlights only the timing of the killing of Daniels. Regarding 1965 and the Voting Rights Act as a watershed in the movement has become a standard interpretation. The PBS documentary series "Eyes on the Prize," for example, divided its two parts at 1965. For other recent examples, see Goldfield, *Black, White, and Southern*, and Weisbrot, *Freedom Bound*.

3. The literature on the civil rights movement is large and growing. A few examples of the types mentioned here include biographies (Lewis, *King*; Garrow, *Bearing the Cross*), organizational studies (Carson, *In Struggle*; Meier and Rudwick, *CORE*), local studies (Chafe, *Civilities and Civil Rights*; Norrell, *Reaping the Whirlwind*), and studies of white opposition (Bartley, *Rise of Massive Resistance*; McMillen, *Citizens' Council*).

4. The only published accounts of Daniels's civil rights activities, of his slaying, or of the trial of Tom Coleman are Schneider's *Jon Daniels Story*, a brief, laudatory biographical account with a collection of some of Daniels's writings; Mendelsohn's "Minding His Own Business, Jonathan Myrick Daniels, August 20, 1965," in *Martyrs*, pp. 196–218; Frady's "A Death in Lowndes County," in *Southerners*, pp. 138–56, based on his reporting in 1965 for *Newsweek*; and the brief discussion in the Southern Poverty Law Center's *Free at Last: A History of the Civil Rights Movement and Those Who Died in the Struggle*, published in 1989 at the time of the dedication of a memorial to Daniels and thirty-nine others who died in the movement. No comparable study of Coleman has appeared, even though he has survived nearly thirty years longer than the man he killed. Erroneous information about Daniels and Coleman abounds. For example, Daniels has been described as "black" (see Walker, *In Defense of American Liberties*, p. 269) and as "the Reverend" (see Weisbrot, *Freedom Bound*, p. 195), and Coleman is repeatedly referred to as a deputy sheriff.

5. For a brief discussion of the various meanings of freedom as related to the civil rights movement, see Richard H. King, "Citizenship and Self-Respect," pp. 7–24, esp. p. 9.

CHAPTER I

1. Interview with Constance Daniels; *Keene Sentinel*, December 28, 1959, January 12, 1984.

2. Interview with Constance Daniels; *Keene Sentinel*, December 28, 1959.

3. Interview with Constance Daniels; *Keene Sentinel*, December 28, 1959.

4. Federal Writers' Project, *New Hampshire*, pp. 184–86; Drenan, "Two Hundred Years of Keene," pp. 37–38, 41, 53; Keene History Committee, *"Upper Ashuelot,"* pp. 312–13, 490, 495–508, 521, 523, 526; "Keene — Profile of a County Seat," p. 62. The stories of two local industries are in Hill, *Beanstalk*, and Proper, *Story of Wright's Silver Cream*.

5. "Keene — Profile of a County Seat," pp. 17, 62; Keene History Committee, *"Upper Ashuelot,"* pp. 191, 190; Interview with Constance Daniels.

6. *Keene Sentinel*, December 30, 1959; Interviews with Constance Daniels, J. Eugene Felch IV, and Emily Daniels Robey.

7. *Keene Sentinel*, December 30, 1959; Interviews with Richard T. Snowman, J. Eugene Felch IV, and Constance Daniels.

8. Interviews with Constance Daniels, Richard T. Snowman, and Emily Daniels Robey.

9. Interviews with Richard T. Snowman, J. Eugene Felch IV, and Emily Daniels Robey.

10. Interviews with Constance Daniels, Emily Daniels Robey, and J. Eugene Felch IV; *Keene Sentinel*, January 12, 1984. Carolyn J. Sturgis, a teenage girlfriend of Jon Daniels, confirmed much of the following description of the Daniels family and home in her "Memories of Jonathan M. Daniels," which she made available to me along with photocopies of other documents that are in her possession (hereafter cited as Carolyn J. Sturgis Papers).

11. Interviews with Emily Daniels Robey, Constance Daniels, Carlton T. Russell, J. Eugene Felch IV, and Edward A. Tulis.

12. Interviews with Emily Daniels Robey and Constance Daniels; Schneider interview with Carolyn Pearce Howard; Sturgis, "Memories of Jonathan M. Daniels"; J. Daniels, "Thorns in the Flesh of C.J.H.S Teachers," clipping from the Central Junior High School newsletter, Carolyn J. Sturgis Papers; Schneider interview with Harold Drew; Jonathan M. Daniels File, Keene Public School Records; FBI in Mobile, Ala., to Director [J. Edgar Hoover], August 21, 1965, 44-30271-13, Federal Bureau of Investigation Papers, Washington, D.C. The FBI discovered the speeding tickets while making a routine check of Daniels's police record after he was killed in Lowndes County.

13. Interviews with Constance Daniels and Emily Daniels Robey. Nearly everyone interviewed in Keene made at least a passing reference to this incident (often saying, "You've heard the story about. . . .").

14. Ibid.; Daniels, "The Shadow," Keene High School *Enterprise*, Winter 1955, p. 14; Daniels, "Autobiography: Phantasmagoria," January 30, 1957, Daniels Papers, Episcopal Theological School, Cambridge (hereafter cited as ETS); Jonathan M. Daniels File, Keene Public School Records.

15. Interviews with Constance Daniels and Emily Daniels Robey.

16. Interviews with Constance Daniels, Emily Daniels Robey, and J. Eugene Felch IV; Keene High School *Salmagundi*, 1955, p. 69, 1956, p. 68, and 1957, pp. 27, 86; *Keene Sentinel*, June 2, December 20, 1956; Keene High School *Informer*, November 1954, p. 3; Daniels, "Autobiography: Phantasmagoria"; Sturgis, "Memories of Jonathan M. Daniels."

17. Merrifield, "A Children's Theatre"; Keene High School *Salmagundi*, 1956, p. 68, 1957, pp. 92–93, 123; *Keene Sentinel*, November 19, 1954, November 19–20, 1956; Interview with Constance Daniels.

18. Daniels, "Autobiography: Phantasmagoria"; Interviews with J. Eugene Felch IV, Carlton T. Russell, Anthony L. Reddington, Constance Daniels, and Emily Daniels Robey; Jonathan M. Daniels File, Keene Public School Records.

19. Patricia Richmond and Jonathan Daniels, "Looking Inside the Covers," Keene High School *Enterprise*, Winter 1954, p. 19. This is the only column written with Richmond. The individual authors' contributions are not signed, but Daniels's parts seem obvious. His column was later titled simply "Inside the Covers." The book was H. A. Overstreet's *Let Me Think*. (See the following reviews: Raymond G. Fuller, "Knowledge Humanized," *Saturday Review*, May 27, 1939, p. 18; Edgar Johnson, "Learn and Like It," *New Republic*, October 11, 1939, p. 276.) No weighty philosophical tome, it was part of *The Peoples Library*, an attempt to educate adults who did not read books regularly but were interested in serious subjects.

20. Interviews with Carlton T. Russell, J. Eugene Felch IV, and Anthony L. Reddington; Sturgis, "Memories of Jonathan M. Daniels."

21. Interviews with J. Eugene Felch IV, Carlton T. Russell, Anthony L. Reddington, and Constance Daniels.

22. Ibid.; Schneider interview with Carolyn Pearce Howard; Daniels, "Autobiography: Phantasmagoria."

23. Jonathan Daniels, "Reality," Keene High School *Enterprise*, Spring 1956, pp. 19–20.

24. Interviews with Constance Daniels, J. Eugene Felch IV, and Carlton T. Russell; Daniels to Carolyn Pearce, [summer 1954?], Sturgis Papers; Proper, *First Congregational Church*, p. 183; Daniels, "IV. Autobiographical Statement [part of application to seminary]," and "Autobiography: Phantasmagoria."

25. Richmond and Daniels, "Looking Inside the Covers," p. 20; Daniels, "Inside the Covers," Keene High School *Enterprise*, Spring 1956. p. 14. The book on Eastern Europe was Joseph Johnson's *God's Secret Armies*.

26. Interviews with Constance Daniels, Emily Daniels Robey, and Rev. J. Edison Pike.

27. Interviews with Constance Daniels and Rev. J. Edison Pike.

28. Interviews with Constance Daniels, Carlton T. Russell, and Rev. J. Edison Pike.

29. Interviews with J. Eugene Felch IV, Carlton T. Russell, Constance Daniels, and Emily Daniels Robey; Richmond and Daniels, "Looking Inside the Covers," and Daniels, "In Memoriam," Keene High School *Enterprise*, Winter 1954, pp. 20, 8–11; Daniels, "Inside the Covers," Keene High School *Enterprise*, Winter 1955, pp. 13–14.

30. Jonathan M. Daniels File, Keene Public School Records; Interviews with Constance Daniels, Emily Daniels Robey, J. Eugene Felch IV, and Carlton T. Russell; Daniels to Col. Herbert N. Dillard, August 18, 1957, English Department Files, VMI. Carolyn J. Sturgis believed that Daniels's mother made the decision for him to attend VMI (Sturgis, "Memories of Jonathan M. Daniels").

31. Interviews with Constance Daniels, Anthony L. Reddington, Rev. J. Edison Pike, Emily Daniels Robey, and Carlton T. Russell; Daniels, "Autobiography: Phantasmagoria."

32. Interviews with Constance Daniels, Emily Daniels Robey, J. Eugene Felch IV, Carlton T. Russell, and Anthony L. Reddington.

33. Federal Writers' Project, *Virginia*, pp. 428–30; VMI, *Official Register for*

1960–61 122, September 1961, p. 45; Wise, *Drawing Out the Man*, pp. 9–48, 93, 347–49; VMI, *Bulletin, 1981–1982* 143, August 1981, pp. 8–11.

34. Wise, *Drawing Out the Man*, pp. 199, 299; VMI, *Official Register for 1957–58* 119, April 1958, p. 167; *VMI Alumni Review*, Fall 1957, pp. 7, 11.

35. *VMI Cadet*, September 26, 1958; Wise, *Drawing Out the Man*, pp. 298–99, 395–97, and passim; VMI, *Official Register for 1960–61* 122, September 1961, p. 30; VMI, *Bulletin, 1981–82* 143, August 1981, pp. 14–15; Daniels to J. Eugene Felch IV, October 10, [1957], in materials provided by Felch (hereafter cited as Felch Papers); Interviews with Constance Daniels, Emily Daniels Robey, William J. Nelms, Douglas E. Ballard, and Noland Pipes, Jr.

36. Jonathan Myrick Daniels's Medical Report, 1957–58, VMI Hospital; Dr. Edgar N. Weaver to Dr. E. N. Bosworth, October 28, 1957; and Official Transcript—all in Daniels File, VMI; Daniels to J. Eugene Felch IV, October 10, [1957], December 13, [1957], and February 25, 1958, Felch Papers; *VMI Bomb*, 1961 [listing for Daniels]; Interviews with William J. Nelms and Noland Pipes, Jr.

37. *The 1984 VMI Register of Former Cadets*, 5th ed. (Lexington: VMI Alumni Association, 1984), pp. 264–68 (the *Register* lists to the day the length of each cadet's stay at VMI); Interviews with Constance Daniels, William J. Nelms, Douglas E. Ballard, and Noland Pipes, Jr.

38. VMI, *Official Register for 1960–61* 122, September 1961, pp. 30–32; Official Transcript, Daniels File, VMI; Daniels to J. Eugene Felch IV, December 10, 1958, Felch Papers; *VMI Cadet*, February 13, 1959; James J. Wilson to William Schneider, April 29, 1966, Daniels Papers, ETS.

39. Jonathan Daniels to his family, April 19, 1959, in materials supplied by his mother (hereafter cited as Constance Daniels Papers); Timmins Music Society, *Newsletter*, September 1960 (apparently the only issue ever produced); Josiah Bunting to William Schneider, February 10, 1966, Daniels Papers, ETS; Interviews with Thomas B. Gentry and William J. Nelms. One night in his junior year he sternly reprimanded a Rat for profaning the room by listening to the "Marines' Hymn" in one of the booths! A few days later, however, Daniels rose above VMI's strong class traditions and his own musical tastes to stop by the lowly Rat's room and apologize for his uncalled-for behavior. See Bunting to Schneider, February 10, 1966. In his sophomore year Daniels also started contributing to the weekly student newspaper, the *VMI Cadet*, first as a staff writer but later as an assistant editor and briefly as feature editor. His work varied from a book review to an abortive attempt at a column—"A Word With You. . . ."—that appeared only once. He never seemed to find his niche on the staff but continued to contribute nonetheless. See *VMI Cadet*, January 9, June 9, December 11, 18, 1959, February 12, 1960.

40. James J. Wilson to William Schneider, April 29, 1966, Daniels Papers, ETS.

41. *VMI Cadet*, May 3, 12, 1958, April 10, 1959; *VMI Bomb*, 1961; Robert Coltrane to William Schneider, [November 1965], in materials supplied by Coltrane (hereafter cited as Coltrane Papers); Coltrane, "My Recollections of Jonathan Myrick Daniels," [1966], and Braithwaite, "Random Recollections of Jon Daniels," April 26, 1966, both in Daniels Papers, ETS; Jonathan Daniels to Col. Herbert N. Dillard, August 18, 1957, English Department Files, VMI; Interviews with George L. Roth, Thomas B. Gentry, and William W. Kelly (all members of

the VMI English Department in the early 1960s) and with William J. Nelms and Douglas E. Ballard.

42. Robert Coltrane, "My Recollections of Jonathan Myrick Daniels"; William Braithwaite, "Random Recollections of Jon Daniels"; James J. Wilson to William Schneider, April 29, 1966, Daniels Papers, ETS.

43. William Braithwaite, "Random Recollections of Jon Daniels"; Robert Coltrane, "My Recollections of Jonathan Myrick Daniels"; James Joseph Wilson to William Schneider, April 29, 1966; Josiah Bunting to William Schneider, February 10, 1966 — all in Daniels Papers, ETS.

44. Interviews with George L. Roth, Thomas B. Gentry, William W. Kelly, and William J. Nelms; [George Roth] and William F. Byers, letters of recommendation for Jonathan Daniels, English Department Files, VMI; Robert Coltrane, "My Recollections of Jonathan Myrick Daniels"; Jonathan Myrick Daniels, Official Transcript, Daniels File, VMI; VMI, *Official Register for 1960–61* 122, September 1961, pp. 108–9; Daniels to J. Eugene Felch IV, December 10, 1958, Felch Papers.

45. William Braithwaite, "Random Recollections of Jon Daniels"; Robert Coltrane, "My Recollections of Jonathan Myrick Daniels"; James J. Wilson to William Schneider, April 29, 1966, Josiah Bunting to William Schneider, February 10, [1966] — all in Daniels Papers, ETS; Jonathan Daniels to Norris Cotton, April 15, 1961, quoted in *Congressional Record*, 89th Cong., 1st sess., 1965, p. 26097; Interviews with Constance Daniels, William W. Kelly, William J. Nelms, and J. Eugene Felch IV; Jonathan Daniels to his family, April 19, 1959, Constance Daniels Papers.

46. Jonathan Myrick Daniels, "Anguish in Action: Notes on the Problem of the Absurd in Selected Writings of Albert Camus" (senior thesis, VMI, 1961), pp. ii, 1–9 (copy in English Department Files, VMI).

47. Ibid., pp. 2, 9–10, 42, 60. The bulk of Daniels's thesis analyzed several of Camus's fictional works.

48. George Roth, letter of recommendation for Jonathan Daniels, English Department Files, VMI.

49. Jonathan Daniels to his family, April 19, 1959, Constance Daniels Papers; Interviews with Constance Daniels, Emily Daniels Robey, William J. Nelms, and J. Eugene Felch IV; Robert Coltrane, "My Recollections of Jonathan Myrick Daniels"; Transcript, Daniels File, VMI; Jonathan Daniels's application for admission to Harvard University, March 3, 1961, Daniels File, Harvard University Archives.

50. William Kelly, "Jonathan Daniels," [1966], in materials provided by Kelly (hereafter cited as Kelly Papers); Col. Herbert N. Dillard to Kenneth I. Brown, March 23, 1961, and copies of letters of recommendation for Daniels by William Kelly, George Roth, and William F. Byers, English Department Files, VMI; Jonathan Daniels to Dean of Admissions, Harvard University Graduate School, February 7, 1961, and Mrs. M. W. Eldridge (Head of Admissions Office) to Jonathan Daniels, March 17, 1961, Daniels File, Harvard University Archives; Jonathan Daniels to Senator Norris Cotton, April 15, 1961, quoted in *Congressional Record*, 89th Cong., 1st sess., 1965, p. 26097; Robert Coltrane, "My Recollections of Jonathan Myrick Daniels"; *VMI Cadet*, April 14, 1961. Josiah Bunting observed that Daniels "wrote with facility but his writing was somewhat precious and contrived" (Bunting to William Schneider, February 10, 1966, in Daniels Papers, ETS).

51. Interviews with George L. Roth, William W. Kelly, William J. Nelms, Douglas E. Ballard, and Edward A. Tulis; William Kelly, "Jonathan Daniels," [1966], Kelly Papers; Josiah Bunting to William Schneider, February 10, 1966, Daniels Papers, ETS.

52. *VMI Cadet*, June 11, 1961.

53. Richard T. Snowman, M.D., to Harvey H. Guthrie, March 28, 1963, Daniels File, ETS; Interviews with Constance Daniels and Emily Robey Daniels; Jonathan Daniels to Norris Cotton, April 15, 1961, quoted in *Congressional Record*, 89th Cong., 1st sess., 1965, pp. 26097–98; Josiah Bunting to William Schneider, February 10, 1966, Daniels Papers, ETS; Jonathan Daniels to his family, July 31, 1961, Constance Daniels Papers; Jonathan Daniels to William W. Kelly, May 16, 196[2], Kelly Papers.

54. Interviews with Emily Daniels Robey, John Potter, and Constance Daniels; Transcript, Daniels File, Harvard University Archives; Jonathan Daniels to Constance Daniels, February 15, 1962, and April 2, 1962[?], Constance Daniels Papers.

55. Jonathan Daniels to Howard A. Reed, May 10, 1962, copy in Constance Daniels Papers.

56. Jonathan Daniels to Howard A. Reed, May 10, 1962; Jonathan Daniels's Application for Admission, Episcopal Theological School, February 17, 1963, Daniels Papers, ETS; Interviews with Constance Daniels and Emily Daniels Robey; Transcript, Daniels File, Harvard University Archives.

57. Reginald H. Phelps to Jonathan Daniels, February 15, June 20, 1962, Daniels File, Harvard University Archives; Jonathan Daniels to Howard A. Reed, May 10, 1962, copy in Constance Daniels Papers; Schneider, *Jon Daniels Story*, pp. 21–22; Interviews with Constance Daniels and John Potter. Daniels's roommate, who had been in New York for Easter, never noticed anything different about Jon when he returned and never heard of the reconversion experience Daniels later described.

58. Interviews with Constance Daniels and John Potter; Jonathan Daniels to Carlton Russell, October 3, 1962, in materials provided by Russell (hereafter cited as Carlton T. Russell Papers).

59. "Monadnock Observer," *Keene Sentinel*, August 17, 1985; Interview with Constance Daniels; Clipping in Scrapbooks, St. James Episcopal Church Records, Keene.

60. Jonathan Daniels to Carlton Russell, October 3, 1962, Russell Papers; Interview with John Potter.

61. Ibid. A psychological examination of Daniels, required of all applicants to Episcopal seminaries, suggested that "[t]here is strong masculine striving but at the same time not yet assuredness in this role." See Dr. Jane M. Kraus, "The Report of Psychological or Psychiatric Examination: Jonathan Daniels," November 15, 1962, Daniels File, ETS. Kraus's report was only half a typewritten page.

62. *Keene Sentinel*, August 12, 1959; Jonathan Daniels to Carlton Russell, October 3, 1962, Russell Papers; Daniels to Dean of Admissions, October 12, 1962, and Daniels's Application for Admission to ETS, February 17, 1963, Daniels File, ETS.

63. Daniels, "IV. Autobiographical Statement [part of application to seminary]," Daniels Papers, ETS; Richard T. Snowman, M.D., to Harvey H. Guthrie,

Jr., March 28, 1965, and Kraus, "Report of Psychological or Psychiatric Examination."

64. *Official Bulletin of the Episcopal Theological School, 1964–65*, pp. 12–13; Blackman, *Faith and Freedom*, pp. 149–72 and passim.

65. *Official Bulletin of the Episcopal Theological School, 1964–65*, pp. 8, 59–67; Interviews with the Reverends Michael Stichwey, John W. Inman, Stephen Weissman, Judith Upham, Harvel Sanders, and Harvey H. Guthrie.

66. Interviews with the Reverends Judith Upham, John W. Inman, Harvel Sanders, Michael Stichwey, Stephen Weissman, and Harvey H. Guthrie. Daniels's first-year roommate was a recent Dartmouth graduate; they never became close because he died of cancer early in their second semester.

67. *Official Bulletin of the Episcopal Theological School, 1964–65*, pp. 13, 16–17.

68. Jonathan Daniels to Constance Daniels, September 24, 1963, Constance Daniels Papers; Jonathan Daniels transcript, Daniels File, ETS.

69. Interviews with the Reverends James Capen, Michael Stichwey, Stephen Weissman, and John W. Inman; Kraus, "Report of Psychological or Psychiatric Examination."

70. *Official Bulletin of the Episcopal Theological School, 1964–65*, p. 22; Jonathan Daniels transcript, Daniels File, ETS; Interviews with the Reverends James Capen, John W. Inman, Harvel Sanders, and Stephen Weissman; Rev. Alan Mason to author, November 29, December 23, 1987.

71. Interview with Rev. Harvel Sanders; Rev. Alan Mason to author, November 29, December 23, 1987.

72. Jonathan M. Daniels, "Field Work Evaluation, Diocese of Rhode Island Inner City Project, Cathedral of St. John, Providence, Rhode Island," December 1963, Daniels File, ETS.

73. Interviews with the Reverends Edward A. Tulis and Michael Stichwey; Newspaper clipping provided by Tulis.

74. Interview with Rev. Edward A. Tulis; Tulis, "Clinical Pastoral Training Report: Jonathan M. Daniels," Summer 1964, Daniels File, ETS.

75. Interview with Rev. Edward A. Tulis; Tulis, "Clinical Pastoral Training Report: Jonathan M. Daniels," Summer 1964, Daniels File, ETS.

76. Daniels to "Folks[?]," Christmas 1964, Constance Daniels Papers; Interviews with the Reverends John W. Inman, Michael Stichwey, James Capen, Stephen Weissman, and Judith Upham; Schneider interview with [?] Holiday, Charles B. Colmore, and Robert A. Oakes.

77. Interviews with the Reverends John W. Inman, Michael Stichwey, James Capen, Stephen Weissman, and Judith Upham; Schneider interview with [?] Holiday, Charles B. Colmore, and Robert A. Oakes.

78. Rev. Alan Mason to author, November 29, December 23, 1987; Interviews with the Reverends Harvel Sanders and Michael Stichwey.

79. Schneider interview with Holiday, Colmore, and Oakes; Interviews with the Reverends William Wolf and Harvel Sanders.

80. Fager, *Selma, 1965*, pp. 91–98; *Official Bulletin of the Episcopal Theological School* 53, May 1965.

81. Jonathan Daniels, "June 22, 1965," Daniels Papers, ETS; *Official Bulletin of the Episcopal Theological School* 53, May 1965; Interviews with the Reverends James Capen, Judith Upham, Michael Stichwey, John W. Inman, and Wil-

liam Wolf. "June 22, 1965" was a paper Daniels prepared for Professor William Wolf's course in theology in the late spring and early summer of 1965. Wolf read it at Daniels's funeral and it was widely reprinted.

CHAPTER 2

1. Standard accounts of the Selma march and other demonstrations can be found in Fager, *Selma, 1965*; Garrow, *Protest at Selma* and *Bearing the Cross*.

2. For the *Brown* case and its predecessors, see Kluger's magisterial *Simple Justice*. On some of the local movements, see Morris, *Origins of the Civil Rights Movement*. For a short survey of the movement, see Sitkoff, *Struggle for Black Equality*.

3. Garrow, *Bearing the Cross*, pp. 173–230. Chapter 4 is appropriately entitled, "Albany and Lessons for the Future, 1961–1962."

4. Ibid., pp. 231–69.

5. Lawson, *Black Ballots*, pp. 278, 284; Garrow, *Bearing the Cross*, pp. 357–60; DeMuth, "Black Belt, Alabama," p. 538.

6. Jackson, *Story of Selma*, pp. 1–37, 82–155, 185–220, and passim; Owen, *History of Alabama*, 1:447–48, 2:1237–38; Hamilton, *Alabama*, pp. 123–25; *Selma Times-Journal*, June 7, 1965. See also Hardy, *Selma*.

7. Jackson, *Story of Selma*, pp. 319–48, 414–60; Owen, *History of Alabama*, 1:451, 2:1237; *Alabama County Statistical Abstracts*, pp. 103–4; NAACP, *Thirty Years of Lynching*, pp. 43–47; "Lynchings by Counties — Alabama," Lynching Records, Tuskegee Institute Archives.

8. Jackson, *Story of Selma*, pp. 492–515; *Selma Times-Journal*, June 7, August 8, 1965.

9. *New York Times*, February 14, 1965; *Selma Times-Journal*, June 7, 1965.

10. DeMuth, "Black Belt, Alabama," pp. 538–39; McMillen, *Citizens' Council*, p. 43; Fager, *Selma, 1965*, pp. 15–16 (first quotation, p. 16); Simcox, "Selma Episcopalians Speak," p. 12 (second quotation); Interview with Rev. Maurice Ouellet.

11. Fager, *Selma, 1965*, pp. 8–9; Garrow, *Protest at Selma*, pp. 31–34; Interview with Rev. Maurice Ouellet.

12. Garrow, *Protest at Selma*, pp. 39–60; Fager, *Selma, 1965*, pp. 22–81.

13. Garrow, *Protest at Selma*, pp. 64–82; Fager, *Selma, 1965*, pp. 86–98.

14. Fager, *Selma, 1965*, pp. 97–100; Garrow, *Protest at Selma*, pp. 78–82.

15. *Official Bulletin of the Episcopal Theological School* 53, May 1965; Interviews with the Reverends James Capen, Judith Upham, Michael Stichwey, and John W. Inman.

16. Interviews with the Reverends Judith Upham, James Capen, John W. Inman, and Stephen Weissman.

17. Interviews with the Reverends Judith Upham, James Capen, John W. Inman, and Stephen Weissman.

18. Ibid.; Garrow, *Protest at Selma*, pp. 83–87.

19. Fager, *Selma, 1965*, pp. 107–11.

20. Ibid., pp. 112–15; Garrow, *Protest at Selma*, pp. 90–92; Interviews with the Reverends Judith Upham, Stephen Weissman, and James Capen.

21. Jonathan Daniels, "June 22, 1965," Daniels Papers, ETS.

22. Interviews with the Reverends Judith Upham, Stephen Weissman, John W. Inman, and James Capen.

23. Judith Upham to Karl Nordling, February 24, 1966, in materials provided by Upham, Syracuse, N.Y. (hereafter cited as Judith Upham Papers); Rev. T. Frank Mathews to Rt. Rev. James A. Pike, June 30, 1965, copy in Bishop C. C. J. Carpenter Papers, Birmingham Public Library; John B. Morris interview with Morris Samuel, [undated, but probably 1966], with Schneider interviews at Episcopal Divinity School, Cambridge; *Houston Chronicle*, March 11, 1965. Mathews strongly objected to the article by Saul Friedman in the *Houston Chronicle*. Though he claimed it "viciously and maliciously and deceptively and deceitfully" reported the meeting (see Mathews to Pike, June 30, 1965), Friedman's story closely parallels other accounts. Even before King began his Selma campaign, Henri A. Stines of ESCRU had visited Mathews to brief him about upcoming events and to assure him that the church would not allow him and his family to suffer hardships if he stood with the civil rights movement, but the Selma rector was not cooperative (Interview with Henri A. Stines).

24. Judith Upham to Karl Nordling, February 24, 1966, in Upham Papers.

25. Interview with Rev. Judith Upham; *Keene Sentinel*, undated clipping, St. James Episcopal Church Records, Keene; Fager, *Selma, 1965*, pp. 132–37. The chronology of Daniels's return to ETS and the start of his second trip to Selma is not clear in the documents, but it seems likely that he flew to Boston on Tuesday, March 16, the day after he marched to the courthouse and heard LBJ's speech.

26. Judith Upham, "Jonathan Daniels — A Recollection," *Episcopal Theological School Journal*, January 1966, pp. 17–18; Interview with Upham; John B. Morris interview with Morris Samuel, [undated but probably 1966], located with Schneider interviews at ETS. The quotation is from Jonathan Daniels to Mary Elizabeth McNaughton, March 27–28, 1965, in materials provided by Mary Bonnet (hereafter cited as Mary Bonnet Papers).

27. Interviews with the Reverends Judith Upham and Joseph Fletcher.

28. Interviews with the Reverends Judith Upham, Joseph Fletcher, Harvey H. Guthrie, William Wolf, John B. Coburn, Michael Stichwey, Harvel Sanders, and Stephen Weissman; *Official Bulletin of the Episcopal Theological School* 57, May 1965; Schneider, *Jon Daniels Story*, p. 31.

29. Interview with Rev. Judith Upham.

30. Ibid.; Interview with Constance Daniels; Judith Upham to Jules [?], June 17, 1965, and to Donna [?], July 10, 1965, Upham Papers.

31. Kater, "Episcopal Society for Cultural and Racial Unity," pp. 31–32; Interview with Rev. John B. Morris.

32. Kater, "Episcopal Society for Cultural and Racial Unity," pp. 37–87; Interviews with the Reverends John B. Morris and Judith Upham.

33. Daniels, "A Burning Bush," pp. 4–5 (quotations) (this essay was written in Selma in April and widely reprinted later in 1965); Upham, "Jonathan Daniels — A Recollection," p. 20; Interview with Rev. Judith Upham.

34. Interview with Rev. Judith Upham; Jonathan Daniels to Constance Daniels, March 26, 1965, Constance Daniels Papers.

35. Garrow, *Protest at Selma*, pp. 95–112; Fager, *Selma, 1965*, pp. 138–49.

36. Jonathan Daniels to Constance Daniels, March 26, 1965, Constance Daniels Papers; Interview with Rev. Judith Upham; Fager, *Selma, 1965*, pp. 150–53.

37. Jonathan Daniels to Constance Daniels, March 26, 1965, Constance Daniels Papers (quotation); Interview with Rev. Morris V. Samuel; Fager, *Selma, 1965*, pp. 153–57; *New York Times*, March 23–25, 1965.

38. Garrow, *Protest at Selma*, p. 116; Fager, *Selma, 1965*, pp. 158–59; Jonathan Daniels to Constance Daniels, March 26, 1965, Constance Daniels Papers (quotations); Jonathan Daniels to Harvel Sanders, [April 1, 1965], in materials provided by Sanders (hereafter cited as Harvel Sanders Papers); interview with Judith Upham; *New York Times*, March 25, 1965.

39. *New York Times*, March 26, 1965 (all quotations from King); Garrow, *Protest at Selma*, pp. 116–17; Fager, *Selma, 1965*, pp. 160–63; Jonathan Daniels to Constance Daniels, March 26, 1965, Constance Daniels Papers (last quotation); Interview with Rev. Judith Upham.

40. Interviews with the Reverends Harvey H. Guthrie and Judith Upham; Jonathan Daniels to Constance Daniels, March 26, 1965, Constance Daniels Papers.

41. For a discussion of some of the whites who stayed in Selma after the march, see Talese, "Where's the Spirit of Selma Now?"

42. Daniels, "Autobiography: Phantasmagoria," January 30, 1957, Daniels Papers, ETS (quotations); Daniels, "June 22, 1965."

43. Interviews with J. Eugene Felch IV, Carlton T. Russell, and Anthony L. Reddington. At the time most people thought that there was only one black family in Keene, but there was one other: a black doctor and his family passed for white. No mention was made of this second family in the interviews conducted with people in or from Keene. See W. L. White, *Lost Boundaries*, a true account of the experiences of the doctor's son.

44. Interview with William J. Nelms.

45. Interview with Rev. T. Frank Mathews; Hamilton, *Seeing Historic Alabama*, p. 148; Hardy, *Selma*, pp. 122–24; Rev. George M. Murray to Rt. Rev. Henry Knox Sherrill, April 2, 1965, Carpenter Papers, Birmingham Public Library.

46. Interviews with Kate J. Gamble, Annette and David McCullough, and Rev. T. Frank Mathews; Vestry Minutes, February 8, 14, 1960, December 9, 1963, St. Paul's Episcopal Church Files, Selma.

47. Vestry Minutes, May 13, June 11, 1963; Interview with Rev. T. Frank Mathews; *Birmingham News*, April 1, 1965.

48. Vestry Minutes, October 6–7, 1963; Harry W. Gamble to B. M. Miller Childers, October 7, 1963, St. Paul's Episcopal Church Files; Interviews with Harry W. Gamble and Rev. T. Frank Mathews.

49. Interviews with Rev. T. Frank Mathews, B. M. Miller Childers, Roswell Falkenberry, and Sam Earle Hobbs; *New York Times*, March 29, 1965; Vestry Minutes, October 7, 1963, St. Paul's Episcopal Church Files.

50. Vestry Minutes, October 7, 1963.

51. Sunday bulletins, January 31, February 7, 1965, St. Paul's Episcopal Church Files; Rev. T. Frank Mathews to Rt. Rev. James A. Pike, June 30, 1965, copy in Carpenter Papers.

52. Vestry Minutes, March 11, 1965, and Sunday bulletin, March 14, 1965, St. Paul's Episcopal Church Files; Rev. T. Frank Mathews to Rt. Rev. James J. Pike, June 30, 1965, and Mathews to Bishop C. C. J. Carpenter, September 17, 1964, Carpenter Papers.

53. Rev. T. Frank Mathews to Bishop George M. Murray, n.d. (probably soon after June 18, 1965), Carpenter Papers; Interviews with Annette and David McCullough, Rev. T. Frank Mathews, B. M. Miller Childers, Harry W. Gamble, and Sam Earle Hobbs. Annette McCullough was a lifelong Episcopalian who for

years was in charge of preparing the linens for the communion services at St. Paul's. For another example of a parishioner who thought that the civil rights movement contained many communists, see Mrs. John Faulk, Jr., to Rt. Rev. George M. Murray, September 25, 1965, Carpenter Papers. For an indication that the communist charge was common in Selma, see Gay Talese's report in the *New York Times*, February 14, 1965.

54. Vestry Minutes, March 18–19, 1965, St. Paul's Episcopal Church Files; Rev. T. Frank Mathews to Bishop George M. Murray, n.d. (ca. July 1965), Carpenter Papers; Interview with Rev. T. Frank Mathews.

55. Vestry Minutes, March 22, 1965, St. Paul's Episcopal Church Files; Rev. T. Frank Mathews to "My dear Fellow Churchmen," March 23, 25, 1965, and Bishop Charles C. J. Carpenter to St. Paul's congregation, March 25, 1965, Carpenter Papers; Interview with Rev. T. Frank Mathews.

56. Fager, *Selma, 1965*, p. 4; *New York Times*, February 14, 1965 (first quotation); DeMuth, "Black Belt, Alabama," p. 536 (second quotation); *Birmingham News*, April 14, 1965 (third quotation), June 17, 1965; Vestry Minutes, March 27, 1965, St. Paul's Episcopal Church Files (fourth quotation).

57. Frances H. Hamilton to Rt. Rev. C. C. J. Carpenter, March 24, 1965, Carpenter Papers. Charges of sexual misconduct during the march were common. See Fager, *Selma, 1965*, pp. 152, 244.

58. Simcox, "Selma Episcopalians Speak," pp. 7, 11–12. Through Rev. Mathews, editor Simcox asked the members of St. Paul's parish "to express themselves freely — and anonymously" — about how they "feel about the issues and controversies which engulfed their community." Twenty replied, and the excerpts from their letters form the basis for this and the next paragraph. In addition, interviews with Rev. T. Frank Mathews, Harry and Kate Gamble, Sam Earle Hobbs, B. M. Miller and Hallie Childers, and Annette and David McCullough confirmed the impression conveyed by Simcox's report.

59. Vestry Minutes, December 9, 1963, May 10, 24, 27, 1965, January 28, 1966, and David N. McCullough to Rev. T. Frank Mathews, April 10, 1965, St. Paul's Episcopal Church Files; *New York Times*, February 4, 7, 1965; Interviews with Rev. T. Frank Mathews, Annette and David McCullough, and others. For evidence of the vestry's awareness of the economic impact of the Selma protests, see Vestry Minutes, April 15, 1965. Hammermill Paper later did hire blacks in Selma, and civil rights leaders then withdrew their objections (see *New York Times*, May 13, 1965).

60. Simcox, "Selma Episcopalians Speak," pp. 11–12.

61. Upham, "Jonathan Daniels — A Recollection," p. 18.

62. Jonathan Daniels to Constance Daniels, March 26, 1965, Constance Daniels Papers; Judith Upham to Karl Nordling, February 24, 1966, Upham Papers; *Selma Times-Journal*, March 28, 1965; *New York Times*, March 29, 1965 (first quotation); *Birmingham News*, April 1, 1965 (other quotations); interviews with the Reverends Judith Upham and T. Frank Mathews.

63. Jonathan Daniels to Mary Elizabeth McNaughton, March 27–28, 1965, Bonnet Papers.

64. Vestry Minutes, March 30, 1965, St. Paul's Episcopal Church Files.

65. Judith Upham to Karl Nordling, February 24, 1966, Upham Papers (first quotation); Jonathan Daniels to Mary Elizabeth McNaughton, April 5–12, 1965, Bonnet Papers (second quotation); Jonathan Daniels and Judith Upham to

"Whom It May Concern," May 12, 1965, copy in Carpenter Papers (third quotation).

66. Jonathan Daniels to Mary Elizabeth McNaughton, April 5–12, 1965, Bonnet Papers (quotation); Judith Upham to Karl Nordling, February 24, 1966, Upham Papers.

67. Rev. George M. Murray to Rt. Rev. C. Kilmer Myers, April 30, 1965, Statement of Bishop Carpenter, n.d., and biographical information—all in Carpenter Papers; Interviews with Rev. T. Frank Mathews and many others; *Birmingham News*, March 19, 1965 (quotations).

68. Vestry Minutes, April 15, 1965, St. Paul's Episcopal Church Files; Rev. T. Frank Mathews to Bishop C. C. J. Carpenter, handwritten note on copy of letter from Mathews to Rev. Robert A. Tourigney, April 17, 1965 (quotations), and Rev. T. Frank Mathews to Rt. Rev. James A. Pike, June 30, 1965—both in Carpenter Papers.

69. Rev. T. Frank Mathews to Rt. Rev. C. C. J. Carpenter, handwritten note on copy of letter from Mathews to Rev. Robert A. Tourigney, April 17, 1965 (quotation), and Mathews to Rt. Rev. James A. Pike, June 30, 1965; Judith Upham to Karl Nordling, February 24, 1966, Upham Papers.

70. Judith Upham to Karl Nordling, February 24, 1966; Jonathan Daniels and Judith Upham to Rt. Rev. C. C. J. Carpenter, April 21, 1965, and to "Whom It May Concern," May 12, 1965 (quotations)—both in Carpenter Papers.

71. Daniels, "A Burning Bush" (first quotation) and "June 22, 1965" (second quotation); Jonathan Daniels and Judith Upham to Rt. Rev. C. C. J. Carpenter, April 21, 1965 (third quotation), and Rev. T. Frank Mathews to Rt. Rev. James A. Pike, June 30, 1965 (copy)—both in Carpenter Papers; Jonathan Daniels to Mary Elizabeth McNaughton, April 5–12, 1965, Bonnet Papers.

72. Jonathan Daniels and Judith Upham to Rt. Rev. C. C. J. Carpenter, April 21, 1965, and Rev. T. Frank Mathews to Rt. Rev. James A. Pike, June 30, 1965, Carpenter Papers.

73. Jonathan Daniels and Judith Upham to Rt. Rev. C. C. J. Carpenter, April 21, 1965, Carpenter Papers.

74. Rt. Rev. C. C. J. Carpenter to Jonathan Daniels and Judith Upham, April 23, 1965, Carpenter Papers.

75. Rev. T. Frank Mathews to Rt. Rev. James A. Pike, June 30, 1965, copy in Carpenter Papers.

76. Jonathan Daniels to Mary Elizabeth McNaughton, May 1, 1965, Bonnet Papers (quotations); Jonathan Daniels and Judith Upham to "Whom It May Concern," May 12, 1965, Carpenter Papers; Jonathan Daniels to Constance Daniels, May 1, 1965, Constance Daniels Papers. Stines recalled that the bishop told him that he should be serving a parish instead of stirring up trouble with the civil rights movement and offered him one of the two black churches in Alabama (Interview with Henri A. Stines).

77. Jonathan Daniels and Judith Upham to Rt. Rev. C. C. J. Carpenter, April 28, 1965 (copy), and Jonathan Daniels to Constance Daniels, May 1, 1965—both in Constance Daniels Papers

78. ESCRU Statement, April 29, 1965, Carpenter Papers.

79. Ibid.; Jonathan Daniels to Mary Elizabeth McNaughton, May 1, 1965, Bonnet Papers.

80. Jonathan Daniels to Constance Daniels, May 1, 1965, Constance Daniels

Papers; Rev. T. Frank Mathews to Rt. Rev. James A. Pike, June 30, 1965, Carpenter Papers; *Birmingham News*, March 30, 1965.

81. Jonathan Daniels to Constance Daniels, May 1, 1965, Constance Daniels Papers; Rev. T. Frank Mathews to Rt. Rev. James A. Pike, June 30, 1965, Carpenter Papers; *Birmingham News*, March 30, 1965; Rev. George M. Murray to William C. Bibb, July 14, 1965, Carpenter Papers; *Birmingham News*, March 29–30, 1965.

82. Rev. T. Frank Mathews to Rt. Rev. James A. Pike, June 30, 1965, Carpenter Papers.

83. Rev. T. Frank Mathews to Rev. George M. Murray, n.d. (probably soon after June 18, 1965), Mathews to Rt. Rev. James A. Pike, June 30, 1965, and Mathews to Rev. K. J. Sharp and Rev. W. G. Workman, June 29, 1965 — all in Carpenter Papers.

84. Jonathan Daniels and Judith Upham to Rev. John B. Morris, May 9, 1965, Carpenter Papers.

85. Jonathan Daniels and Judith Upham to Rev. John B. Morris, May 9, 1965, Carpenter Papers; Interview with Gloria Larry House.

86. Rev. T. Frank Mathews to Rev. George M. Murray, n.d. (probably July 1965), and Rt. Rev. C. C. J. Carpenter to Rev. T. Frank Mathews, August 12, 1965 — both in Carpenter Papers; Interview with Gloria Larry House.

87. Rev. T. Frank Mathews to Rev. George M. Murray, n.d. (probably July 1965), Mathews to Murray, July 27, 1965, and Mathews to Murray and Rt. Rev. C. C. J. Carpenter, August 1, 1965 — all in Carpenter Papers.

88. Rev. T. Frank Mathews to Rt. Rev. C. C. J. Carpenter and Rev. George M. Murray, August 1, 1965, Carpenter Papers; Mathews to St. Paul's Congregation, August 15, 1965, in Vestry Minutes, St. Paul's Episcopal Church Files; Interview with Rev. T. Frank Mathews.

89. "You and Your Church," talk by Rev. T. Frank Mathews, August 8, 1965, in Vestry Minutes, August 10, 1965, St. Paul's Episcopal Church Files.

CHAPTER 3

1. Daniels, "A Burning Bush," p. 4. For discussion of the racial etiquette, see Doyle, *Etiquette of Race Relations*, and Myrdal, *An American Dilemma*. A more recent assessment of racial etiquette appears in Goldfield, *Black, White, and Southern*.

2. Jonathan Daniels to Mary Elizabeth McNaughton, April 5, 1965, Bonnet Papers (first quotation); Daniels to Molly D. Thoron, April 12, 1965, Constance Daniels Papers (second and fourth quotations); Jonathan Daniels to Harvel Sanders, [April 1, 1965], Sanders Papers (third and fifth quotations).

3. Jonathan Daniels to Constance Daniels, March 26, 1965, and May [?], 1965, Constance Daniels Papers (first two quotations); Daniels to Mary Elizabeth McNaughton, March 27, April 5, 1965, Bonnet Papers (last quotation).

4. *Birmingham News*, March 16–17, 21, 1965; Interview with Rev. Morris V. Samuel.

5. *Washington Post*, April 1, 1965; *New York Times*, April 2 (quotation), 3, 6, 8, 1965; *Montgomery Advertiser*, April 6, 1965; *Birmingham News*, April 8, 1965.

6. Jonathan Daniels to Molly D. Thoron, April 12, 1965, Constance Daniels Papers; Jonathan Daniels to Mary Elizabeth McNaughton, April 5–12, 1965,

Bonnet Papers; *Birmingham News*, April 8, 1965; *New York Times*, April 8, 1965; Judith Upham, "Jonathan Daniels — A Recollection," *Episcopal Theological School Journal*, January 1966, p. 21; John B. Morris interview with Rev. Morris V. Samuel, Daniels Papers, Episcopal Theological School, Cambridge; Author interview with Samuel.

7. Jonathan Daniels to Molly D. Thoron, April 12, 1965 (quotation); Daniels to Mary Elizabeth McNaughton, April 5–12, 1965.

8. Jonathan Daniels, "Foreclosure of a Mortgage: Reflections from a Point on the Way of the Cross: A Meditation in Theological Ethics," May 31, 1965, Constance Daniels Papers. Daniels wrote this paper for Professor Joseph Fletcher's class on Christian ethics.

9. Ibid.

10. Interview with Rev. Morris V. Samuel; *Atlanta Daily World*, April 13, 1965, clipping in Facts on Film; Jonathan Daniels to Mary Elizabeth McNaughton, April 5–12, 1965, Mary Bonnet Papers (first quotation); Jonathan Daniels to Constance Daniels, March 26, 1965, Constance Daniels Papers (second and third quotations).

11. Interview with Rev. Judith Upham; Upham, "Jonathan Daniels — A Recollection," p. 20.

12. Ibid. Numerous people commented in interviews about the seminarian's collar worn by Daniels, and many referred to him as "Reverend Daniels." Judith Upham recalled that the long trip to Mobile "was well worth taking because it was in [the store in] Mobile that we first had a chance to talk to a genuine white Southern integrationist" (Upham, "Jonathan Daniels — A Recollection," p. 21).

13. *Selma Times-Journal*, November 23, 1986 (article on the celebration of Brown Chapel's 120 years); Interviews with Rev. Judith Upham and Marc Oliver. For many references to Brown Chapel as a meeting place for the movement, see Fager, *Selma, 1965*, and Garrow, *Protest at Selma*.

14. Information provided by the Selma Housing Authority during a personal visit to the offices.

15. Interview with Rev. Judith Upham.

16. *New York Times*, June 22, 1965; *Selma Times-Journal*, June 28, 1965 (quotation); *Jubilee*, September 1965, pp. 16–23; *Atlanta Daily World*, December 25, 1964, clipping in Facts on Film; Interviews with the Reverends Maurice Ouellet and Morris V. Samuel.

17. *New York Times*, June 22, 1965; *Selma Times-Journal*, June 28, 1965; *Jubilee*, September 1965, pp. 16–23; *Atlanta Daily World*, December 25, 1964, clipping in Facts on Film; Interviews with Rev. Maurice Ouellet and Rev. Morris V. Samuel; *Selma Times-Journal*, February 7, June 27, 1965; *New York Times*, February 7, 1965; DeMuth, "Black Belt, Alabama," p. 536.

18. *New York Times*, June 22, 1965; *Selma Times-Journal*, June 28, 1965; *Jubilee*, September 1965, pp. 16–23; *Atlanta Daily World*, December 25, 1964, clipping in Facts on Film; Interviews with the Reverends Maurice Ouellet and Morris V. Samuel; *Selma Times-Journal*, February 7, June 27, 1965; *New York Times*, February 7, 1965; DeMuth, "Black Belt, Alabama," p. 536.

19. Jonathan Daniels, "June 22, 1965," Daniels Papers, ETS; Interviews with Rev. Judith Upham, Rev. Maurice Ouellet, and Alice M. West; *Selma Times-Journal*, June 28, 1965; Jonathan Daniels to Constance Daniels, May 1, 1965, Constance Daniels Papers.

20. Interview with Rev. Maurice Ouellet.

21. Interviews with Rev. Maurice Ouellet and Rev. Judith Upham; Jonathan Daniels to Constance Daniels, May 1, 1965, Constance Daniels Papers.

22. Jonathan Daniels to Molly D. Thoron, April 12, 1965, Constance Daniels Papers (quotations); Jonathan Daniels to Mary Elizabeth McNaughton, April 5–12, May 1, 1965, Bonnet Papers; Judith Upham to Ruth Johnson, April 16, 1965, Upham Papers.

23. Rev. T. Frank Mathews to Rt. Rev. C. C. J. Carpenter and Rev. George M. Murray, July 22, 1965, Carpenter Papers (quotation); Interview with Rev. T. Frank Mathews.

24. Interview with Harry and Kate Gamble.

25. Ibid.

26. Daniels, "A Burning Bush," p. 5 (written in April 1965).

27. Interviews with B. M. Miller Childers and Roswell Falkenberry. The incident referred to by Childers must have occurred in January 1965 (see *New York Times*, January 23, 1965).

28. Jonathan Daniels to Harvel Sanders, [April 1, 1965], Sanders Papers (quotations); Upham, "Jonathan Daniels — A Recollection," p. 19.

29. Interviews with Harry and Kate Gamble, B. M. Miller Childers, Roswell Falkenberry, Rev. T. Frank Mathews, and Sam Earle Hobbs.

30. Longenecker, *Selma's Peacemaker*, pp. 70, 88; Interviews with Harry and Kate Gamble, B. M. Miller Childers, and Rev. T. Frank Mathews.

31. Daniels, "A Burning Bush," p. 6.

32. Ibid., p. 5. Another, longer version of this essay, located in the Daniels Papers at ETS, contains the remarks about the photographers.

33. Ibid., p. 5.

34. Ibid., p. 6.

35. Ibid., p. 7; Information provided by the Selma Housing Authority during a personal visit to its offices.

36. Daniels, "A Burning Bush," p. 8.

37. Jonathan Daniels to Constance Daniels, March 26, 1965, and May [?], 1965, Constance Daniels Papers; Jonathan Daniels to Mary Elizabeth McNaughton, April 5–12, 1965, Bonnet Papers; Upham, "Jonathan Daniels — A Recollection," p. 20. Judith Upham admitted, "We invariably also took time to eat a decent meal. Unfortunately our stomachs weren't able to identify as closely with the culture in which we existed as we would have liked."

38. *Baltimore Afro-American*, April 10, 1965, clipping in Facts on Film; *Birmingham News*, May 16, 1965; Jonathan Daniels to Mary Elizabeth McNaughton, May 1, 1965, Bonnet Papers.

39. *New York Times*, May 16, 1965; Rowland Evans and Robert Novak, "Inside Report," *Birmingham News*, May 3, 1965 (quotations).

40. *Selma Times-Journal*, April 18, 1965; *New York Times*, May 16, 1965; Evans and Novak, "Inside Report"; Jonathan Daniels to Constance Daniels, May [?], 1965, Constance Daniels Papers; Jonathan Daniels to Judith Upham, [August 3, 1965?], Upham Papers; Interview with Marc Oliver.

41. Interview with Rev. Morris V. Samuel; Jonathan Daniels to Mary Elizabeth McNaughton, May 1, 1965, Bonnet Papers (quotation).

42. Interviews with Alice West and Lonzy West.

43. Interviews with Alice West, Rev. Judith Upham, and Lonzy West; Daniels, "A Burning Bush," p. 7.

44. Interviews with Alice West, Rev. Judith Upham, Lonzy West, and Rev. Maurice Ouellet.

45. Interviews with Alice West, Rev. Judith Upham, and Marc Oliver; Jonathan Daniels, "A Burning Bush," p. 7.

46. Interviews with Alice West, Judith Upham, and Rev. Morris V. Samuel.

47. Webb and Nelson, *Selma, Lord, Selma*, pp. 51–53 (quotations, pp. 51, 130); Jonathan Daniels to Constance Daniels, May [?], 1965, Constance Daniels Papers; Jonathan Daniels, "June 22, 1965"; Upham, "Jonathan Daniels — A Recollection," pp. 15–6; Interviews with Alice West and Rev. Judith Upham.

48. Webb and Nelson, *Selma, Lord, Selma*, p. 131.

49. Ibid., p. 153.

50. Ibid.

51. Upham, "Jonathan Daniels — A Recollection," p. 20.

52. Jonathan Daniels to Mary Elizabeth McNaughton, April 5–12, 1965, Bonnet Papers; Daniels to Constance Daniels, March 26, 1965, and Daniels to Molly D. Thoron, April 12, 1965 (quotation) — both in Constance Daniels Papers; Upham, "Jonathan Daniels — A Recollection," p. 20; Interviews with Rev. Judith Upham, Alice West, and Rev. Morris V. Samuel.

53. Jonathan Daniels to Constance Daniels, May [?], 1965, Constance Daniels Papers; Daniels to Mary Elizabeth McNaughton, May 1, 1965, Bonnet Papers; Interviews with Alice West, Rev. Judith Upham, Lonzy West, and Rev. Morris V. Samuel.

54. Jonathan Daniels to Mary Elizabeth McNaughton, April 5–12 (first quotation), May 1, 1965 (second quotation), Bonnet Papers; Daniels to Constance Daniels, March 26, May 1, 1965, Constance Daniels Papers; Mary-Virginia Shaw to Judith Upham, March 29, May 11, 1965, Frances E. Bailey to Jonathan Daniels and Judith Upham, April 10, 1965, and Hugh Flesher to Judith Upham, April 29, 1965 — all in Upham Papers.

55. Daniels to Mary Elizabeth McNaughton, May 1, 1965, Bonnet Papers (first, second, and fourth quotations); Jonathan Daniels to Constance Daniels, May 1, [?], 1965, Constance Daniels Papers (third quotation); Interview with Rev. Judith Upham.

56. Jonathan Daniels, "June 22, 1965."

57. Ibid. (quotations); Upham, "Jonathan Daniels — A Recollection," p. 21.

58. Jonathan Daniels, "June 22, 1965" (quotation); Daniels to Judith Upham, June 14, 1965, and Sarah Grant Ellis to Upham, [June 1965] — both in Upham Papers; Interview with Rev. Judith Upham.

59. *Keene Sentinel*, August 21, 1965; Jonathan Daniels, "June 22, 1965" (quotations).

60. *Keene Sentinel*, August 21, 1965; Jonathan Daniels, "Notes on Talk at Geneva Point," June 24, 1965, Upham Papers; Daniels, "June 22, 1965.

61. Carlton Russell to Rev. William Wolf, September 13, 1965, in Russell Papers; Judith Upham to Donna [?], July 10, 1965, Upham Papers; Interviews with the Reverends John W. Inman, Stephen Weissman, and Judith Upham.

62. Interview with Eugene Pritchard.

63. Judith Upham to Donna [?], July 10, 1965, Upham Papers; Interview with Marc Oliver.

64. Interview with Marc Oliver; Garrow, *Protest at Selma*, p. 91 (quotation); Fager, *Selma, 1965*, pp. 28, 108.

65. Interviews with Eugene Pritchard and Marc Oliver.

66. Interviews with Lonzy West, Eugene Pritchard, and Alice West.

67. Interviews with Marc Oliver and Eugene Pritchard; John B. Morris interview with Oliver, located with Schneider interviews; Judith Upham to Jules [?], June 17, 1965, Upham Papers.

68. Interview with Marc Oliver; Newspaper clippings, n.d., in materials provided by Oliver (hereafter cited as Marc Oliver Papers); Jonathan Daniels to Judith Upham, [August 3, 1965?], Upham papers; *Birmingham News*, May 21, 1985, November 21, 1986; *Montgomery Advertiser*, November 30, 1985; *Selma Times-Journal*, November 20–21, 1986. Clippings and other biographical data on Dumont and Mulder were supplied by Alston Fitts III of the Edmundite Mission in Selma.

69. Jonathan Daniels and Eugene Pritchard, "Community Resources for Public Assistance," July 30, 1965, Upham Papers; Interview with Eugene Pritchard.

70. Jonathan Daniels and Eugene Pritchard, "Community Resources for Public Assistance," July 30, 1965, Upham Papers; Interview with Eugene Pritchard.

71. Jonathan Daniels and Eugene Pritchard, "Community Resources for Public Assistance," July 30, 1965, Upham Papers; Interview with Eugene Pritchard.

72. Newspaper clipping, n.d., Oliver Papers; Interviews with Marc Oliver and Eugene Pritchard. When I interviewed him, Pritchard still had 1965 government pamphlets on "Civil Rights under Federal Programs: An Analysis of Title VI [of the 1964 Civil Rights Act]" and "Equal Opportunity in Hospitals and Health Facilities: Civil Rights Policies under the Hill-Burton Program."

73. Notarized statement of Robert Jefferson Henderson, September 22, 1965, Thomas McIntyre Papers, University of New Hampshire Archives, Durham. The reason for Henderson's sworn statement about his contacts with Daniels remains a mystery. A slightly different version was reprinted in the *Birmingham Independent*, October 8, 1965 (see clipping in Carpenter Papers). See also Clark, *The Jim Clark Story*, pp. 107–12. The account in Henderson's statement cannot be verified from other sources, but large parts of it are consistent with more general impressions derived from other sources. Portions of the statement, however, seem incredible; for instance, Henderson reported that Daniels constantly referred to him and his wife as "Baby" (which Henderson interpreted as "beatnik-type speech") and that Daniels "made liberal use of mild profanity . . . [h]is language at times bordered on being offensive." All other reports indicate that Daniels was invariably courteous and polite, especially in front of women.

74. Notarized statement of Robert Jefferson Henderson.

75. Ibid.; Jonathan Daniels to Judith Upham, [August 3, 1965], Upham Papers.

76. Jonathan Daniels to Judith Upham, [August 3, 1965]. For a contemporary assessment of Selma at the end of July, see the article by David Gordon in the *Southern Courier*, July 23, 1965. A weekly newspaper covering the southern civil rights movement, the *Southern Courier* was edited by northern college students and began publication on July 16, 1965. See R. Jefferson Norrell, "Reporters and Reformers."

CHAPTER 4

1. Interview with a confidential source.

2. For an example, see *Washington Post*, May 9, 1965. Innumerable people in

interviews used the term *bloody Lowndes*. For a black man's first-person account of violence in Lowndes County in the 1920s and 1930s and of race relations generally in the Alabama Black Belt, see Denby [Matthew Ward], *Indignant Heart*, pp. 1–86.

3. Owen, *History of Alabama*, 2:909.

4. Abernathy, *Formative Period in Alabama*, pp. 16–17, 24–32; Owen, *History of Alabama*, 1:432, 611, 2:909; Russell, *Lowndes County Court House*, p. 3.

5. For discussions of Lowndes and Hayne, see Wallace's three-volume *History of South Carolina*. For the context of the Hayne-Webster debate and the shifting views of South Carolina politicians, see Freehling, *Prelude to Civil War*. Early years in Hayneville are covered by Russell, *Lowndes County Court House*.

6. Boyd, *Alabama*, p. 12 (quotation); Gibson, "Alabama Black Belt"; Richardson, *Alabama Encyclopedia*, p. 285.

7. Boyd, *Alabama*, p. 12; Gibson, "Alabama Black Belt"; Richardson, *Alabama Encyclopedia*, p. 285.

8. Davis, *Cotton Kingdom*, pp. 7, 11–12; Abernathy, *Formative Period in Alabama*, p. 58; Sisk, "Alabama Black Belt," p. 78; U.S. Bureau of the Census, *Fifth Census*, pp. 23, 99, 101, *Sixth Census; or, Enumeration of the Inhabitants*, p. 245, *Sixth Census: Compendium of the Inhabitants*, pp. 215–17, 219, 221, *Seventh Census*, pp. 430–31, *Eighth Census: Population*, p. 8; *Eighth Census: Agriculture*, p. 3.

9. Owsley, *Plain Folk*, pp. 182–87; Sellers, *Slavery in Alabama*, pp. 11–12, 21–28; U.S. Bureau of the Census, *Eighth Census: Population*, p. 8; Davis, *Cotton Kingdom*, p. 39. In examining the Alabama Black Belt, Owsley looked at seven counties, including Lowndes. My figures are from either Owsley's examination of Lowndes or his detailed work on Perry County, which he suggests was typical of the Black Belt (and, therefore, probably not much different from Lowndes).

10. Moore, *History of Alabama*, p. 357 (quotation). The literature on slavery is immense. For an overview of recent scholarship, see Dew, "The Slavery Experience," p. 1261. For Alabama, the standard — but now old — account is Sellers, *Slavery in Alabama*. Sellers devotes one chapter to "The Defense of Slavery" (pp. 332–60).

11. Sellers, *Slavery in Alabama*, pp. 215–41; Moore, *History of Alabama*, pp. 374–77; Davis, *Cotton Kingdom*, pp. 92–116.

12. Moore, *History of Alabama*, pp. 382–84; Hamilton, *Seeing Historic Alabama*, pp. 137–39 (quotation, p. 139); Sisk, "Alabama Black Belt," p. 8.

13. Russell, *Lowndes County Court House*, pp. 5–15 (quotations, p. 10).

14. Kennedy, "Black Belt Aristocrats," pp. 81–83 (quotations); Moore, *History of Alabama*, p. 381. One of the clearer statements of this belief is Kennedy, pp. 80–85. Kennedy wrote from Camden in Wilcox County, adjacent to Lowndes.

15. Confederate monument in courthouse square, Hayneville, Ala.; Russell, *Lowndes County Court House*, pp. 99–110; Jones, *Yankee Blitzkreig*, pp. 103–6 and passim; Moore, *History of Alabama*, pp. 434–36. See also Fleming, *Civil War and Reconstruction*; Wiggins, *Scalawag in Alabama Politics*; Kolchin, *First Freedom*.

16. Wiggins, *Scalawag in Alabama Politics*, pp. 70, 84, 99, and passim; Going, *Bourbon Democracy*, pp. 214–23; Russell, *Lowndes County Court House*, pp. 125–32; Loren Schweninger, *James T. Rapier*, pp. 167–68. See also Gilmour, "The Other Emancipation," and Wiggins, *Scalawag in Alabama Politics*.

17. Sisk, "Alabama Black Belt," p. 15 and passim; U.S. Bureau of the Census, *Ninth Census*, 3:96, and *Tenth Census*, 3:213.

18. Gilmour, "The Other Emancipation," pp. 126–28; Ransom and Sutch, *One Kind of Freedom*, pp. 78–80. Glenn Sisk argues that after the Civil War, the Lowndes plantation system broke up and large holdings were replaced by more numerous small farms. He seems to have confused actual ownership and units of production (see Sisk, "Alabama Black Belt," pp. 26–27).

19. Quoted in Litwack, *Been in the Storm So Long*, p. 396.

20. Sisk, "Alabama Black Belt," p. 27; Ransom and Sutch, *One Kind of Freedom*, pp. 81–90. Although Ransom and Sutch's findings may be safely applied to most regions of the South, their work is particularly appropriate for Lowndes County because they included it in their sample of representative counties of the cotton South (see p. 291).

21. U.S. Bureau of the Census, *Thirteenth Census . . . : Agriculture*, p. 43; Ransom and Sutch, *One Kind of Freedom*, p. 170.

22. Ransom and Sutch, *One King of Freedom*, pp. 106–70; Daniel, *Shadow of Slavery*, pp. 19–21.

23. Daniel, *Shadow of Slavery*, pp. 59–60.

24. Ibid., p. 60.

25. On racial segregation generally, see Woodward, *Strange Career of Jim Crow*, esp. p. 99, and Williamson, *Crucible of Race*. No monograph has been written on race relations in Alabama in the late nineteenth and early twentieth centuries.

26. Sisk, "Alabama Black Belt," p. 273; Schweninger, *James T. Rapier*, pp. 115–16, 145–50, 156–57, and passim; Smith, *The Negro in Congress*, pp. 78–85.

27. Kousser, *Shaping of Southern Politics*, pp. 130–38 and passim; Hackney, *Populism to Progressivism*, pp. 32–39; McMillan, *Constitutional Development in Alabama*, pp. 223–25, 284 (quotation), and passim.

28. McMillan, *Constitutional Development in Alabama*, pp. 260–62, 348–52, and passim (quotation, pp. 261–62 n. 93); Kousser, *Shaping of Southern Politics*, pp. 165–71. As McMillan points out, Lowndes had 5,500 black and 1,000 white voters, yet the county voted for the constitutional convention to restrict the suffrage by a vote of 3,226 for to 338 against; whites must have, in effect, "voted" the blacks for their own disfranchisement (McMillan, p. 262).

29. McMillan, *Constitutional Development in Alabama*, pp. 262, 352; Kousser, *Shaping of Southern Politics*, p. 169 and passim; Fleming, *Civil War and Reconstruction*, p. 806.

30. Denby, *Indignant Heart*, p. 19. Lowndes County tax assessments for 1947 list Dickson as the owner of more than ten thousand acres. Numerous Lowndes natives referred to Dickson's violent ways. See also notes of Jonathan Worth Daniels on a trip through Alabama in the mid-1930s, in Daniels Papers, Southern Historical Collection, University of North Carolina at Chapel Hill.

31. Marie Reese, "A Near Miracle," interview with Bettie D. McCall, January 1, 1939, Work Progress Administration Federal Writers' Project of Alabama, Alabama Department of Archives and History.

32. Couto, *Ain't Gonna Let Nobody Turn Me Round*, pp. 235–36.

33. *Atlanta Constitution*, December 19, 1914, January 7, 1915; *New York Times*, December 19, 1914; *Montgomery Advertiser*, December 31, 1914. Char-

les Denby comments on two unreported lynchings of the period in *Indignant Heart*, pp. 40–43.

34. *New York Times*, December 19, 1914; *Atlanta Constitution*, December 19, 1914, January 7, 1915; *Montgomery Advertiser*, December 31, 1914, January 6, 1915 (quotations). In 1919 former Governor O'Neal attended an antilynching conference in New York City that touched off a push for federal legislation against the practice (see Tindall, *Emergence of the New South*, p. 173).

35. For the Powell lynchings, see *Montgomery Advertiser*, July 24–25, 1917; *Montgomery Journal*, July 26, 1917; *Birmingham Weekly Voice*, July 28, 1917. All newspaper accounts come from Lynching Records, Tuskegee Institute Archives.

36. *Montgomery Advertiser*, July 24–25, 1917; *Montgomery Journal*, July 26, 1917 (quotation); *Birmingham Weekly Voice*, July 28, 1917.

37. *Montgomery Advertiser*, July 26, 1917; *Mobile Register*, July 26, 1917; *Birmingham Age-Herald* quoted in *Birmingham Weekly Voice*, July 28, 1917.

38. *Atlanta Constitution*, August 31, 1931; *New York Times*, August 31, 1931.

39. Couto, *Ain't Gonna Let Nobody Turn Me Round*, pp. 101–2, 179, 365–67 n. 62. In trying to assess the effects of the Sharecroppers' Union (SCU) on the later civil rights movement in Lowndes County, Robin D. G. Kelley has written: "How much these young activists [Stokely Carmichael, Jon Daniels, and others] knew about the SCU, the Communists, or the 1935 cotton pickers' strike in Lowndes before their arrival is difficult to determine. . . . The fact is, the events of 1935 comprised part of the collective memory of Lowndes County blacks in 1965. The armed and poor sharecroppers who followed Carmichael's lead brought a lot of their past to the new movement, including what the CP and SCU had left behind" (Kelley, *Hammer and Hoe*, p. 230). Charles Smith, who was involved in protests in the 1930s and 1960, agreed with Kelley's conclusion (see See Couto, *Ain't Gonna Let Nobody Turn Me Round*, p. 102). In interviews with Smith and others in Lowndes County — black and white, natives and outside activists — the SCU and the 1935 strike was never mentioned, even when individuals discussed their lives in the 1930s and the history of race relations and agriculture in the county. For natives of Lowndes, the connection between the events of the 1930s and the civil rights movement seems, therefore, tenuous at best; for outside activists, the relationship is probably nonexistent.

40. Sisk, "Alabama Black Belt," pp. 160, 418 (quotation), 326–28; Russell, *Lowndes County Court House*, pp. 159–60, 165.

41. Sisk, "Alabama Black Belt," pp. 376, 396, 403, 411–12; Russell, *Lowndes County Court House*, pp. 134–35, 163. One commentator said, "Many of the men of this section enjoyed chicken fights, dueling, women-chasing, horse races, poker, politics, barbecues and liquor drinking as great sports" (Kohn, *The Cradle*, p. 21).

42. U.S. Bureau of the Census, *Ninth Census*, pp. 11–12, and *Twelfth Census*, 1:9, 529; Sisk, "Alabama Black Belt," pp. 195, 449–50; *Alabama State Gazette and Business Directory, 1887–8* (Atlanta: R. L. Polk and Co., n.d.), p. 411.

43. Sisk, "Alabama Black Belt," pp. 91–92, 195–98; Ellis, "The Calhoun School."

44. Sisk, "Alabama Black Belt," pp. 52–54 (quotation, p. 52), 61, 527–28, 533–36.

45. U.S. Bureau of the Census, *Twelfth Census*, 6:430, and *Thirteenth Census*,

6:50; Sisk, "Alabama Black Belt," pp. 435–38; Fite, *Cotton Fields No More*, pp. 6–7, 48, 94–95.

46. Sisk, "Alabama Black Belt," pp. 437–49, 456. For a similar county, see Rubin, *Plantation County*.

47. Tower, "Alabama's Shifting Cotton Belt"; Bond, *Negro Education in Alabama*, pp. 2–3, 133, 238, and passim.

48. McMillan, *Constitutional Development in Alabama*, pp. 358, 368–69.

49. Sisk, "Alabama Black Belt," pp. 455–75; Gilmour, "The Other Emancipation," pp. 169–70.

50. U.S. Bureau of the Census, *Thirteenth Census*, 6:36, 43, *Fourteenth Census*, 6:42, *Fifteenth Census*, 2:975, *Sixteenth Census*, 1:293, *United States Census of Agriculture, 1925, The Southern States*, p. 785, and *United States Census of Agriculture, 1935, The Southern States*, p. 637. See also the analysis in Rubin, *Plantation County*.

51. U.S. Bureau of the Census, *Thirteenth Census*, 6:36, 43, *Fourteenth Census*, 6:42, *Fifteenth Census*, 2:975, *Sixteenth Census*, 1:293, *United States Census of Agriculture, 1925, The Southern States*, p. 785, *United States Census of Agriculture, 1935, The Southern States*, p. 637, and *United States Census of Agriculture, 1945, Alabama*. For a valuable discussion of the overall changes in the cotton culture in the twentieth century, see Daniel, *Breaking the Land*. See also Street, *New Revolution in the Cotton Economy*, and Fite, *Cotton Fields No More*.

52. U.S. Bureau of the Census, *Thirteenth Census*, 2:54, *Fourteenth Census*, 3:63, *Fifteenth Census*, 3:102, and *Sixteenth Census*, 2:238.

53. U.S. Bureau of the Census, *United States Census of Agriculture, 1945*, pp. 27, 39, 48, 59, 73, 87, 97, *United States Census of Agriculture, 1954*, pp. 65, 71, 84, 89, 101, 107, 113, 119, 137, *United States Census of Agriculture, 1959*, pp. 133, 145, 151, 157, 163, 175, 185, 191, 197, 209, 233, *United States Census of Agriculture, 1964*, pp. 259, 275, 283, 291, 307, 321, 339, 345, 351, 373, *Sixteenth Census*, 2:238, *Seventeenth Census*, 7:2–87, and *Eighteenth Census*, 1:2–193; Richardson, *Alabama Encyclopedia*, p. 395. See also, Street, *New Revolution in the Cotton Economy*.

54. Sisk, "Alabama Black Belt," pp. 480, 527 (quotation).

55. U.S. Bureau of the Census, *United States Census of Housing, 1960*, pp. 2–78; *Alabama Official and Statistical Register, 1963*, p. 497; Richardson, *Alabama Encyclopedia*, pp. 503, 924, 936–43.

56. U.S. Bureau of the Census, *United States Census of Housing, 1960*, pp. 2–83, 2–78.

57. U.S. Commission on Civil Rights, *Hearing*, pp. 255–65. The doctor testifying was Alan C. Mermann, a pediatrician with the Yale University Medical School, who had conducted a survey of Lowndes for the Tuskegee Institute Community Education Program in the summer of 1966.

58. Ibid., pp. 258, 273 (quotation). The local doctor was Robert B. Griffin of Fort Deposit.

59. U.S. Bureau of the Census, *Eighteenth Census*, 1:2-140-2, 2-233-35.

60. Daniel, *Breaking the Land*, p. xiv.

61. *Wall Street Journal*, January 20, 1965; Interviews with a confidential source, Tom L. Coleman, and John Hulett. More generally, see Rubin, *Plantation County*.

62. Interviews with a confidential source, Tom L. Coleman, and John Hulett; *Chicago Sun-Times*, March 3, 1965 (quotation).

63. *Alabama Official and Statistical Register, 1963*, pp. 468–69; *New York Times*, May 3, 1965; *Washington Post*, March 23, 1965; *Chicago Sun-Times*, March 3, 1965; *Wall Street Journal*, January 20, 1965; Rubin, *Plantation County*, pp. 96–100.

64. *Southern Courier*, February 19–20, 1966; Kopkind, "Lair of the Black Panther," p. 10 (quotation); *Wall Street Journal*, January 20, 1965; Interview with Hulda Coleman.

65. *Wall Street Journal*, January 20, 1965.

66. Ibid.

67. *Washington Post*, March 23, 1965 (quotation); *Chicago Sun-Times*, March 3, 1965; *New York Times*, March 23, 1965.

68. *Selma Times-Journal*, March 23, 1965; Interview with C. Frank Ryals.

69. *Birmingham News*, March 18–19, 1965; *New York Times*, March 23, 1965; *New York Herald-Tribune*, March 21, 1965.

70. Fager, *Selma, 1965*, pp. 159–60; Garrow, *Protest at Selma*, p. 117; Mendelsohn, *Martyrs*, pp. 176–95.

71. Fager, *Selma, 1965*, pp. 163–64; Garrow, *Protest at Selma*, pp. 117–18; Mendelsohn, *Martyrs*, pp. 176–95.

72. *Selma Times-Journal*, May 3, 1965; *New York Times*, May 7, 1965; *Birmingham News*, May 7, 1965; *Arkansas Gazette*, May 5, 1965.

73. *Selma Times-Journal*, May 2, 1965 (first two quotations); *Chicago Sun-Times*, May 2, 1965 (last quotation).

74. *New York Times*, May 7, 1965 (third quotation); *Birmingham News*, May 7, 1965. Local blacks must have wondered whether the prosecution would have been so outspoken if the Klansmen had killed Leroy Moton instead of Viola Liuzzo. Certainly in the past blacks had been killed without a white being convicted for the crime and whites did not worry that justice was forgotten and that the fear of God was abandoned.

75. *New York Times*, May 7, 1965 (quotations); *Birmingham News*, May 7, 1965.

76. *New York Times*, May 8, 1965; *Birmingham News*, May 9, 1965. The jury reported a 10–2 split in favor of conviction.

CHAPTER 5

1. The subtitle of this chapter ("A Genuine Social and Political Revolution") comes from a report by James K. Batten, writing from Hayneville: "Here in Lowndes County and others nearby there is developing a genuine social and political revolution, in the fullest sense of that overworked word" (*Miami Herald*, June 20, 1965). Later in the summer, after the first black registered to vote in Lowndes, Gillis Morgan wrote, "Registration of the lone Negro was a social and political revolution within itself" (*Birmingham News*, August 21, 1965).

2. Kopkind, "Lair of the Black Panther," p. 10. Kopkind observed, "Of all the Black Belt counties, Lowndes is the very heart of darkness . . . there are a lot of dead souls in Lowndes County."

3. Interviews with John Hulett and Robert L. Strickland; Carson, *In Struggle*, p. 164.

4. Interview with John Hulett; Carson, *In Struggle*, pp. 162–64; Kopkind, "Lair of the Black Panther," p. 11.

5. *Selma Times-Journal*, January 1, February 26, 1965. For the larger Selma story, see Garrow, *Protest at Selma*.

6. *Birmingham News*, March 2, 1965; *New York Times*, March 2, 1965 (quotation); *Baton Rouge State Times*, March 24, 1965; Kopkind, "Lair of the Black Panther," p. 11; Fager, *Selma, 1965*, p. 84.

7. Fager, *Selma, 1965*, p. 84 (first quotation); *Birmingham News*, March 2, 1965 (second quotation); *New York Times*, March 2, 1965 (third quotation); *Baton Rouge State Times*, March 24, 1965; Kopkind, "Lair of the Black Panther," p. 11.

8. *Birmingham News*, March 16–17, 21, 1965; *Chicago Sun-Times*, March 3, 1965. In the *Sun-Times*, Charles Bartlett explicitly compares the experiences of Lowndes and Wilcox counties in the voting rights campaign.

9. *Baton Rouge State Times*, March 24, 1965 (first two quotations); *Birmingham News*, March 17, August 21, 1965 (last quotation); Interview with John Hulett.

10. *Southern Courier*, April 2–3, 1966; Interviews with John Hulett, Charles Smith, and Rosceno M. Haralson. The organization's name was clearly patterned after the Alabama Christian Movement for Human Rights, which Fred L. Shuttlesworth of Birmingham had started after the state of Alabama effectively barred the NAACP.

11. Interview with John Hulett.

12. Ibid.

13. Ibid.

14. Interview with Charles Smith; Couto, *Ain't Gonna Let Nobody Turn Me Round*, p. 88; Ellis, "The Calhoun School."

15. Interview with Charles Smith; Couto, *Ain't Gonna Let Nobody Turn Me Round*, pp. 99–100.

16. Interview with Charles Smith.

17. Kopkind, "Lair of the Black Panther," p. 13; Interview with Robert L. Strickland.

18. Interview with Robert L. Strickland.

19. Interview with Sarah B. Logan.

20. Ibid.

21. Interview with Lillian McGill-Bogarty.

22. Ibid.

23. Interviews with John Hulett, Charles Smith, Robert L. Strickland, Sarah B. Logan, John Jackson, Rosceno M. Haralson, and others; Carmichael and Hamilton, *Black Power*, p. 101.

24. Interviews with John Hulett, Charles Smith, Robert L. Strickland, Sarah B. Logan, John Jackson, Rosceno M. Haralson, and others; Carmichael and Hamilton, *Black Power*, p. 101.

25. Fager, *Selma, 1965*, pp. 153–57; *Houston Chronicle*, March 22 (first two quotations), 23 (last quotation), 1965; Garrow, *Protest at Selma*, p. 69; Interview with Gardenia S. White.

26. FBI in Mobile, Ala., to Registrars of Voters in Dallas, Wilcox, Lowndes, and Montgomery Counties, Ala., April 2, 1965, 44-12831-771, *Centers of the Southern Struggle*, Federal Bureau of Investigation Papers, Washington, D.C.; *Southern Courier*, April 2–3, 1966; *New York Times*, March 29, 1965.

27. Carson, *In Struggle*, pp. 162–63; Viorst, *Fire in the Streets*, pp. 347–57. See also Carmichael and Hamilton, *Black Power*.

28. Carson, *In Struggle*, pp. 162–63 (quotation); Viorst, *Fire in the Streets*, pp. 361–62; Carmichael and Hamilton, *Black Power*, pp. 96–101.

29. Interviews with Bob Mants, Stokely Carmichael, and Ruby N. Sales.

30. Carmichael and Hamilton, *Black Power*, pp. 96–106 (quotations, pp. 100–101); Viorst, *Fire in the Streets*, pp. 362–63; Carson, *In Struggle*, pp. 162–64.

31. Interviews with Stokely Carmichael, Bob Mants, Ruby N. Sales, and John Hulett.

32. Carmichael and Hamilton, *Black Power*, pp. 101–3; Interviews with Stokely Carmichael, Bob Mants, and John Hulett.

33. Interviews with Stokely Carmichael, Bob Mants, Ruby N. Sales, and John Hulett; Carmichael and Hamilton, *Black Power*, pp. 103–4 (quotations).

34. *Southern Courier*, April 2–3, 1966; Interviews with Stokely Carmichael, John Hulett, Bob Mants, and Charles Smith.

35. Transcription of recorded interview with Carmichael, April [?], 1966, in SNCC Papers, Martin Luther King Center Library, Atlanta (hereafter cited as Carmichael interview in SNCC Papers); Interviews with Stokely Carmichael, Bob Mants, John Hulett, and Charles Smith. On the problems involved in obtaining telephones for blacks, see *Southern Courier*, July 23, 1965. For twenty years blacks in the Mosses community had tried to get phones, and in the summer of 1965 the telephone company asked for the payment of two years' service charges in advance.

36. Interviews with Stokely Carmichael and Bob Mants; Carmichael interview in SNCC Papers. Mants emphasized that it took eighteen years for him to realize that the school principal had *not* been the person who called the sheriff.

37. Stokely Carmichael interview and Lowndes County WATS report, April 4, 1965 — both in SNCC Papers.

38. Lowndes County WATS report, April 4, 1965, SNCC Papers; *New York Times*, May 3–4, 1965; *Houston Chronicle*, March 15, 1965. Lowndes County was not unique; a comparable situation existed in adjacent Wilcox County, where no blacks were registered and white registrants exceeded the eligible white population.

39. *Chicago Sun-Times*, March 3, 1965.

40. Strong, *Registration of Voters in Alabama*, pp. 25–34; *New York Times*, May 4, 1965; *Baton Rouge State Times*, March 24, 1965; *Houston Chronicle*, March 15, 1965. For the history of restrictions on black suffrage and of black efforts to attain the right to vote in the South, see Lawson, *Black Ballots*.

41. *Baton Rouge State Times*, March 24, 1965.

42. This story was recounted in the *Houston Chronicle*, March 15, 1965.

43. *New York Times*, May 4, 1965; Lowndes County WATS report, May 20, 1965, SNCC Papers.

44. Lowndes County WATS reports, May 20, July 6–7, 9, 1965, and SNCC news release, July 8, 1965 (quotations), SNCC Papers; *Southern Courier*, July 16, 1965.

45. Jonathan Daniels to Judith Upham, [August 3, 1965], Upham Papers. The evidence dealing with Daniels's work in Lowndes County before the demonstration on August 14, 1965, is sketchy. The story has been pieced together primarily from his co-workers' recollections, which are necessarily incomplete.

46. Carson, *In Struggle*, pp. 191–211 (Carmichael quotation from *New York*

Times, p. 204); Interviews with Stokely Carmichael, Bob Mants, James Rogers, Jr., and Ruby N. Sales.

47. Jonathan Daniels to Judith Upham, [August 3, 1965], Upham Papers; Interviews with Ruby N. Sales, Bob Mants, and John Hulett.

48. Interviews with Ruby N. Sales, Bob Mants, and Stokely Carmichael.

49. Jonathan Daniels to Judith Upham, [August 3, 1965], Upham Papers; Kopkind, "Lair of the Black Panther," p. 11.

50. Interview with Ruby N. Sales; McAdam, *Freedom Summer*, p. 79 (quotation). The account of voter registration efforts comes from Robert Feinglass, a volunteer during Mississippi's Freedom Summer in 1964, in a letter to his father. Though about Mississippi, its description fits with impressions gained from interviews about the same work in Lowndes County a year later.

51. Jonathan Daniels to Judith Upham, [August 3, 1965], in Upham Papers; U.S. Commission on Civil Rights, Alabama State Advisory Committee, *Agricultural Stabilization and Conservation Service in the Alabama Black Belt* (hereafter cited as *ASCS in the Alabama Black Belt*), pp. v (quotation), 1–2; *Southern Courier*, September 25–26, 1965. The report of the Alabama State Advisory Committee resulted from an open meeting held in Selma on May 26–27, 1967.

52. *ASCS in the Alabama Black Belt*, pp. 1, 7–9; *Southern Courier*, September 25–26, 1965.

53. *ASCS in the Alabama Black Belt*, pp. 10–11 (first quotation); *Southern Courier*, September 25–26, 1965 (second quotation).

54. *Southern Courier*, September 25–26, 1965 (quotation); *ASCS in the Alabama Black Belt*, pp. 10, 27.

55. *Southern Courier*, September 25–26, 1965; *ASCS in the Alabama Black Belt*, pp. 10, 27.

56. *Southern Courier*, September 25–26, 1965 (quotation); Lowndes County weekly report, August 5, 1965, SNCC Papers; *ASCS in the Alabama Black Belt*, pp. 14–15. The SNCC worker's prediction came true — the Lowndes County ASCS committee nominated seventy-five blacks and none was elected, though three were elected outright and eight others as alternates to community committees (see *ASCS in the Alabama Black Belt*, pp. 11, 15, 46).

57. Interviews with Ruby N. Sales, John Hulett, and Bob Mants; Corry, "A Visit to Lowndes County," p. 31.

58. The account of mass meetings comes from Belfrage, *Freedom Summer* (quotations, pp. 52–55). Numerous interviews confirmed that Belfrage's description of mass meetings in Mississippi in 1964 was typical of the meetings in Lowndes County during the summer of 1965.

59. Ibid.

60. Interviews with John Hulett, Bob Mants, and Ruby N. Sales; Unidentified Freedom Summer volunteer, quoted in McAdam, *Freedom Summer*, p. 92.

61. Douglas Harris to Constance Daniels, November 20, 1965, Upham Papers; Interviews with John Hulett, Bob Mants, and Ruby N. Sales. Harris, a SNCC staffer, sent Constance Daniels a picture of her son and described the mass meeting where the photograph had been taken.

62. Douglas Harris to Constance Daniels, November 20, 1965, Upham Papers.

63. Unidentified Freedom Summer volunteer, quoted in McAdam, *Freedom Summer*, p. 92.

64. Interview with Hulda Coleman; *Southern Courier*, August 13, 1965, February 19–20, 1966.

65. Interview with Hulda Coleman; *Southern Courier*, August 13, 1965, February 19–20, 1966.

66. Lowndes County WATS report, July 26, 1965, SNCC Papers; *Southern Courier*, August 13, 1965 (quotation); Interview with Sarah B. Logan.

67. Lowndes County WATS report, July 26, 1965, SNCC Papers; *Southern Courier*, August 13, 1965; Interview with Hulda Coleman.

68. Lowndes County weekly report, August 5, 1965, SNCC Papers; *Southern Courier*, August 13, 1965; Interview with Sarah B. Logan.

69. Johnson quoted in *Congressional Record*, 89th Cong., 1st sess., 1965, pp. 4924–26. For background on the voting rights proposal, see Lawson, *Black Ballots*, pp. 288–312 and passim, and Garrow, *Protest at Selma*, pp. 36–106.

70. Lawson, *Black Ballots*, pp. 312–14; Garrow, *Protest at Selma*, pp. 105–10 and passim.

71. Lawson, *Black Ballots*, pp. 315–21; Garrow, *Protest at Selma*, pp. 123–32.

72. Lowndes County WATS reports, July 7, 9, 26, August 3, 1965, Lowndes County weekly report, August 5, 1965, and Carmichael interview — all in SNCC Papers.

73. Walling Keith, "In Hayneville's Roots," *Birmingham News*, August 26, 1965.

74. Ibid. (first quotation); *Southern Courier*, August 13, 1965.

75. *Miami Herald*, June 20, 1965.

76. Ibid.

77. *New York Times*, May 3, 1965.

78. *Washington Post*, June 30, 1965.

79. *Race Relations Law Reporter* 10 (1965): 1364. In later interviews, several whites still referred to Jon Daniels and Rev. Richard Morrisroe as "those so-called priests."

80. *Sex and Civil Rights*; *New York Herald-Tribune*, August 22, 1965 (quotations). The author of the news account was William Bradford Huie, a white Alabamian who had written widely in support of civil rights.

81. Interviews with Richmond Flowers and Tom Coleman; Richmond M. Flowers, Attorney General of Alabama, "Preliminary Results of Investigation of Alabama United Klans of America, Incorporated, Knights of the Ku Klux Klan and other Klan Organizations, October 18, 1965," pp. 1–4, 8, and passim, Thomas McIntyre Papers, University of New Hampshire Archives, Durham (hereafter referred to "Investigation of Klan"); Lowndes County WATS report, June 5, July 12, 26, August 9, 1965, and Lowndes County weekly report, August 5, 1965, SNCC Papers. Coleman readily admitted attending meetings of the Citizens' Council but denied being a member of the Klan.

CHAPTER 6

1. Lawson, *Black Ballots*, pp. 321, 329; *Birmingham News*, August 10, 1965; *Selma Times-Journal*, August 10, 1965 (quotation).

2. *Birmingham News*, January 4 (quotations), October 3, 1962; *Alabama Journal*, April 14, November 25, 1964, May 10, June 23, 1965; *Mobile Register*, May 1, 1965; *Southern Courier*, August 28–29, 1965; Interview with Richmond Flowers.

3. *Birmingham News*, August 10–11, 1965; *Selma Times-Journal*, August 10 (quotation), 12, 1965.

4. On the Watts riots, see David O. Sears and John B. McConahay, *The Politics of Violence – The New Urban Blacks and the Watts Riots* (Boston: Houghton-Mifflin, 1973).

5. *New York Herald-Tribune*, August 22, 1965.

6. *Birmingham News*, August 9–12, 1965.

7. Ibid., August 11–12, 15, 1965.

8. Edward Clarke Jackson to Constance Daniels, August 30, 1965, Constance Daniels Papers; Schneider interview with Richard F. Morrisroe; *Chicago Tribune*, August 21, 1965.

9. *Chicago Tribune*, August 21–22, 1965; Chicago *Defender*, August 21–27, 1965; Interview with Richard F. Morrisroe.

10. Interview with Richard F. Morrisroe; *Chicago Tribune*, August 21, 1965; *Chicago Defender*, June 9–12, August 21–27, 1965; *Chicago Tribune*, August 21, 1965.

11. Interview with Richard F. Morrisroe; Morris interview with Morrisroe.

12. Interview with Richard F. Morrisroe; Morris interview with Morrisroe.

13. Lowndes County WATS report, August 9, 1965, SNCC Papers, Martin Luther King Center Library, Atlanta.

14. Interviews with James Rogers, Jr., and Bob Mants; "Lowndes County: Prelude to Murder," *National Guardian*, August 28, 1965. The account in the *National Guardian* was written by Patricia Brooks before the death of Jon Daniels.

15. *McMeans v. Mayor's Court*; *Student Voice*, August 30, 1965, p. 2; Lowndes County WATS report, August 14, 1965, SNCC Papers; Interviews with Joe Frank Bailey, Bob Mants, and Ruby N. Sales. The court case, discussed later in this volume, challenged the arrests of the demonstrators. Judge Frank Johnson handed down his decision in federal court in Montgomery on September 30, 1965.

16. Lowndes County WATS report, August 11, 1965 (first quotation), and John Lewis to Governor George C. Wallace (telegram), August 12, 1965, Governor George C. Wallace Papers, Alabama Department of Archives and History, Montgomery; Interviews with Ruby Sales, James Rogers, Jr., and Bob Mants.

17. Interviews with Richard F. Morrisroe, Sarah B. Logan, and Geraldine Logan Gamble; Morris interview with Morrisroe.

18. *Southern Courier*, August 20, 1965 (quotation); Lowndes County WATS report, August 14, 1965, SNCC Papers; *National Guardian*, August 28, 1965; Interviews with Joe Frank Bailey, William A. Price, Sanford J. Ungar, Joyce Bailey Dozier, Gloria Larry House, and others.

19. FBI in Mobile, Ala., "Racial Situation in State of Alabama, Lowndes County, Alabama," August 16, 1965, 157-6-61-1027, *Centers of the Southern Struggle*, Federal Bureau of Investigation Papers, Washington, D.C.

20. Ibid.; *Student Voice*, August 30, 1965, p. 2

21. Lowndes County WATS report, August 14, 1965, SNCC Papers; *Southern Courier*, August 20, 1965; *National Guardian*, August 28, 1965 (quotations);

Interviews with James Rogers, Jr., Joe Frank Bailey, Geraldine Gamble Logan, Ruby N. Sales, Wilbur Jenkins, Willie Jenkins, Gloria Larry House, and Joyce Bailey Dozier; Schneider interview with David Gordon.

22. Lowndes County WATS report, August 14, 1965, SNCC Papers; Interviews with William A. Price and Sanford J. Ungar. William Price and Patricia Brooks were the *National Guardian* correspondents, Sanford Ungar represented *Life*, and David Gordon and Ed Rudd covered the story for the *Southern Courier*. Apparently no representative from either the wire services or a major daily newspaper was in Fort Deposit on the day of the protest. On reporters' fears in Lowndes County, see also interview with Arlie Schardt (another *Time* reporter).

23. *McMeans v. Mayor's Court*; *Southern Courier*, August 20, 1965; *National Guardian*, August 28, 1965; Statement of Facts, *State of Alabama v. Tom L. Coleman*; Interviews with Joyce Bailey Dozier, Gloria Larry House, Joe Frank Bailey, Wilbur Jenkins, Richard F. Morrisroe, James Rogers, Jr., and others; Schneider interview with David Gordon.

24. FBI in Mobile, Ala., "Racial Situation in State of Alabama, Lowndes County, Alabama," August 16, 1965; *Southern Courier*, August 20, 1965 (first quotation); *McMeans v. Mayor's Court* (second quotation); Lowndes County WATS report, August 14, 1965, SNCC papers; *National Guardian*, August 28, 1965; *Student Voice*, August 30, 1965, p. 2; Interviews with Joe Frank Bailey, Gloria Larry House, Joyce Bailey Dozier, Ruby N. Sales, and Richard F. Morrisroe. The penalty for violating the town ordinance was a fine of at least $100 or a jail term of six months of hard labor, or both.

25. FBI in Mobile, Ala., "Racial Situation in State of Alabama, Lowndes County, Alabama," August 16, 1965; *Southern Courier*, August 20, 1965; Lowndes County WATS report, August 13, 1965, SNCC Papers; Interview with Sanford J. Ungar.

26. Interview with Stokely Carmichael; *McMeans v. Mayor's Court*; *Southern Courier*, August 14, 1965.

27. *Southern Courier*, August 20, 1965; *National Guardian*, August 28, 1965; *McMeans v. Mayor's Court*; *Student Voice*, August 30, 1965, p. 2; Interviews with Joe Frank Bailey, Ruby N. Sales, Richard F. Morrisroe, Wilbur Jenkins, Gloria Larry House, Joyce Bailey Dozier, and William A. Price; Schneider interview with David Gordon.

28. "Register of Prisoners Committee to County Jail, Lowndes County," August 14, 1965, County Courthouse, Hayneville; *National Guardian*, August 28, 1965; Interviews with Joyce Bailey Dozier, Gloria Larry House, Ruby N. Sales, James Rogers, Jr., and Joe Frank Bailey.

29. *National Guardian*, August 28, 1965 (quotation); Interview with William A. Price.

30. Lowndes County WATS report, August 14, 1965, SNCC Papers; *National Guardian*, August 28, 1965.

31. Lowndes County WATS reports, August 14, 16, 1965, and statement by Scott B. Smith, August 16, 1965, SNCC Papers; *National Guardian*, August 28, 1965.

32. Interviews with Richard F. Morrisroe, James Rogers, Jr., Gloria Larry House, Ruby N. Sales, and others; Morris interview with Morrisroe.

33. Interviews with Ruby Sales, Gloria Larry House, Geraldine Logan Gamble, and Joyce Bailey Dozier.

34. Interviews with Wilbur Jenkins, Willie Jenkins, and Joe Frank Bailey.

35. Interviews with Ruby N. Sales, James Rogers, Jr., Willie Jenkins, Joe Frank Bailey, Gloria Larry House, and Joyce Bailey Dozier.

36. Interviews with Ruby N. Sales, James Rogers, Jr., Willie Jenkins, Joe Frank Bailey, Gloria Larry House, and Joyce Bailey Dozier.

37. Interviews with Ruby N. Sales, James Rogers, Jr., Willie Jenkins, Joe Frank Bailey, Gloria Larry House, and Joyce Bailey Dozier; Selma WATS report, August 16, 1965, SNCC Papers; *State of Alabama v. Tom L. Coleman*; Schneider interview with David Gordon. The interviews produced slightly different versions of the period in jail. Some remembered being visited by a number of people, including lawyers, whereas others thought nobody managed to see them.

38. James H. Horn to Shirley Walker and Peter Hall, August 20, 1965, and Lowndes County WATS report, August 16, 1965, SNCC Papers; Interviews with Bob Mants and Richard F. Morrisroe; Morris interview with Morrisroe.

39. Interviews with the Reverends Francis X. Walters and Henri A. Stines. Walters's recollection is that he visited Daniels on either Wednesday or Thursday. Thursday seems the more likely because he did not remember seeing Carmichael in the jail, but Stines believed that their visit was two days before Daniels was shot.

40. Interviews with Rev. Francis X. Walters, Rev. Henri A. Stines, Ruby N. Sales, and Richard F. Morrisroe.

41. Selma WATS report, August 16, 1965, SNCC Papers; Interviews with Richard F. Morrisroe, Ruby N. Sales, Joyce Bailey Dozier, Wilbur Jenkins, Joe Frank Bailey, and C. Frank Ryals; Morris interview with Morrisroe.

42. Lowndes County WATS report, August 16, 1965, SNCC Papers; Interviews with Bob Mants and John Hulett; Schneider interview with David Gordon.

43. *Keene Sentinel*, August 30, 1965 (quotation); *Chicago Defender*, August 28–September 3, 1965; *McMeans v. Mayor's Court*; Interview with C. Frank Ryals. The two newspapers carried lengthy accounts by UPI. A number of the jailed demonstrators later charged that their release was a part of a conspiracy by local authorities to have some of them killed. They seemed unaware, at the time and in later interviews, of the legal proceedings involving their case. For example, see *Keene Sentinel*, August 30, 1965.

44. Interview with Tom L. Coleman; *State of Alabama v. Tom L. Coleman*.

45. Affadavit of James Rogers, Jr., n.d. (probably August 21 or 22, 1965), and Alabama Daily Report, August 20, 1965, SNCC Papers; *State of Alabama v. Tom L. Coleman*; *Southern Courier*, August 27–28, 1965; Interviews with Richard F. Morrisroe, Ruby N. Sales, James Rogers, Jr., Joyce Bailey Dozier, Gloria Larry House, Joe Frank Bailey, Willie Jenkins, and Wilbur Jenkins.

46. All sources given in n. 45.

47. All sources given in n. 45; *Keene Sentinel*, August 28, 1965.

48. *State of Alabama v. Tom L. Coleman*; *New York Times*, August 21, 1965; *Keene Sentinel*, August 28, 1965; Interviews with Tom L. Coleman and Virginia Varner. Varner later said that Tom Coleman had never been to her store before that afternoon.

49. Alabama Daily Report, August 20, 1965, SNCC Papers; *State of Alabama v. Tom L. Coleman*; UPI photograph of the Cash Store, Bettmann Newsphotos.

50. *State of Alabama v. Tom L. Coleman*; Interviews with Ruby N. Sales, Richard F. Morrisroe, and Joyce Bailey Dozier.

51. *State of Alabama v. Tom L. Coleman*; Interviews with Ruby N. Sales, Richard F. Morrisroe, Joyce Bailey Dozier, and Tom L. Coleman.

52. Alabama Daily Report, August 20, 1965, SNCC Papers; Interviews with James Rogers, Jr., Ruby N. Sales, Joyce Bailey Dozier, Gloria Larry House, Joe Frank Bailey, Willie Jenkins, and Wilbur Jenkins.

53. *State of Alabama v. Tom L. Coleman*.

54. Ibid.

55. Ibid.; T. J. Ward, "Supplementary Offense Report, Police Department, Montgomery, Alabama," August 20, 1965, P. J. Dumas Papers, Duke University; *Birmingham News*, August 21, 24, 1965. Officers T. J. Ward and P. J. Dumas briefly interviewed Morrisroe at Baptist Hospital and then went to the funeral home. I am grateful to J. Mills Thornton for making available to me a copy of the report by Officer Ward.

56. Interview with Constance Daniels.

57. All quotations from *Keene Sentinel*, August 24, 1965.

58. *New York Times*, August 23, 1965 (quotation); *Keene Sentinel*, August 23, 1965; *Chicago Tribune*, August 24, 1965.

59. *Southern Courier*, August 27–28, 1965 (quotation); Lowndes County WATS report, August 23, 1965, SNCC Papers.

60. *Selma Times-Journal*, August 24, 1965 (quotations); *Living Church*, September 5, 1965, pp. 4–5; *Keene Sentinel*, August 23, 1965; Vestry Minutes, August 22, 1965, St. Paul's Episcopal Church Files, Selma; Interview with Rev. T. Frank Mathews.

61. *Birmingham News*, August 28, 1965; *Keene Sentinel*, August 28, 1965; Interviews with Rev. Charles F. Hall and Rev. John B. Coburn.

62. *Keene Sentinel*, August 23, 1965; Interview with Rev. John B. Morris.

63. *Keene Sentinel*, August 23–24, 1965; "In Memorium, Jonathan Myrick Daniels," August 24, 1965, Constance Daniels Papers; Interviews with Ruby N. Sales, Rev. Judith Upham, Rev. John B. Morris, James Rogers, Jr., Stokely Carmichael, and Alice M. West.

64. "In Memorium, Jonathan Myrick Daniels"; *Keene Sentinel*, August 25, 1965; *Living Church*, September 5, 1965, p. 4; Book of Common Prayer, pp. 324, 331.

65. Jonathan Daniels, "Theological Reflections on My Experience in Selma," June 22, 2965, Daniels Papers, Episcopal Divinity School, Cambridge.

66. Ibid., *Keene Sentinel*, August 25, 1965.

67. "In Memorium, Jonathan Myrick Daniels"; *Keene Sentinel*, August 25, 1965; Interviews with the Reverends Henri A. Stines and Judith Upham. The singing of "We Shall Overcome" immediately after the religious service caused some consternation among friends of Jon Daniels who thought it very inappropriate. Interviews with the Reverends Judith Upham and John W. Inman.

CHAPTER 7

1. "Memorandum for Biographical Sketch of Jesse Albert Coleman," Alabama Department of Archives and History, Montgomery; Manuscript censuses for Lowndes County, 1880, 1900, and 1910; Interviews with Tom L. Coleman and Hulda Coleman.

2. "Memorandum for Biographical Sketch of Jesse Albert Coleman," Ala-

bama Department of Archives and History, Montgomery; Manuscript censuses for Lowndes County, 1880, 1900, and 1910; Interviews with Tom L. Coleman and Hulda Coleman. For details of the lynching incident, see chapter 4.

3. Interview with Hulda Coleman.

4. Interviews with Tom L. Coleman and Hulda Coleman.

5. Interviews with Tom L. Coleman and Hulda Coleman.

6. Interview with Tom L. Coleman.

7. Ibid.

8. Ibid.; Interviews with Virginia Varner and John Robert Varner.

9. Interviews with Tom L. Coleman, Virginia Varner, and John Robert Varner.

10. Interviews with Tom L. Coleman, Virginia Varner, and John Robert Varner.

11. Interviews with Tom L. Coleman, Virginia Varner, and John Robert Varner.

12. Interviews with Coralie C. Coleman and Tom L. Coleman.

13. Interview with Hulda Coleman.

14. Interview with Tom L. Coleman.

15. Ibid.

16. Interviews with Tom L. Coleman and Tom L. Coleman, Jr.; *New York Herald-Tribune*, September 29, 1965.

17. Interview with Tom L. Coleman.

18. Ibid.

19. *Los Angeles Times*, October 15, 1965; Interview with Tom L. Coleman. Although many residents of Hayneville undoubtedly recalled the shooting incident, it was not mentioned in the coverage of Daniels's slaying until Jack Nelson of the *Los Angeles Times* uncovered the case two weeks after Coleman's acquittal.

20. Interview with Tom L. Coleman.

21. Interview with Roy Reed; *New York Times*, August 22, 1965. The other reporter, according to Reed, was Nicholas Von Hoffman, who certainly did not appear to be a southerner. See also Reed, "George Wallace's Bid for the New South," *New York Times Magazine*, September 5, 1982, pp. 15–16, where he mentions meeting Coleman.

22. Interview with Tom L. Coleman; Lowndes County WATS Report, June 5, 1965, in SNCC Papers; McMillen, *The Citizens' Council*, pp. 46–47.

23. Interview with Tom L. Coleman; James G. Clark, Jr., to Coleman, June 28, 1965, in Coleman Papers.

24. UPI wire service report, August 21, 1965, in Richmond Flowers Papers (quotations); *Memphis Commercial-Appeal*, August 22, 1965; *New York Herald-Tribune*, September 29, 1965. Coleman did not recall the incident (Interview with Tom L. Coleman).

25. Interviews with Hulda Coleman, Tom L. Coleman, and C. Frank Ryals; *New York Herald-Tribune*, September 29, 1965 (second quotation).

26. Interviews with Tom L. Coleman, Virginia Varner, and John Robert Varner.

27. *Chicago Tribune*, August 21, 1965; *Selma Times-Journal*, August 22, 1965; *New York Times*, August 22, 1965; *State of Alabama v. Tom L. Coleman*; Interviews with Tom L. Coleman and Tom L. Coleman, Jr. Recollections of the telephone calls remained imprecise, but the above appears the most likely sce-

nario. The transcript of the trial of Tom Coleman, prepared by the official court reporter, Charles R. Higgins, contained numerous errors. The transcript, for example, frequently said "irrelevant" when clearly the lawyer must have said "relevant." In addition, many names were misspelled. The mistakes have been corrected without the use of "[sic]" or any other designation.

28. *Birmingham News*, August 21, 1965; *Memphis Commercial-Appeal*, August 21, 1965; Interview with Coralie Coleman.

29. *Birmingham News*, August 21 (quotation), 22, 1965.

30. FBI in Mobile, Ala., to Director [J. Edgar Hoover] (urgent teletype), August 20, 1965, 44-30271-4, 44-30271-6, and August 21, 1965 (quotation), 44-30271-2, 44-30271-3; FBI Director [J. Edgar Hoover] to Attorney General [Nicholas de B. Katzenbach], August 24, 1965, 44-30271-5 — all in Federal Bureau of Investigation Papers, Washington, D.C.; *Birmingham News*, August 22, 1965. Materials from FBI files in Washington, D.C., were obtained under the Freedom of Information and Privacy Act (hereafter cited as FBI Papers). Numbers are to individual documents in the FBI files; file 44 pertains to civil rights, particularly investigations of suspected violations of federal civil rights laws. For an explanation of the system, see Garrow, *The FBI and Martin Luther King*, pp. 230–31.

31. *Selma Times-Journal*, August 22, 1965; *New York Times*, August 22, 1965; *Chicago Tribune*, August 22, 1965 (first two quotations); FBI in Mobile to Director [J. Edgar Hoover] (urgent teletype), August 21, 1965, 44-30271-2, 44-30271-8, FBI Papers; *Birmingham News*, August 21, 1965 (last quotation).

32. *New York Times*, August 22, 1965 (first two quotations); *Selma Times-Journal*, August 22–23 (last quotation), 1965; *Birmingham News*, August 22, 1965; Interview with Richmond Flowers; FBI in Mobile to Director [J. Edgar Hoover] (urgent teletype), August 22, 1965, 44-30271-11, FBI Papers. Of the surviving lawyers involved in the case, Arthur E. Gamble, the circuit solicitor, and Vaughan Hill Robison refused to be interviewed and Robert E. Black gave a brief, unrecorded interview.

33. *Chicago Tribune*, August 22, 1965; FBI in Mobile, Ala., to Director [J. Edgar Hoover] (urgent teletype), August 21, 1965, 44-30271-2 (first quotation), 44-30271-8, FBI Papers; *Selma Times-Journal*, August 22, 1965 (second quotation); *Birmingham News*, August 22, 1965; *New York Herald-Tribune*, August 22, 1965.

34. *Birmingham News*, August 21 (first six quotations), 23 (last quotation), 1965; *New York Times*, August 22, 1965 (seventh and eighth quotations); *Southern Courier*, August 27–28, 1965.

35. *New York Herald-Tribune*, August 22, 1965 (first two quotations); *Southern Courier*, August 27–28, 1965 (last four quotations); *Birmingham New*, August 23, 1965.

36. FBI in Mobile, Ala., "Racial Situation in State of Alabama, Lowndes County, Alabama," September 23, 1965, 157-6-61-1062, *Centers of the Southern Struggle*, Federal Bureau of Investigation Papers, Washington, D.C.; WTN news film, August 21, 1965, Worldwide Television News; *Birmingham News*, August 21, September 12, 1965; *Selma Times-Journal*, August 26, 30, 1965; *New York Herald-Tribune*, August 22, 1965 (quotation); *Washington Post*, October 2, 1965; U.S. Commission on Civil Rights, *Voting Rights Act*, pp. 37, 54.

37. *Southern Courier*, September 25–26, 1965. White farmers in Lowndes

County tried to subvert the process by nominating 135 blacks for 30 committee positions on committees in six Lowndes communities. Blacks nonetheless managed to elect 3 committeemen and 8 alternates. U.S. Commission on Civil Rights, Alabama State Advisory Committee, *Agricultural Stabilization and Conservation Service in the Alabama Black Belt*, pp. 12, 46.

38. *Selma Times-Journal*, August 30–31, 1965; *Southern Courier*, September 4–5, 1965; Interview with Hulda Coleman.

39. *Selma Times-Journal*, August 31, 1965; *Southern Courier*, September 4–5, 1965 (quotations); Interview with Hulda Coleman.

40. *Southern Courier* (quotations), September 4–5, 1965, July 9–10, September 10–11, 1966; Interview with Hulda Coleman.

41. *McMeans v. Mayor's Court*; *Selma Times-Journal*, October 1, 1965.

42. *Los Angeles Times*, August 26, 1965; *Birmingham News*, August 26, 1965; Plaintiffs' Complaint, August 25, 1965, *White v. Crook*; Morgan, *One Man, One Voice*, pp. 39, 41; *Newsweek*, November 8, 1965, p. 33 (quotations); Interview with Charles Morgan, Jr.

43. Plaintiffs' Complaint and Order of Chief Judge Elbert P. Tuttle, U.S. Fifth Circuit Court of Appeals, August 30, 1965, *White v. Crook*, U.S. Federal Court, Montgomery, Ala. (quotations); *Los Angeles Times*, August 26, 1965; Interview with Charles Morgan, Jr. The U.S. Federal District Court in Montgomery retrieved the records of *White v. Crook* from the National Archives in Atlanta (hereafter cited as Records, *White v. Crook*).

44. *Selma Times-Journal*, August 31, 1965.

45. Director [J. Edgar Hoover] to Mobile FBI (urgent teletype), August 23, 1965, 44-30271-12 (quotation), and (urgent radiogram), August 26, 1965, 44-30271-20, FBI Papers.

46. FBI, Mobile, Ala., to Director [J. Edgar Hoover] (urgent teletype), August 24, 1965, 44-30271-22, FBI Papers; John Doar to Acting Attorney General, February 1, 1967, U.S. Department of Justice Papers, Washington, D.C. As will be explained, the Justice Department pursued the Coleman case for more than a year.

47. FBI, Mobile, Ala., to Director [J. Edgar Hoover] (urgent teletype), August 22, 1965, 44-30271-11, FBI Papers. In the light of later evidence of the FBI's opposition to the civil rights movement, the credibility of the bureau's investigation remains somewhat problematic. See Kenneth O'Reilly, *"Racial Matters": The FBI's Secret File on Black America, 1960–1972* (New York: Free Press, 1989). O'Reilly makes no mention of the Daniels-Coleman case.

48. *Birmingham News*, September 12, 1965; *Selma Times-Journal*, August 23, September 13, 15, 1965.

49. *Southern Courier*, September 25–26, 1965; *Birmingham News*, September 15, 1965.

50. *New York Times*, September 16, 1965; *Selma Times-Journal*, September 15, 1965; *Birmingham News*, September 16, 1965.

51. *Selma Times-Journal*, September 15, 1965 (quotations); *Birmingham News*, September 15, 1965; *New York Times*, September 16, 1965.

52. *New York Times*, September 16, 1965 (first and third quotations); *Southern Courier*, September 25–26, 1965 (second quotation); Interviews with Richmond Flowers and Joe Breck Gantt.

53. *Selma Times-Journal*, September 16, 1965 (first quotation); *Southern Courier*, September 25–26, 1965 (all other quotations).

298 • NOTES TO PAGES 203-9

54. *Alabama Register*, undated clipping [probably 1963], Proper Name File, Alabama Department of Archives and History, Montgomery; *Birmingham News*, November 11, 1943, May 30, 1962, January 4, 1963; Interview with Richmond Flowers.

55. *Birmingham News*, October 3, 1962, April 6, 1964; *Alabama Journal*, October 6, 1962, April 14, November 25, 1964, May 10, June 23, July 6, 24, August 10, 1965; *Montgomery Advertiser*, April 4, 1965; *Southern Courier*, August 28 (quotations), 29, 1965; Interview with Richmond Flowers. See also Kopkind, "Alabama Unbound." *New Republic*, November 27, 1965, pp. 12–16.

56. Kopkind, "Alabama Unbound," p. 14 (quotations); *Southern Courier*, September 25–26, 1965.

57. *Birmingham News*, September 16, 1965.

58. *Birmingham News*, September 17, 1965 (first two quotations); *Selma Times-Journal*, September 17, 1965 (last quotation); Interviews with Richmond Flowers and Joe Breck Gantt.

59. *Los Angeles Times*, September 22, 1965; *Selma Times-Journal*, September 24, 1965; *Birmingham News*, September 25, 1965; Interviews with Richmond Flowers and Joe Breck Gantt.

60. Interview with Tom L. Coleman.

61. Ibid.

62. Marie Reese, "Court House, Lowndes County," Federal Writers' Project of Alabama, Works Progress Administration Papers, Alabama Department of Archives and History, Montgomery; Goldsmith, *Fort Deposit*, p. 13; Hamilton, *Seeing Historic Alabama*, p. 140; *Birmingham News*, May 3, 1965; *New York Times*, May 3, 1965; *Wall Street Journal*, January 20, 1965; Personal observation.

63. Interviews with Roy Reed, Richard Valeriani, Marshall Frady, and Arlie Schardt; *New York Herald-Tribune* (international ed.), September 18–19, 1965. The FBI also had a representative attending the trial who filed reports with the Washington headquarters.

64. *Alabama Journal*, September 28, 1965.

65. Sayers, *Who's Who in Alabama*, p. 432; "Memorandum for Biographical Sketch of Thomas Werth Thagard," October 28, 1955, Alabama Department of Archives and History, Montgomery; *Montgomery Advertiser*, September 6, 1952; *Arkansas Gazette*, May 5, 1965; Interview with Tom L. Coleman.

66. *Montgomery Advertiser*, September 14, 1952; *Greenville Advocate*, September 18, 1952; *Lowndes Signal*, September 4, 1975; Interview with Tom L. Coleman.

67. *Birmingham News*, May 7, 1965; Interviews with Richmond Flowers and Joe Breck Gantt.

68. *Alabama Journal*, April 3, 1965; *Martindale-Hubbell*, vol. 1, 1965, pp. 76–77; *Alabama Official and Statistical Register, 1943*, pp. 255–56; Interview with Robert C. Black.

69. *Montgomery Advertiser*, April 24, 1913 (first quotation), May 18, 1956; *Alabama Journal*, May 4, 1949 (second quotation); *Birmingham News*, May 1, 1932.

70. *Alabama Journal*, October 21, 1941 (the drafting of Robison made the headline), October 25, 1949, September 12, 1958, September 28, 1965; *Montgomery Advertiser*, July 12, 1945, May 31, 1950 (first quotation), June 1, 1950 (second quotation), January 13, 1953, January 14, 1959; *Birmingham News*, Sep-

tember 4, 1955; "Biographical Memorandum," April 15, 1952, Alabama Department of Archives and History, Montgomery. For background on the Hill family, see Hamilton, *Lister Hill*, chapter 1.

71. *Selma Times-Journal*, September 27, 1965 (quotations); *Birmingham News*, September 27, 1965; *Los Angeles Times*, September 28–29, 1965; *New York Herald-Tribune* (international ed.), September 28, 1965; Interview with Joe Breck Gantt.

72. *Birmingham News*, September 27, 1965 (first quotation); *Selma Times-Journal*, September 27, 1965 (second quotation); *Los Angeles Times*, September 27, 1965; *New York Herald-Tribune* (international ed.), September 28, 1965; Interview with Joe Breck Gantt; *Washington Post*, September 28, 1965 (third quotation).

73. *Selma Times-Journal*, September 27, 1965; *Birmingham News*, September 27, 1965; *Los Angeles Times*, September 27, 1965; *New York Herald-Tribune* (international ed.), September 28, 1965 (all quotations); *Washington Post*, September 28, 1965; Interview with Joe Breck Gantt.

74. News film from Hayneville, September 27, 1965, ABC News Film, Sherman Grinberg Film Libraries.

75. Amended complaint, plaintiffs' motion (first quotation), and affidavits of Henri Stines and Orzell Billingsley (second quotation), September 23, 1965, in Records, *White v. Crook*; *Birmingham News*, September 25, 1965.

76. Defendants' answer and motion, motion to strike affidavits, defendants' brief and argument, and affidavits of Carl Bunton and Cleveland Moorer, September 27, 1965, in Records, *White v. Crook*.

77. District Court Order, September 27, 1965, in Records, *White v. Crook*; *Memphis Commercial-Appeal*, September 28, 1965.

CHAPTER 8

1. Interview with Coralie C. Coleman.

2. *Los Angeles Times*, September 29, 1965; *Birmingham News*, September 28, 1965; *Selma Times-Journal*, September 28, 1965; Frady, "A Death in Lowndes County," in *Southerners*, p. 139.

3. *Birmingham News*, September 28, 1965; *Los Angeles Times*, September 29, 1965; *State of Alabama v. Tom L. Coleman*. Unless otherwise noted, all quoted testimony in the Coleman trial is taken from the trial transcript.

4. *State of Alabama v. Tom L. Coleman*; *Los Angeles Times*, September 29, 1965; *Selma Times-Journal*, September 28, 1965; *Birmingham News*, September 28, 1965; Interview with Joe Breck Gantt.

5. *State of Alabama v. Tom L. Coleman*; *Selma Times-Journal*, September 28, 1965; *Birmingham News*, September 28, 1965; Interview with Joe Breck Gantt.

6. *State of Alabama v. Tom L. Coleman*; *Birmingham News*, September 28, 1965; Interview with Joe Breck Gantt.

7. *State of Alabama v. Tom L. Coleman*; *New York Times*, May 7, 1965.

8. *State of Alabama v. Tom L. Coleman*.

9. Ibid.

10. Plaintiff-Intervenor's Brief and Proposed Findings of Fact and Proposed Conclusions of Law, filed December 23, 1965, in Records, *White v. Crook*. The intervenor was John Doar, assistant attorney general, for the U.S. Department of

Justice. The federal government joined the case on October 27, 1965. Charles R. Nesson of the Justice Department reconstructed the jury rolls and analyzed them to discover the pattern of jury service (Interview with Charles R. Nesson).

11. Records, *White v. Crook*; Deposition of Mrs. Kelly D. Coleman, clerk of the Lowndes County jury commission, November 22, 1965 [?], in hearings for *White v. Crook*, U.S. District Court, November 26, 1965, in Records, *White v. Crook*.

12. Plaintiff-Intervenor's Brief and Proposed Findings of Fact and Proposed Conclusions of Law, filed December 23, 1965, in Records, *White v. Crook*.

13. Ibid.

14. *State of Alabama v. Tom L. Coleman*; *Chicago Tribune*, October 1, 1965; *New York Times* (international ed.), October 1, 1965.

15. *State of Alabama v. Tom L. Coleman*; *Los Angeles Times*, September 29, 1965; *Keene Sentinel*, September 29, 1965; Frady, "A Death in Lowndes County," p. 140.

16. *Selma Times-Journal*, September 28, 1965; *Los Angeles Times*, September 29, 1965; Interview with Rev. John B. Morris.

17. *Los Angeles Times*, September 29, 1965; *Montgomery Advertiser*, October 3, 1965; *Birmingham News*, September 29, 1965; Frady, "A Death in Lowndes County," p. 140.

18. *Montgomery Advertiser*, October 3, 1965; *St. Louis Post-Dispatch*, September 30, 1965; Frady, "A Death in Lowndes County," pp. 141–42.

19. *State of Alabama v. Tom L. Coleman*; *Los Angeles Times*, September 29, 1965; *Southern Courier*, October 9–10, 1965; Frady, "A Death in Lowndes County," p. 140.

20. *State of Alabama v. Tom L. Coleman*.

21. Ibid.; *Los Angeles Times*, September 29, 1965; Frady, "A Death in Lowndes County," p. 140.

22. *State of Alabama v. Tom L. Coleman*.

23. Ibid.; *Birmingham News*, September 29, 1965.

24. *State of Alabama v. Tom L. Coleman*; *Birmingham News*, September 29, 1965.

25. *State of Alabama v. Tom L. Coleman*; *Birmingham News*, September 29, 1965; *Newsweek*, October 11, 1965, p. 36; *Los Angeles Times*, September 29, 1965; Frady, "A Death in Lowndes County," p. 141.

26. *State of Alabama v. Tom L. Coleman*; *New York Herald-Tribune* (international ed.), September 30, 1965.

27. *State of Alabama v. Tom L. Coleman*.

28. Ibid.; *New York Herald-Tribune* (international ed.), September 30, 1965. The writer for the *Herald-Tribune* was William Bradford Huie of Alabama.

29. *State of Alabama v. Tom L. Coleman*; *Los Angeles Times*, September 29, 1965; *Birmingham News*, September 29, 1965; Frady, "A Death in Lowndes County," p. 142.

30. *State of Alabama v. Tom L. Coleman*; *Los Angeles Times*, September 29, 1965; *Birmingham News*, September 29, 1965; Frady, "A Death in Lowndes County," p. 142.

31. *State of Alabama v. Tom L. Coleman*; *Birmingham News*, September 29, 1965; *Selma Times-Journal*, September 29, 1965; Frady, "A Death in Lowndes County," pp. 142–43.

32. *State of Alabama v. Tom L. Coleman*; *Montgomery Advertiser*, October 3, 1965; *Los Angeles Times*, October 1, 1965.

33. Interviews with Robert B. Smith and Richard Valeriani.

34. News film from Montgomery, September 28, 1965, ABC News (Sherman Grinberg Film Libraries), CBS News, and Worldwide Television News; *Los Angeles Times*, September 29, 1965; Frady, "A Death in Lowndes County," pp. 140–41; *Birmingham News*, September 29, 1965.

35. *Memphis Commercial-Appeal*, September 29, 1965; *New York Post*, September 29, 1965; *Congressional Record*, 89th Cong., 1st sess., September 29, 1965, p. 25448.

36. *State of Alabama v. Tom L. Coleman*; *Washington Post*, September 30, 1965; *Time*, October 8, 1965, p. 34.

37. *State of Alabama v. Tom L. Coleman*; *Selma Times-Journal*, September 29, 1965; *Birmingham News*, September 29, 1965; Frady, "A Death in Lowndes County," p. 144; *Los Angeles Times*, October 1, 1965. The trial transcript incorrectly refers to the witness as Crockett.

38. *State of Alabama v. Tom L. Coleman*; *Birmingham News*, September 29, 1965; *Washington Post*, September 30, 1965.

39. *State of Alabama v. Tom L. Coleman*; *Birmingham News*, September 29, 1965; *Chicago Tribune*, September 30, 1965.

40. *State of Alabama v. Tom L. Coleman*.

41. Ibid.

42. Ibid.; *New York Times* (international ed.), October 1, 1965; Interview with Joyce Bailey Dozier.

43. *State of Alabama v. Tom L. Coleman*; *New York Times* (international ed.), October 1, 1965; *Birmingham News*, September 29, 1965; Frady, "A Death in Lowndes County," pp. 146–47.

44. *State of Alabama v. Tom L. Coleman*; *Birmingham News*, September 29, 1965; Frady, "A Death in Lowndes County," p. 147.

45. *State of Alabama v. Tom L. Coleman*; *Birmingham News*, September 29, 1965; Frady, "A Death in Lowndes County," p. 147 (last quotation).

46. *State of Alabama v. Tom L. Coleman*; *Birmingham News*, September 29, 1965; Frady, "A Death in Lowndes County," p. 147.

47. *State of Alabama v. Tom L. Coleman*; Frady, "A Death in Lowndes County," pp. 147–48; *Birmingham News*, September 29, 1965. The trial transcript incorrectly identifies the witness as James Lee Beaty.

48. *State of Alabama v. Tom L. Coleman*; *Birmingham News*, September 29, 1965; Frady, "A Death in Lowndes County," p. 147.

49. *State of Alabama v. Tom L. Coleman*.

50. *Los Angeles Times*, September 29, 1965; Frady, "A Death in Lowndes County," p. 149; *Montgomery Advertiser*, September 30, 1965; *Selma Times-Journal*, September 30, 1965; Interviews with Roy Reed and Robert B. Smith.

51. *State of Alabama v. Tom L. Coleman*. Evening newspapers, especially the *Birmingham News* and the *Selma Times-Journal*, provided slight coverage of the afternoon session because their Thursday editions focused on the outcome of the trial.

52. *State of Alabama v. Tom L. Coleman*.

53. Interview with Ruby N. Sales; *Southern Courier*, October 9–10, 1965. According to the *Southern Courier*, Sales's testimony "caused the biggest stir in the courtroom. She refused to be afraid of Vaughan Hill Robison."

54. *State of Alabama v. Tom L. Coleman*. For some inexplicable reason, Marshall Frady does not mention Sales's testimony in his account of the trial (see "A Death in Lowndes County").

55. *State of Alabama v. Tom L. Coleman*; *Alabama Journal*, May 4, 1949; *Montgomery Advertiser*, undated clipping in Alabama Department of Archives and History.

56. *State of Alabama v. Tom L. Coleman*.

57. Ibid.; *Chicago Tribune*, September 30, 1965; *Southern Courier*, October 3–4, 1965.

58. *State of Alabama v. Tom L. Coleman*.

59. Ibid.

60. Ibid.

61. Ibid.

62. *Southern Courier*, October 9–10, 1965; *Chicago Tribune*, September 30, 1965.

63. *State of Alabama v. Tom L. Coleman*; *Chicago Tribune*, September 30, 1965.

64. *State of Alabama v. Tom L. Coleman*.

65. Ibid.

66. Frady, "A Death in Lowndes County," pp. 145–46.

67. Ibid., p. 148; *State of Alabama v. Tom L. Coleman*.

68. *State of Alabama v. Tom L. Coleman*.

69. Frady, "A Death in Lowndes County," pp. 148–49; *State of Alabama v. Tom L. Coleman*. Frady (p. 149) suggested that Coker was part of "some vagrant subgenus of the race" that had developed in the community.

70. *State of Alabama v. Tom L. Coleman*.

71. Ibid.; *Newsweek*, October 11, 1965, p. 36.

72. *State of Alabama v. Tom L. Coleman*.

73. Ibid.

74. Ibid.

75. Ibid.

76. Ibid.

77. Ibid.; *Los Angeles Times*, October 1, 1965; *New York Herald-Tribune* (international ed.), September 29, 1965. The *Herald-Tribune* said that it took fifty-four minutes for the defense to present its case, whereas the Associated Press reported that the defense lasted seventy minutes (see *Atlanta Constitution*, September 30, 1965).

78. *Memphis Commercial-Appeal*, September 30, 1965 (first quotation); *Los Angeles Times*, September 30, 1965 (second quotation). The trial transcript did not include the lawyers' summations to the jury.

79. *New York Times* (international ed.), October 1, 1965; *Nashville Tennessean*, September 30, 1965 (first quotation); *Memphis Commercial-Appeal*, September 30, 1965 (second quotation); *Birmingham News*, September 30, 1965 (third quotation); Frady, "A Death in Lowndes County," p. 150.

80. *Birmingham News*, September 30, 1965 (first and third quotations); *New York Times* (international ed.), October 1, 1965; *Memphis Commercial-Appeal*, September 30, 1965 (second quotation); Frady, "A Death in Lowndes County," p. 150.

81. Frady, "A Death in Lowndes County," pp. 151 (first quotation), 150

(second quotation); *Southern Courier*, October 3–4, 1965 (other quotations); *Nashville Tennessean*, September 30, 1965.

82. *Southern Courier*, October 3–4, 1965; Frady, "A Death in Lowndes County," pp. 150–51 (first two quotations); *Nashville Tennessean*, September 30, 1965 (third quotation); *Newsweek*, October 11, 1965, pp. 36 and 41 (last quotation).

83. Frady, "A Death in Lowndes County," p. 151 (first quotation); *Southern Courier*, October 3–4, 1965 (second quotation).

84. *Southern Courier*, October 3–4, 1965 (first quotation); *Los Angeles Times*, September 30, 1965; Frady, "A Death in Lowndes County," p. 151 (second quotation).

85. *Nashville Tennessean*, September 30, 1965 (first quotation); *Southern Courier*, October 3–4, 1965 (second quotation).

86. *State of Alabama v. Tom L. Coleman*.

87. Ibid. At the request of the defense, Thagard also presented to the jury a list of written charges against the defendant and how the law should be applied to them.

88. *Birmingham News*, September 30, 1965; *Los Angeles Times*, September 30, October 1, 1965; *New York Herald-Tribune* (international ed.), September 30, 1965; Frady, "A Death in Lowndes County," pp. 153–54; Interview with Tom L. Coleman.

89. *Birmingham News*, September 30, 1965; *Los Angeles Times*, October 1, 1965; Frady, "A Death in Lowndes County," p. 152; *Chicago Tribune*, October 1, 1965; *State of Alabama v. Tom L. Coleman*.

90. *Los Angeles Times*, October 1, 1965 (first, third, and fifth quotations); *Birmingham News*, September 30, 1965; *Selma Times-Journal*, September 30, 1965; *Keene Sentinel*, September 30, 1965; Frady, "A Death in Lowndes County," pp. 152–53 (second and fourth quotations); *New York Times* News Service dispatch by John Herbers, September 30, 1965.

91. Frady, "A Death in Lowndes County," pp. 152–53 (first and second quotations); *Selma Times-Journal*, September 30, 1965 (third quotation); *Los Angeles Times*, October 1, 1965 (fourth quotation); *Birmingham News*, September 30, 1965; *Keene Sentinel*, September 30, 1965; *New York Times* News Service dispatch by John Herbers, September 30, 1965; News film from Hayneville, September 30, 1965, ABC News (Sherman Grinberg Film Libraries) and Worldwide Television News.

92. *Congressional Record*, 89th Cong., 1st sess., September 30, 1965, p. 25590.

93. News film from Chicago, October 1, 1965, CBS News (first four quotations); *New York Herald-Tribune*, October 1, 1965 (fifth and sixth quotations); *Birmingham News*, October 1, 1965; *Time*, October 8, 1965 (last quotation); *Memphis Commercial-Appeal*, October 1, 1965; *Atlanta Constitution*, October 1, 1965. Dr. Louis River, one of Morrisroe's physicians, told Nelson Benton of CBS that Morrisroe would be unable to travel to Alabama for at least sixty days and that he could not have returned for Coleman's trial: "I think he probably would have died. He is so weak that I think the stress of having to go back there and attempt to testify would have been completely beyond his capabilities at this time."

94. New film from Montgomery, September 30, 1965, ABC News.

95. *Living Church*, October 17, 1965, pp. 5–6.

96. News film from Hayneville, September 30, 1965, Worldwide Television News; *Memphis Commercial-Appeal*, October 1, 1965; *Birmingham News*, October 1, 1965.

97. *Keene Sentinel*, September 30, 1965 (first quotation); News film from Hayneville, October 4, 1965, ABC News (all other quotations).

98. *New York Post*, October 1, 1965; *St. Louis Post-Dispatch*, October 3, 1965; *Atlanta Constitution*, October 5, 1965; *New York Amsterdam News*, October 9, 1965.

99. *Washington Post*, October 7, 1965.

100. *Nashville Tennessean*, October 1, 1965; *Memphis Commercial-Appeal*, October 1, 1965; *Atlanta Constitution*, October 2, 7, 1965.

101. *Los Angeles Times*, October 1, 1965; *New York Times* News Service dispatch by John Herbers, September 30, 1965.

102. *McMeans v. Mayor's Court*; *Selma Times-Journal*, October 1, 1965; *Time*, October 8, 1965, p. 35.

CHAPTER 9

1. *New York Times*, January 13, 1966. Several months after the shootings, Morrisroe was still too ill to return to Alabama for a trial and could visit his parents' home in Chicago only briefly (Interview with Richard F. Morrisroe).

2. Director [J. Edgar Hoover] to FBI in Mobile, Ala., November 2, 1965, 44-30271-50; A. Rosen to Belmont, November 2, 1965, 44-30271-53; Report from FBI in Mobile, November 16, 1966, 44-30271-56 — all in FBI Papers, Washington, D.C. In addition to the federal government's continuing interest in the case, private lawyers in Boston and New York suggested that the acquittal of Coleman need not be the end of the case involving Jon Daniels. Working with New Hampshire's Senator Thomas McIntyre, they recommended that the Daniels family and others bring a civil case against Coleman in federal court for the wrongful death of Daniels. No civil suit, however, was ever filed. See Harold Horovitz to Senators McIntyre and Norris Cotton, November 3, 1965, and Gray Thoron to Alan S. Novins, Thomas McIntyre Papers, University of New Hampshire Archives, Durham.

3. *Montgomery Advertiser*, May 10–11, 1966; *New York Times*, September 14, 1966; *Southern Courier*, September 17–18, 1966 (first quotation); *Vancouver Sun*, October 7, 1966, clipping in Governor George C. Wallace Papers, Alabama Department of Archives and History, Montgomery (second quotation, by William Bradford Huie).

4. *New York Times*, September 24, 27, 1966; *Southern Courier*, October 1–2, 1966 (quotation).

5. *New York Times*, September 28, 1966; Rev. John B. Morris to the *New York Times*, September 30, 1966, ESCRU Papers, Martin Luther King Center Library, Atlanta.

6. John Doar to Acting Attorney General, February 1, 1967, 144-2-493, U.S. Department of Justice Papers, Washington, D.C.; Interviews with Tom L. Coleman and Coralie Coleman.

7. *Selma Times-Journal*, October 15, 30–31, 1965; Records of *White v. Crook*, U.S.; Interview with Charles Nesson.

8. Records, *White v. Crook*, U.S. Federal District Court, Montgomery; *New York Times*, February 8, 13, 1966. The case also significantly benefited the rights of women. Fred P. Graham hailed the decision as a "windfall" for women since the plaintiffs' real issue involved race (see *New York Times*, February 13, 1966).

9. *Southern Courier*, January 1–2 (quotations), 1966; U.S. Commission on Civil Rights, *Hearing*, pp. 655–87.

10. *Southern Courier*, January 1–2, 1966; U.S. Commission on Civil Rights, *Hearing*, pp. 655–87; *New York Times*, December 10, 1965.

11. *Southern Courier*, January 1–2, 1966; *New York Times*, January 6, February 5, April 1, 1966.

12. *New York Times*, January 11, February 12, April 1, 1966; *Southern Courier*, April 9–10, 1966.

13. *Southern Courier*, April 9–10, May 7–8, 1966; Campbell, "The Lowndes County (Alabama) Freedom Organization," pp. 43–77; Walton, *Black Political Parties*, pp. 138–49; Hulett, "How the Black Panther Party Was Organized," pp. 8–9, 15 (all quotations except last) (Hulett made his comments at a May 22, 1966, antiwar meeting in Los Angeles); Long, "Black Power," p. 23 (last quotation); Interviews with John Hulett and Charles Smith. The only significant secondary source on the Lowndes County Freedom Organization is the master's thesis by David Campbell.

14. *Southern Courier*, May 7–8, 1966; Campbell, "The Lowndes County (Alabama) Freedom Organization," pp. 43–77; Walton, *Black Political Parties*, pp. 138–49; Hulett, "How the Black Panther Party Was Organized"; Long, "Black Power," p. 23; Interviews with John Hulett and Charles Smith.

15. Walton, *Black Political Parties*, pp. 148–49; Kopkind, "The Great Fear Is Gone," p. 12; Interviews with John Hulett and Charles Smith.

16. Interview with John Hulett.

17. Kopkind, "Lair of the Black Panther," p. 13, and "The Great Fear Is Gone," p. 53; *Southern Courier*, July 16–17, 1966.

18. U.S. Bureau of the Census, *Census of Housing, 1980*, pp. 2–125; Edds, *Free at Last*, p. 83.

19. Edds, *Free at Last*, pp. 80, 85, 96; U.S. Bureau of the Census, *Census of Population, 1980*, pp. 2–130.

20. Interview with Tom L. Coleman. At least at the time of my interview with him in the late 1980s, Coleman had never talked with his wife or sisters about the shootings.

21. For suggestions about the relationship between violence and different cultures in the North and the South, see Wyatt-Brown, *Southern Honor*, and Ayers, *Vengeance and Justice*.

22. Interview with Tom L. Coleman.

23. News film from Hayneville, September 29, 1966, CBS News.

24. Interviews with Tom L. Coleman and John Hulett.

25. On martyrdom, see Klausner, "Martyrdom"; Riddle, *The Martyrs*; Helen C. White, *Tudor Book of Saints and Martyrs*; Frend, *Martyrdom and Persecution*; Loades, *The Oxford Martyrs*; and Byman, "Ritualistic Acts." Most of the literature on martyrs was written about earlier times and has little applicability to Jon Daniels because, as Byman has pointed out, "the sixteenth-century milieu of these martyrs was quite different from our own" (p. 642).

26. *Keene Sentinel*, September 15, 1965, and "Monadnock Observer" [maga-

zine supplement], August 17–23, 1985; *New York Times*, February 21, 1966; *Official Bulletin of Episcopal Theological School*, May 1966, p. 16; Interviews with Constance Daniels, Alice West, William J. Schneider, Eugene Felch IV, and Richard F. Morrisroe. This is by no means an exhaustive list of the ways Jon Daniels has been memorialized.

27. *Keene Sentinel*, June 22, 1979; John A. Simpson to author, August 4, 1989; Interview with Constance Daniels.

28. Interviews with Noland Pipes, Jr., and Henri A. Stines.

BIBLIOGRAPHY

MANUSCRIPTS

Atlanta, Georgia
American Civil Liberties Union
  State of Alabama v. Tom L. Coleman (trial transcript)
Martin Luther King Center Library
  Episcopal Society for Cultural and Racial Unity (ESCRU) Papers
  Student Nonviolent Coordinating Committee (SNCC) Papers (microfilm edition)

Birmingham, Alabama
Birmingham Public Library
  Charles Colcock Jones Carpenter Papers

Cambridge, Massachusetts
Episcopal Divinity School (formerly Episcopal Theological School)
  Jonathan Myrick Daniels File
  Jonathan Myrick Daniels Papers
Harvard University Archives
  Jonathan Myrick Daniels File

Chapel Hill, North Carolina
Southern Historical Collection, University of North Carolina
  Jonathan Worth Daniels Papers

Durham, New Hampshire
University of New Hampshire Archives
  Norris Cotton Papers
  Thomas McIntyre Papers

Durham, North Carolina
Duke University Library
  P. J. Dumas Papers

Keene, New Hampshire
Keene Public School Records
  Jonathan Myrick Daniels File
St. James Episcopal Church Records
  Scrapbooks

Lexington, Virginia
Virginia Military Institute
  Alumni Records

Jonathan Myrick Daniels File
English Department Files

Montgomery, Alabama
Alabama Department of Archives and History
   Federal Writers' Project of Alabama, Works Progress Administration Papers
   Proper Name File
   Governor George C. Wallace Papers
U.S. Federal District Court
   Records, *White v. Crook*

Selma, Alabama
St. Paul's Episcopal Church Files
   Vestry Minutes

Tuskegee, Alabama
Tuskegee Institute Archives
   Lynching Records

Washington, D.C.
Federal Bureau of Investigation Papers
   Centers of the Southern Struggle: FBI Files on Montgomery, Albany, St. Augustine, Selma, and Memphis. Edited by David J. Garrow. Frederick, Md.:
      University Publications of America, 1988 (microfilm).
   File on Civil Rights, Violence, Jonathan Myrick Daniels
U.S. Department of Justice Papers

The individuals listed below made available to the author materials that remain in their possession. To ensure the privacy of some individuals, the locations of these materials are not listed.

Mary Elizabeth McNaughton Bonnet
Tom L. Coleman
Robert Coltrane
Constance Daniels
J. Eugene Felch IV
Richmond Flowers
William W. Kelly
John B. Morris
Marc Oliver
Carlton T. Russell
Harvel Sanders
Carolyn P. Sturgis
Judith Upham

GOVERNMENT PUBLICATIONS

Congressional Record
McMeans v. Mayor's Court, Fort Deposit, Alabama, 247 F. Supp. 606 (1965).
State of Alabama v. Tom L. Coleman, Second Judicial District of Lowndes
   County, Ala.
U.S. Bureau of the Census. *Fifth Census; or, Enumeration of the Inhabitants of
   the United States, 1830.* Washington, D.C., 1832.

————. *Sixth Census: Compendium of the Inhabitants of the United States. 1840*. Washington, D.C., 1841.

————. *Sixth Census; or, Enumeration of the Inhabitants of the United States, 1840*. Washington, D.C., 1841.

————. *The Seventh Census of the United States, 1850*. Washington, D.C., 1853.

————. *The Eighth Census: Agriculture in the United States in 1860*. Washington, D.C., 1864.

————. *The Eighth Census: Population of the United States in 1860*. Washington, D.C., 1864.

————. *Ninth Census, 1870*. Vol. 1, *The Statistics of the Population of the United States*. Vol. 3, *The Statistics of the Wealth and Industry of the United States*. Washington, D.C., 1872.

————. *Tenth Census, 1880*. Vol. 3, *Report on the Productions of Agriculture*. Washington, D.C., 1883.

————. *Twelfth Census of the United States, 1900*. Vol. 1, *Population*. Washington, D.C., 1901.

————. *Twelfth Census of the United States, 1900*. Vol. 6, pt. 2, *Agriculture*. Washington, D.C., 1902.

————. *Thirteenth Census of the United States, 1910*. Vol. 2, *Population*. Vol. 6, *Agriculture*. Washington, D.C., 1913.

————. *Fourteenth Census of the United States, 1920*. Vol. 3, *Population*. Washington, D.C., 1922.

————. *Fourteenth Census of the United States, 1920*. Vol. 6, pt. 2, *Agriculture*. Washington, D.C., 1921.

————. *United States Census of Agriculture, 1925*. Pt. 2, *The Southern States*. Washington, D.C., 1927.

————. *Fifteenth Census of the United States, 1930*. Vol. 2, pt. 2, *Agriculture: The Southern States*. Vol. 3, pt. 1, *Population, Alabama-Missouri*. Washington, D.C., 1932.

————. *United States Census of Agriculture, 1935*. Vol. 1, pt. 2, *The Southern States*. Washington, D.C., 1936.

————. *Sixteenth Census of the United States, 1940*. Vol. 2, *Population*. Washington, D.C., 1943.

————. *Sixteenth Census of the United States, 1940*. Vol. 1, pt. 4, *Agriculture*. Washington, D.C., 1942.

————. *United States Census of Agriculture, 1945*. Vol. 1, pt. 21, *Alabama*. Washington, D.C., 1946.

————. *Seventeenth Census of the United States, 1950*. Vol. 7, pt. 2, *Characteristics of the Population: Alabama*. Washington, D.C., 1952.

————. *United States Census of Agriculture, 1954*. Vol. 1, pt. 21, *Alabama*. Washington, D.C., 1956.

————. *United States Census of Agriculture, 1959*. Vol. 1, pt. 32, *Alabama*. Washington, D.C., 1961.

————. *Eighteenth Census of the United States, 1960*, Vol. 1, pt. 2, *Characteristics of the Population: Alabama*. Washington, D.C., 1963.

————. *United States Census of Housing, 1960*, Vol. 1, pt. 2, *States and Small Areas: Alabama-Connecticut*. Washington, D.C., 1963.

————. *United States Census of Agriculture, 1964*. Vol. 1, pt. 32, *Alabama*. Washington, D.C., 1967.

———. *United States Census of Housing, 1980.* Vol. 1, chap. b. Washington, D.C.: Government Printing Office, 1982.

U.S. Commission on Civil Rights. *The Voting Rights Act . . . The First Months.* Washington, D.C.: Government Printing Office, 1965.

———. Alabama State Advisory Committee. *The Agricultural Stabilization and Conservation Service in the Alabama Black Belt.* N.p., April 1968.

———. *Cycle to Nowhere.* Washington, D.C.: Government Printing Office, 1968.

———. *Hearing before the United States Commission on Civil Rights.* Montgomery, Ala., April 27–May 2, 1968. Washington, D.C.: Government Printing Office, 1968.

———. *Political Participation.* Washington, D.C.: Government Printing Office, 1968.

———. *Fifteen Years Ago . . . Rural Alabama Revisited.* Washington, D.C.: Government Printing Office, 1983.

White v. Crook, 251 F. Supp. 401 (1966).

NEWSPAPERS AND OTHER SERIALS

Atlanta Constitution
Birmingham News
Birmingham Weekly Voice
Chicago Sun-Times
Chicago Tribune
Episcopal Theological School Journal
Greenville Advocate
Houston Chronicle
Keene (N.H.) High School *Enterprise*
Keene (N.H.) *Sentinel*
Living Church
Los Angeles Times
Lowndes Signal
Memphis Commercial-Appeal
Mobile Register
Montgomery Advertiser
Montgomery Journal
National Guardian
New York Herald-Tribune
New York Times
Official Bulletin of the Episcopal Theological School
Selma Times-Journal
Southern Courier
Student Voice
Timmons Music Society *Newsletter* (VMI)
VMI Alumni Review
VMI Bomb
VMI Bulletin
VMI Cadet
VMI Official Register
Washington Post

All other newspaper references were located in Facts on Film (Southern Education Reporting Service).

NEWS FILM

CBS News, CBS News Archives, New York City
CBS News Film
   John Hart reporting from Hayneville, Ala., September 28, 1965
   John Hart reporting from Hayneville, Ala., September 30, 1965
   Nelson Benton reporting from Oak Park Hospital, Chicago, Ill., October 1, 1965
   John Hart reporting from Hayneville, Ala., September 29, 1966

Sherman Grinberg Film Libraries, Inc., New York City
ABC News Film
   Film footage (place undetermined), August 27, 1965
   Film footage from Hayneville and Montgomery, Ala., September 28, 1965
   Film footage from Hayneville and Montgomery, Ala., September 30, 1965
   Film footage from Hayneville, Ala., October 4, 1965
   Tom Jarrell reporting from Montgomery, Ala., September 27, 1965

Worldwide Television News, New York City
WTN News Film
   Film footage from Hayneville, Ala., August 21, 1965
   Film footage from Hayneville, Ala., September 28, 1965
   Film footage from Hayneville, Ala., September 30, 1965

INTERVIEWS

The individuals listed below were interviewed between 1982 and 1992. The locations of these meetings have been omitted to protect the privacy of some of the participants. All the interviews were in person except those noted by telephone. The author conducted all interviews except those noted by William J. Schneider. The tapes of the author's interviews and transcripts for some of them are in the possession of the author. Transcripts of Schneider's interviews are at the Episcopal Theological School in Cambridge, Massachusetts.

Margaret Ackerman
Joe Frank Bailey
Douglas Ballard
Robert C. Black
Mary Elizabeth McNaughton Bonnet
William F. Byers
Rev. James Capen
Stokely Carmichael
S. Mac Champion
B. M. Miller Childers
Hallie Jones Childers
Rev. John B. Coburn

Coby C. Coleman
Coralie C. Coleman (Mrs. Tom L.)
Hulda Coleman
Kelly Coleman
Tom L. Coleman
Tom L. Coleman, Jr.
Charles B. Colmore (by Schneider)
Constance Daniels
George Dansby
Joyce Bailey Dozier
Harold Drew (by Schneider)
Roswell Falkenberry
Ethel S. Felch
J. Eugene Felch IV
Rev. Joseph Fletcher
Richmond M. Flowers
Marshall Frady
Geraldine Logan Gamble
Harry W. Gamble
Kate J. Gamble
Joe Breck Gantt (telephone)
Thomas B. Gentry
David Gordon (by Schneider)
Rev. Harvey H. Guthrie
Rev. Charles F. Hall
Rev. Tod Hall
Harrell Hammonds
Rosceno M. Haralson
Douglas Harris
Sam Earle Hobbs
[?] Holiday (by Schneider)
Gloria Larry House
Carolyn Pearce Howard (by Schneider)
John Hulett
Rev. John W. Inman (telephone)
John Jackson
Wilbur Jenkins
Willie Jenkins
William W. Kelly
Sarah B. Logan
Rev. Chandler McCarty
Annette McCullough
David McCullough
Abby MacDonald (tape)
Lillian McGill-Bogarty (telephone)
Bob Mants
Rev. T. Frank Mathews
Frank E. Miles, Sr.
Charles Morgan, Jr.

Rev. John B. Morris
Richard F. Morrisroe (by author and by Schneider)
William J. Nelms
Charles R. Nesson
Robert A. Oakes (by Schneider)
Marc Oliver (telephone)
Rev. Maurice Ouellet
Joseph Phelps
Rev. J. Edison Pike
Rev. Noland Pipes, Jr.
John Potter (telephone)
William A. Price
Eugene Pritchard
Anthony L. Reddington
Roy Reed (telephone)
Emily Daniels Robey
James Rogers, Jr.
George L. Roth
Carlton T. Russell
C. Frank Ryals
Ruby N. Sales
Rev. Morris V. Samuel (telephone)
Rev. Harvel Sanders (telephone)
Arlie Schardt
William J. Schneider
Charles Smith
Robert B. Smith
Richard T. Snowman, M.D.
Rev. Michael Stichwey (telephone)
Rev. Henri A. Stines
Robert L. Strickland
Winifred H. Sullivan
Rex N. Thomas
John B. Tillson
Kwame Toure (Stokely Carmichael)
Rev. Edward A. Tulis (telephone)
Sanford J. Ungar (telephone)
Rev. Judith Upham
Richard Valeriani
John Robert Varner
Virginia Varner
Rev. Francis X. Walters
Rev. Stephen Weissman (telephone)
Alice M. West
Lonzy West
Gardenia S. White
James W. Wible
Rev. William Wolf
Lamar S. Woodham

SECONDARY SOURCES

Abernathy, Thomas Perkins. *The Formative Period in Alabama, 1815–1828.* Montgomery: Alabama State Department of Archives and History, Historical and Patriotic Series No. 6, 1922.

Alabama County Statistical Abstracts. University: University of Alabama Bureau of Business Research, 1941.

Alabama Official and Statistical Register, 1943. Montgomery: Walker Publishing, 1943.

Alabama Official and Statistical Register, 1963. Montgomery: Walker Printing Co., 1963.

Alexander, Charles B., and Duckworth, Peggy J. "Alabama Black Belt Whigs during Secession: A New Viewpoint." *Alabama Review* 17 (July 1964): 181–97.

Ayers, Edward L. *Vengeance and Justice: Crime and Punishment in the Nineteenth-Century South.* New York: Oxford University Press, 1984.

Bartley, Numan V. *The Rise of Massive Resistance: Race and Politics in the South during the 1950s.* Baton Rouge: Louisiana State University Press, 1969.

Bass, Jack. *Unlikely Heroes.* New York: Simon and Schuster, 1981.

Belfrage, Sally. *Freedom Summer.* New York: Viking Press, 1965.

Belknap, Michael. *Federal Law and Southern Order: Racial Violence and Constitutional Conflict in the Post-Brown South.* Athens: University of Georgia Press, 1987.

Blackman, George L. *Faith and Freedom: A Study of Theological Education and the Episcopal Theological School.* New York: Seabury, 1967.

The Black Panther Party. New York: Merit, 1966.

Blumberg, Rhoda Lois. *Civil Rights: The 1960s Freedom Struggle.* Boston: Twayne, 1984.

Bond, Horace Mann. *Negro Education in Alabama: A Study in Cotton and Steel.* New York: Associated Publishers, 1939.

Boyd, Minnie Clare. *Alabama in the Fifties: A Social Study.* New York: Columbia University Press, 1931.

Branch, Taylor. *Parting the Waters: America in the King Years, 1954–1963.* New York: Simon and Schuster, 1988.

Brittain, Joseph M. "Negro Suffrage and Politics in Alabama since 1870." Ph.D. dissertation, Indiana University, 1958.

———. "The Return of the Negro to Alabama Politics, 1930–1954." *Negro History Bulletin* 20 (May 1959): 196–99.

———. "Some Reflections on Negro Suffrage and Politics in Alabama—Past and Present." *Journal of Negro History* 47 (April 1962): 127–38.

Burnham, Walter Dean. *Presidential Ballots, 1836–1892.* Baltimore: Johns Hopkins University Press, 1955.

Byman, Seymour. "Ritualistic Acts and Compulsive Behavior: The Pattern of Tudor Martyrdom." *American Historical Review* 83 (June 1978): 625–43.

Campbell, David. "The Lowndes County (Alabama) Freedom Organization: The First Black Panther Party, 1965–1968." M.A. thesis, Florida State University, 1970.

———. "The Lowndes County Freedom Organization: An Appraisal." *New South* 27 (Winter 1972): 37–42.

Carmichael, Stokely, and Hamilton, Charles V. *Black Power: The Politics of Liberation in America.* New York: Random House, 1967.

Carson, Clayborne. *In Struggle: SNCC and the Black Awakening of the 1960s.* Cambridge: Harvard University Press, 1981.

Carter, Kit Carson, Jr. "A Critical Analysis of the Basis of Party Alignment in Lowndes County, Alabama, 1836–1860." M.A. thesis, University of Alabama, 1961.

"Catalyst for Reconciliation." *Christian Century,* September 8, 1965.

Chafe, William H. *Civilities and Civil Rights: Greensboro, North Carolina, and the Black Struggle for Freedom.* New York: Oxford University Press, 1980.

Clark, James G. *The Jim Clark Story: I Saw Selma Raped.* Selma: Selma Enterprises, 1966.

Colburn, David R. *Racial Change and Community Crisis: St. Augustine, Florida, 1877–1980.* New York: Columbia University Press, 1985.

Corry, John. "A Visit to Lowndes County, Alabama." *New South* 27 (Winter 1972): 28–36.

Costain, Thomas B. *The Silver Chalice.* Garden City, N.Y.: Doubleday, 1952.

Couto, Richard A. *Ain't Gonna Let Nobody Turn Me Round: The Pursuit of Racial Justice in the Rural South.* Philadelphia: Temple University Press, 1991.

Daniel, Pete. *The Shadow of Slavery: Peonage in the South, 1901–1969.* Urbana: University of Illinois Press, 1973.

———. *Breaking the Land: The Transformation of Cotton, Tobacco, and Rice Cultures since 1880.* Urbana: University of Illinois Press, 1985.

Daniels, Jonathan. "A Burning Bush." *New Hampshire Churchman,* June 1965.

Davis, Charles S. *The Cotton Kingdom in Alabama.* Montgomery: Alabama State Department of Archives and History, 1939.

DeMuth, Jerry. "Black Belt, Alabama: Total Segregation." *Commonweal,* August 7, 1964.

Denby, Charles. *Indignant Heart: A Black Worker's Journal.* Boston: South End Press, 1978.

Dew, Charles B. "The Slavery Experience." In *Interpreting Southern History: Historiographical Essays in Honor of Sanford W. Higginbotham,* edited by John B. Boles and Evelyn Thomas Nolen, pp. 120–61. Baton Rouge: Louisiana State University Press, 1987.

Douglas, Lloyd C. *The Robe.* Boston: Houghton-Mifflin, 1942.

Doyle, Bertram Wilbur. *The Etiquette of Race Relations in the South: A Study in Social Control.* Chicago: University of Chicago Press, 1937.

Drenan, Sprague W. "Two Hundred Years of Keene . . . From Settlement to City." *New Hampshire Profiles* 2 (June 1953): 37–73.

Edds, Margaret. *Free at Last: What Really Happened When Civil Rights Came to Southern Politics.* Bethesda, Md.: Adler and Adler, 1987.

Ellis, Rose Herlong. "The Calhoun School: Miss Charlotte Thorn's 'Lighthouse on the Hill' in Lowndes County, Alabama." *Alabama Review* 37 (July 1984): 183–201.

Evans, Edward A. "A Study of Some Phases of Social and Economic Conditions of the Free Inhabitants of the Alabama Black Belt in 1860." M.A. thesis, University of Alabama, 1940.

Fager, Charles E. *Selma, 1965: The March That Changed the South.* 1974. 2d ed. Boston: Beacon Press, 1985.

Fairclough, Adam. *To Redeem the Soul of America: The Southern Christian Leadership Conference and Martin Luther King, Jr.* Athens: University of Georgia Press, 1987.

Federal Writers' Project. *New Hampshire*. Boston: Houghton Mifflin, 1938.

―――. *Virginia: A Guide to the Old Dominion*. New York: Oxford University Press, 1940.

Feldman, Paul. "How the Cry for 'Black Power' Began." *Dissent* 13 (September–October 1966): 472–77.

Fite, Gilbert. *Cotton Fields No More: Southern Agriculture 1865–1980*. Lexington: University of Kentucky Press, 1984.

Fitts, Alston, III. *Selma: Queen City of the Black Belt*. Selma: Clairmont Press, 1989.

Fleming, Walter L. *Civil War and Reconstruction in Alabama*. New York: Columbia University Press, 1905.

―――. "The Servant Problem in a Black Belt Village." *Sewanee Review* 13 (January 1905): 1–17.

Frady, Marshall. *Southerners: A Journalist's Odyssey*. New York: New American Library, 1980.

Freehling, William W. *Prelude to Civil War: The Nullification Controversy in South Carolina, 1816–1836*. New York: Harper and Row, 1966.

Frend, W. H. C. *Martyrdom and Persecution in the Early Church: A Study of a Conflict from the Maccabees to Donatus*. New York: New York University Press, 1967.

Garrow, David J. *Protest at Selma: Martin Luther King, Jr., and the Voting Rights Act of 1965*. New Haven: Yale University Press, 1978.

―――. *The FBI and Martin Luther King, Jr.: From "Solo" to Memphis*. New York: Norton, 1981.

―――. *Bearing the Cross: Martin Luther King, Jr., and the Southern Christian Leadership Conference*. New York: Morrow, 1986.

Gibson, J. S. "The Alabama Black Belt: Its Geographic Status." *Economic Geography* 17 (January 1941): 1–23.

Gilmour, Robert Arthur. "The Other Emancipation: Studies in the Society and Economy of Alabama Whites During Reconstruction." Ph.D. dissertation, Johns Hopkins University, 1972.

Going, Allen Johnston. *Bourbon Democracy in Alabama, 1874–1890*. University: University of Alabama Press, 1951.

Goldfield, David R. *Black, White, and Southern: Race Relations and Southern Culture, 1940 to the Present*. Baton Rouge: Louisiana State University Press, 1990.

Goldsmith, Glenn Davis. *Fort Deposit: History and Happenings*. N.p., 1982.

Graham, Hugh Davis, and Gurr, Ted Robert, eds. *Violence in America: Report of the Task Force on Historical and Comparative Perspectives to the National Commission on the Causes and Prevention of Violence*. Washington, D.C.: Government Printing Office, 1969.

―――. *Violence in America: Historical and Comparative Perspectives*. Rev. ed. Beverly Hills: Sage, 1979.

Hackney, Sheldon. *Populism to Progressivism in Alabama*. Princeton, N.J.: Princeton University Press, 1969.

Hamilton, Virginia Van der Veer. *Alabama: A Bicentennial History*. New York: Norton, 1977.

———. *Seeing Historic Alabama*. University: University of Alabama Press, 1982.

———. *Lister Hill: Statesman from the South*. Chapel Hill: University of North Carolina Press, 1987.

Hardy, John. *Selma: Her Institutions and Her Men*. 1879. Reprint. Spartanburg, S.C.: Reprint Co., 1978.

Harris, Trudier. *Exorcising Blackness: Historical and Literary Lynching and Burning Rituals*. Bloomington: Indiana University Press, 1984.

"The Hayneville Incident." *Christianity Today*, October 22, 1965.

Hill, Evan. *Beanstalk: The History of Miniature Precision Bearings, Inc., 1941– 1966*. N.p. 1966.

Hulett, John. "How the Black Panther Party Was Organized." In *The Black Panther Party*. New York: Merit Publishers, 1966.

Hurd, D. Hamilton, ed. *History of Cheshire and Sullivan Counties, New Hampshire*. Philadelphia: J. W. Lewis and Co., 1886.

Jackson, Walter M. *The Story of Selma*. Birmingham: Birmingham Printing Co., 1954.

Johnson, Freddie Eugene. "A Statistical Analysis of the Black Belt Area of Alabama." M.A. thesis, University of Alabama, 1962.

Johnson, Joseph. *God's Secret Armies within the Soviet Empire*. New York: Putnam, 1954.

Jones, James Pickett. *Yankee Blitzkreig: Wilson's Raid through Alabama and Georgia*. Athens: University of Georgia Press, 1976.

Kater, John L., Jr. "The Episcopal Society for Cultural and Racial Unity and Its Role in the Episcopal Church, 1959–1970." Ph.D. dissertation, McGill University, 1973.

Keene History Committee. *"Upper Ashuelot": A History of Keene, New Hampshire*. N.p. 1968.

"Keene — Profile of a County Seat." *New Hampshire Profiles* 11 (May 1962): 16–25.

Kelley, Robin D. G. *Hammer and Hoe: Alabama Communists during the Great Depression*. Chapel Hill: University of North Carolina Press, 1990.

Kennedy, Renwick C. "Black Belt Aristocrats: The Old South Lives on in Alabama's Black Belt." *Social Forces* 13 (October 1934): 80–85.

King, Mary. *Freedom Song: A Personal History of the 1960s Civil Rights Movement*. New York: William Morrow, 1987.

King, Richard H. "Citizenship and Self-Respect: The Experience of Politics in the Civil Rights Movement." *Journal of American Studies* 22, no. 1 (1988): 7–24.

Klausner, Samuel Z. "Martyrdom." In *The Encyclopedia of Religion*, edited by Mircea Eliade, pp. 230–38. New York: Macmillan, 1986.

Kluger, Richard. *Simple Justice: The History of "Brown v. Board of Education" and Black America's Struggle for Equality*. New York: Knopf, 1976.

Kohn, Peter. *The Cradle: Anatomy of a Town — Fact and Fiction*. New York: Vantage, 1969.

Kolchin, Peter. *First Freedom: The Responses of Alabama Blacks to Emancipation and Reconstruction*. Westport, Conn.: Greenwood, 1972.

Kopkind, Andrew. "Alabama Unbound: Will Flowers Bloom in the Spring?" *New Republic*, November 27, 1965.

———. "The Lair of the Black Panther." *New Republic*, August 13, 1967.

———. "Lowndes County, Alabama: The Great Fear Is Gone." *Ramparts*, April 1975, pp. 8–12, 53–54.

Kousser, J. Morgan. *The Shaping of Southern Politics: Suffrage Restriction and the Establishment of the One-Party South, 1880–1910.* New Haven: Yale University Press, 1974.

Lawson, Steven F. *Black Ballots: Voting Rights in the South, 1944–1969.* New York: Columbia University Press, 1976.

———. *In Pursuit of Power: Southern Blacks and Electoral Politics, 1965–1982.* New York: Columbia University Press, 1985.

———. *Running for Freedom: Civil Rights and Black Politics in America since 1941.* New York: McGraw-Hill, 1991.

Lewis, David L. *King: A Critical Biography.* New York: Praeger, 1970.

Litwack, Leon F. *Been in the Storm So Long: The Aftermath of Slavery.* New York: Knopf, 1979.

Loades, D. M. *The Oxford Martyrs.* New York: Stein and Day, 1970.

Long, Margaret. "Black Power in the Black Belt." *The Progressive* 30 (October 1966): 20–24

Longenecker, Stephen L. *Selma's Peacemaker: Ralph Smeltzer and Civil Rights Mediation.* Philadelphia: Temple University Press, 1987.

Louis, Debbie. *And We Are Not Saved: A History of the Movement as People.* Garden City, N.Y.: Doubleday, 1970.

McAdam, Doug. *Political Process and the Development of Black Insurgency, 1930–1970.* Chicago: University of Chicago Press, 1982.

———. *Freedom Summer.* New York: Oxford University Press, 1988.

McMillan, Malcolm Cook. *Constitutional Development in Alabama, 1798–1901: A Study in Politics, the Negro, and Sectionalism.* Chapel Hill: University of North Carolina Press, 1955.

McMillen, Neil R. *The Citizens' Council: Organized Resistance to the Second Reconstruction, 1954–64.* Urbana: University of Illinois Press, 1971.

Meier, August, and Rudwick, Elliott. *CORE: A Study in the Civil Rights Movement.* New York: Oxford University Press, 1973.

Mendelsohn, Jack. *The Martyrs: Sixteen Who Gave Their Lives for Racial Justice.* New York: Harper and Row, 1966.

Merrifield, Gladys. "A Children's Theatre . . . and How It Grew." *Family Circle*, October 1951.

Moore, Albert Burton. *History of Alabama.* University, Ala.: University Supply Store, 1934.

Morgan, Charles, Jr. *A Time to Speak.* New York: Harper and Row, 1964.

———. *One Man, One Voice.* New York: Holt, Rinehart and Winston, 1979.

Morris, Aldon. *The Origins of the Civil Rights Movement: Black Communities Organizing for Change.* New York: Free Press, 1984.

Myrdal, Gunnar. *An American Dilemma: The Negro Problem and Modern Democracy.* New York: Harper and Row, 1944.

National Association for the Advancement of Colored People (NAACP). *Thirty Years of Lynching in the United States, 1889–1918.* 1919. Reprint. New York: Arno Press, 1969.

Nelson, Jack. "The Talk Is a Little Different These Days." *New South* 21 (Winter 1966): 47–53.

Norrell, R. Jefferson. "Reporters and Reformers: The Story of the *Southern Courier*." *South Atlantic Quarterly* 79 (Winter 1980): 93–104.

Norrell, Robert J. *Reaping the Whirlwind: The Civil Rights Movement in Tuskegee*. New York: Knopf, 1985.

Oates, Stephen B. *Let the Trumpet Sound: The Life of Martin Luther King, Jr.* New York: Harper and Row, 1982.

Owen, Thomas McAdory. *History of Alabama and Dictionary of Alabama Biography*. Vols. 1–2. Chicago: S. J. Clark, 1921.

Owsley, Frank Lawrence. *Plain Folk of the Old South*. Baton Rouge: Louisiana State University Press, 1949.

Peltason, J. W. *Fifty-eight Lonely Men: Southern Federal Judges and School Desegregation*. New York: Harcourt, Brace and World, 1961.

Proper, David R. *History of the First Congregation Church*. Keene, N.H.: Sentinel Publishing Co., 1973.

———. *The Story of Wright's Silver Cream, 1873–1973*. Lunenburg, Vt.: Stinehour Press, 1973.

Ransom, Roger L., and Sutch, Richard. *One Kind of Freedom: The Economic Consequences of Emancipation*. Cambridge: Cambridge University Press, 1977.

Reed, Roy. "George Wallace's Bid for the New South," *New York Times Magazine*, September 5, 1982.

Richardson, James M., ed. *Alabama Encyclopedia*. Northport, Ala.: American Southern Publishing, 1965.

Riddle, Donald W. *The Martyrs: A Study in Social Control*. Chicago: University of Chicago Press, 1931.

Robinson, Henry M. *The Cardinal*. New York: Simon and Schuster, 1950.

Rothschild, Mary Aickin. *A Case of Black and White: Northern Volunteers and the Southern Freedom Summers, 1964–1965*. Westport, Conn.: Greenwood, 1982.

Rubin, Morton. *Plantation County*. Chapel Hill: University of North Carolina Press, 1951.

Russell, Mildred Brewer. *Lowndes County Court House: A Chronicle of Hayneville, an Alabama Black Belt Village, 1820–1900*. Montgomery, Ala.: Paragon Press, 1951.

Sayers, John W., comp. *Who's Who in Alabama*. Birmingham: Sayers Enterprises, 1969.

Schneider, William J., ed. *The Jon Daniels Story, with His Letters and Papers*. New York: Seabury, 1967.

Schweninger, Loren. *James T. Rapier and Reconstruction*. Chicago: University of Chicago Press, 1978.

Sellers, James Benson. *Slavery in Alabama*. University: University of Alabama Press, 1950.

Sex and Civil Rights: The True Selma Story. Montgomery: ESCO Corporation, 1965.

Shapiro, Herbert. *White Violence and Black Response: From Reconstruction to Montgomery*. Amherst: University of Massachusetts Press, 1988.

Simcox, Carroll E. "Selma Episcopalians Speak: An Editorial Report." *Living Church*, June 27, 1965.

Sisk, Glen N. "Alabama Black Belt: A Social History, 1875–1917." Ph.D. dissertation, Duke University, 1951.

——. "Social Aspects of the Alabama Black Belt, 1875–1917." *Mid-America* 37 (January 1955): 31–47.

Sitkoff, Harvard. *The Struggle for Black Equality, 1954–19890.* New York: Hill and Wang, 1981.

Smith, Samuel Denny. *The Negro in Congress, 1870–1901.* Chapel Hill: University of North Carolina Press, 1940.

Street, James H. *The New Revolution in the Cotton Economy: Mechanization and Its Consequences.* Chapel Hill: University of North Carolina Press, 1957.

Strong, Donald S. *Registration of Voters in Alabama.* University, Ala.: Bureau of Public Administration, 1956.

Talese, Gay. "Where's the Spirit of Selma Now?" *New York Times Magazine,* May 30, 1965.

Tindall, George Brown. *Emergence of the New South, 1913–1945.* Baton Rouge: Louisiana State University Press, 1967.

Tower, J. Allen. "Alabama's Shifting Cotton Belt." *Alabama Review* (January 1948): 27–38.

Viorst, Milton. *Fire in the Streets: America in the 1960s.* New York: Simon and Schuster, 1979.

Walker, Samuel. *In Defense of American Liberties: A History of the ACLU.* New York: Oxford University Press, 1990.

Wallace, David Duncan. *History of South Carolina.* New York: American Historical Society, 1934.

Walton, Hanes, Jr. *Black Political Parties: An Historical and Political Analysis.* New York: Free Press, 1972.

Wasserman, Miriam. "White Power in the Black Belt." *New South* 22 (Winter 1967): 27–36.

Webb, Sheyann, and Nelson, Rachel West. *Selma, Lord, Selma: Girlhood Memories of the Civil-Rights Days.* University: University of Alabama Press, 1980.

Weisbrot, Robert. *Freedom Bound: A History of America's Civil Rights Movement.* New York: Norton, 1989.

White, Helen C. *The Tudor Books of Saints and Martyrs.* Madison: University of Wisconsin Press, 1963.

White, W. L. *Lost Boundaries.* New York: Harcourt Brace, 1948.

Wiggins, Sarah Woolfolk. *The Scalawag in Alabama Politics, 1865–1881.* University: University of Alabama Press, 1977.

Wilhoit, Francis M. *The Politics of Massive Resistance.* New York: George Braziller, 1973.

Williamson, Joel. *The Crucible of Race: Black-White Relations in the American South since Emancipation.* New York: Oxford University Press, 1984.

Winn, Margaret. "Keene — All American City." *New Hampshire Profiles* 14 (July 1965): 42–43.

Wise, Henry A. *Drawing Out the Man: The VMI Story.* Charlottesville: University Press of Virginia (for the VMI Alumni Association), 1978.

Woodward, C. Vann. *The Strange Career of Jim Crow.* 3d rev. ed. New York: Oxford University Press, 1974.

Wyatt-Brown, Bertram. *Southern Honor: Ethics and Behavior in the Old South.* New York: Oxford University Press, 1982.

ACKNOWLEDGMENTS

On a Saturday morning in the summer of 1981, I went to the Southern Historical Collection at the University of North Carolina to check some footnotes in a manuscript that would be published the following year (*Jonathan Daniels and Race Relations: The Evolution of a Southern Liberal* [Knoxville: University of Tennessee Press, 1982]). The subject was Jonathan Worth Daniels, the longtime liberal editor of the Raleigh (N.C.) *News and Observer*, whose papers were deposited in the Southern Historical Collection at Chapel Hill. I was the first researcher in the collection that morning and hurriedly signed the register as working on "JDaniels." A few minutes after I started to work, a short black woman whom I had never seen before put her materials on a table not far from mine and immediately came over to me. She asked quietly but with intense excitement if I was the person who had signed in to work on "JDaniels." When I said yes, she wanted to know if it was "Jonathan Daniels" and then "THE Jonathan Daniels." Sensing a bit of confusion, I explained who "my" Jonathan Daniels was. Her enthusiasm vanished. When I inquired about her interest in Jonathan Daniels, she told me that she had hoped I had been working on the Jon Daniels who had been killed in Lowndes County, Alabama, in 1965. Though I had heard of the "other" Jonathan Daniels, I repeated that my study focused on the newspaper editor. Convinced of the importance of her Jon Daniels, she told me I should take on the civil rights worker after I finished with the editor.

A few days later we had lunch and discussed the man whom I was beginning to call the "second Jonathan Daniels." Once again she encouraged me to study number two and gave me the names of several people who could help me in the research. Our conversation was a wrenching experience for her because it was the first time she had talked about the death of Jon Daniels with anyone other than family and close friends. She had been standing next to Daniels when he was killed. Her name was Ruby Sales.

My conversations with Sales led directly to this book. She told me how to contact Daniels's mother, referred me to John Hulett in Hayneville, and told me about people at ETS in Cambridge. In the years thereafter, my research took me to New England, to VMI in Lexington, Virginia, and finally to Alabama—Montgomery, Selma, and Lowndes County. The trips included interviews with acquaintances of Daniels, activists in the Lowndes civil rights movement, and residents of Selma and Lowndes County. Everyone was cordial and, with only a few exceptions (primarily lawyers involved in the Coleman trial), helpful. I am grateful to the more than one hundred people who took time to talk, sometimes extensively, with me about my research; their interest and cooperation was indispensable to this project. There are too many to thank individually here, but their names appear in the bibliography. Many individuals, including a number with whom I only spoke on the telephone, combed their personal files to retrieve old letters, clippings, and documents to share with me. I particularly appreciate the help of Constance Daniels, Emily Daniels Robey, Tom Coleman, Hulda Coleman, Richard Morrisroe, and Ruby Sales—their conversations with me were often difficult for them but they persevered.

In addition to the many people who granted me interviews and corresponded with me, thanks are due to archivists and librarians at ETS, the Alabama Department of Archives and History in Montgomery, the Martin Luther King Center in Atlanta, the University of New Hampshire, VMI, and the public libraries in Selma, Birmingham, and Keene. The staff of St. James Episcopal Church in Keene kindly made available materials at the church, and the Reverend Peter Hawes arranged for me to examine the vestry records of St. Paul's Episcopal Church in Selma.

During the years of work on this project I was fortunate to receive the kind of support that can only come from bright and talented people. Clayborne Carson, David J. Garrow, and Nancy J. Weiss helped me gain a year-long fellowship that allowed me to begin writing. Gaines M. Foster, Daniel J. Singal, J. Mills Thornton, David Garrow, Neil R. McMillen, and Duncan M. Gray III each gave the manuscript a thorough reading and offered valuable criticism and suggestions. Dan T. Carter and Waldo E. Martin, Jr., who read the manuscript for the University of North Carolina Press, provided sound advice and guidance.

Financial support came from the American Association for State and Local History for transcribing some interviews, from the American Council of Learned Societies for a year-long fellowship (supplemented by my dean), from Southeast Missouri State University for my initial trip to New England, and from the University of Mississippi, where the Department of History, the College of Liberal Arts, and the Graduate School provided small grants for research.

I have benefited from the hospitality of several people in addition to those whom I interviewed. In Montgomery, J. Mills Thornton and Michael and Theresa Fitzsimmons made my visits more enjoyable. My brother, Loren, and his family supplied a happy and comfortable place to stay at their home in New Jersey during a research trip to New York City, as did David Garrow in the city.

The most important people to thank are the members of my family. Throughout my work on this book—from the first research trips to New England and Lowndes County to the last words written—my most sensible adviser, most perceptive critic, and most ardent supporter has been my wife, Brenda. Over the past decade our conversations about this project have so thoroughly affected my research, my thinking, and my writing that her contributions to the final product can only be described as profound and pervasive. Our two sons, on the other hand, remain innocent of both my work and the social problems it tries to address. In their own ways, however, Daniel and Benjamin speeded the work along by making life so enjoyable. My parents, to whom this book is dedicated, first introduced me to many racial questions. Not only did I grow up in the South, but we often visited relatives in small-town Minnesota and in rural eastern North Carolina—places as different in many ways as Keene and Hayneville.